剑桥应用语言学年度评论 2000
Annual Review of Applied Linguistics

作为新兴学科的应用语言学
Applied Linguistics as an Emerging Discipline

主编 〔美〕William Grabe

导读 何伟

2016年·北京

Originally published by Cambridge University Press in 2000. This reprint edition is published with the permission of the Syndicate of the Press of the University of Cambridge, Cambridge, England.
原书由英国剑桥大学出版社于 2000 年出版。
本版经英国剑桥大学出版社授权出版。

This edition is licensed for sale in the People's Republic of China only (excluding Hong Kong SAR, Macao SAR and Taiwan Province). No part of this publication may be reproduced or distributed by any means, or stored in a database or retrieval system, without the prior written permission of the publisher.
本版仅限在中华人民共和国境内(不包括香港特别行政区、澳门特别行政区及台湾)销售。未经出版者书面许可,不得以任何方式复制或发行本书的任何部分。

剑桥应用语言学年度评论
专家委员会

主　任　胡壮麟

副主任　田贵森　朱永生

委　员　曹　进　何　伟　靳　琰　赖良涛　李战子
　　　　　彭宣维　齐振海　孙迎晖　王振华　辛志英
　　　　　杨信彰　于　晖　张　辉　张　琳　张　薇
　　　　　郑　萱

Contents

总序 ··· 1
导读 ·· 何伟 11
FOREWORD
··· William Grabe i

APPLIED LINGUISTICS AND ARAL

APPLIED LINGUISTICS AND THE *ANNUAL REVIEW OF APPLIED LINGUISTICS*
·· Robert B. Kaplan and William Grabe 3

LANGUAGE TEACHING AND LANGUAGE TEACHER EDUCATION

OBJECT LANGUAGE AND THE LANGUAGE SUBJECT: ON THE MEDIATING ROLE OF APPLIED LINGUISTICS
·· Henry G. Widdowson 23
LANGUAGE TEACHER EDUCATION
·· JoAnn (Jodi) Crandall 39

LANGUAGES FOR SPECIFIC PURPOSES

LANGUAGES FOR SPECIFIC PURPOSES
··· John M. Swales 67

LSP IN NORTH AFRICA: STATUS, PROBLEMS AND, CHALLENGES
··· Mohamed Daoud 88

LITERACY

WRITING, LITERACY, AND APPLIED LINGUISTICS
.... Ilona Leki 113
DESIGN AND PRACTICE: ENACTING FUNCTIONAL LINGUISTICS
.... James R. Martin 132

LANGUAGE POLICY AND LANGUAGE ASSESSMENT

LANGUAGE POLICY AND PLANNING
.... Sauli Takala and Kari Sajavaara 147
ASSESSMENT AND TESTING
.... Caroline Clapham 168

SECOND LANGUAGE ACQUISITON AND SECOND LANGUAGE PROCESSING

SECOND LANGUAGE ACQUISITION AND APPLIED LINGUISTICS
.... Diane Larsen-Freeman 187
STILL WRESTLING WITH "CONTEXT" IN INTERLANGUAGE THEORY
.... Elaine Tarone 207
FRENCH IMMERSION RESEARCH IN CANADA: RECENT
CONTRIBUTIONS TO SLA AND APPLIED LINGUISTICS*
.... Merrill Swain 227
A CRITICAL REVIEW OF THE CRITICAL PERIOD RESEARCH
.... Thomas Scovel 243
PSYCHOLINGUISTICS IN APPLIED LINGUISTICS: TRENDS
AND PERSPECTIVES
.... Kees de Bot 256

CONCLUDING SUMMARY

CONCLUDING THOUGHTS: APPLIED LINGUISTICS AT THE
JUNCTURE OF MILLENNIA
.... G. Richard Tucker 275

总　　序

自 2013 年 8 月起，商务印书馆与剑桥大学出版社开始商洽在大陆出版《应用语言学年度评论》(Annual Review of Applied Linguistics)事宜，至 2014 年春末签约。此后，商务印书馆英语编辑室领导栾奇和马浩岚并责任编辑杨子辉博士先后来访，约我办三件事，一是代为组织国内学者为各卷写导读，二是承担导读的审稿任务，三是为商务版《应用语言学年度评论》写一个总序。作为对我的照顾，同意我邀请复旦大学朱永生教授[①]和北京师范大学田贵森教授[②]参加导读审定工作。就总序而言，多次思考之后，想谈以下四个方面。

一、刊物方针

《应用语言学年度评论》(以下简称《年度评论》)是美国应用语言

---

① 朱永生：复旦大学教授、博导，杭州师范大学钱塘学者，高校功能语言学研究会副会长，高校语篇分析研究会副会长，Linguistics and Human Sciences 编委及《中国外语》等杂志编委。曾任苏州大学外语系主任、复旦大学外文系主任和国际文化交流学院院长、国际系统功能语言学研究会执委、国务院学科评议组成员、全国高校外语教学指导委员会委员等职务。著有《系统功能语言学多维思考》《系统功能语言学再思考》《语境动态研究》《系统功能语言学概论》等。
② 田贵森：北京师范大学外文学院教授、博导，中国功能语言学学会常务理事、中国社会语言学学会理事。1976 年河北师范大学外语系毕业后留校任教，1987 年北京外国语大学硕士，1991 年纽约市立大学硕士，1997 年北京大学博士。曾任河北师大外国语学院院长，河北省高校外语教学研究会会长，中国教育学会外语教学专业委员会副理事长。著有《禁忌语的功能研究》《英语专业毕业论文写作教程》《新编英语词汇学教程》等。

学学会（American Association for Applied Linguistics，简称 AAAL）主办的一部书刊结合的出版物，自 1980 年起每年一卷，至 2014 年已出版 34 卷。该刊最初由 Newbury House 出版社出版，自第 5 卷起改为剑桥大学出版社出版，延续至今。美国南加州大学美国语言研究所主任 Robert B. Kaplan 教授筹划第 1 卷《年度评论》时，邀请犹他州布里格姆-扬大学日耳曼语系 Randall L. Jones 教授和华盛顿大学应用语言学中心主任 G. Richard Tucker 教授三人合作主编。在他们领导下的编委会对办刊宗旨确定这样一个基本认识：尽管 1941 年美国密执安大学率先成立了将语言学理论应用于语言教育的英语学院，1956 年英国爱丁堡大学成立了应用语言学系，1959 年美国华盛顿大学建立了应用语言学中心，1966 年 TESOL Quarterly 出版，1977 年美国应用语言学学会成立，《年度评论》编委会无意选定其中之一作为应用语言学界共同遵循的蓝图，而是决定走自己的路。在此基础上编委会确定的方针有如下特点：（1）《年度评论》不是杂志，因为它一年只出一本；它又被看作是一本杂志，因为它由出版社的杂志部负责编辑、发行事务。①（2）该出版物不对应用语言学做面面俱到的报道，而是对应用语言学学科的现状进行专题评论、综述和文献式的归纳。（3）应用语言学具有高度的跨学科性，因此该刊重点结合双语教育、语言教育学、心理语言学和社会语言学四个方面进行选题。考虑到这四个学科枝叶蔓生，年刊会对一个学科的某一领域做全面的综述和评论。（4）即使上述四个学科也不是应用语言学的唯一研究领域，因为该刊遵循美国应用语言学学会所倡导的功能导向，着眼于具体应用更甚于理论。（5）所有的文章由编委会组织某一领域的专家撰写，不转载已在其他刊物上发表的文章，也不采用在某个学术会议上已经宣读的论文，更不对某一部具体的学术著作进行评论。因此，《年度评论》的主要任务是收集和突出被学术界很少报道或研究的领域，不重复已有工作，更不企图贬低某一

---

① 《应用语言学年度评论》问世后，受到国际学术界的高度重视，被权威的《社会科学引文索引》（SSCI）、《艺术和人文科学引文索引》（AHCI）和《科学引文索引》（SCI）所收录。

个方面，或对本学科内某项研究的价值进行排队。这样，《年度评论》对二语习得和语言干扰等内容谈得不多，因为这方面的研究成果已经发表很多。反之，微语言学、符号语言学、计算机辅助教学等受到重视。（6）《年度评论》本身应当正确面对来自不同领域实践者的认同或挑战。①② 鉴于上述情况，《年度评论》每卷都有一个主题，如"语言和语言教育政策"（卷2）、"书面话语"（卷3）、"读写教育"（卷4）等。这些选题均具有学术性、实用性、时代性和独特性。与此同时，该刊每隔四五年会有一卷就应用语言学的整体研究从不同方面进行总结式的调研和讨论，内容涉及语言学习和教学、话语分析、教学创新、二语习得、计算机辅助教学、职场语境下的语言用途、社会语言学、语言政策和语言评估（如卷1、5、10、15、19等）。每年向读者提供500多个新的文献，以帮助本学科教学科研人员能深入掌握情况，点面结合。《年度评论》原计划的第1卷在1980年出版，由于组稿和印刷的原因，实际上在1981年问世。这一脱节现象直到1994年第14卷才得到扭转，即每卷标明的年度与出版年度取得一致。③

二、主编更迭

三十多年来，《年度评论》的总主编大约十年更换一次。美国南加利福尼亚大学美国语言研究所主任 Robert B. Kaplan 教授从创刊起任总主编，连续十年。Kaplan 曾任美国应用语言学会会长、英语作为第二语言教

---

① Rota, A. (1982). ANNUAL REVIEW OF APPLIED LINGUISTICS (ARAL). Robert B. Kaplan (Gen. Ed.); Randall L. Jones and G. Richard Tucker (Co-Eds.). *TESOL Quarterly*, *16*, 398–404.
② Kaplan, Robert B. (1980). Introduction. *Annual Review of Applied Linguistics*, *1*, vii–xi.
③ Kaplan, Robert B. and William Grabe. (2000). Applied Linguistics and the Annual Review of Applied Linguistics. in *Annual Review of Applied Linguistics*, *20*, 3–17. Cambridge University Press.

学学会会长、《牛津应用语言学手册》总主编、《国际语言学百科全书》编委等。① 在 Kaplan 主编的《牛津应用语言学手册》中,他认为应用语言学家至少应该具备以下领域的一些知识:人类学、社会学、经济学、政治学、教育学、老年人学、历史学、国际关系、语言学习和教学、词典编纂学、政策研究、心理学和神经科学、公共管理、教师培训和文本生成等。此外,每一位应用语言学家都应精于计算机使用,能够对数据进行统计分析。②③

自第 11 卷起,William Grabe 任主编。Grabe 是美国北亚利桑那州大学负责科研的副校长,曾先后在该校英语系和应用语言学系任教。Grabe 认为应用语言学的核心是"试图解决人们在日常生活中遇到的与语言相关的问题",是一种"研究现实世界语言问题的、实践驱动的学科"。④ 鉴于这个原因,应用语言学必然是一个交叉学科,涉及许多其他领域。这可见之于他对每卷的选题,如"读写教育"(卷 12)、"二语教学"(卷 13)、"语言政策和规划"(卷 14)、"技术和语言"(卷 16)、"多语现象"(卷 17)、"二语教育基础"(卷 18)、"应用语言学的学科性"(卷 19,20)。Grabe 任总主编至 2000 年卸任。在他最后一次负责的第 20 卷,他和 Robert Kaplan 合写了一篇回顾应用语言学和《年度评论》发展历程的总结性文章。

自 2001 年起任总主编的是北亚利桑那大学英语系的 Mary McGroarty 教授。她主要研究双语现象、语言政策、语言教育和课堂研究、社会语言学、二语教学的文化影响等。由于第一次出任主编,McGroarty 邀请了美

---

① Bruthiaux, Paul, Dwight Atkinson, William G. Egginton, William Grabe, Viadehi Ramanathan. Eds. (2005). *Directions in Applied Linguistics in Honour of Robert B. Kaplan*. Clevedon: Multilingual Matters Ltd.
② Kaplan, Robert B. (1999). *The Oxford Handbook of Applied Linguistics*. Edinburgh: Edinburgh University Press.
③ 刘海涛. 从比较中看应用语言学. 北华大学学报(社会科学版),2007,8(2):4.
④ Grabe, William. (2000). Introduction. *Annual Review of Applied Linguistics*, 20, 1–2. Cambridge University Press.

国著名外语教学法专家 Wilga M. Rivers 为第 21 卷"语言和心理学"写序,题为"沿着记忆巷道的漫长旅程"。此后,McGroarty 在她任期内主编了"话语和对话"(卷 22)、"语言接触和演变"(卷 23)、"语言教育学的进展"(卷 24)和"通用语言言"(卷 26)。《年度评论》第 27 和 28 卷的主题分别为"语言与科技"和"神经语言学和认知语言处理",但未见到这两卷本应由总主编执笔的引言,在目录中也未出现,原因不详。作为总主编的 McGroarty 在第 29 卷"语言政策和语言评估"中再次出现,不过她邀请了著名学者 Bernard Spolsky 作为客座主编。Spolsky 教授长期在以色列的 Bar-Ilan 大学任教,曾任该校人文学院院长,并创建语言政策研究中心。在编辑业务方面,他曾任国际刊物 *Language Policy*(《语言政策》)的总主编,*Asia TEFL*(《亚洲英语作为外语教学》)杂志的出版部主任和总编辑。Spolsky 的专著都与语言政策和语言教育有关,如《教育语言学导论》(1978)、《二语学习的条件》(1991)、《社会语言学》(1998)、《以色列诸语言:政策、意识和实践》(1999)、《语言政策》(2004)、《语言管理》(2009)等。[①] 由此看来,Spolsky 无力全心投入《年度评论》的编辑工作,这次只是扮演一次客串角色而已。

自第 30 卷起,总主编一职由美国密执安州立大学的 Charlene Polio 教授担任。Polio 的主要研究领域为二语写作、二语习得、外语课堂话语、新技术和有经验教师之间的行为差异。她在编辑工作上有较多经验,除接受《年度评论》的总主编任务外,也是 *Modern Language Journal*(《现代语言杂志》)的编辑,此前曾为 *Journal of Second Language Writing*(《二语写作杂志》)和 *TESOL Quarterly* 杂志编委会委员。[②] Polio 为《年度评论》各卷确定的选题为"应用语言学专题"(卷 30)、"第二语言教育研究"(卷 31)、"公式化语言研究"(卷 32)、"多语现象研究"(卷 33)、"研究方法专题"(卷 34)。这体现了她作为总主编延续了该刊创办时的主导思

---

① Spolsky, Bernard. Homepage. http://www.biu.ac.il/faculty/spolsky/. 2015. 1. 3.
② Polio, Charlene. http://www.wsu.edu/~oikui/. 2015. 1. 5.

想,即每卷的稿子都是就某一领域的特定问题而精选的。

为《年度评论》写稿的作者中不乏名人,如 Henry G. Widdowson、James R. Martin、Bernard Spolsky、Alan Davies 等都是国际著名语言学家。

三、国人参与

我国大陆、港台地区和国际华人圈对《应用语言学年度评论》很为重视。

台湾学者郑锦全(Chan-chuan Cheng)在第 7 卷上发表"语言和计算机"一文。郑当时任台湾师范大学华语文教学研究所讲座教授、台湾地区研究院语言所研究员和人文社会科学研究中心通信研究员(Cheng, 2014)。[①]另一位是台湾清华大学培养的许静芬(Ching-fen Hsu)博士,现在台湾华梵大学人文学院师资培养研究中心工作,专攻威廉姆斯综合征(Williams Syndrome)发育障碍的语言习得研究,是第 28 卷"威廉姆斯综合征:基因型和认知表型描述"一文的第一作者。[②]香港教育学院语言教学研究中心主任的李楚成(David C. S. Li)教授在第 26 卷上发表"作为大中华通用语的汉语"一文。[③]在《年度评论》第 30 卷独立发表有关传承语学习的社会文化维度一文的何纬芸(Agnes Weiyun He)教授,早期毕业于北京外国语大学,现为 Stony Brook 大学应用语言学和亚洲研究专业的教授,筹建了该校多语和跨文化交际中心。何纬芸主要研究语言语境和语篇的结合,人们如何通过日常互动逐步构建和重构概念、社团和文化。近十年来,她专门研究不同时期和不同背景下汉语作为传承语的社会化。[④]在《年度评论》第 27 卷与 John Flowerdew 联名发表"多语制和二语写作在电

---

① Cheng, Chan-chuan(郑锦全). http://doc88.com/P-795557797523.html. 2014.12.9.
② Hsu, Ching-fen(许静芬). http://www.docin.com/p-2898691.html & key. 2015.1.5.
③ Li, David, C. S.(李楚成). http://dfl.shufe.edu.cn/structure/ xueshu-com-142410-1.htm. 2014.12.9.
④ He, Agnes Weiyun(何纬芸). http://www.stonybrook.edu/commcms/asian/PROGRAMS.html. 2014.12.9.

子时代的关系"一文的李咏燕博士（Yongyan Li）任教于香港大学教育学院英语教育系，其研究范围包括专业写作、多语学者的研究和发表实践、言而有据的写作、科学文章的整篇抄袭现象、在职教育等。[①] 令人瞩目的是，上述学者与大陆高校和研究单位保持良好的学术联系，如郑锦全教授曾担任四川大学文学与新闻学院兼职教授、厦门大学嘉庚学院中文系兼职教授、北京大学汉语语言学研究中心兼职研究员；李楚成教授曾在上海财经大学举行关于中国外语学习者和使用者常见错误的纠正讲座；何纬芸教授与上海交通大学苗瑞琴副教授合作编写了"继承语之习得及其社会化"一文。[②]

大陆学者对《年度评论》也做出了应有的反应和贡献。早在1981年《年度评论》第1卷问世后，我国学者左焕琪教授便在国内语言学权威刊物《当代语言学》上作了报道，既介绍了编者 Kaplan 的背景，也对该卷四个部分作了近似导读的介绍。作者当时就以敏锐的眼光指出这是"近年来美国应用语言学领域引人瞩目的新刊物"。[③] 较近的可举2012年方秀才的"程式语面面观介绍"一文，对《年度评论》第32卷从认知视角、教学应用、社会学进展和未来展望四个部分深入介绍。作者特别注意到，为了从多种视角讨论程式语这一主题，总主编没有限定程式语的定义、内涵，也没有统一术语，让每篇文章的作者采用自己认同的术语和定义，[④] 这表明《年度评论》并没有因为总主编的变动而放弃原有的风格。

行文至此，有必要提一下以 Charlene Polio 为首的新编委会所作的一个重大决定，那就是她代表编委会聘请了我国广东外语外贸大学王初明教授从第31卷起任《年度评论》顾问委员会的委员。这是对我国应用语言

[①] Li, Yongyan（李咏燕）. http://www_researchgate.net/profile/Yongyan_Li/publications. 2014.12.9.
[②] 何纬芸，苗瑞琴. 继承语之习得及其社会化. 载姬建国，蒋楠主编：应用语言学（西方人文社会科学前沿述评）. 北京：中国人民大学出版社，2007. 239–255.
[③] 左焕琪. 应用语言学年度评述(1980).《国外语言学》, 1983,（3）: 46–49.
[④] 方秀才.《程式语面面观》介绍.《当代语言学》, 2013, 15（4）: 492–495.

学研究发展和水平的肯定。我与王初明教授结识于 1995 年 9 月，当时我是香港中文大学的访问学者，他是英语系的博士生。我们经常一起讨论学术问题。长江后浪推前浪，2011 年我从北京外国语大学中国外语教育研究中心学术委员会主任退下后，他接替了此职。王初明教授现在的学术兼职有国务院学位委员会外国语言文学学科评议组成员、中国高等教育学会外语教学研究分会副会长。他的主要研究方向为第二语言习得研究及其在外语教学中的应用，主要学术创见有外语写长法、语境补缺假说、外语语音学习假设、外语学习的学伴用随原则、读后续写的理论和应用价值。

四、"商务"特色

除保留剑桥版《应用语言学年度评论》的原有特色外，商务版《应用语言学年度评论》有它自己的特色。

商务版《年度评论》从第 20 卷开始，而不是从第 1 卷开始。我认为商务印书馆此举着眼于让读者以更多的精力把握应用语言学在新世纪的发展，急读者之所急。我们还应该看到，《年度评论》第 20 卷实际上起到承前启后的作用。在该卷中，为上世纪创刊时立下汗马功劳的 Robert Kaplan、William Grabe 和 G. Richard Tucker 分别对应用语言学和《年度评论》在二十年中的发展作了系统的总结，帮助读者对前二十年有个总体了解，又寄厚望于这门新学科在新世纪、新千年的发展，把握前进的方向。其次，商务版《年度评论》增加了满足中国读者需求的新内容，那就是每卷都有一篇 1.5 万字左右的中文导读。这便于帮助读者掌握每卷的基本内容和背景材料，特别是汉语界的教师、研究者和学生。

参与此任务的导读作者有国内外语界著名学者，也有新生代的中青年学者。这些专家学者对自己撰写的内容比较熟悉。作为此项目的组织者，我没有向他们摊派任务，而是让各位学者根据自己熟悉的领域自由选题。对各位作者的努力我在此谨表谢意。如前所述，导读初稿完成后均由上海复旦大学朱永生教授和北京师范大学田贵森教授分别先行审读。对两位教授退休后仍能不辞辛苦、鼎力相助的感激之情,难以言表。

由于《年度评论》涉及多个学科和领域,各卷原版的体例不全相同,而各位导读作者的学术生涯也不尽相同,我们对导读编写体例上只作大致要求,不强调绝对统一。总的印象是,每位导读作者对本卷各章内容都能做提纲挈领的介绍和解释,帮助读者理解和抓住要点,这是共同的优点。导读作者各自的特色则表现在:(1)能在正文之前对本卷的总主编、客座编辑做介绍,并对总主编的引言深入分析,起到画龙点睛的作用;(2)对本卷主题进行了解释;(3)对有关主题在20世纪的研究状况或《年度评论》已经发表过的专辑作必要回顾;(4)对每卷论文内容进行归纳,指出其特点;(5)坦率指出某卷内容的不足之处;(6)结合国内现状进行讨论,并进行反思;(7)在讨论中,引入当代先进理论;(8)向我国学界和领导部门提出今后有待深入展开研究的问题。

在结束本序之际,再次感谢各位导读作者,以及永生教授和贵森教授的共同努力,使本项艰巨任务得以顺利完成;祝贺商务版《应用语言学年度评论》正式出版;祝愿商务印书馆今后在应用语言学和理论语言学等领域为外语教育界和学术界做出更多更大贡献!

北京大学蓝旗营寓所
2015年元月

导　读

何　伟[①]

一、引言

《应用语言学年度评论》（*Annual Review of Applied Linguistics*，简称 *ARAL*）第 20 卷是 William Grabe 作为十年总主编而编辑出版的最后一卷。与以往几卷不同，Grabe 把本卷的主题定为"作为新兴学科的应用语言学"。正如他和 Robert Kaplan 在第 1 篇中所回顾的应用语言学和《年度评论》在此二十周年的发展历程，也正如 Richard Tucker 在第 15 篇"结束语"中所论述的处于千年之交的应用语言学今后如何谋求进一步的发展，Grabe 和他的学术界朋友，力图论证应用语言学是一门名副其实的新兴学科，而且前途无量。

在这个背景下，Grabe 对本卷组稿的计划与以往也有所不同。他要求被邀请供稿的专家学者就本卷的主题具体回答一些问题，如应用语言学与第二语言习得（SLA）、作为外语的英语教学（TESOL）、专门用途语言（LSP）、专门用途英语（ESP）、语言政策及规划（LPLP）等领域之间究竟存在什么样的关系？在教师教育中，社会语境起什么样的作用？在语言

[①] 何伟，北京外国语大学中国外语教育研究中心教授，博士生导师，*Journal of World Languages* 联合主编，*Functional Linguistics* 副主编，《北京科技大学学报》语言学栏目主编，中山大学功能语言学研究所客座教授，香港城市大学兼职教授，中国英汉比较研究会一级学会理事，功能语言学专业委员会常务理事，英汉语篇分析专业委员会秘书长，北京市优秀教师，教育部新世纪优秀人才。主持完成多项国家及省部级课题，已发表 100 多项成果。
联系方式：北京市海淀区西三环北路 2 号，北京外国语大学中国外语教育研究中心

学习或读写能力发展中，包括社会心理因素在内的社会身份是如何影响语言的接受和产出的？在应用语言学研究中，英语的地位独一无二，相应地，其他语言被忽视了，而我们是否也应该给予其他语言一定的地位？在语言教育及学习中，我们的研究范式如何得以扩展？应用语言学的前景如何？Grabe 特别要求撰稿者把自己研究领域里的问题摆出来。

从本卷的框架看，除 William Grabe 本人的引言外，共选用 15 篇文章，包括上面谈到的第 1 篇和第 15 篇。这些述评文章主要围绕以上问题对 2000 年之前几年（尤其是前两三年）的应用语言学领域的发展动态和研究成果进行了回顾和评述。参加写作的有不少是国际上的著名学者，如 Henry G. Widdowson（第 2 篇），JoAnn（Jodi）Crandall（第 3 篇），John M. Swales（第 4 篇），James R. Martin（第 7 篇），Diane Larsen-Freeman（第 10 篇），Elaine Tarone（第 11 篇），Merrill Swain（第 12 篇）等。本书内容丰富，涵盖面广，是应用语言学领域的学者和广大语言教师了解该领域前沿理论和研究动态的重要参考文献。

二、正文介绍

1. 应用语言学与《应用语言学年度评论》

本卷第 1 篇系 Robert B. Kaplan 和 William Grabe 撰写的"应用语言学与《应用语言学年度评论》"。Kaplan 和 Grabe 通过回顾 1999 年在东京召开的应用语言学国际大会（AILA Congress）的情况，为读者介绍了与会专家学者对应用语言学学科的界定，并在此基础上追述了《应用语言学年度评论》的创刊历史，明晰了该刊在应用语言学学科发展中的架构作用。

应用语言学这个术语究竟指什么？应用语言学的范围和地位如何？应用语言学是如何成为一个学科的？这些问题一直萦绕在应用语言学家及众多学者的脑海中。因此，参加 1999 年应用语言学国际大会的专家学者对这些问题进行了研讨。绝大多数专家学者一致认为应用语言学应具有以下八个特点：第一，应用语言学拥有作为一个学科的标志，包括专业期刊、专业协会、作为一个领域的国际认同、研究课题的资助资金、大量的自认为是应用语言学研究学者的个体、训练有素的从业人员等；第二，语言学是应用语言学的一个主要理论知识基础；第三，应用语言学研究由现实世界实际问题驱动，比如语言使用、语言评估、语言接触、语言政策以及语言教学方面的实际问题；第四，应用语言学除了需要语言学理论作为支撑外，还需要其他学科知识来解决语言问题，比如心理学、教育学、人类学、政治学、社会学、文学、经济学等；第五，应用语言学具有跨学科性质，主要是由于诸多语言实际问题的解决不能仅依靠单一学科知识；第六，应用语言学领域的核心议题涉及语言教学、语言教师训练与语言课程发展；第七，应用语言学包括双语研究、语料库语言学、法律语言学、语言接触研究、语言测试、语言翻译、职场语境下的语言使用、词典编纂学、读写能力发展、二语习得以及二语写作研究等分支学科；第八，应用语言学还涉及与语言相关的研究领域，比如母语读写能力研究、语言与文学、语言病理学以及自然语言处理。

上述八个特点看起来基本界定了应用语言学领域，然而事实上仍然使该学科处于一个模糊不清的状态，仍然没有厘清应用语言学和语言学的界限。

也有一些专家学者提出，对应用语言学作为一个学科的界定，应从包括学校、研究中心、协会以及期刊等组织机构对知识建构所做的贡献这一视角来进行，该观点认为任何一个学科领域都具有其决定性的基本架构。Kaplan 和 Grabe 认为《应用语言学年度评论》刊物在应用语言学的发展中就起到了这样一个重要的架构作用，这就是他们综述该刊物对应用语言学学科所做贡献的根本所在。

在综览《应用语言学年度评论》20 年的发展历程中，他们首先介绍了该刊物与美国应用语言学协会以及《应用语言学》（AL）期刊的历史渊源，较为详细地陈述了美国应用语言学协会的发展历史，提到 1973 年系美国应用语言学协会的发起时间，不过正式成立时间是四年后的 1977 年，第一届执行委员会的情况如下：主席 Wilga Rivers，副主席 Roger Shuy，秘书 Bernold Spolsky，成员 Charles Ferguson、Betty W. Robinett、Albert Valdman 和 G. Richard Tucker。该协会在成立之后不久，即 1978 年国际应用语言学学会（AILA）在加拿大蒙特利尔召开的第五次大会（该大会每三年召开一次）上，成为国际应用语言学学会的一个分支机构。

应用语言学目前拥有两个重要的学术期刊，即《应用语言学》和《应用语言学年度评论》。《应用语言学》创刊于 1980 年，由美国应用语言学协会和英国应用语言学协会共同资助，由牛津大学出版社出版，由来自北美和英国的专家学者做联合主编，每年 1 卷，主要发表在应用语言学领域具有重要影响的论文，同时也发表一些书评和专题文章。该期刊很好地体现了应用语言学作为一个学科的发展状况。

《应用语言学年度评论》在 1981 年创刊时，由 Robert B. Kaplan、Randall Jones 和 G. Richard Tucker 担任第一卷的编辑，1981 年至 1990 年期间由 Robert B. Kaplan 担任主编，每一卷的前言也就由他撰写，1991 年至 2000 年期间 William Grabe 接任主编，同样这期间的前言由他撰写，之后 Mary McGroarty 接任主编。该刊物为学界提供的有关应用语言学发展状况的综述性文章很好地体现了该学科已有的研究范围、核心话题以及存在的种种问题，并影响了该学科领域的未来发展方向。

2. 客体语言和语言主体：应用语言学的中介作用

本卷第 2 篇文章是 Henry G. Widdowson 撰写的"客体语言和语言主体：应用语言学的中介作用"。Widdowson 通过引述 Chomsky（1988）、Halliday（Halliday, et al. 1964）、Hymes（1972）等形式语言学和功能语言学家的观点，以及通过回顾 Sinclair（1997）等语料库语言学家的看法，提出了应用语言学在语言学和实际语言教学之间扮演"中介"角色的观点。

在 2000 年之前的 30 多年时间里，语言学研究的内容逐渐从抽象的语言符号转向具体的语言使用，这意味着语言学关注的现象与实际生活相关。然而，我们不能断定语言学描述的客体语言与语言使用者实际接受和产出的语言是一回事，二者之间的不同正是应用语言学研究的话题。

Widdowson 认为教师教授的语言不同于语言学家研究的语言,无论形式语言学、功能语言学、语用学等语言学学科提供了多么完好的语言描述原则,这些原则都不能直接应用于语言教学。他同样认为语料库语言学为我们提供的仅仅是部分语言实例,与实际语言教学仍不相同。在他看来,语言学描述的客体语言只是"正常"社会交往中语言使用者所经历的语言现实,语言主体与其不同,是一定语境下的语言现实。语言描述和教学设计之间不匹配的关系引发了应用语言学的"中介"作用,也就是说,应用语言学的任务不是将语言学研究的结果直接"转移"(transfer)到语言教学领域,而是将其"转化"(translate)到语言教学领域。在转化过程中,应用语言学专家学者所起的"中介"作用就是"演示"(demonstrate),即使用应用语言学领域的专门术语阐释清楚语言学所提供的语言见解,这样的"演示"视角就是教学法。语言教师根据应用语言学家提供的教学法设计自身的教学材料和具体教学方法及技巧。

3. 语言教师教育

本卷第 3 篇文章系 JoAnn(Jodi)Crandall 撰写的"语言教师教育"。Crandall 通过参阅近百种相关文献,圈点出了语言教师教育在 2000 年之前 10 年中的变化趋势,其中也表明了自身对语言教师教育发展的看法。

语言教师教育课程一般情况下由应用语言学系、教育系或语言文学系提供,不过,在 2000 年之前的 10 年中,普通教育学对准教师和在职教师教育影响很大,主要体现为对以下内容的关注:强调包括观察、实践教学、课程设计和教学材料选择等方面的实际经历;强调课堂为中心以及教师研究;强调教师信念及认知的作用。教师教育中的变化趋势体现了教师教育理论和实践的发展。这些趋势主要涉及四个方面的转变:

第一,学习、教学以及语言教学理论由过去的以知识传授、产品为取向转为现在的以建构和过程为取向。Crandall 与学界一致,认为这种转变是有益的:过去教师是被动的知识传授者,而现在教师的主观能动性得以发挥出来。第二,人们越来越意识到过去的语言教师教育课程过于理想化，其提供的方法手段等不能应对课堂现实。和许多专家学者一样，Crandall认为在为准教师提供相关教育课程的同时，为他们提供教学实践的机会，这样就能为他们的理论学习提供相应的实践化语境，有利于教学实践问题的解决。第三，学界愈发认识到教师的学习经历对他们的教学实践有着很大的影响。因此，Crandall认同Freeman（1991，1996）及其他学者提出的建议，鼓励教师在教学过程中经常进行自察和自省活动。第四，人们逐渐意识到教学和医学、法律一样，是一种专门的职业，从业者需要继续学习、不断开展研究等，以更好地与时俱进。Crandall在论述在职培训的重要性时，特别提及了Freeman（Freeman and Richards 1996）对教师在职培训功能的论述，认为在职培训可促使教师转变陈旧的教学理念，发展新的教学模式，更新已有的教学材料等。

4. 专门用途语言

John M. Swales撰写了本卷第4篇文章："专门用途语言"。Swales简单回顾了1964年以后30多年来专门用途语言作为应用语言学一个分支领域的发展状况，指出世界范围内越来越多的专家学者和教师参与到专门用途语言的研究和教学实践中。

通过综览Johns（1997）、Douglas和Selinker（1994）以及Whyte（1995）等专家学者的研究，Swales指出，截至2000年，专门用途英语/语言的地位不明确。专门用途英语/语言与语篇分析和语用学的关系非常密切，同时也与语言评估和交际语言教学较为相关，不过，它与二语习得之间的共性比较少——这也就是为什么《应用语言学年度评论（第19卷）》辟有不同的章节分别探讨它们。基于这种特点，在美国，专门用途英语/语言基本上是作为一种职业存在的，不过，在澳大利亚、巴西、英国、中国香港等国家和地区，它的发展趋向比较好，可以说是作为应用语言学领域的一个分支学科而存在。

通过回顾和引述Atkinson（1999）、Gibbons（1999）、Hyden和Mishler（1999）等专家学者的研究，Swales为读者呈现了专门用途语言与科学、医学和法律研究之间越来越密切的关系，指出许多专家学者结合语言与其他学科提出了语类（genre）概念，并开展了科学语言、医学语言、法律语言等语类结构及特征的研究。读者从中可以看出，专门用途语言的研究范围越来越宽广。

通过概述 Dudley-Evans 和 St John（1998）、Smart（1998）等专家学者的研究，Swales 认为商业用途英语的发展势头良好，不过，其质量与学术英语研究之间没什么大的区别。在对比专门用途英语和其他语言时，Swales 与 Phillipson（1999）看法一致，认为在专门用途语言的发展中，英语已呈现独占鳌头的情势，他们提倡扩展对其他专门用途语言的研究。

5. 专门用途英语在北非：地位、问题及挑战

本卷第 5 篇文章系 Mohamed Daoud 撰写的"专门用途英语在北非：地位、问题及挑战"。Daoud 通过综述相关文献，归纳总结了专门用途英语在北非所处的实际地位，遇到的主要问题以及面临的重要挑战。

在回顾 Battenberg（1997）、Walters（1999）等众多专家学者研究的基础上，Daoud 指出，尽管在北非社会对专门用途语言专业人员的需求越来越大，然而专门用途语言，尤其是英语的地位还没有得到应有的肯定，无论是政府，还是学校以及其他相关机构还没有采取必要而充分的措施保障专门用途语言，尤其是英语的发展和实践。他认为，专门用途语言，尤其是英语的发展，在北非遇到四个方面的问题和挑战：第一，由于历史原因，北非大部分国家仍然比较抵制英语的使用；第二，专门用途语言（包括英语）的教学实践是临时性的，缺乏课程设计、教师培训、评估等活动的支撑；第三，与世界其他地区一样，北非国家对商务及职场语言的培训需求日益高涨；第四，对于从事应用语言学研究的人员来说，如何平衡理论和实践之间的关系以及如何做到这两个方面的相长，都是比较棘手的问题和挑战。

在展望未来时，Daoud 指出，北非学者从来没有怀疑过专门用途英语在研究范围上的国际性，但是许多人鉴于专门用途英语在英美等国家的研

究和实践与本土之间的相关性以及本土的研究和实践对英美等国家专门用途英语理论研究和实践的贡献程度两个方面，质疑专门用途英语的国际性质。

在北非，从事专门用途英语教学和实践的人员对该领域的专家颇有责备，认为他们的研究太过理论性，而没有针对北非的现实情况提供适宜的解决方案。另一方面，学界提倡从业人员自身通过语言学的学习、文化素养的提高等，结合当地的政治、经济以及行政现实状况，设计可行的解决方案；学界同时提倡本土从业人员在借鉴国外研究和实践成果的基础上，在开展本土实践和研究的过程中，不断总结和提升，以形成很好的成果表述，并予以发表。这样，专门用途英语的国际性质才能得到真正体现。

不过，Daoud 也指出，国际学者发表的一些成果，尤其是教材，其内容的呈现形式有时不适合北非的当前现状，比如在科技文献中的一些非言语表达形式的使用等，对本土从业人员的理解造成了很大的困惑。由此，Daoud 与许多本土学者观点一致，认为一方面北非的从业人员应加强自身的学习，另一方面呼吁学界提供一些有关教学技能和策略以及翻译技能等方面的培训课程，以帮助本土从业人员更好地借鉴国际研究和实践成果，同时也能在国际学界发表本土研究成果。

6. 写作、读写能力与应用语言学

第 6 篇"写作、读写能力与应用语言学"由 Ilona Leki 撰写。Leki 首先描述了写作和读写能力研究者对自身研究与应用语言学学科之间的关系，指出他们内部存在两种观点，一种是把自身看作应用语言学家及学者，一种是认为自身不是应用语言学阵营里的一员，尤其是北美的写作和读写能力教师及研究者——他们认为应用语言学研究科学性差，过度强调定量研究，而缺乏深度分析和解释。不过，Leki 本人认为从事写作和读写能力教学及研究的人员属于应用语言学这一大的圈子。

接着，Leki 通过综述相关文献，指出在应用语言学框架内，对包括语类研究、对比修辞研究、高等教育中第二语言读写能力需求种类研究、母语对二语学习的影响研究以及纠错研究等在内的需求分析的必要性和可行性的看法,因学者而异。然后,Leki 通过回顾 Fairclough(1998)、Ivanic(1998)等人的研究,指出在对二语写作和读写能力进行研究时,不少专家学者开始关注学习者身份这一因素,特别提出在以后研究中,学界应对同时作为学习者和教师这一类人员在学习和教学过程中身份的冲突问题进行探讨。再者,Leki 通过回顾 Harklau(1999)、Spack(1997)以及自己(Leki 1999)分别对 4 名美国高中生、1 名日本大学生和 1 名在美国读过高中和大学的波兰语学生的多年跟踪观察和研究,指出类似的个案纵向研究对于学习者读写能力的整体认识有着建设性意义。最后,Leki 在参阅诸多相关文献的基础上,得出:主流应用语言学的实践和研究基本限于英语以及英语作为单一语言的国家,这对二语读写能力的研究是不利的。与 Pattanayak(参见 Pennycook 1994)意见一致,Leki 从而提出应用语言学家及学者应拓展实践和研究的范围。

7. 设计与实践:功能语言学运用

本卷第 7 篇系 James R. Martin 撰写的"设计与实践:功能语言学运用"。Martin 依据 Halliday(1985, 1994)的观点,首先陈述了这样一个认识:语言学运用是一种社会行为,这种运用消除了语言学与应用语言学之间相互对立的壁垒,相反证实了理论与实践之间的辩证关系。基于这种认识,Martin 回顾了应用语言学领域的写作能力研究状况。

Martin 带领悉尼大学语言学系及来自其他学校的研究人员以 Halliday 创建的系统功能语言学为理论指导,尤其是 Martin(1993)本人在系统功能语言学框架中提出的语类概念(genre),重新设计了澳大利亚中学的课程大纲及教学法。他们[比如 Coffin(1996)、Veel 和 Coffin(1996)]制作了多个学科的语类系统,根据这些系统,他们发展了学习者的学习路径,比如在历史科目学习中,学习者首先学习如何叙述语类,然后学习因果关系从而解释语类,再后学习如何论证语类,最后了解有关历史的语类谱系。在这样一个学习路径中,研究人员需要讲解清楚语法隐喻概念，因为该概念在学习者读写能力发展中起到至关重要的作用。根据学科语类系统，他们发展了教／学整个循环过程，其中有三个关键阶段——解构、联合建构和独立建构，与它们相关的是语类的社会语境及相关知识的建构，该教／学模式的核心目的是促使学习者通过了解相关社会文化语境知识来批判性地掌握一个语类。

除了语类概念，Martin认为教师和学生需要掌握一定的功能语法知识，熟悉语篇及语域分析的方法，另外，需要懂得评价语言的特点。在谈及如何有效地运用语言学理论时，Martin提出人们应该学习和了解新的语言学理论，比如系统功能语言学理论新的发展内容、新维果茨基（neo-Vygotskyan）学习理论、批评话语分析和积极话语分析等，以新的理论知识来指导实践，反过来，也可以看到实践问题是如何促进理论发展的。最后，Martin谈到对于下一代人的培养，应该加强有关元语言的教育，即应该让学习者尽可能地学习一些语言学理论术语，将理论知识运用到各科目的学习中。在众多语言学理论中，他极力推荐Halliday及其同事和全球范围内的追随者所发展的系统功能语言学，原因是该理论构建的目的是语篇分析，而应用语言学研究以语篇分析为取向。

8. 语言政策与规划

本卷第8篇为Sauli Takala和Kari Sajavaara撰写的"语言政策与规划"。Takala和Sajavaara与Haugen（1966）、Kloss（1969）、Tauli（1968）、Fishman（1974）等专家学者一样，一致认为语言政策与规划是应用语言学学科的一个分支领域。两位作者在本章主要结合欧洲斯堪的纳维亚和波罗的海地区国家的语言政策和规划情况，探讨并归纳总结了有关外语指导体系及不同社会语境中外语使用的预定变化及原因，特别讨论了语言政策与规划以及规划与评估之间的关系。

在欧洲，尤其是斯堪的纳维亚和波罗的海地区，政府及其教育主管部门对语言特别是外语的使用关注度比较高，原因有多种：第一，全球化提高了对外语的需求程度；第二，公共部门及机构为了加强人们之间的沟通,推出了相关规定。比如欧盟在 1995 年发布的白皮书中提到,欧洲人应在母语外,至少学习两门欧洲语言。这样一来,许多国家的教育部门或机构都对语言政策做出了相应的调整;第三,学习外语也是人们因旅游及移民需要而做出的选择。当然,语言政策及规划的变化也反映了人们的政治诉求。

语言政策与规划作为应用语言学的一个重要研究领域,在《应用语言学年度评论》中得到了充分的体现,比如说在第 2、6、10、14 和 17 卷中都刊有相关文章,然而此分支领域在应用语言学中的地位还没有得到很好的稳固,仍然需要进一步发展。Takala 和 Sajavaara 认为,学者们今后应更加系统地参考广义的而不只是语言政策研究文献。另外,两位作者指出,语言规划可以有多种形式,至于哪种形式好以及哪种形式不好,需要一定的标准来界定。他们提出界定标准应至少应对 4 种问题:如何建立规划体系?规划过程中,如何确定使用的原则、价值以及如何制订相应的程序?对具体的规划,如何进行公共审议和讨论?如何进行规划实施情况的合理监控?同时,他们认为语言规划可由行政部门来制订,也可以由大学研究机构来制订,这种语言规划可分为战略规划(strategic planning)和实施规划(operational planning)。

规划和评估密切相关,可以说,评估是规划的一个内在部分。至于如何进行评估,两位作者特别提到了 Stufflebeam(1975)建构的 CIPP 模式。CIPP 系 context(语境)、input(输入)、process(过程)和 product(结果)4 个单词的首字母缩略语。此评估模式所涵盖的 4 项评估要素针对的是规划全过程中的 4 种决定:规划(planning)、建构(structuring)、实施(implementing)和重建(recycling)。

简单地讲,语境评估是最基本的评估内容,旨在为规划目的提供逻辑依据。此项评估需界定相关的语言社区,描述理想和实际的语言环境条件,确定已满足的需求以及未得到利用的机会,诊断出阻碍或干预需求实现以及制约机会得以合理利用的困难因素等。相关问题的确定能为规划目的的达成提供必要的基础。输入评估也是一项基础评估内容。此项工作需要识别和评估负责规划机构的能力、实现规划目标的策略以及实施策略的方案。过程评估的目的是为负责实施规划的人员定期提供反馈意见，以帮助实施人员找到现有的问题或预测将来可能出现的问题，为其改善实施方案提供必要的信息等。结果评估，顾名思义，指的是对规划实施的结果进行评估和解释。

两位作者一致认为，相关部门或机构在制定语言政策和规划时，不应只对目前的现状进行评估，还应重视对预期带来的变化开展相应的评估工作，这样才能确保新的语言政策和规划在实施方面的及时性、有效性、持续性等。

9. 评估与测试

本卷第 9 篇系 Caroline Clapham 撰写的"评估与测试"。Clapham 着重探讨了应用语言学与评估的关系以及评估与测试之间的关系。

通过概览专家学者们对应用语言学的解释和界定，比如 Widdowson（1980）、Johnson 和 Johnson（1998）、Bachman 和 Cohen（1998）、Hudson（1999）等，Clapham 总结：语言评估是应用语言学学科的一个重要领域，它为应用语言学研究者提供分析语料及数据，最终促进理论的发展和完善；语言测试不限于二语学生的语言水平，应该也包括对使用诱导技术（elicitation techniques）收集来的语料的信度及效度等方面的测试。

通过引述 Bachman 和 Palmer（1996）以及 Alderson 和自己（1992）等人的研究，Clapham 得出评估方法影响课堂教学，新的学习及教学理论也会导致测试在方法和内容方面的变化。在探讨测试与评估之间的关系时，Clapham 不赞同学界对二者之间关系的对立做法——把测试看做能保证信度和效度的一种正式测评方式，而把其他的非正式测评方式归为评估。她认为在未来应用语言学的发展中，鉴于教学材料愈发趋于真实性，语言能力测试（performance test）愈发盛行，测试与评估之间的裂隙会逐渐弥合起来。

为了能充分说明测试与评估之间的关系，Clapham 对测试者（tester）和评估员（assessor）各自的关注点做了解释。测试者指那些在设计测试内容时关注效度和信度标准的人员，评估员指那些在设计评估内容时非有意识地受效度和信度标准限制的人员。尽管评估员认为测试者过于纠结于数据分析，以至于对测试的内容和实施方式等没有给予充分的重视，从而测试本身是非交际性的，其实际意义不大；也尽管测试者认为评估员使用的评估方法比较新颖有趣，而由于缺少预测试环节，从而其评分标准未必系统一致，其结果不一定能达到预期目的——总之，尽管两者互不信任，然而他们之间不存在本质的区别，根本原因在于他们目的一致性，均是检验语言学习的能力和结果，并为语言教学提供相应的反馈意见。这也就是 Clapham 有时交替使用测试和评估两个术语的理据所在。

10. 二语习得与应用语言学

撰写本卷第 10 篇"二语习得与应用语言学"的是著名学者 Diane Larsen-Freeman。他认为，作为应用语言学的一个分支领域，二语习得与应用语言学一样，在理论上具有多学科性质，在实践上具有经验性质。

在本篇中，Larsen-Freeman 首先回顾了 30 多年以来的二语习得研究的理论基础，提到母语习得、语言学、心理学、社会语言学、教育学等理论均对二语习得研究的贡献比较大，特别指出其中的母语迁移现象以及句法系统发展在二语习得研究中比较普遍。他另外指出研究者们从动机、态度、天资、年龄、认知类型、策略、个性等来解释二语学习者学习效果之间的层级差异。接着，Larsen-Freeman 总结了主流二语习得研究所面临的挑战：第一，二语习得过程研究脱离语境，具有反社会（asocial）取向；第二，把二语学习者看做被动的接受者，忽视了他们在语言学习中的主观能动性；第三，把解释语法能力看做二语习得研究的终极目标，忽视了认知方式、学习策略等因素对二语习得的影响。再者，在谈到二语习得未来的发展时，Larsen-Freeman 提出研究者们应认真面对上述挑战，认清二语习得的本质，拓宽研究视野，并综合各种理论视角，来呈现二语习得过程本身的复杂性、动态性以及非线性特点。

最后，Larsen-Freeman 就未来应用语言学学者的培养和发展，提出以下认识：从二语习得角度，在研究工作中，应用语言学学者应精通各种研究范式，深入讨论各种观点的优势和局限性；在学习过程中，应用语言学学生应被教授各种研究方法，包括定性的和定量的，也应被提供充分的实践机会，并且配有教师亲自指导；教学界甚至可通过提供一些有关政治方面的课程，来培养应用语言学学生的社会正义观（social-justice perspective），从而鼓励他们在二语习得教学受到某些现实条件的限制时，可发表有理有据的观点。

11. 中介语理论是否应涉及"语境"因素

Elaine Tarone 撰写了本卷第 11 篇，即"中介语理论是否应涉及'语境'因素"。学界普遍认为，社会语境因素是否影响二语习得过程是二语习得研究领域中一个很棘手的问题。Tarone 在本章围绕此问题，回顾总结了三个方面的研究，得出了相应的结论。

第一，部分从事应用语言学其他领域研究的专家学者以及二语习得研究者，比如 Firth 和 Wagner（1997）、Rampton（1995）等，认为二语习得研究者忽视了二语习得过程中社会语境因素所起的重要影响；第二，包括二语习得研究者在内的部分应用语言学专家学者，比如 Peirce（1995）、Platt 和 Troudi（1997）、Bayley 和 Preston（1996）等，从社会语境及建构主义视角开展了相关实验，结论是社会语境因素对二语习得过程的影响不够确定，还有一些研究者，比如 de Bot（见本卷第 14 篇）、Scovel（见本卷第 13 篇）等，从心理语言学及认知角度开展了相关实验，结论是社会语境因素与二语习得过程不相关；第三，许多研究学者，比如 Swales（1990）、Bhatia（1993）、Cohen（1997）、Tarone 和 Swain（1995）等，从变换二语学习者的社会语境这个角度进行了多项实验研究，他们认为在不同社会语境中二语学习者接受的语言输入材料涉及不同的语法规则，并且正式程度以及是否有输入干预等都不相同，同时也有学者，包括 Kormos（1999）、Gass（1997）等，通过观察二语习得过程的变化，指出二语习得过程中的纠错、发展序列、意义协商等均受到社会因素的制约。

通过上述综述，作者 Tarone 指出未来的二语习得研究似乎应该将社会语境因素和心理习得过程结合起来，正如同 Preston（1996）以及 Larsen-Freeman（1997）所强调的那样，二语习得研究应将心理语言学和社会语言学整合起来，放置在一个框架下，以用作理论基础。

12. 近年来加拿大的法语沉浸式教育研究对二语习得及应用语言学的贡献

本卷第 12 篇"近年来加拿大的法语沉浸式教育研究对二语习得及应用语言学的贡献"的作者是 Merrill Swain。截至 2000 年，法语沉浸式教育项目在加拿大已开展了 30 多年，其研究成果对二语习得的理解有什么贡献？对更为广泛的应用语言学又有什么贡献？在今后的研究中，还需要关注哪些方面？在本篇，Swain 就上述问题主要围绕 2000 年之前几年的相关研究，来综述法语沉浸式教育项目对二语习得及应用语言学的贡献。

法语沉浸式教育在加拿大有多种形式，其中以其他科目知识为内容而以法语为载体的教育形式最为普遍，包括 Swain 和 Johnson（1997）、Genesee（1987）等在内的专家学者的相关研究成果促进了这种教育方式的进一步发展。同时，许多研究表明，这种教育方式加深了人们对社会条件在双语教育过程中所起影响的理解，例证了跨学科知识及相关研究范式对应用语言学发展所起的积极作用，说明了相关研究成果对应用语言学其他领域的发展有着借鉴性的价值。

在探讨法语沉浸式教育对二语习得的贡献时，Swain 通过综述学界的相关研究，指出在学生的语言输出、教师在课堂中针对学生的参与给出什么样的反馈、学生对语言形式的关注、母语在二语学习中的角色、学习者年龄因素、语言测试形式和内容等多个方面的具体数据材料，说明了这种教育方式是二语习得的一种很好的形式，增强了人们对二语习得过程的认识。在谈及未来的发展趋势时，Swain 建议在观察的基础上加强实验研究，考察毕业生在工作场合对法语的使用情况，增加对魁北克与加拿大其他地区的法语沉浸式教育的效果的比较研究等。

13. 关键期假设研究评介

本卷第 13 篇系 Thomas Scovel 撰写的"关键期假设研究评介"。自 1963 年加拿大神经外科医生 Penfield 提出人们越早学习外语,效果越好的观点后,应用语言学界、语言学界、生物医学界等都对此表示出了很大的研究兴趣,从而语言学习关键期假设(Critical Period Hypothesis)就成了应用语言学领域的一个经久不衰的重要研究话题。

Scovel 着重围绕四个问题对相关文献进行了综述:第一,学界的绝大多数研究是否都支持关键期假设?第二,从口语角度看,是否存在关键阶段?第三,从句法角度看,是否存在关键期?第四,如果上述答案是肯定的,如何解释因年龄差别而导致的学习效果区别?回顾表明:对上述问题的回答均存在较大的分歧,部分前期研究成果支持关键期假设,部分不支持,而大部分近期研究成果比较支持该假设;部分研究成果对第二和第三个问题的回答是肯定的,部分是否定的;部分研究成果表明儿童与成人不同——儿童是习得(acquire)语言,而成人是学习(learn)语言,有人认为这种不同应归于生理差别,而有人认为与生理差别无关。

值得关注的是,在本篇结语中,鉴于学界对关键期假设看法的分歧,Scovel 提议父母、教育部门或机构在考虑如何运用这些研究成果做出相关决定时,应持非常慎重的态度,应用语言学专家学者在看待该假设时应持批评性的态度而了解全部信息,不能失之偏颇。

14. 应用语言学中的心理语言学:趋势及视角

本卷第 14 篇系 Kees de Bot 撰写的"应用语言学中的心理语言学:趋势及视角"。Kress(1991:1)曾提到:"心理语言学研究指从心理角度对语言展开的研究",而 de Bot 在本篇将心理语言学限定于语言产出和接受过程这一研究领域,并主要讨论了心理语言学和应用语言学之间的关系以及多语处理过程所涉及的关键问题。

心理语言学关注二语习得及其使用的处理机制,尤其是学习者习得和使用多种语言的处理机制,应用语言学则同样对二语习得及使用机制感兴趣,也就是说对二语学习者为什么有这样或那样的表现很关注。尽管心理语言学是认知科学中的一个分支领域,但它对应用语言学的发展起到了理论支撑作用。

双语词汇结构是多语处理过程所涉及的一个关键问题。现在学界一般认为不同语言的单词在词汇记忆域中是分门别类组织起来的,并且呈现三种层次——概念、词汇和音系。产出和接受过程中的语言选择是另一个关键问题。学界一般认为在产出过程中语言选择呈现出一个自上而下的方式,而在接受过程中呈现出一个自下而上的方式。第三个关键问题是语言状态。Grosjean(1997)认为语言状态是一个连续体,由单一语言状态到双语状态,再到多语状态。在语言使用中到底是哪一种语言状态被激活,取决于社会环境和说话者的交际目的。有关这三个关键问题,de Bot 指出学界存在不同的声音,它们均需进一步探讨。

关于未来发展趋势,de Bot 通过综述相关文献,讨论了认知过程和二语习得之间的关系,指出输入和输出之间不存在直接的关系,因为两个方面的认知处理过程不一样,有关具体关系,需学界进一步研究。在概述语言处理和语言测试之间的关系时,de Bot 认为语言处理重在过程研究,而语言测试重在结果检查,提出今后的研究应尽可能地将二者结合起来。目前社会心理因素是如何影响语言处理的,还没有得到学界的重视,de Bot 认为这也是今后研究中的一个方向。还有,现在的语言处理研究没有真正揭开手语和双语之间关系的复杂性,双语处理中的神经意象研究也处于初步阶段,这些话题均是今后研究的方向。

15. 终结思考:千年之交的应用语言学

本卷压轴的是 Richard Tucker 对全卷的总结,意义深远,因为 Tucker 是《应用语言学年度评论》第 1 卷的三位编者之一。Kaplan 既然已参与开卷之作,让 Tucker 享受这个殊荣理所当然,而且他毕竟是了解《应用语言学年度评论》创始过程的元老之一。

Tucker 首先感谢了应用语言学的先驱,已故 Charles A. Ferguson(1921—1998)。Ferguson 于 1978 年 12 月在波士顿召开的第一届美国应用语言学大会,即在庆祝美国应用语言学协会成立一周年纪念日上做了主题发言"语言学的应用:语言学界面临的问题和挑战"。他在后面几届大会上的发言,和在成立应用语言学中心等方面都起了关键作用,因而对应用语言学的发展和方向有着很重要的影响。然后,Tucker 总结了全卷的研究主题,包括 Daoud、Kaplan 和 Grabe、Larsen-Freeman、Leki、Scovel、Takala 和 Sajavaara、Widdowson 等人所做的学科发展思考;一些主要话题的探讨,比如 Crandall、Larsen-Freeman、Leki、Martin、Swain、Takala 和 Sajavaara、Widdowson 等人关注的社会语境, de Bot、Larsen-Freeman、Leki 等人关注的社会身份, Swales、Widdowson、Crandall、Daoud、de Bot 等人关注的对英语以外的其他语言、对发展中国家和地区学者的职业培训或对手语研究的忽视等;以及包括 Clapham、Crandall、de Bot、Kaplan 和 Grabe、Larsen-Freeman、Leki、Martin、Takala 和 Sajavaara、Widdowson 等人对学科领域未来发展方向的预测和评述。通过上述总结,Tucker 指出在可预见的将来,语言教育仍然必不可缺,这对国家发展起着很重要的作用;双语教育愈发重要,这呼应了各个领域全球化的需求。鉴于这种情势,应用语言学专家学者应从多视角,对以下问题开展持续跟踪研究:第一,二语学习中,母语的作用如何?第二,什么样的教学方法对哪些学习者有效?第三,科技如何有效地服务于语言教学?第四,教师发展与课堂教学质量及学习者的表现有什么样的关系?第五,成人特别语言课程有什么短期及长期影响?第六,现有的评估手段如何有效而可信地反映学习者水平能力上的变化?

三、结束语

"应用语言学"这一概念最早是由波兰语言学家 Baudouin de Courtenay 于 1870 年提出的,目的是将应用语言学和纯粹语言学(pure linguistics,

即理论语言学)区分开来。在 20 世纪 60 年代以前,即在 1964 年国际应用语言学学会(Association Internationale de Linguistique Appliquée)成立以前,应用语言学的主要任务是关注语言教学,尤其是英语教学,之后发展到广义的语言学理论的应用,再到 20 世纪末及 21 世纪初以来,发展到拥有自身独立的研究范围和研究框架。可以讲,应用语言学已成为一门独立的学科,也是语言学界最大的学科之一(桂诗春 2010,唐树华 王光林 2012)。

人们习惯地认为一门应用学科就是把本学科的理论、方法与成果应用于实践领域。在本卷第一篇评述性文章中,Widdowson 指出这种认识不限于一般的学者,一些语言学家也持这样的观点,但是他认为应用语言学并不是理论语言学的直接应用,应用语言学家及学者所起的作用应该是转化,语言教师的角色是演示。在中国应用语言学的发展中,越来越多的学者也认识到,应用语言学要在应用中不断总结和提炼自己的理论,并以此来丰富理论语言学的知识宝库(于根元 1999,冯志伟 2003)。"应用语言学与理论语言学的关系不是单向的,而是一种双向互动的关系"(曹春春 2010 : 27)。

在本书中,Clapham、Crandall、de Bot、Daoud、Kaplan 和 Grabe、Larsen-Freeman、Leki、Martin、Scovel、Takala 和 Sajavaara、Widdowson 等作者对应用语言学学科的发展做了一些思考,抑或对该学科领域未来发展方向做了相应的预测和评述。在他们的探讨中,我们可以清晰地看到,他们认为应用语言学的研究基础不仅涉及语言学理论,而且还涉及心理学、神经生理学、社会学、人类学、教育学、哲学、计算机科学、逻辑学、统计学、传播学等学科理论和研究方法。不过应用语言学所涉及的不是这些学科的整体框架,而是这些学科与语言使用和研究相关的领域。高素珍和刘海燕(2005)、曹春春(2010)等在综述应用语言学的发展时,也都提到了应用语言学理论基础的多学科性。

Cook 和 Barbara(1995)认为应用语言学研究应确保其综合性与开放性特点的呈现,确保理论与实践的紧密结合。在本卷中,Crandall、

Larsen-Freeman、Leki、Martin、Swain、Takala 和 Sajavaara、Widdowson 等作者探讨的社会语境与语言的关系，de Bot、Larsen-Freeman、Leki 等作者探讨的社会身份与语言的关系，Swales、Widdowson、Carandall、Daoud、de Bot 等作者指出的学界对英语以外其他语言研究的忽视，这些话题均说明了这样一个事实：应用语言学研究要重视语言和各种环境因素之间的相互影响关系，应用语言学的研究过程不是一个静态的简单的单向活动，而是一个动态的复杂的互动过程。

在应用语言学研究内容方面，本卷既包括狭义的应用语言学所讲的语言教学，比如 Swales 的专门用途语言教学，Leki 的语言读写能力发展，Larsen-Freeman 的二语习得，Swain 的法语沉浸式教育等，也包括广义的应用语言学所涵盖的话题，比如 Crandall 的语言教师教育，Takala 和 Sajavaara 的语言政策与规划，Clapham 的评估与测试，Scovel 的关键阶段假设研究，de Bot 的应用语言学中的心理语言学等。

综上所述，《应用语言学年度评论》第 20 卷所刊发的文章，无论是从理论基础的探讨，还是从研究内容和范围方面的讨论等角度看，都很好地反映了应用语言学的跨学科性质，充分体现了应用语言学学科的综合性和开放性特点，而这些反映和体现均顺应了应用语言学学科的发展趋势。因此，《应用语言学年度评论》第 20 卷为应用语言学学科的发展起到了梳理和总结已有研究成果，从而引领未来发展的作用，起到了本卷前言作者 Grabe 及其他专家学者所提出的对应用语言学学科的架构作用。故而，《应用语言学年度评论》第 20 卷是对应用语言学感兴趣的广大教师和学习者，甚至专家和学者，要洞悉该学科的发展历程以及了解其研究内容的变化，而需参考的重要文献。

参考文献：

Alderson, J.C. and C. Clapham. 1992. Applied linguistics and language testing: A case study of the ELTS test. *Applied Linguistics*. 13. 149–167.

Atkinson, D. Language and science. 1999. In W. Grabe, *et al.* (eds.) *Annual Review of Applied*

Linguistics, 19. Survey of applied linguistics. New York: Cambridge University Press. 193–214.

Bachman, L.F. and A. Cohen. 1998. Language testing—SLA interfaces: An update. In L.F. Bachman and A. Cohen (eds.) *Interfaces between second language acquisition and language testing research.* Cambridge: Cambridge University Press. 1–31.

Bachman, L.F. and A. Palmer. 1996. *Language testing in practice.* Oxford: Oxford University Press.

Battenburg, J.D. 1997. English vs. French: Language rivalry in Tunisia. *World Englishes.* 16. 281–290.

Bayley, R. and D. Preston (eds.) 1996. *Second language acquisition and linguistic variation.* Amsterdam: J. Benjamins.

Bhatia, V.K. 1993. *Analysing genre: Language use in professional settings.* London: Longman.

Chomsky, N. 1988. *Language and problems of knowledge.* Cambrige, MA: MIT Press.

Coffin, C. 1996. *Exploring literacy in school history.* Sydney: Metropolitan East Disadvantaged Schools Program.

Cohen, A. 1997. Developing pragmatic ability: Insights from the accelerated study of Japanese. In H.M. Cook, K. Hijirida and M. Tahara (eds.) *New trends and issues in teaching Japanese language and culture.* Honolulu: University of Hawaii, Second Language Teaching and Curriculum Center. 137–163.

Cook, G. and S. Barbara. 1995. *Principles and practice in applied linguistics.* Oxford: Oxford University Press.

Douglas, D. and L. Selinker. 1994. Native and nonnative teaching assistants: A case study of discourse domains and genres. In C.G. Madden and C.L. Myers (eds.) *Discourse and performance of international teaching assistants.* Alexandria, VA: TESOL. 221–230.

Dudley-Evans, T. and M.J. St John. 1998. *Developments in English for specific purposes.* Cambridge: Cambridge University Press.

Fairclough, N. 1998. Discourse across disciplines: Discourse analysis in researching social change. *AILA Review.* 12. 3–17.

Firth, A. and J. Wagner. 1997. On discourse, communication, and (some) fundamental concepts in SLA research. *Modern Language Journal.* 81. 285–300.

Fishman, J. (ed.) 1974. *Advances in language planning.* The Hague: Mouton.

Freeman, D. 1991. Three views to teachers' knowledge. *IATEFL Teacher Development Newsletter.* December, 1–4.

Freeman, D. 1996. Redefining the relationship between research and what teachers know. In K.M. Bailey and D. Nunan (eds.) *Voices from the language classroom.* Cambridge: Cambridge University Press. 88–115.

Freeman, D. and J.C. Richards (eds.) 1996. *Teacher learning in language teaching.* Cambridge:

Cambridge University Press.

Gass, S. 1997. *Input, interaction and the second language learner*. Mahwah, NJ: L. Erlbaum.

Genesee. F. 1987. *Learning through two languages: Studies of immersion and bilingual education*. Rowley, MA: Newbury House.

Gibbons, J. 1999. Language and the law. In W. Grabe, *et al.* (eds.) *Annual Review of Applied Linguistics, 19. Survey of applied linguistics*. New York: Cambridge University Press. 156–173.

Grosjean, F. 1997. Processing mixed language: Issues, findings and models. In A. de Groot and J. Kroll (eds.) *Tutorials in bilingualism*. Hillsdale, NJ: L. Erlbaum. 225–254.

Halliday, M.A.K. 1985. Systemic Background. In J.D. Benson and W.S. Greaves (eds.) *Systemic perspectives on discourse. Volume 1: Selected theoretical papers from the 9th International Systemic Workshop*. Norwood, NJ: Ablex. 1–15.

Halliday, M.A.K. 1994. *An introduction to functional grammar.* 2nd ed. London: Edward Arnold.

Halliday, M.A.K., A. McIntosh and P. Strevens. 1964. *The linguistic sciences and language teaching*. London: Longman.

Harklau, L. 1999. From the "good kids" to the " worst" : Representations of English language learners across educational settings. *TESOL Quarterly.* 34.

Haugen, E. 1966. Linguistics and language planning. In W. Bright (ed.) *Sociolinguistics*. The Hague: Mouton. 50–71.

Hudson, R. 1999. E-mail message to the Linguistics Association of Great Britain (LAGB) listserve. [see http://www. phon.ucl.ac.uk/home/dick/AL. html]

Hyden, L.-C. and E.G. Mishler. 1999. Language and medicine. In W. Grabe, *et al.* (eds.) *Annual Review of Applied Linguistitics, 19. Survey of applied linguistics*. New York: Cambridge University Press. 174–192.

Hymes, D.H. 1972. On communicative competence. In J. Pride and J. Holmes (eds.) *Sociolinguistics: Selected readings*. Harmondsworth: Penguin Books. 269–293.

Ivanic, R. 1998. *Writing and identity.* Pheiladelphia: J. Benjamins.

Johns, A.M. 1997. *Text, role and context.* New York: Cambridge University Press.

Johnson, K. and H. Johnson (eds.) 1998. *Encyclopedic dictionary of applied linguistics*. Malden, MA: Blackwell.

Kloss, H. 1969. Research possibilities on group bilingualism. A report. Quebec: Center for Research on Bilingualism.

Kormos, J. 1999. Monitoring and self-repair in a second language. *Language Learning*. 49. 303–342.

Kress, J. 1991. *Psycholinguistics: Psychology, linguistics and the study of natural language.* Amsterdam: J. Benjamins.

Leki, I. 1999. " Pretty much I screwed up" : Ill-served needs of a permanent resident. In L.

Harklau, K. Losey and M. Siegal (eds.) *Generation 1.5 meets college composition.* Mahwah, NJ: L. Erlbaum. 17–43.

Martin, J.R. 1993. Genre and literacy: Modelling context in educational linguistics. In W. Grabe, *et al.* (eds.) *Annual Review of Applied Linguistics, 13. Issues in teaching and learning.* New York: Cambridge University Press. 141–172.

Peirce, B.N. 1995. Social identity, investment, and language learning. *TESOL Quarterly.* 29. 9–32.

Pennycook, A. 1994. *The cultural politics of English as an international language.* New York: Longman.

Phillipson, R. 1999. Voice in global English: Unheard chords in crystal loud and clear. *Applied Linguistics.* 20. 265–272.

Platt, E. and S. Troudi.1997. Mary and her teachers: A Grebo-speaking child's place in the mainstream classroom. *Modern Language Journal.* 81. 28–49.

Rampton, B. 1995. *Crossing: Language and ethnicity among adolescents.* London: Longman.

Sinclair, J.M. 1997. Corpus evidence in language description. In A. Wichmann, S. Fligelstone, T. McEnery and G. Knowles (eds.) *Teaching and language corpora.* London: Longman. 27–39.

Smart, G. 1998. Mapping conceptual worlds; Using interpretive ethnography to explore knowledge-making in a professional community. *The Journal of Business Communication.* 35.1. 111–127.

Spack, R. 1997. The acquisition of academic literacy in a second language. *Written Communication.* 14. 3–62.

Stufflebeam, D.K. 1975. *The CIPP model of evaluation.* Kalamazoo, MI: Western Michigan University, Evaluation Center.

Swain, M. and R.K. Johnson. 1997. Immersion education: A category within bilingual education. In R.K. Johnson and M. Swain (eds.) *Immersion education: International perspectives.* Cambridge: Cambridge University Press. 1–16.

Swales, J.M. 1990. *Genre analysis: English in academic and research settings.* Cambridge: Cambridge University Press.

Tarone, E. and M. Swain. 1995. A sociolinguistic perspective on second-language use in immersion classrooms. *Modern Language Journal.* 79. 166–178.

Tauli, V. 1968. *Introduction to a theory of language planning.* Stockholm: Almqvist and Wiksell.

Veel, R. and C. Coffin. 1996. Learning to think like a historian: The language of secondary school history. In R. Hasan and G. Williams (eds.) *Literacy in society.* London: Longman. 191–231.

Walters, K. 1999. "New year happy": Some sociolinguistic observations on the way to the

"Anglicization" of Tunisia. In M. Jabeur, A. Manai and M. Bahloul (eds.) *English in North Africa*. Tunis: TSAS Innovation Series, TSAS and the British Council. 33–63.

Whytes, S.1995. Specialist knowledge and interlanguage development: A discourse domain approach to text construction. *Studies in Second Language Acquisition*. 17. 153–183.

Widdowson, H.G.1980. Models and fictions. *Applied Linguistics*. 1. 165–170.

曹春春. 论应用语言学的跨学科性. 山东外语教学, 2010, (2): 26–30.

冯志伟. 应用语言学新论. 北京: 当代世界出版社, 2003.

高素珍, 刘海燕. 应用语言学综观. 济南大学学报, 2005, (5): 59–64.

桂诗春. 应用语言学思想: 缘起、变化和发展. 外语教学与研究, 2010, (3): 163–169.

唐树华, 王光林. 应用语言学的范围、方法与趋势——劳特利奇应用语言学手册述评. 外国语, 2012, (5): 80–84.

于根元. 应用语言学理论纲要. 北京: 华语教学出版社, 1999.

FOREWORD

William Grabe

OVERVIEW OF VOLUME 20

The twentieth volume of *ARAL*, as an anniversary edition, explores the evolving discipline of applied linguistics from a variety of perspectives. Rather than ask fifteen authors to provide general positions on the status of applied linguistics, the invitation to contribute to *ARAL 20* asked authors to consider the status of applied linguistics from the perspective of their own fields of study and major topical issues. Contributors received a small set of questions asking them to situate their own fields of study within a framework informed by applied linguistics. For example, contributors were asked 1) how their own research sub-fields were located within applied linguistics, 2) how applied linguistics will make the strongest contributions in the coming decade—from the perspective of their own sub-fields, and 3) what obstacles confront their sub-fields and applied linguistics more generally. Some of the authors have addressed these issues explicitly while others have recognized more implicitly the frame of reference that is provided by applied linguistics.

In a number of cases, the natural tensions generated by a relatively ill-defined and interdisciplinary domain such as applied linguistics have led to a questioning of the role that applied linguistics plays in certain fields (e.g., literacy, second language acquisition); other authors have noted a complementary tension—the umbrella of applied linguistics may be fragmenting to a number of more autonomous sub-fields (e.g., second language acquisition, language testing). The tensions are even apparent in discussions of language teacher education with its shift away from the pervasive influence of linguistic foundations as a given orientation and a movement toward general teacher education and reflective practices—a move from methods to methodology and from language knowledge to teaching knowledge.

I will refrain, at this point, from offering an extended perspective on applied linguistics since such a perspective is offered in the first chapter of the volume. I will simply point out that a range of views on the status and scope of applied linguistics as a discipline appears in many of the chapters to follow. In particular, Widdowson and Tucker provide extended explorations of this very topic. Widdowson draws on Hymes' theory of communicative competence to make a persuasive argument that applied linguists are uniquely positioned to mediate issues of language knowledge and use in relation to their applications in real-world contexts, particularly with respect to language teaching and teacher training. Tucker notes that there are many conflicts and tensions with any disciplinary interpretation of applied linguistics, and there are dangers that the conceptual center is under centrifugal pressure with a real potential to separate into many smaller disconnected domains. Nevertheless, he remains confident that, over the next decade, applied linguistics will strengthen, supported by the central role of language for learning in all fields, the interdisciplinary advantages inherent to applied linguistics, and the real applications and realistic solutions that it can offer. As Tucker notes, "at some point, policy makers and prospective funders will come to realize the centrality of language issues for educational and national development."

ARAL 20 presents perspectives from a number of research fields: Chapters cover language teaching and teacher training, literacy, language policy, language assessment, second language acquisition, and second language processing. In some respects, then, the volume is like other past overview volumes of ARAL (see Volumes 10, 15, 19). However, it differs in one major respect: The authors of each chapter consider how their fields are situated within applied linguistics, and whether or not such positioning is problematic.

On reviewing the many contributions to this volume, it is clear that no one person will have all the answers to the many questions raised about the future role and status of applied linguistics, and, if nothing else, this volume is a testament to the many interpretations available as well as the complexities involved. One goal of the volume, given this multivocal complexity, is to allow readers to find positions and views, both explicit and implicit, that will accord with their own sense of applied linguistics as a discipline. In this respect, the volume is intended to generate discussion that advances our understanding of applied linguistics, expands the range of research that can be carried out under its umbrella, and promotes the potential for interdisciplinary connections.

PROCEDURAL NOTES

Since the *ARAL* series is, in part, meant to be a research reference tool, the following procedural notes are intended as a guide. All bibliographic entries follow the basic format of the Linguistic Society of America (LSA), although a unique citation form has emerged for the *ARAL* series. With respect to internal citation, the two types of bibliographies—*annotated* and *unannotated*—should be viewed as integrated, so that in instances where there is more than one entry for a given author for a particular year (e.g., 1990a; 1990b), it is possible that either of the entries may occur in either of the bibliographies; that is, 1990a may be in the annotated bibliography while 1990b may be in the unannotated bibliography, or vice versa. No items are duplicated between the two separate bibliographic lists; that is, the item identified as 1990a will *not* occur in both the annotated and the unannotated bibliography. Both types of bibliography—annotated and unannotated—are arranged in strict alphabetical order by the last name of the first author. Individual entries will precede works co-authored or co-edited by that same author (or set of authors). Repeated authors are indicated by the use of a solid line [_____] of the same length as the name (or names) it replaces. Sources that include cited articles may not necessarily be represented in either bibliographic list if they are not in general germane to the particular area under discussion; in general, belletristic works cited as examples (or for more literary purposes) are not included in either bibliographic list, though they are identified in detail in the article in which they occur. In all texts contributed to the *ARAL* series, an editorial effort has been made to conform generally to the usages and spellings common in the United States. Where possible, English translations of all non-English sources are provided. All contributed papers have been composed specifically for publication in the *ARAL* series and have not (unless otherwise specifically noted) appeared elsewhere previously, although their contents may have been used in whole or in part in oral presentations by the author(s).

The Editorial Directors do not assume responsibility for the positions taken by contributors. Contributions often involve issues of policy as well as more clearly language-related issues. The Editorial Directors wish to be held blameless for opinions and errors of fact expressed by any contributor. The Editor apologizes in advance for any editorial errors that may have crept into the texts and accepts full responsibility for any such editorial errors, but not for substantive errors which are the sole responsibility of each contributor. Bibliographies are prepared and submitted by the contributors; the Editor makes every effort to assure the accuracy of each bibliographic entry that appears in every volume of *ARAL*, but in the case of materials not readily available through libraries or other bibliographic sources in the United States, the Editor is dependent upon the accuracy of material submitted by the contributors. In some few instances, inclusive pages for cited articles, which originally appeared in anthologies or collections, are not given; such omissions occur only when the original source is not available to the Editor and/or when the contributor has not supplied the appropriate pagination. In materials listed in well-known storage and retrieval networks like ERIC and the British Council's ELT Documents, reference numbers are also provided; when titles available only through electronic data bases are cited, every effort is made to provide an accession number (e.g., ERIC files).

This twentieth volume of *ARAL* continues the practice, first established in the third volume, of including a running index of authors cited and topics covered in previous issues of *ARAL*. However, this list became so large that it has become necessary to eliminate the listings from the earliest volumes. Thus, Volume 6 included a cumulative bibliography of Volumes 1 through 5; beginning with Volume 7 as each new year is added, the oldest year's citations have been dropped from the list. In this issue (Volume 20), the cumulative citation listing will include citations from Volumes 15 through 19. Beginning with Volume 5, a Contributor Index was added to the series; in each issue, previous contributors to *ARAL* are indexed in a single alphabetical list. With the *ARAL* series now in its second decade, the Contributor Index lists articles appearing in the previous ten years (Volume 10 through Volume 19). There is also a ten-year Subject Index.

The indices are presented separately—an *Author* Index, a *Subject* Index, and a *Contributor* Index—at the end of each volume. The Author Index cites every item that has appeared in the bibliographies accompanying each article. Each author citation is accompanied by one or more Roman numerals and Arabic numbers (e.g., Sharp, D. X/120). The Roman numeral represents the number of the *ARAL* volume in which the author is cited, and the Arabic number represents the page(s) in that volume in which the citation occurs. Thus, X/120 means that Sharp is cited in *ARAL* *X* (the volume published in 1990). Multiple sets of numbers (e.g., Bazerman, C. X/156; XI/72, XI/82, aXI/109) mean that the author is cited in more than one place. The prefixed lower case "a" (e.g., in aXI/109) indicates that the citation occurs in an annotated bibliography. To the extent that *ARAL* may be said to represent the field accurately, the Author Index may be used as a citation index and be a supporting criterion for merit and promotion evaluation in U.S. institutions.

The Subject Index provides the traditional alphabetical list of topics covered, giving inclusive pages by volume for the point at which the discussion occurs (e.g., X/274–276); this entry indicates that the subject is covered on pp. 274–276 in Volume X. Multiple number sets (e.g., Variationist sociolinguistics: V/48–53; XI/3–16) indicate that the subject (*variationist sociolinguistics*, in this case) is discussed in two places in the series, once in Volume V on pp. 48–53, and again in Volume XI on pp. 3–16.

The Contributor Index provides a traditional alphabetical listing of all contributors to the *ARAL* series for the previous ten years. The citation includes the complete title of the contribution as well as the name of the contributor. Each entry, as in the other indices, carries two designations (e.g., X/163); the first number designates the volume in which the contribution occurs (in this case Volume X), and the second number indicates the page in that volume on which the contribution begins.

ACKNOWLEDGEMENTS

This twentieth volume is my last as Editor of *ARAL*. Beginning with Volume 21, Mary McGroarty, Northern Arizona University, will assume the Editorship. During the ten years that I have been Editor, I have been very fortunate to have been able to draw upon the experience and insights of the Editorial Directors of *ARAL*: Charles Ferguson, Robert Kaplan, Mary McGroarty, Merrill Swain, Dick Tucker, Henry Widdowson, and Janice Yalden. Their guidance and support have allowed *ARAL* to grow significantly as an applied linguistics publication. Over the last ten years, I have also been aided by the suggestions and comments of the Advisory Board, and I thank them for their willingness to support and promote *ARAL* and my work as Editor. They have served as a very important resource for planning and for the nomination of *ARAL* contributors.

Closer to home, I would like to thank my Editorial Assistant, Beth Yule, for all the extra time and effort that is required to keep *ARAL* running smoothly. It would not be possible for me to produce *ARAL* without her, and for ten years she has managed to keep her sense of humor throughout the entire process. I would like to thank Jeffrey Popko, Latricia Trites, and Harley Stoller for proofreading the manuscript and pointing out many editorial matters that I had overlooked. I would also like to thank Julie McCormick for computer consultation, for editorial assistance, and for putting the final copy through a page layout program. Finally, I would like to acknowledge the support and assistance of the Department of English and the College of Arts and Sciences at Northern Arizona University. For ten years, they have provided the Editor with the basic facilities and have absorbed some of the incidental costs associated with the production of this series.

William Grabe
Flagstaff, Arizona
December 1999

APPLIED LINGUISTICS
AND ARAL

APPLIED LINGUISTICS AND THE *ANNUAL REVIEW OF APPLIED LINGUISTICS*

Robert B. Kaplan and
William Grabe

INTRODUCTION

The *Annual Review of Applied Linguistics* is celebrating its 20th anniversary. and we are happy to report that applied linguistics is still with us. We also believe that the field of applied linguistics is here to stay much as psychology and English literature are disciplinary fixtures after having developed in the early 20th century. The development of a disciplinary field, however, is a messy undertaking, typically driven by needs and purposes that extend beyond individual goals or planned group purposes. In the case of applied linguistics its continued development can only be channeled and planned indirectly. Moreover, full disciplinary acceptance will only occur to the extent that applied linguistics responds to wider societal needs and its expertise is valued by people beyond the professional field. Applied linguistics, as an inter-disciplinary field faces the additional challenge of trying to cohere around a set of central notions with which a diverse group of practitioners can identify. So, while some may want an orderly blueprint for disciplinary development, and acceptance, and some practitioners may generate discussions around such orderly expectations none is likely to arise. At the same time, certain events and institutional structures help to shape and form the discipline without recourse to any neat blueprint. Examples include the establishment of the English Language Institute at the University of Michigan in 1941, the establishment of the Department of Applied Linguistics at Edinburgh in 1956, the establishment of the Center for

Applied Linguistics in Washington, DC in 1959, the formation of the TESOL organization in 1966, and the formation of the American Association for Applied Linguistics in 1977.

Also among the shapers of this new field are the various journals that have promoted the work of applied linguists and that, as a secondary force, have helped determine what counts as applied linguistics. The first such journal, *Language Learning*, is now in its 50th year of publication. The emergence of *TESOL Quarterly* in the 1960s created an important research voice for second language researchers and practitioners. In the late 1970s and early 1980s, a number of journals more specifically devoted to applied linguistics made their appearance and helped shape a newly forming field: *Applied Linguistics, Applied Psycholinguistics, Australian Review of Applied Linguistics, English for special Purposes, Studies in Second Language Acquisition*, and the *Annual Review of Applied Linguistics (ARAL)*. As the two Editors of the first 20 volumes of the *ARAL* series, we believe that *ARAL* has contributed to the emergence of "messy" applied linguistics as a disciplinary field. In the sections to follow, we examine the complexities and difficulties involved in granting disciplinary status to applied linguistics, the role of *ARAL* as a contributor to the development of applied linguistics, and a small set of predictions for the future of applied linguistics. After twenty years of intense professional development beyond the early decades, applied linguistics is still a discipline in search of broader recognition and internal stability. The difficulties in describing the status of applied linguistics were also apparent at the 1999 *Association Internationale de Linguistique Applique* (AILA) Congress in Tokyo, Japan.

APPLIED LINGUISTICS: THE ONGOING DEBATES

At the recent 1999 AILA Congress in Tokyo, there were several public discussions of "the field of applied linguistics" : on its scope, on its status, on its emergence as a field, and on its viability as a discipline. There were also several discussions concerning the paradigms that inform the field, the political place of the field in the academic landscape, and the means and content for training the next generation(s) of applied linguists. Not surprisingly, participants in these debates agreed on only a small set of key points and differed considerably on a large number of issues. The commonalities, while few and seemingly meager, nonetheless, provide the anchor for discussing applied linguistics as an inter-disciplinary field. Most applied linguists would agree on the following points:

First, applied linguistics has many of the markings of an academic discipline: professional journals, professional associations, international recognition for the field funding resources for research projects, a large population of individuals who see themselves as applied linguists, trained professionals who are hired in academic institutions and elsewhere as applied linguists, students who want to become applied linguists, and recognized means for training these students to become applied linguists.

Second, there is a general recognition that linguistics needs to be included as a core knowledge base in the work of applied linguistics, even though the purpose of most applied linguistics work is not merely to "apply linguistics" to achieve a solution.

Third, applied linguistics is grounded in real-world language-driven problems and concerns (primarily by linkages to practical issues involving language use, language evaluation, language contact and multilingualism, language policies, and language learning and teaching). There is also, however, recognition at these practically driven problems have extraordinary range, and this range tends to dilute any sense of common purpose or common professional identification among practitioners.

Fourth, applied linguistics needs to incorporate other disciplinary knowledge beyond linguistics in its efforts to address language-based problems. Applied linguists commonly draw upon, and are often well trained in, psychology, education, anthropology, political science, sociology, measurement, computer programming, literature, and/or economics.

Fifth, following from points three and four above, applied linguistics is an interdisciplinary field since few practical language issues can be addressed through the knowledge resources of any single discipline, including linguistics.

Sixth, applied linguistics commonly includes a core set of issues and practices that are readily identified as work done by many applied linguists (language teaching, language teacher preparation, and language curriculum development).

Seventh, applied linguistics generally incorporates or includes several further identifiable sub-fields of study: bilingual studies, corpus linguistics, forensic linguistics, language contact studies, language testing, language translation and interpretation, language use in professional contexts, lexicography and dictionary making, literacy, second language acquisition, and second language writing research. Some members of these fields do not see themselves as applied linguists though their work clearly addresses practical language issues.

Eighth, applied linguistics often defines itself in such a way as to include additional fields of language-related studies (e.g., first language composition studies, first language literacy research, language and literature, language pathology, and natural language processing). The large majority of members of these fields do not see themselves as applied linguists, but the broad definition gives license for applied linguists to roam across these disciplines for their own goals.

The commonalities above, in and of themselves, also point out the difficulties involved in defining applied linguistics, determining its scope, identifying its membership, highlighting its practices, and preparing new members for the field. At one level, defining applied linguistics can be relatively easy; one could say that applied linguistics is the field characterized by the above eight common points. At another level, the term *applied linguistics*, raises fundamental difficulties, if for no other reason than that it is difficult to decide on what counts as "linguistics." Does linguistics incorporate the range of competing theoretical views of language description commonly discussed as linguistic theories? Does linguistics include the work of descriptive grammarians and corpus linguists? Does linguistics include the work of prescriptive grammarians and stylists? Does linguistics include the so-called hyphenated sub-fields: computational linguistics, critical linguistics, forensic linguistics, historical linguistics, pragmatics, psycholinguistics, sociolinguistics, and so on? Does linguistics center on sentences and smaller structural units, or does it center on discourse patterns and language uses? Perhaps, more importantly, what underlying assumptions are held by competing views of what counts as linguistics? The answer to many of these questions, it would seem, is "it depends." Given these difficulties within linguistics proper, it is perhaps unfair to expect clean solutions and clear delimitations for defining applied linguistics.

One alternative perspective to adopt in defining applied linguistics is to examine the contributions made by institutional structures (schools, research centers, associations, journals) to knowledge building. They represent important, if sometimes covert, defining structures within a discipline. We believe that *ARAL* has played such a role, and its history is one that parallels the evolution of applied linguistics as a discipline. We therefore see it as a fitting introduction to this exploratory volume to set the stage by examining the contribution that *ARAL* has made to the field of applied linguistics.

THE *ANNUAL REVIEW OF APPLIED LINGUISTICS*: 20 YEARS AND COUNTING

1. The background

ARAL is twenty years old. This seems an appropriate time to record its history before all the players become inaccessible. The history of *ARAL* is intimately intertwined with the history of the American Association for Applied Linguistics (AAAL) and with the history of the journal *Applied Linguistics* (*AL*), all of them being of essentially the same vintage. Additionally, several of the key players have been involved in all three activities. We hope that the historical narrative that follows offers a coherent interpretation of the development of *ARAL* and, by implication, of events in the more recent development of applied linguistics as well.

2. The history of AAAL

At the TESOL conference in San Juan, Puerto Rico, in early May of 1973, a small group of people came together (not in a formal sense, but in a casual series of informal hallway and dinner conversations) to discuss the desirability of forming an American Association for Applied Linguistics (originally conceived of as an Association of Applied Linguists) and a journal for the field. (For a listing of key dates in the history of applied linguistics, see Kaplan 1997: 19.) Among the people involved were Edward Anthony, Thomas Buckingham, Peter Collier, David Eskey, Robert Kaplan, Joe Darwin Palmer, Bernard Spolsky, and Peter Strevens. It seemed clear to that group that the need for such an organization existed. In the 1970s, applied linguists really had no professional home in which to meet and to discuss their work. The Applied Linguistics Interest Section (not created until 1975) in TESOL suffered (as it perhaps still does) from inadequate budget and inadequate presentation, meeting, and discussion time within the framework of the annual Teachers of English to Speakers of Other Languages (TESOL) conference, being in competition with a growing number of other Interest Sections and activities of the association. (It must be noted that the *T* in TESOL stands for *Teachers*; thus, TESOL was and remains primarily a teachers' association, not a scholarly, research oriented body.)

There was, in addition, a serious fragmentation of the field because those applied linguists working in the context of teaching English as a second (or foreign) language (TESL/TEFL) came to the TESOL conferences, but those working in other areas did not. Instead, they often attended meetings of the American Council on the Teaching of Foreign Languages (ACTFL); the then Association of Teachers of English as a Second Language (now Administrators and Teachers in English as a Second Language [ATESL]; a section of the (then) National Association for Foreign Student Affairs [NAFSA], now NAFSA: Association of International Educators); the Conference on College Composition and Communication (CCCC); the Linguistic Association of Canada and the United States (LACUS); the Linguistic Society of America (LSA); the Modern Language Association (MLA); the National Association for Bilingual Education (NABE); the National Council of Teachers of English (NCTE), The Speech Association of America (SAA), not to mention a number of associations of teachers of particular languages (e.g. French [AATF], German [AATG], Japanese [ATJ], etc.). Applied linguists also regularly attended non-associational structures such as the Georgetown University Roundtable on Languages and Linguistics (GURT). But even in the reasonably "affluent" 1970s, the notion of attending more than two conferences a year was prohibitive both in terms of financial support and in terms of time away from primary responsibilities. In addition, there was a strong sense among applied linguists that the United States ought to belong to the *Association Internationale de Linguistique Appliqué* (The International Association of Applied Linguistics); none of the associations mentioned above were eligible for such membership. Some 100 applied linguists across the United States were polled, and there was a clear sentiment for the establishment of such a new association. (Initially, the Center for Applied Linguistics served as the official American representative organization associated with AILA from AILA's inception in 1964 to 1978, at which time AAAL assumed this role.)

As a result of these pressures to organize, a more general open meeting was convened in conjunction with the Summer Institute of the Linguistic Society of America (LSA) in Ann Arbor, Michigan, on 3 August 1973. The reaction at the open meeting was somewhat less enthusiastic, and the following day, at the business meeting of the LSA, a resolution was passed requesting the LSA Executive to study the possibility of convening a subsection concerned with applied linguistics within the LSA. At the regular annual business meeting of the LSA on 29 December 1973, the matter was discussed again; the LSA Executive suggested that applied linguists were welcome at LSA meetings so long as they adhered to its quality standards. It was further agreed that there would be no special section of the LSA for applied linguists; it was also decided that, for at least two years, no further action would be taken and that the receptivity of the LSA to the idea would be re-evaluated on the basis of the experience of those years. (In fact, the matter was overtaken by time and allowed to lapse for lack of interest on the part of the LSA Executive.)

During that two year hiatus, the constitution of TESOL was amended (1975) to permit the existence of special interest sections. Among the first special interest sections to be established was one in applied linguistics; Bernard Spolsky was appointed first chairperson of the group. Subsequently its next five elected chairs were, in chronological order, Robert Kaplan, David Eskey, Thomas Buckingham, Joe Darwin Palmer, and Eugene Brière. For a time, it was hoped that this interest section would obviate the necessity for a separate organization. The LSA did, in fact, also include, in its annual meeting in San Francisco in December 1975, a section on language acquisition intended to serve the needs of applied linguists. The TESOL Applied Linguistics Interest Section also mounted a special program segment at the New York convention in 1976, at the Miami convention in 1977, and at the Mexico City convention in 1978. The first two of these program segments were largely concerned with English for Special Purposes and were organized with the close cooperation and assistance of the British Council.

It became clear, however, that these various efforts did not serve the broader needs of the applied linguistics community and that a new independent organization was desirable. At the TESOL Convention in Miami in April 1977, a round table discussion of the "scope of applied linguistics" was convened. The participants in that roundtable were H. Douglas Brown, S. Pit Corder, Paul Holtzman, Robert Kaplan, Tony Robson, Bernard Spolsky, Peter Strevens, and G. Richard Tucker. In addition, Thomas Buckingham and David Eskey, acting as the officers of the Applied Linguistics Interest Section of TESOL, collected in advance a series of statements on the scope of applied linguistics from well-known scholars in the field. (In addition to roundtable participants, those invited included Edward Anthony,

Russell Campbell, Francisco Gomes de Matos, Stephen Krashen, and John Oller. All the papers of the roundtable were published as Kaplan [1980]; a paper by David Ingram of Australia was added.)

At the conclusion of the several presentations, there was again an open discussion of the desirability of forming a new association. That discussion was quite positive, and out of it grew a mandate to move forward with the notion. During the summer months of 1977, an executive committee (Randall Jones, Robert Kaplan, Wilga Rivers, Bernard Spolsky, G. Richard Tucker) and several interim committees were formed. A formal constitutional convention was convened in conjunction with the ACTFL Conference in San Francisco on 24 November 1977, and the American Association for Applied Linguistics (AAAL) came into existence; Wilga Rivers was elected its first president (Roger Shuy was VP; Bernold Spolsky was S/T; Executive Committee members were Charles Ferguson, Betty W. Robinett, Albert Valdman, and G. Richard Tucker). AAAL became an affiliate of AILA soon after AILA held its fifth triennial world congress in Montreal in August 1978.

As a kind of footnote to the discussion, James Alatis (then Executive Secretary of TESOL) was strongly opposed to the formation of a new association. He rightly feared that a new association would draw applied linguists away from TESOL. Over time, his fear has been justified; applied linguists have largely deserted TESOL (and many of the other associations mentioned above). In the early years of its existence, AAAL elected to meet annually with the LSA, but that proved—for a variety of reasons—to be an unsatisfactory arrangement. In 1991, in New York, AAAL began to meet contiguously with TESOL; that arrangement continues at the present time (Kaplan 1998).

3. The history of two applied linguistic journals

There could not have been so much activity surrounding the creation of a new organization without comparable discussion of the vehicle(s) through which the new association was to voice its views. Among the various conversations that took place at the critical Puerto Rico TESOL conference in 1973, some dealt directly with the question of a journal (largely those involving Peter Collier). At the time that those discussions were being held, the British Association of Applied Linguistics (BAAL) had been in business for some five years, but it did not yet have a journal of its own. About 1976, serious discussions began toward the creation of a journal of applied linguistics. These discussions, always centering on Oxford University Press (OUP), involved J. P. B. (Patrick) Allen, Simon Murison-Bowie (then of OUP), Robert Kaplan, Bernard Spolsky, Henry Widdowson, and others. The notion was to create a 'transatlantic' journal serving the needs of both AAAL and BAAL.

Applied Linguistics: The journal *Applied Linguistics* (*AL*) was founded in 1980. It was jointly sponsored by AAAL and BAAL, was published by OUP, and has regularly had joint editors, normally one from North America and one from the UK. In the late 1970s, some individuals at OUP felt the need for a journal to support the kind of applied linguistics textbook publishing effort under way at OUP.[1] The only journal OUP had in the general area was *The English Language Teaching Journal* (*ELTJ*), which, while being the most respected and oldest journal for language teachers, did not address the more theoretical bases of the profession. At the time, OUP also distributed the *International Review of Applied Linguistics* (*IRAL*), but this journal has not consistently served the wider applied linguistics community.

At the time when these discussions were taking place, OUP had for a number of years worked with J. P. B. Allen (for example, on the *Edinburgh Course in Applied Linguistics*, 4 vols., 1972–1977) and H. G. Widdowson (for example, *Teaching Language as Communication*, 1978), and both of them indicated an interest in editing a new journal of the sort being discussed. The aim of that journal, as stated on the inside back cover of vol. 1, No. 1, and still regularly noted in every issue, was:

> ...to promote a principled approach to language education and other language related concerns by encouraging inquiry into the relationship between theoretical and practical studies. The journal is less interested in the ad hoc solution of particular problems and more interested in the handling of problems in a principled way by reference to theoretical studies...

The idea was tested out on a number of linguists and applied linguists, seeking geographic as well as professional spread, and testimonials were solicited. A proposal to publish the journal was approved by the Delegates of OUP (a board of university appointees chaired by the Vice Chancellor). From the earliest stages of the journal, OUP sought to link subscription to *AL* to membership in professional associations. The British Association for Applied Linguistics (BAAL) was the first organization to enter into such a relationship, and the American Association for Applied Linguistics (AAAL) soon followed, so that Vol. 1, No. 1, published in the Spring 1980, was jointly sponsored by those two bodies. As a consequence of that relationship, Bernard Spolsky (then on the faculty at the University of New Mexico) joined J. P. B. Allen and H. G. Widdowson as editors. An editorial board of 22 academics (representing Australia, Canada, Finland, Germany, Israel, Poland, Singapore, Sweden, Switzerland, the United Kingdom, and the United States), plus two representatives of OUP (Simon Murison-Bowie was one), was formed. Both AAAL and BAAL had the right to nominate a board member. The board remained essentially unchanged for the first seven years of its existence, though Alan Davies and Elaine Tarone replaced J. P. B. Allen and H. G. Widdowson from Vol. 6. Beginning from Vol. 8 (1987), a number of administrative changes were introduced. Bernard Spolsky resigned as editor and was replaced by a reviews editor; Kari Sajavarra, from Finland, was the first holder of that post. The original 22-person board was replaced by an Advisory Board consisting of the BAAL and AAAL representatives (initially John Trim and Susan Gass, respectively). Christina Whitecross at OUP became the publisher. An eight-person editorial panel was appointed. From Vol. 6 (1985) the International Association of Applied Linguistics (AILA) added its formal support to the journal; that support was duly approved at the 1984 AILA Congress in Brussels.

From the beginning, *AL* has published a number of seminal articles for the applied linguistics field. In Vol. 1, No. 1, the article "Theoretical bases of communicative approaches, " by M. Canale and M. Swain appeared, and a number of other key articles have been published over the years. Through a balanced mix of articles, reviews, and thematic issues, *AL* has mapped the development of the discipline in a serious and non-trivial way.

Annual Review of Applied Linguistics: The *Annual Review of Applied Linguistics* (*ARAL*) has had a rather different history. In 1978, when AAAL was created and discussions of a journal were being widely held, Henry Birnbaum (now deceased, originally a mathematician, later a United States government science administrator and ultimately international advisor to the President of the University of Southern California) suggested to Robert Kaplan that no scientific field could long survive without an annual review of research. The idea captured Kaplan's imagination. He held conversations with a number of people, and eventually asked Randall Jones (Brigham Young University) and G. Richard Tucker (by then Director of the CAL) to join him as the first editors of an annual review. Having an editorial board, a general plan for the journal evolved—a full review of the field every fifth year and special topical issues in the interim years. Kaplan approached Rupert Ingram, then owner and publisher of Newbury House, with the idea. Ingram was interested. The editorial board decided on approximately a dozen topics to be covered in the first volume—bilingualism, computer-assisted instruction, language testing, macro-sociolinguistics and micro-sociolinguistics, notional-functional teaching approaches, pidginization and creolization, structural—cognitive teaching approaches, psycholinguistics, second-language acquisition, sign language, and theoretical issues in sociolinguistics. The editorial board identified a number of authors to be invited to submit contributions in these areas, and contributions were ultimately received from Jenny Barnett, H. Douglas Brown, Alfonso Caramazza and Michael McCloskey, Joshua Fishman, Francisco Gomes de Matos, Matthias Hartig, Lilith Haynes, Braj Kachru, Rachel Mayberry, John Oller, Frank Otto, Jack Richards, and Loreto Todd. The editor, Robert Kaplan, wrote the introduction to the first volume, as he did for the next nine volumes.

In 1985, a misunderstanding with Newbury House caused Kaplan to enter into discussions with Cambridge University Press [CUP]. All subsequent volumes of *ARAL*, beginning with volume 5, have been published by Cambridge University Press. Unfortunately, the first four volumes are no longer available. The ongoing relationship with CUP has been quite successful though the nature of ARAL does cause some marketing problems. *ARAL* looks like a journal and is produced by the journals division, but it is an annual and not really a journal. This has led to some regrettable confusion. *ARAL* has, for quite a number of years, been made available at reduced rates to members of AAAL, BAAL, and TESOL. Somewhat more than 1,000 copies of *ARAL* are sold annually by CUP (including back issues).

The *ARAL* Editorial Board has, over the years, made several strategic innovations; the journal would have a running bibliography of all works cited, a topical index (a listing that has begun to serve as a definition of the scope of applied linguistics—see Grabe and Kaplan 1992: 3-4), and a contributor index. (As the series grew longer, certain compromises have had to be made to prevent the three indices from overwhelming the volumes.)

 ARAL would always publish only solicited articles (no unsolicited contributions), and—since all articles were, by definition, review articles accompanied by extensive reference lists—it would not publish separate book reviews. The primary focus of the review articles was to be on critical research in the preceding two to three years, but with the assumption that reference lists were free to cite seminal works in the area regardless of date of publication. Reference lists have always consisted of annotated and unannotated entries. The series would publish in American English, but it would strive for broad international representation. Beginning with Volume 6, each issue has carried a running index of authors cited and subjects covered; because the author index and the subject index became overwhelming, only the preceding five years' citations are available in any given volume after number 7. A contributor index was also added beginning with Volume 5; it now lists contributors from the preceding decade. It was the intent that these several indices would become citation indices for the field.

 The first issue appeared in 1981 with a title showing the preceding year (1980). Beginning in 1994, the cover date was adjusted to reflect the year of publication rather than the year covered in the research (e. g. , Volume 13, published in 1993, carried the cover date 1992, Volume 14, the transitional issue published in 1994, carried a cover date of 1993–94, and Volume 15, published in 1995, carried the cover date 1995). (Incidentally, 1981 was the only year in which a hardback version was published.) From Volume 1, the first issue, through Volume 8, Kaplan, with the able assistance of his wife, Audrey Kaplan, produced camera-ready typescript copy. It was not until Volume 9 that manuscript preparation was shifted to electronic word-processing. Over the years, there was only one single issue (Volume 8) which utilized a guest editor; Christopher Brumfit edited that volume, a special issue on Communicative Language Teaching. Otherwise, the full editorial responsibility rested with Kaplan as the editor-in-chief through 1991.

 The Editorial Directors, meeting annually in face-to-face conversation, usually during the AAAL or TESOL conferences, identify the focus of each volume, the topics to be covered, and the individuals to be solicited to contribute, based on discussions of ideas circulated in advance by the editor-in-chief. The Editorial Directors are thus always working with three years of ARAL. Each time they meet—one that is about to appear (or has just appeared), one that is well along in the editorial process, and one that is in its formative stage, two-years out.

Gradually, the role of the Editorial Directors has evolved, and the members of the Board have changed—fixed terms were instituted beginning with Volume ten. Over the years—in addition to Jones (who withdrew after Volume one), Kaplan, and Tucker—Alison d'Anglejan, J. Ronayne Cowan, Charles Ferguson, William Grabe, Braj Kachru, Mary McGroarty, Merrill Swain, H. G. Widdowson, and Janice Yalden have at various times served as Editorial Directors for varying periods of time. Grabe, Kaplan, Tucker, and Widdowson, have served for the longest terms. The composition of the Editorial Directors has always striven for international representation and gender balance. In 1989 (Volume 9), an Editorial Advisory Board was added, normally consisting of approximately 10 internationally recognized scholars. The first advisory board included Aura Bocaz (Chile), Moira Chimombo (Malawi), Michael Clyne (Australia), Biodun Goke-Pariola (Nigeria), Andrew Gonzalez (Philippines), Sayyid Hurreiz (Sudan), Peter Nelde (Belgium), Bernard Spolsky (Israel), R. N. Srivastava (India), and John Kwock-ping Tse (Taiwan). The function of the advisory board has been to suggest areas and contributors for scholarship to be covered.

With the completion of the eleventh volume (1991—jointly edited by Kaplan and Grabe), Kaplan resigned as editor-in-chief (though he remained on the editorial board through Volume 20, at which point he retired from service to *ARAL*) and was succeeded by William Grabe as editor-in-chief. Grabe, in turn has served ten years as editor-in-chief and, with this twentieth volume, relinquishes that role to Mary McGroarty .

4. Topics covered in *ARAL*

The shaping influence of a broader interpretation of applied linguistics is partly reflected in the thematic volumes produced in the *ARAL* series, and also the themes repeated over ten-year cycles. For example, the first ten years covered language and language-in-education policy (Volume 2), discourse analysis (3), literacy (4), multilingualism (6), language use in the professions (7), communicative language teaching (8), and second language acquisition (9). In the second decade, a number of basic themes were revisited: language policy, literacy, discourse analysis, and multilingualism. In addition, a volume was developed to examine technology and language and two volumes were devoted to language teaching concerns. An effort was made to plan for a language-teaching-related volume to appear every fifth year (beginning with Volume 8). Beginning with Volume 15, a plan has been developed to produce overview volumes with a greater consistency of topical coverage; so overview Volumes 15 and 19 both include sections on second language acquisition, language assessment, and language uses in various professional and public contexts. This consistency of topical coverage also meant that *ARAL* does not need to publish separate thematic volumes on second language acquisition, language assessment, or language use in professional and public contexts. Rather, the inclusion of these topics in regular overview volumes ensures a more frequent updating of changes and innovations in these areas, particularly since overview volumes are now to be published every four years rather than every five years.

Aside from the general field coverage of applied linguistics projected by volume themes and overviews, the specific topical coverage of the volumes is meant to reflect evolving perspectives among applied linguistics. This currency of topics is reflected in the subject index at the back of each *ARAL* volume, providing a snapshot of the issues addressed in the prior five years. Because the *ARAL* subject index changes completely over a period of five years, shifts, trends, and continuities in applied linguistics can be explored in one way by comparing the subject indexes from Volumes 9, 14, and 19, for example. Of course, a similar content analysis approach could be applied to other key applied linguistics journals, and a multiple journal comparison might be instructive for the field.

We have argued in this section that *ARAL*, along with a few other publications, has had and is having a consistent shaping influence on the field of applied linguistics. This influence is not one that can be readily demonstrated in any simple way since such a demonstration would belie the complex and messy nature of a disciplinary field's development and evolution. The topics emphasized in *ARAL* over the past two decades reflect the central sub-fields that are typically included under applied linguistics in discussions and debates. The related fields that are only sometimes incorporated into applied linguistics definitions by applied linguists themselves have also received a lesser recognition in *ARAL* volumes. By this reasoning, second language acquisition, language testing, language policy studies, multilingualism, literacy, and language uses in professional and public contexts are all fields firmly within the discipline of applied linguistics (in addition to language teaching and language-teacher training). Other fields may also be located within applied linguistics, but perhaps less clearly so by this reasoning. A further corollary implication is that applied linguistics is not a cover term simply for language teaching and language-teacher training.

THE FUTURE OF APPLIED LINGUISTICS

Applied linguists of most persuasions tend to shy away from speculating on the future of applied linguistics. However, the opportunity to influence and shape the thinking of others often falls to those who are willing to prognosticate (and who do so fairly effectively, if not completely accurately). So, in closing, we will offer a small set of tentative indications on future directions in applied linguistics research. In doing so, we wish to call attention to the fact that we are perhaps better qualified to write the history presented here (having lived it); scholars working on the cutting edges of the field should be invited to write about its future.[2] Having made our apologies for reading the future, we see four trends increasing in the coming years.

In the future, the field of applied linguistics will be defined by greater uses of technology and computer applications. Computer literacy will become an essential component of training for new applied linguists. These computer uses will be seen in new statistical approaches, computer-based testing and language learning, connectionist research on learning, technology and literacy development, corpus linguistics research and lexicography, and translation research. Tied to computer uses and technology applications will be changes in testing that better reflect recent views on validity and performance assessment. Assessment practices will take on new dimensions with the development of appropriate technology resources that are not yet ready for application or that have not yet been developed in practical ways. The rapid growth in computational power available to everyone will bring these changes about sooner rather than later. Technology resources will also influence task designs for research studies in a wide variety of ways and for a broad range of research purposes, some of which cannot even be envisioned at the present time.

A second major trend that has begun and will increase will be a move toward a more powerful version of descriptive linguistics as the central linguistic resource for research. The development of corpus linguistics is now revealing facts about language use and language variation across registers that are essential for addressing practical issues but that may be largely incompatible with many current theoretical models in linguistics. Applied linguists, who must be anchored in a "realistic" linguistics that is discourse based, contextually framed, and grounded in attested occurrences, will move back toward analyzing new data rather than arguing new theory (though theory building is certainly possible within a descriptive-data framework; cf. Widdowson, this volume). Goals will center around understanding new facts about language rather than having language facts forced to fit preconceived theory. In the face of this disjuncture, descriptive linguistics, with its new power to enhance our understanding of language uses, will provide more fertile ground for applied linguistics. The return to descriptively powerful research will be enhanced by computer applications; by studies of language uses in legal, medical, scientific, and business contexts; by research at the discourse level (as the basic analytic unit); and by the power of descriptive analysis to provide relatively theory—neutral data for future linguistic theorizing.

A third important trend will be the increasing importance of evaluation and assessment practices. The centrality of construct validity as a driving force in language testing is already spreading beyond the boundaries of testing and into other areas of applied linguistics. In second language acquisition, there is a growing recognition that validity of task and test data is a central concern—researchers need to collect and interpret responsible evidence in support of theoretical claims (Bachman and Cohen 1998, Clapham, this volume). The critical importance of careful and thorough evaluative practices is relevant to language policy and planning efforts as well. Takala and Sajavaara (this volume) argue strongly for the central role of evaluation in the planning and implementation of language policies. The importance of evaluation practices is also being felt in classrooms and in curriculum planning. National standards efforts and the increasing demand for standardized assessments in many states in the U.S. and elsewhere highlight validity and reliability issues that will directly impact instructional practices and learning processes (Brindley 1998). Evaluation and assessment issues are no longer only the concern of language testers, and sophisticated evaluation and assessment practices will be a key concern for all future applied linguistics research.

A final area in which applied linguistics will change in new ways is in student learning. This trend will manifest itself both for all students learning languages and for undergraduate and post-graduate students studying applied linguistics. Language students will become familiar with new technologies for learning. They will become more engaged in autonomous learning while also working collaboratively within groups. They will have greater access to resources to support their learning, and they will receive more rapid feedback on their learning progress. All of these features of language learning will be even more prominent among programs that train applied linguists. Students of applied linguistics will need to master a wide range of technological skills as central components of their training. They will need to work collaboratively on research projects, as inter-disciplinary cooperation and the common use of research teams become essential to deal with larger problems implicating a broader range of disciplines and human resources. Students will engage in research practices that require strong knowledge of both quantitative and qualitative methods and their complementary contributions to knowledge making. Students will need to engage in field-work projects as applications take on larger roles than do standard knowledge-bases in training programs. Of course, these students of applied linguistics will also need current and broad knowledge of linguistics and, in all likelihood, of at least one related field. While these demands on new students may seem daunting, they are probably no more demanding than new and increasing expectations in other disciplines. It is an exciting time to be an applied linguist, and also an exciting time to learn to become one.

We believe that *ARAL*, under the guidance of its future editors and editorial directors, will continue to chart the field, to contribute to its development, and to serve as an important resource both to practitioners and to future applied linguists.

NOTES

1. We are deeply indebted to Simon Murison Bowie (personal communication) for much of the information contained in this brief sketch of the history of *Applied Linguistics*.

2. We will together undertake one more volume, outside of *ARAL*, intended to move toward a definition of the field by giving full play to its scope (Kaplan, to appear).

UNANNOTATED BIBLIOGRAPHY

Allen, J. P. B. 1972–1977. *Edinburgh course in applied linguistics*. 4 vols. Oxford: Oxford University Press.

Annual Review of Applied Linguistics. 1981–2000. R. B . Kaplan and W. Grabe, *et al.* (eds .) New York: Cambridge University Press.

Applied Linguistics. 1980–2000. Oxford: Oxford University Press.

Bachman, L. F. and A. Cohen (eds.) 1998. *Interfaces between second language acquisition and language testing research*. New York: Cambridge University Press.

Brindley, G. 1998. Outcomes-based assessment and reporting in language learning programmes. *Language Testing*. 15.45–85.

Grabe, W. 1994. Applied linguistics. In A. Purves (ed.) *Encyclopedia of English studies and language arts*. New York: Scholastic Leadership Policy Research. 60–62.

———— and R. B. Kaplan (eds.) 1992. *Introduction to applied linguistics*. Reading, MA: Addison Wesley.

Kaplan, R. B. 1997. An IEP is a many-splendored thing. In M. A. Christison and F. Stoller (eds.) *A handbook for language program administrators*. Burlingame, CA: Alta Book Center. 3–19.

———— 1998. On TESOL and research. *TESOL Matters*. 8.3. 16.

———— (ed.) 1980. *On the scope of applied linguistics*. Rowley, MA: Newbury House.

———— (ed.) 2002. *Handbook of applied linguistics*. New York: Oxford University Press.

Rampton, B. (ed.) 1997. *Retuning applied linguistics*. [Special issue of *International Journal of Applied Linguistics*. 7.1 .]

Widdowson, H. G. 1978. *Teaching language as communication*. Oxford: Oxford University Press.

LANGUAGE TEACHING AND
LANGUAGE TEACHER EDUCATION

OBJECT LANGUAGE AND THE LANGUAGE SUBJECT: ON THE MEDIATING ROLE OF APPLIED LINGUISTICS

Henry G. Widdowson

INTRODUCTION

As linguistics has extended its scope over the past thirty years from an exclusive concern with knowledge of the abstract code, what Chomsky referred to as Internalized (I) language, to a consideration of the way this knowledge is actualized in Externalized (E) language (Chomsky 1988), so it has inevitably gained in face validity as an area of inquiry relevant to practical life. A linguistics that deals with real, as distinct from ideal, speaker-listeners has a more obvious applicability to the problems real people actually have with language. Nevertheless, one cannot just assume a direct correspondence between the E externalized language the linguist describes and the E experienced language that is a reality for the user. The applicability of linguistic descriptions is a potential that has to be realized, and this is where applied linguistics comes in.

My purpose in this contribution is to look into this question of applicability as it relates to language pedagogy. My concern, in particular, is with L2 learners as a particular kind of language user: At issue is the extent to which linguistic descriptions can adequately account for their reality for learners and so provide a point of reference for the design of language courses.

LINGUISTICS AND LANGUAGE TEACHING

In traditional ways of thinking, applicability does not appear to be a problem.

Since language is both what L2 teachers teach and linguists describe, it would seem self-evident that the findings of linguistics should be relevant to how the content of language courses is to be defined. Linguistics has always in fact been deferred to as the accepted authority on these matters, the assumption being that the language subject is derived from the linguistic discipline and that the units of description constitute the units for learning. On the face of it, this seems reasonable enough: If teachers cannot draw on linguistic descriptions in the design of their instruction, where else, after all, can they turn? But they need to know what such descriptions have to offer, and this is something that applied linguists can inform them about. In this view, the content of the language subject is necessarily dependent on linguistic description.

The assumption of necessary dependency goes back a long way. The following can be taken as a representative statement:

He (the language teacher) is not teaching linguistics. But he is teaching something which is the object of study of linguistics, and is described by linguistic methods. It is obviously desirable that the underlying description should be as good as possible, and this means that it should be based on sound linguistic principles (Halliday, *et al.* 1964:66).

The something that the teacher is teaching, the language subject, is here equated with the linguist's object of study, the object language. But this object is, as I have indicated, describable, and definable, in different ways. The methods and principles employed by taxonomic structuralists, for example, are very different from those of generativists of the Chomsky stamp, which are, again, very different from those of functional grammarians, variationists, pragmaticists, and so on, all of whom would claim that their descriptions are good and sound. So which object of study is to be depended upon to provide the basis for the language subject? In practice, it has been the one in current vogue. Thus, when structuralist linguistics was in the ascendancy, the content of language courses was specified in terms of sentence patterns. With the shift to the pragmatic functioning of language, the units of courses were specified in terms of communicative functions.

It seems to me that this assumption of dependency is mistaken. I want to argue that what the language teacher teaches is not the same as the object of study of linguistics, and that what is a 'good' description in reference to 'sound linguistic principles' cannot be assumed to be good for language pedagogy, which has its own principles to refer to. I want to argue, furthermore, that it is precisely because there is a necessary disparity between the principles of language pedagogy and those of the linguistic discipline that applied linguistics has a role to play. In this view, the purpose of applied linguistics is not to assume relevance but to question it, not to engage in application, but to inquire into applicability.

A convenient way of talking about the object of study of linguistics is in reference to Hymes' well known formulation of the components of communicative competence: the formally possible in respect to the resources of the code available, the feasible in respect to mental processibility, the appropriate in respect to the context, and the done or attested in respect to actual occurrence (Hymes 1972). The first two can be seen as features of I-language, the second two as features of E-language. Different approaches to linguistic description can be seen as giving prominence to one feature rather than another, and, as I have suggested, pedagogy has generally followed suit. Thus, with the extension of linguistic description to account for E-language, we shift from a 'structuralist' pedagogy of the possible to a 'communicative' pedagogy of the appropriate. What has been generally disregarded is that in Hymes' scheme the possible is also an intrinsic aspect of communication. This is, in part at least, because Hymes presents these different features as separate components and does not inquire into their relationship. I have discussed this elsewhere (Widdowson 1989), and this is not the place to deal with it again in detail, but we need to note that this matter of relationships is a crucial one, for in a normal experience of language, all of the features Hymes mentions come into play and interact in complex ways. If the object of description is fixated on one feature, then it cannot correspond with user reality, and this, in turn, raises questions about the relevance of any linguistic theory as a model for pedagogy.

CORPUS LINGUISTICS, AUTHENTIC LANGUAGE, AND TASK-BASED INSTRUCTION

The concern over linguistic objects of description is not limited to formal generative linguistics. Rather, this concern also extends to what is in many ways the most important and influential development in E-language description over recent years, that of corpus linguistics. The 'goodness' of a linguistic description is now increasingly being measured against corpus analyses. The computer provides us with the capability of accumulating and analyzing vast amounts of language that users have actually produced. We no longer have to depend on our own intuitions about the language that people use, or on eliciting from them what they think they use. We can now establish patterns of usage as a matter of observed fact. This trend is, par excellence, the description of the attested in the Hymes scheme. It is obviously a highly significant development which has already had momentous effects on linguistic description. Nobody these days would contemplate writing a grammar or dictionary which did not take account of corpus findings. But we need to note that for all the facts they reveal, and in spite of what is often claimed, these findings are confined to one feature of language, namely the attested. They do not capture an absolute reality but a partial one. So, although they provide additional information of immense interest, it would be a mistake to suppose, in our enthusiasm, that they thereby make all other accounts of language null and void.

We should recognize, to begin with, that corpus analysis is not a different and improved way of dealing with the object of study of linguistics, it changes the object of study itself. There is a radical shift from one kind of reality to another— from language internalized as competence, as something people know, to language externalized as performance, what people do. This, one might say, is a salutary shift. There was in the past too much emphasis on knowledge dissociated from behavior, too exclusive an attention paid to the possible (the encoded resources of the language as known by its users), without regard to the actually attested (what the users actually produce in the way of message forms drawn from these resources). This limitation may be conceded. But then we should be wary about going to the other extreme and denying any significance to the possible that is not attested, of taking up a neo-behaviorist position that denies any validity to knowledge that is not acted upon and overtly realized, and that takes reality to be only what can be quantitatively measured (see Widdowson 1991).

We need to note too that the object of study in corpus linguistics is a particular language in itself, *sui generis*, not as representative of language in general. We get detailed information about patterns of occurrence of English (or French, or Spanish) but nothing in the way of underlying abstract categories which might relate them since these, obviously enough, are never directly manifested in behavior.

Corpus analysis, then, can only, of its nature, reveal what is overtly done (the attested message forms), not what is covertly known (the possible or encoded potential of the language). Moreover, it cannot reveal what is meant by what is done either. We come here to a third of Hymes dimensions of communicative competence: the appropriate, the keying of language in with context. Now we may accept that formalist linguistics, with its exclusive concern with the abstractions of the possible, is bound to represent language as remote from the experience of its users, since this knowledge only becomes a reality for users when it is actualized as behavior. But just the same point applies to the dissociation of the attested from the appropriate. What is attested is text. This is the perceptible trace of discourse enactment—that pragmatic activity whose meaning is realized in relation to contextual conditions of various kinds. It is this meaning achievement that constitutes language reality for users. People do not set out to produce texts: Texts simply occur incidentally as a consequent by-product of the discourse process. So to isolate texts from the contextual conditions of their production is necessarily to create an analytic construct which cannot represent language reality as experienced by users quite simply because users do not experience texts in contextual isolation.

The description that corpus analysis provides, then, is necessarily partial in that it privileges one aspect of language. It deals with the attested message forms, but not with the possible or potential of the code from which they are drawn, and not with the contextually appropriate conditions whereby message forms are assigned pragmatic meaning. Now it is important to stress that this view does not deny the validity of such text description, but only to recognize that, as with descriptions that privilege other aspects of language, its validity is bound to be limited. Corpus linguistics has enormous appeal, of course. It provides a genuinely innovative set of discovery procedures for revealing textual facts not immediately accessible to introspection or elicitation. But its very appeal should make us wary of any claims it might make to be a comprehensive account of language.

So far, I have discussed the descriptive adequacy of corpus accounts of language. What of its applicability for language teaching? How far can it, or should it, determine the specification of course content? In some people's minds, the relevance is self-evident, and to question it is to encourage the complacent reliance on outmoded approaches to description. This view, following the well established tradition that I referred to earlier, assumes that the language object that is described is the same as the language subject that is to be taught, and since corpus linguistics provides the best possible description, accounting for 'real' language rather than some idealized version of it, it stands to reason that its findings should determine the content of language courses. So it is that John Sinclair, who, more than anybody else, has inspired the development of corpus based descriptions of text, proposes the following precept for language teachers:

> Present real examples only (Sinclair 1997:30).

Real examples of what, though? As I have argued, all that corpus descriptions can yield are examples of text, and text only has reality for its producers when it contracts a relationship with context in the discourse process, in other words when the attested is related to the appropriate. So if textual examples are to be drawn from actually occurring usage, they can only be made real as communication if there is some context that they can be appropriately related to. In this respect, examples of the attested are no different from examples of the possible. Consider the following:

> 1) I have a little book here by a lady called Mystic Meg.
> 2) I have a little book. The book is here.

The first example is from the COBUILD Dictionary of actually occurring English and so a real example and to be deemed suitable for pedagogic presentation. The second example is a pair of sentences that I have invented myself and in this respect unreal and so presumably unsuitable. But in both cases what we have are stretches of inert language which need to be activated by some kind of appropriate contextual connection for them to be realized as meaningful. It is of course true that the first, as an instance of the attested, an extract from text, did originally have appropriate contextual connections, whereas the second, as an instance of the possible derived directly from the code, never did. But this distinction is pedagogically irrelevant since the original context of the first is unknown, and even if it were known could not be replicated in the classroom anyway. So in both cases the teacher has to somehow contrive an appropriate context of some kind which would make the examples meaningful to learners, and this contextualizing would be infinitely easier to do for the second example than for the first. Indeed, 'unreal' examples like the second are expressly contrived to make them realizable in the contextual conditions of the classroom. In other words, the likelihood is that the 'unreal' example can be more readily made real for learners than the 'real' one.

In spite of the clear benefit with the use of 'unreal' examples, there is a persistent prejudice against such contrivance. For example, Willis (1990) notes the following:

> Contrived simplification of language in the preparation of materials will always be faulty, since it is generated without the guide and support of a communicative context. Only by accepting the discipline of using authentic language are we likely to come anywhere near presenting the learner with a sample of language which is typical of real English (1990:127).

But the 'real' examples of attested text are also simplified: They are message forms that are dissociated both from their source in the code potential of the possible and from the complexity of the normal contextual conditions that made them communicatively appropriate in the first place. The original communicative context that constituted their 'guide and support' is no longer in evidence. A context has to be reconstituted in some way, and it has to be appropriate to classroom conditions. In classroom settings, it is not the case that contrived language is 'generated without the guide and support of a communicative context.' It is simply that the communicative context itself has to be contrived so as to be real for learners and effective for learning. I would argue that we must have the discipline to deny ourselves the easy assumption—that authenticity is transferable intact in the text from one context to another. What we need to recognize is that it makes no sense to present learners with 'real' examples of text unless they can make them real for themselves.

Returning to the general point, it is misleading to suppose that the object of linguistic description is the same as the subject of language teaching. What linguists produce are partial accounts of language, and different approaches to description are partial in different respects. The question is what insights can be drawn from these accounts that are relevant to the pedagogic design of language courses. Corpus description, as one kind of account, has enormous appeal. A description that promises to provide real English for the first time is bound to be appealing to teachers. Who wants to be accused of teaching unreal English? *Real, authentic, naturally occurring* are expressions which have (in corpus linguistic terms) a positive prosody, and *unreal, inauthentic, contrived, artificial* a negative one. The appeal is difficult to resist.

This allure is all the more reason for questioning its validity for language teaching. The direct application of corpus description to language teaching is rooted in a misconception about the nature of the language subject. The language subject is not the same as the language as known and experienced by its users. It is something which is necessarily designed to account for the fact that the language is foreign. The reality of the language for its users is a function of its familiarity. The reality of the language for people learning it is precisely the opposite: It is a function of its unfamiliarity, its foreignness, something that primary language users cannot possibly experience. And the language will, of course, be foreign in different ways for different groups of learners. It is this foreignness that the language subject has to be designed to accommodate. So there are two kinds of language reality here. The interesting question is how they are to be related, what relevance the description of one might have for the design of the other. But it will not do to conflate the two, or seek to impose one on the other by fiat.

It is not only in the specification of course content that we find what we might call the dogma of the authentic, the uncritical belief in the transferability of reality from the context of use to the context of instruction. We find it too in the design of classroom activities where language is not just presented but engaged with so as to activate the learning process. The activity which has been particularly commended over recent years is the task. This involves the learner in using language contingently to solve a problem and, as such, is defined as distinct from an exercise, which simply requires the learner to solve a language problem *per se*. The design of a task has to satisfy two crucial pedagogic conditions. One is that the problem that is set has to engage learners in what they will take as purposeful activity; in other words, it has to be appropriate to their reality. The second is that it has to be effective in activating their learning, which means that it has to develop their knowledge of the possible, the meaning-making potential of the code. Neither of these conditions depends on replicating the reality of user experience. And yet those who talk about tasks regularly invoke this reality as a necessary design feature. Thus it appears as one of the criteria that Skehan (1998) specifies as definitive of a task

...a task is regarded as an activity which satisfies the following criteria:
Meaning is primary.
There is a goal which needs to be worked towards.
The activity is outcome-evaluated.
There is a real-world relationship (1998:268).

He comments on this issue as follows:

...the real-world relationship implies that an activity focussed on language itself cannot be a task. A transformation drill, for example, is an activity which fills class time, but does not happen in the real world and so fails to meet this criterion (1998:268).

The assumption Skehan makes here is that, as with Willis's communicative contexts, there is only one real world—that of the language user—and this must be replicated if the learning activity is to be valid. However, this assumption ignores the fact that what happens in the real world of language users may be utterly unreal for learners, for they inhabit quite different worlds. Furthermore, learners are quite capable of creating worlds of their own, of appropriating the language to their own purposes and making it real for themselves on their own terms. Even such activities as a transformation drill can be converted by learners into something real and meaningful whereby they exploit the very foreignness of the language (see Kramsch and Sullivan 1996, Sullivan to appear). Learners can engage with language, and learn from it, without reference to the kind of transactional goals and outcomes by which user-language use is evaluated. They may indeed subvert presumed goals and outcomes by language play, which, as Cook (1997; 2000) argues, has a powerful reality of its own and is an effective device for learning for children and adults alike.

LINGUISTICS, LANGUAGE TEACHING, AND APPLIED LINGUISTICS

The object language which linguists describe is, then, one kind of reality: that of user experience in the contexts of 'normal' social interaction. The language subject is another and quite different reality, one which has to be contrived to be appropriate to other contextual conditions. Looking into the relationship between them, between linguistic description and pedagogic design, is a matter of mediating between two domains of inquiry, each with its own principles and conditions of adequacy. It is this mediation which is the central business of applied linguistics. In the past, the orthodox view was that the language subject and the object language of description were the same and that, since linguists were expert in description, they had the authority to tell teachers what to teach. Given the academic prestige of linguistics, and the relatively humble status of pedagogy, teachers have tended to concede the authority. This persistent belief in unmediated application necessarily denies any distinctive role for applied linguistics and simply equates it with linguistics applied (see Widdowson 1980), which linguists can do for themselves: Mediation is merely meddling. Such a position would seem to be John Sinclair's view:

> Applied linguists, I have the impression, see themselves as mediators between the abstract and heady realms of linguistic theory and the humdrum practical side of language teaching (1998:84).

As far as I am concerned at least, the impression is entirely correct. As an applied linguist, I do indeed see myself as a mediator. From the perspective of outsiders, linguistic theory may indeed be a heady realm, and language teaching humdrum practice. And this is just the kind of difficulty that mediation has to deal with by showing that what is commonly dismissed as heady and abstruse can also be interpreted as providing a legitimate intellectual perspective, that theory can be relevantly related to language teaching (as to other areas of practical life) to make it more meaningful and less humdrum. Without mediation, the domains remain self enclosed: The heady just remains heady, the humdrum humdrum.

One might, of course, accept the need for mediation but deny the need for mediators, arguing that linguists are perfectly capable of doing it for themselves. The evidence would seem to indicate, however, that they find this difficult to do. This is not surprising, actually, for it would require them to distance themselves from their own disciplinary perspective and relate linguistic knowledge to a quite different perspective. Linguists have authority in their own domain: They describe language on their own terms and in their own terms. There is no reason why they should assume the responsibility of acquiring expertise and authority in the quite different domain of language pedagogy. It is not their business. The linguist, qua linguist, is in no position to judge the pedagogic relevance of linguistic theory and description, and some linguists recognize this well enough. Chomsky is one of them.

It is often pointed out that Chomsky, in a talk at a teachers' conference in 1965, expressed his own skepticism about the relevance of linguistics for language teaching (and by implication the validity of applied linguistics), and his remarks are frequently cited, with some glee, as if they settled the question once and for all. But Chomsky, as linguist, has no authority to pronounce on the matter, and right at the beginning of his talk he makes his position quite plain:

I should like to make it clear from the outset that I am participating in this conference not as an expert on any aspect of the teaching of languages, but rather as someone whose primary concern is with the structure of language and, more generally the nature of cognitive processes (1966:43).

And later in his talk we find the following disavowal:

It is possible—even likely—that principles of pyschology and linguistics, and research in these disciplines, may supply insights useful to the language teacher. But this must be demonstrated, and cannot be presumed. It is the language teacher himself who must validate or refute any specific proposal. There is very little in psychology or linguistics that he can accept on faith (Chomsky 1966:46).

As we have seen, not all linguists would be so cautious and deferential. Some would assume usefulness without further ado and presume to propose precepts for teachers based on linguistic authority. One might, of course, retort that what Chomsky says applies to his linguistics, a linguistics only of the possible, an idealized, armchair abstraction which everybody knows is useless because it does not describe use. With linguistic description that deals with attested reality, the situation is different.

But how is it different? To begin with, a moment's reflection will reveal that Chomsky's linguistics was not useless at all. It had an enormous influence on how people concerned with pedagogy thought about language. His insights effectively led to a fundamental reconceptualization of the nature of the language learning process, and consequently of how language was to be defined as a subject. It was Chomsky who challenged the orthodox pedagogic view of the time that learning was a matter of habit formation to be induced by pattern practice and structural drill whereby learners were constrained into conformity. He made us conceive of learning in a totally different way, as an essentially cognitive and creative process in which there was room for learner initiative. This reorientation, in turn, led to a revision of the concept of error and a radical reappraisal of teacher and learner roles. All of the ideas about autonomous learning, problem solving, the distinction between overt participation and covert engagement, and the defining of classroom activities in terms of tasks rather than exercises can be traced back to Chomsky's insights about the nature of language.

These pedagogic consequences, however, were not a matter of direct application but of indirect implication. As has been frequently pointed out, attempts to formulate course content in reference to formalist categories proved to be misguided. What was significant about Chomsky's ideas was that they led those concerned with pedagogy to redefine the nature of the language subject in cognitive rather than behaviorist terms. It is a nice irony that the current rejection of his linguistics of the possible in favor of the linguistics of the attested marks a return to behaviorist principles. Clearly, however, students do not learn a language by accumulating message forms, but only by inferring from them some underlying encoded potential; in other words, they learn by relating the attested to the possible, and the subject has to be designed in such a way as to guide them to do this. But learning cannot occur if it is determined directly by a description that only deals with overt attested behavior, particularly if this behavior is only that of the experienced language of the user. Here we return to the distinction made earlier between the object language of user experience and the language subject as designed for learners. The point I made about the language subject was that it was essentially concerned with the foreignness of the language and so could not be equated with the language of familiar user experience. Since this foreignness can only be recognized in relation to another language, it follows that English (or French, or Spanish) as a foreign language is necessarily a bilingual subject. Students learn the foreign language in relation to the language (or languages) they already know. They can only relate the language they know to the language they do not by reference to abstract categories of the possible.

To the extent that the language subject must incorporate the possible, it cannot be defined in reference only to descriptions of the attested. Both aspects of language have to be taken into account. And both, as I indicated earlier, have to be related to the appropriate. Whether one is drawing the content of courses from message forms which are contrived exemplifications of the code, or from message forms which are sampled from actually occurring text, they need to be made real for the learner. The message forms have to be made locally appropriate to the different classroom contexts in which learners find themselves.

What I have said about the necessary adequacy of linguistic descriptions as models for course design applies both to formalist approaches and to the findings of corpus analysis. Both provide insights into language of immense interest, but their pedagogic usefulness for the language subject 'must,' in Chomsky's words, 'be demonstrated, and cannot be presumed.' The only difference is that the proponents of one approach do not presume, whereas those of the other do.

It seems to me that Chomsky, that arch fiend of useless formalist linguistics, gives us a clearer indication of the role of the linguist than many who claim a necessary pedagogic relevance for their partial descriptions of 'real' language. What he says in this regard also allows us to see where the applied linguist comes in. 'The usefulness of insights that linguistics supplies must be demonstrated,' he says, and he never said a truer word. But then who is it that does the demonstrating? Who is to be the agent? The teacher? But how do teachers recognize these insights in the first place? Linguists, as I have said, describe language on their own terms and in their own terms; in other words, they develop their own specialist discourses to suit their own disciplinary perspective on language. They would not have insights of any interest to offer if they did not. Their perspective, however, is not a pedagogic perspective. So whatever insights might be forthcoming cannot simply be supplied, retailed from one discourse domain to another. A third party, a mediating agent, must make these insights intelligible in ways in which their usefulness can be demonstrated. In other words, we need the applied linguist.

I have been talking here about mediating a relationship between linguistics and language teaching, the principle of mediation applies more generally to the relationship between any disciplinary discourse and the areas of its potential applicability, between abstraction and the actuality of experience. There is never any direct transference. Disciplines can, of course, and routinely do, use human beings empirically as a source of data. But you cannot then reconstitute, or replicate, human beings from the data. As we have seen, the language data that corpus linguists describe may reflect one kind of reality, but it is not one that can be equated with the reality that students experience when they are learning a foreign language in the classroom. Whatever insights such description offers, they are a function not of transference but of translation, mediated into a form where their usefulness might be realized. They cannot just be supplied.

So linguistic insights are created by mediation. But, equally, so is the usefulness. Applied linguistics is often said to be concerned with the investigation of real-world problems in which language is implicated. But this seems to suggest that problems, like insights, are somehow there, that somebody in the real world supplies a problem, the linguist supplies an insight, and the applied linguist matches them up. But things are not like that. To begin with, problems are perceived and formulated in culturally marked ways; in other words, they belong to particular discourses, and it is likely that they will need to be reformulated so as to make them amenable to investigation. It may indeed be the case that what people identify as a problem is simply the symptom of another one that they are not aware of. In a sense then, investigation, which of its nature belongs to a discourse other than that of the problem, will necessarily reformulate it, and change it into something else, which in turn may create problems that were not perceived at all in the first place. Just as linguistic insights are a function of the mediation, so are the problems they are related to. The process brings together two discourses, or two versions of reality, and this requires an adjustment of fit whereby an area of convergence is created, compounded of elements of both discourses but belonging exclusively to neither.

Since the area of convergence belongs to neither discourse, proponents of both are likely to be somewhat ambivalent about it. Thus language teachers, for example, may, and indeed often do, think of mediation as an unwanted, and unwarranted, intrusion on their domain. And there are times when it is: when we get linguistics applied, as distinct from applied linguistics, the process whereby linguistic findings are foisted on pedagogy on just the presumption of relevance that Chomsky warns us against. Conversely, linguists may feel that the area of convergence is a misrepresentation that disfigures their discipline. Applied linguists thus find themselves in an anomalous position, in a no-man's land they have made for themselves, and not infrequently under fire from both sides. It is not surprising that they should so often feel insecure, nor is it surprising that the straightforward unmediated process of linguistics applied should be so appealing. You only have to be a linguist to do that.

UNANNOTATED BIBLIOGRAPHY

Chomsky, N. 1966. Linguistic theory. In R. Mead (ed.) *Language teaching: Broader contexts. Northeast Conference reports.* [Reprinted in J. P. B. Allen and P. van Buren (eds.) *Chomsky: Selected readings.* Oxford: Oxford University Press. 1971. 152–159.]

─────── 1988. *Language and problems of knowledge.* Cambridge, MA: MIT Press.

Cook, G. 1997. Language play, language learning. *English Language Teaching Journal.* 51.224–231.

─────── 2000. *Language play, language learning.* Oxford: Oxford University Press.

Halliday, M. A. K., A. McIntosh and P. Strevens. 1964. *The linguistic sciences and language teaching.* London: Longman.

Hymes, D. H. 1972. On communicative competence. In J. Pride and J. Holmes (eds.) *Sociolinguistics: Selected readings.* Harmondsworth: Penguin Books. 269–293.

Kramsch, C. and P. Sullivan. 1996. Appropriate pedagogy. *English Language Teaching Journal.* 50.199–212.

Sinclair, J. M. 1997. Corpus evidence in language description. In A. Wichmann, S. Fligelstone, T. McEnery and G. Knowles (eds.) *Teaching and language corpora.* London: Longman. 27–39.

─────── 1998. Large corpus research and foreign language teaching. In R. Beaugrande, M. Grosman, and B. Seidlhofer (eds.) *Language policy and language education in emerging nations.* Stamford, CT: Ablex. 79–86.

Skehan, P. 1998. *A cognitive approach to language learning.* Oxford: Oxford University Press.

Sullivan, P. To appear. Language play and communicative language teaching in a Vietnamese classroom. In J. Lantolf (ed.) *Sociocultural theory and second language learning.* Oxford: Oxford University Press.

Widdowson, H. G. 1980. Models and fictions. *Applied Linguistics.* 1.165–170.

─────── 1989. Knowledge of language and ability for use. *Applied Linguistics.*

10.128–137.

Widdowson, H. G. 1991. The description and prescription of language. In J. Alatis (ed.) *Linguistics and language pedagogy: The state of the art*. Georgetown: Georgetown University Press. 11–24.

Willis, D. 1990. *The lexical syllabus*. London: Collins.

LANGUAGE TEACHER EDUCATION

JoAnn (Jodi) Crandall

INTRODUCTION[1]

Language teacher education programs are likely to be housed in departments of applied linguistics, education, or languages and literature: These three disciplines provide the knowledge base and opportunities for developing skills and dispositions for both prospective and experienced teachers. Until recently, applied linguistics (psycholinguistics, sociolinguistics, discourse analysis, language description, and language teaching and testing methodology) formed the core of language teacher education, not unexpected, since language teaching has historically been the primary focus of applied linguistics (Bardovi-Harlig and Hartford 1997, Crandall 1995; 1996). However, during the last decade, general educational theory and practice have exerted a much more powerful influence on the direction of the education of both preservice and inservice language teacher education, resulting in a greater focus on: 1) practical experiences such as observations, practice teaching, and opportunities for curriculum and materials development (Crandall 1994, Johnson 1996b, Pennington 1990, Richards 1990, Richards and Crookes 1988); 2) classroom-centered or teacher research (Allwright and Bailey 1991, Chaudron 1988, Edge and Richards 1993, Nunan 1989, van Lier 1988); and 3) teacher beliefs and teacher cognition in language teacher education (Freeman 1996; 1998, Freeman and Johnson 1998a, Richards and Nunan 1990). In fact, the last decade can be viewed as a search for a theory of language teaching and, by extension, of language teacher education at both the micro and macro levels (Freeman and Johnson 1998b, Johnson 1996a, Larsen-Freeman 1990, Richards 1990). Language teacher education is a microcosm of teacher education, and many of the trends in current language teacher education derive from theory and practice in general teacher education.

These trends include at least four major shifts.

First, there is a shift from transmission, product-oriented theories to constructivist, process-oriented theories of learning, teaching, and teacher learning. Traditional, transmission-oriented teaching involves top-down approaches which present best practices for teachers to understand and imitate in their teaching (Richards 1990, Widdowson 1997). Traditional teacher education views teachers as passive recipients of transmitted knowledge rather than active participants in the construction of meaning (in learning by reconstruction). Nor does it take into account the thinking or decision-making of teachers. A shift to a constructivist perspective of teaching and teacher learning makes teachers a primary source of knowledge about teaching, reflected in an increasing focus on teacher cognition (Johnson 1999, Kleinfeld 1992, Richards and Lockhart 1994), the role of reflection in teacher development (Bartlett 1990, Freeman and Richards 1993, Schon 1983; 1987), and the importance of teacher inquiry and research throughout teacher education and development programs (Crandall 1994, Freeman 1998, Wright 1992).

Second, there is a growing sense that language teacher education programs have failed to prepare teachers for the realities of the classroom. As a result, efforts are being made to transform teaching through a focus on situated teacher cognition and practice (Bruner 1986, Lave 1988) and the development of concrete, relevant linkages between theory and practice throughout the teacher education program. The host of differences in learners, programs, curricula, materials, policies, and the socio-cultural environment that teachers are likely to encounter in their careers calls into question any set of "best practices" appropriate for all contexts or any attempts to transfer the knowledge and practice from teacher education programs directly to teaching (Casanave and Schecter 1997, Freeman 1989, Holliday 1994). Decontextualized theory fails to consider the multi-dimensionality and unpredictability of the classroom environment (Bailey and Nunan 1996, Doyle 1986, Johnson 1996b). Partnerships between programs of language teacher education and language teaching programs or schools provide opportunities for contextualizing and integrating preservice and inservice teacher education, encouraging prospective and experienced teachers, administrators, and researchers to learn together as they also provide enhanced programs for language learners (Crandall 1994, Darling-Hammond 1994, Holmes

Group 1986).

Third, there is a growing recognition that teachers' prior learning experiences (what Lortie [1975] refers to as "the apprenticeship of observation") play a powerful role in shaping their views of effective teaching and learning and their teaching practices. These preconceptions are remarkably resistant to change unless awareness of that prior learning is developed in the teacher education program and opportunities for practical experiences and conscious reflection upon those experiences are provided throughout the program (Freeman 1991; 1996, Freeman and Richards 1996, Johnson 1994, Kennedy 1987, Richards and Lockhart 1994). Similarly, one can expect that the way teacher educators were taught will be replicated in their teacher education programs unless conscious reflection upon teacher-education practice also takes place. Self-observation and reflection on practice can help teachers move from a philosophy of teaching and learning developed during their 16 or so years as a learner to a philosophy of teaching consistent with their emerging understandings of the language learning and teaching processes (what Freeman has referred to as InterTeaching, analogous to a language learner's development of interlanguage).

Fourth, there is a growing concern that teaching be viewed as a profession (similar to medicine or law) with respect for the role of teachers in developing theory and directing their own professional development through collaborative observation, teacher research and inquiry, and sustained inservice programs, rather than the typical short-term workshop or training program (Crandall 1993; 1994; 1996, Darling Hammond 1994, The Holmes Group 1986). Candlin and Widdowson, in their introduction to each volume of their series, *Language teaching: A scheme for teacher education*, sum up this trend in the following way: "If language teaching is to be a genuinely professional enterprise, it requires continual experimentation and evaluation on the part of practitioners whereby, in seeking to be more effective in their pedagogy, they provide at the same time—and as a corollary—for their own continuing education." Freeman (in Freeman and Richards 1996) argues that one function of inservice training for teachers is to enable them to be "bilingual," that is, to rename what they have been previously doing in light of what they are learning in their training, and by so doing, to function bilingually, adding professional language to the local language they use in their schools.

CONCEPTIONS OF LANGUAGE TEACHING AND MODELS OF LANGUAGE TEACHER EDUCATION

Traditional language teacher education has involved a delicate balancing act between education and training. The former addresses the development of language knowledge and language teaching and learning. The latter emphasizes the development of skills to apply this knowledge in the practice of language teaching, with a limited opportunity to observe and practice that theory in actual classrooms or simulated contexts such as microteaching (Crandall 1998). Those involved in preparing prospective language teachers refer to themselves as either teacher trainers or teacher educators. Widdowson (1997) describes teacher training as solution-oriented, with the "...implication that teachers are to be given specific instruction in practical techniques to cope with predictable events..." while teacher education is problem-oriented, with the implication of "...a broader intellectual awareness of theoretical principles underlying particular practices" (1997:121). In both orientations, the prospective or experienced teacher is viewed as a passive recipient of transmitted knowledge; omitted is any understanding of the role that language teachers play in their own development, which teacher research has begun to demonstrate as being of considerable importance (Edge and Richards 1993, Woodward 1991). Teacher development is a life-long process of growth which may involve collaborative and/or autonomous learning, but the important distinction is that teachers are engaged in the process and they actively reflect on their practices. According to Wallace (1991), "The distinction is that training or education is something that can be presented or managed by others; whereas development is something that can be done only by and for oneself" (p.3).

Wallace (1991) identifies three major models of language teacher education: 1) a craft or apprenticeship model by which less experienced teachers learn through observing those with more experience; 2) an applied science or theory-to-practice model by which knowledge is learned from experts and then applied in real-world contexts; and 3) a reflective model by which teachers reflect upon, evaluate, and adapt their own practice. These three models broadly correspond to the three views of teaching identified by Freeman (1991; 1996): 1) teaching as doing (a behavioral model emphasizing what teachers do and encouraging a skills or craft model of teacher education); 2) teaching as thinking and doing (a cognitive model emphasizing what teachers know and how they do it, encouraging both theory and skills development and craft and applied science models of teacher education); and 3) teaching as knowing what to do (an interpretivist view emphasizing why teachers do what they do in different contexts, encouraging the addition of reflection and the development of frameworks of interpretation to theory and skill development in teacher education). Wallace's three models of language teacher education are likely to be needed in all teacher development, but in different degrees, depending upon teacher experience and understanding. However, neither traditional education nor training are sufficient; also needed are opportunities for teachers to reflect upon their beliefs and practices and to construct and reconstruct their personal theories of language teaching and learning (Bailey 1992, Flowerdew, *et al.* 1992, Freeman and Richards 1996, Sachs, *et al.* 1996). "Teaching depends upon the application of appropriate theory, the development of careful instructional designs and strategies, and the study of what actually happens in the classroom" (Richards 1990:vii).

FROM METHODS TO METHODOLOGY AND THE IMPORTANCE OF CONTEXT

The core of traditional language teacher education has long been the methods course, a course which presents the theoretical rationale and practical implications of language teaching approaches, methods, procedures, and techniques (Anthony 1963, Blair 1982, Celce-Murcia 1991, Larsen-Freeman 1986, Oller 1993, Oller and Richard-Amato 1983, Richards and Rodgers 1982; 1986, Rivers 1981, Stevick 1980). Methods courses often discuss the rationale for, and instructional practices reflected in "innovative" methods (e.g., Silent Way, Community Language Learning, Natural Approach, Content-based Language Instruction) as well as "traditional" ones (Grammar-Translation, Audio-Lingual, Communicative), and they often combine this discussion with specific attention to techniques for teaching the four skills (listening, speaking, reading, and writing). Sometimes specific courses in oral or written skills are provided, as are courses in assessment and evaluation.

While courses in language teaching methods are still central to language teacher education, there is growing concern that they not be taught in prescriptivist terms, as recipes or cookbooks for effective teaching. Rather, they need to investigate the range of instructional options language teachers have available in their repertoires and, through case studies, interviews, or introspection, examine the kinds of decisions teachers make in planning and carrying out instruction (Richards 1990, Roberts 1998, Stevick 1998, William and Burden 1997). The shift from methods to methodology is consonant with constructivist theories of learning—a shift away from a top-down approach to methods as "products" for teachers to learn and "match" and toward a bottom-up approach to methodology as reflections on experiences. The shift involves prospective teachers in "...exploring the nature of effective teaching and learning, and discovering the strategies used by successful teachers and learners in the classroom" (Richards 1990:vii).

While few language teacher educators believed that the role of the traditional methods course was to make future teachers into "methods" teachers (cf. "methods actors"), the counter view, that prospective teachers should pick and choose from among the techniques described in an "eclectic approach," conveyed little coherence. Several recent core texts for methodology courses (Brown 1994, Nunan 1991; 1999, Omaggio Hadley 1993) are more cognizant of the role of context and the need to engage prospective and experienced teachers in analyzing their own theories of teaching and learning as they practice, discuss, and reflect upon instructional techniques (Graves 2000, Hartman 1998, Nunan and Lamb 1996). Collections of "what works" or "new ways" of teaching or educating teachers (e.g., Freeman and Cornwell 1993) continue to provide teachers with practical options, but analysis and evaluation of teaching and learning strategies that teachers use in a variety of contexts help bring coherence to the process. Focusing on teachers—their beliefs about teaching, learning, or classroom interaction—can help balance more top-down, product-oriented conceptions of language teaching, with more nuanced, bottom-up, process-oriented descriptions of specific language teaching events. Studies of teachers, either undertaken by teachers themselves or in collaboration with researchers (Shulman 1992), can help illuminate the processes by which language teachers plan and make decisions about their teaching (Woods 1996). Central to these studies is the need to examine underlying teacher beliefs and teacher thinking.

1. Teacher cognition and beliefs

Traditional teacher education has largely ignored the substantial set of beliefs about teaching, learning, teacher-student roles, and the like which teacher candidates bring to their program from their experiences as students and language learners. Teachers do not engage in mere implementation of routinized procedures, but are constantly engaged in thinking, problem-solving, and decision-making. While content knowledge and pedagogical content knowledge remain important underpinnings of language teacher education, also needed are opportunities for prospective teachers to become aware of their own beliefs about effective teaching and learning, and they need opportunities to acquire the ways of thinking (general strategies, personal orientation, and habits of mind) that characterize being a member of the language teaching community. Case studies and teacher narratives, teaching videos, and teacher journals offer windows into that thinking (Kennedy 1987, Richards and Lockhart 1994, Woods 1996).

Teacher cognition is "situated" in practice (Lave 1988); thus, it is important to consider the effects of context upon teacher decision-making and teaching and learning. Traditional language teacher education programs have attempted to capture some of the diversity of language teaching situations in broad terms through courses and texts which look at learners with respect to common patterns of variation: different ages (teaching young children or adults), different levels of proficiency (teaching beginners or advanced learners), different purposes for learning (academic, professional, or "general"), and different contexts (second or foreign language; intensive or occasional). But these attempts are not likely to provide sufficient preparation for the heterogeneity of learners or contexts that teachers actually encounter. Fanselow (1987; 1992), Head and Taylor (1997), and others offer a number of activities to make teachers' underlying beliefs more explicit and to encourage the development of alternative perspectives.

Studies of teachers and teaching reveal the number of decisions which teachers make, often with competing demands and not much time to think back to principles or applications derived from teacher education programs (Burns 1995, Freeman and Richards 1996, Kleinfield 1992). Woods (1996), in the first major study of teacher cognition in language teaching, describes how teachers rely upon experience and call into play their beliefs, assumptions, and knowledge in that decision-making. Richards (1996) identifies eight maxims or principles derived from experience which teachers use to explain the decisions they make during teaching. Often tacit, these maxims need to be made explicit if teachers are to consider new techniques or changes in practices.

2. The role of reflection

What is often missing from traditional language teacher education is recognition of the role that the teacher plays in generating knowledge through teaching experience and reflection (conscious recollection and evaluation of that experience; Bartlett 1990, Freeman and Richards 1993, Wallace 1991). As Bruner (1986; 1990) explains, universities have traditionally focused on scientific knowledge which is abstract, decontextualized, and impersonal, but teachers also need access to narrative ways of knowing which relate theory to specific practices in concrete, contextualized, and personal ways. In focusing on "how," language teacher education has ignored the important "what" and "why" questions which can only be answered by teacher reflection and research. Bartlett (1990) suggests a cycle (similar to action-research cycles) moving from observation, to interpretation, introspection and questioning, to consideration of alternatives, and then to adaptation of instruction. Wallace (1991) also provides a scheme by which teachers can recall their practice and engage in critical reflection. Fanselow (1987) suggests that teachers "break rules" and then observe and reflect upon the consequences. Reflection on experience provides a means for prospective and experienced teachers to develop more informed practice, making tacit beliefs and practical knowledge explicit, articulating what teachers know and leading to new ways of knowing and teaching. Long ignored, teacher inquiry and reflection are now viewed as important to the development of language teaching theory and appropriate language teacher education.

3. Teacher narratives and case studies

Many ways of tapping into teachers' knowledge and helping teachers to make explicit their own beliefs about teaching have been proposed, including analyses of teacher logs, diaries, or journals; audio or video recordings of teaching; interviews; and teacher narratives or case studies of teacher practice (Kleinfield 1992). Narratives (stories, cases, lessons, anecdotes, and extended examples), long a part of teacher education, were dismissed as "practitioner lore" by scientific positivism, and have only recently been brought back into teacher education (Shulman 1992, Wideen, *et al.* 1998). Teaching case studies and stories (like those used in the medical, legal, or business education) provide a means of bridging theory and practice and demonstrating the complexity of teaching as a profession. They provide contextualized portraits of the many factors which influence teacher decision making and behavior in the classroom.

Teacher narratives, or "stories" that teachers tell about their classroom experiences, convey the daily experiences of teachers and the ways in which they try to make sense of these experiences through talking or writing about them (Bailey and Nunan 1996, Casanave and Schecter 1997, Hartman 1998, Plaister 1993, Richards 1998). Teachers avoid abstract theoretical statements in talking with each other about their work because these lack connection to classroom experience. Stories help teachers understand students; they address the dilemmas of teaching and the competing roles that teachers carry out; and they provide professional development through reflection on practice. Narratives represent a primary way in which teachers organize and understand the complexities of their profession, involving competing demands, constraints, policies, and power relations. In working with case studies, prospective and experienced teachers become actively involved in the kinds of decision-making they face in their language teaching (Plaister 1993). Case studies also offer a way to help teacher educators avoid the imposition of culturally inappropriate teaching philosophies (Bax 1995a; 1995b).

4. The role of practical experience

The growing respect for the situated knowledge of the teacher, the recognition of the teacher as central in the teaching and learning process, and the crucial roles of the teacher as program and materials developer, needs analyst, decision-maker, problem-solver, and researcher of his or her own classroom (Richards 1990), has led to a call for teacher preparation programs to create opportunities for prospective teachers to access this knowledge and test theories and principles with actual practice. Practica (practical experiences such as observations, internships, apprenticeships, student teaching, or other teaching practice) have long been a part of most language teacher education programs. Richards and Crookes (1988) found that 75 percent of the language teacher education programs they reviewed included a practicum experience, ranging from observing experienced teachers or peers, being observed by or conferencing with supervising or mentor teachers, participating in peer or microteaching, or being responsible for classroom instruction. However, these experiences are often too few, too late, and not sufficiently focused on the realities of the classroom, the program, or the school (Crandall 1996). A number of language teacher educators (Crandall 1994, Johnson 1996b, Richards 1990) have called for more extensive and intensive practical experiences to be integrated throughout the teacher education program, providing prospective teachers with greater opportunities to link theory with practice and to receive support and learn from experienced teachers, while also offering experienced teachers an opportunity to learn from their new counterparts (Stoynoff 1999). Within general teacher education, prospective teachers spend more time in real teaching situations than is often the case in language teacher preparation programs, especially those housed outside of education departments. Partnerships between university-based teacher education departments and schools offer prospective and experienced teachers opportunities for engaging in collaborative research and teaching, while also benefitting the language learners in the classroom. (See Crandall 1994; 1995 for a description of a professional development center approach which engages prospective and experienced language teachers in research, program planning, curriculum development, and teaching to benefit secondary school immigrant students as well as improve teacher education and development.)

Observation of mentor teachers or peers and self-observation through video recordings, accompanied by reflective activities such as journal writing and feedback or discussion sessions, are especially important for language teacher preparation and continuing teacher development (Crandall 1994, Fanselow 1987). Unfortunately, because observation is characteristically used in teacher supervision and evaluation, the self-knowledge it can provide has too often been ignored. A number of observation schemes and instruments have been developed that enable teachers and researchers to focus attention on specific aspects of classroom interaction, management, or instruction, and construct or reconstruct understandings of language teaching and learning.

Teacher-education programs can also provide practical experiences that encourage prospective teachers to continue their professional development after leaving the program. These experiences help prepare them for a variety of professional activities: writing for publication, developing proposals for conference presentations or grant funding, or working on public speaking and professional presentations (Crandall 1996).

5. The role of research

Classroom research, research that is carried out in the second or foreign language classroom to answer questions about teaching and learning, plays an increasingly important role in both initial teacher preparation and ongoing teacher development. This research can focus on teachers (e.g., questioning strategies, teacher decision-making, error correction, or teacher modifications); learners (e.g., learning styles and strategies, learner interaction, affective variables, or language output from specific tasks); or the interaction between teachers and learners (Burns 1995, Nunan 1989, van Lier 1988). Research on language acquisition and learning was traditionally conducted by university researchers (sometimes in collaboration with language teachers) and reflected their research traditions, using experimental, ethnographic, discourse, or interactional analyses (Chaudron 1988), often with a goal of identifying "best practices" in language teaching or learning. Studies of teachers attempting to implement these best practices reveal that teachers adapt them substantially to fit their specific teaching contexts. This adaptation process has led to the addition of action or teacher research grounded in the specifics of individual teacher contexts. Allwright and Bailey (1991) offer a number of suggestions for small-scale and large-scale research and provide guidance on conducting research and analyzing findings. Such research can be undertaken collaboratively by teacher educators/researchers and teachers or individually by teachers researching their own classrooms (Crandall 1994; 1995). Research undertaken by teachers and focused on observation, analysis, and potential changes of one's own teaching represents one means by which teachers can reconsider their assumptions and practices and enhance teacher professionalism. Often, this research is most successful when teachers collaborate in the research process or engage in inquiry or study groups which meet periodically to discuss findings; otherwise, the daily responsibilities of teaching may take precedence. The publication of the results of teacher research in journals, stories, or case studies can also provide opportunities for other teachers to explore changes in their own practice as well.

ASSESSMENT IN LANGUAGE TEACHER EDUCATION

Congruent with increased emphasis on performance assessment in language teaching is the increasing focus on performance assessment of prospective and experienced teachers, especially in new teacher-evaluation schemes resulting from the standards movement (Johnson 1996b). These performance assessments may include audio- or videotapes of classroom teaching; examples of student work; lesson plans, curriculum guides, or syllabi; entries from a teaching log or journal; statements of a personal (evolving) philosophy of teaching; or simulated performances such as microteaching, role plays, or interviews. Frequently, these documentations of performance are combined into a teaching portfolio (along with a curriculum vita, transcripts, letters of reference, teaching evaluations, and brief annotations or reflections on the significance of the contents of the portfolio), providing concrete evidence of teacher capability and ongoing development. In some teacher education programs, the teaching portfolio serves as documentation of the student teaching experience; in others, it is integrated into the entire program and serves as one of the final evaluation criteria.

NATIVE- AND NON-NATIVE-SPEAKING PROFESSIONALS IN SECOND AND FOREIGN LANGUAGE CONTEXTS

Another concern in language teacher education which is receiving a great deal of attention in both the foreign and second language teaching communities is the role of the native speaker (Kramsch 1997). Because of the globalization of English, the growing prominence of World Englishes, and the increasing need for English teachers around the world, the issues of appropriate competencies, expectations, and roles for native- and non-native-speaking teachers have received frequent discussion (Braine 1998, Cook 1999, Medgyes 1992; 1994). Determining who is a "native speaker" is not quite so simple as previously imagined, and the linkage between native-speaking proficiency and professional competence is also often misconstrued (when teachers are hired not because of their preparation, but because they are "native speakers"). Recently, a number of researchers and language-teacher educators have called for the rejection of near native-speaker proficiency as a model for language education (Cook 1999) and have pointed out the advantages of non-native speakers. Teachers who share the same linguistic and cultural experiences with their students can provide a good model for them, anticipating problems and sharing strategies they have used in their own language learning (Kahmi-Stein, *et al.* 1999, Medgyes 1994).

Research has also documented the concerns that non-native-speaking teacher candidates have in teaching in a context in which most of the teachers are native speakers (Kahmi-Stein, *et al.* 1999, Polio and Wilson-Duffy 1998), including a lack of self-confidence about target-language proficiency, perceived bias in favor of native speakers in hiring, and, when engaged in teacher education outside their own country, a lack of role models and voice in their own profession. Ways to address these issues include pairing non-native and native-speaking students in field experiences and other practica; assigning non-native-speaking teacher candidates to non-native-speaking mentor teachers; integrating issues related to non-native speakers throughout the curriculum; and addressing language-proficiency needs. Similarly, language teacher education programs need to address foreign-language contexts, especially the more problematic situations involving large classes, limited materials and resources, and unfamiliar educational policies and teaching practices (Braine 1998).

SOME SPECIAL CONSIDERATIONS FOR EXPERIENCED TEACHERS

While much of the above discussion has focused more on inexperienced teachers and teacher preparation, as well as inservice teacher education and development, there are a number of studies which address the specific issue of teacher development with experienced teachers. These studies include the importance of shared responsibility for the design and delivery of inservice programs, sustained time for learning and reflection, and opportunities for feedback and reflection (Bax 1995a; 1995b, Darling-Hammond 1994, Hayes 1995). In discussing an inservice teacher-training program in Thailand, Hayes (1995) argues that sessions should be task-based, classroom-centered, and practical, focusing not only on the application of theory to practice, but also including awareness-raising sessions, with shared responsibility in both the design and the implementation of the program. Teachers should also have opportunities to practice innovations through microteaching, peer teaching, and poster sessions before returning to their classrooms and, where possible, engage in follow-up sessions.

NOTES

1. Reviewing any field requires difficult decisions, but this is especially true of language teacher education. The last decade has witnessed the publication of hundreds of books and articles in this field. In choosing among these, I have drawn more from the ESL/EFL teacher-education resources, especially those written about the United States context, because I know that literature best. However, much of what is written about English language teacher education may be applicable to other language teacher education if issues of cultural appropriateness or cultural appropriation are taken into consideration.

ANNOTATED BIBLIOGRAPHY

[The large number of texts and articles published in the last ten years on language teacher education make it impossible to be comprehensive. In the references, I have explicitly eliminated discussion of texts related to teaching specific language skills (listening, speaking, reading, or writing) or specific language systems (pronunciation, grammar, vocabulary) except as these are discussed in more general methods texts. I have also not included texts focused specifically on a particular method or approach or the use of corpora, technology, or other new resources. It was also necessary to eliminate texts focused on specific learners (children or adult, beginners or advanced, school or university, or students with special needs such as learning disabilities). The fact that hundreds of these resources have been published in the last ten years is one demonstration of the increasing professionalism of the language teacher education field.]

Bailey, K. M. and D. Nunan (eds.) 1996. *Voices from the language classroom.* Cambridge: Cambridge University Press.

This collection of stories told by language teachers and teacher educators in a wide range of contexts (ESL classes in Pakistan, KwaZulu high school classrooms in South Africa, dual-language classrooms in Hungary, junior high classes in the US, and bilingual classrooms in Peru) is intended for prospective and experienced teachers, teacher educators, and researchers in second and foreign language education. Using data from observational field notes, teachers' and learners' journals, interviews, stimulated recall protocols, and lesson plans and transcripts, the stories provide an opportunity to listen to teachers talk about their understandings of teaching and learning, and the interpretations they make of their own experiences in thinking, problem-solving, and decision-making in a variety of contexts. Issues such as class size, student anxiety in class participation, fear of failure in a writing classroom, student and teacher reactions to changes in curriculum, and the effects of different pedagogies or program structures are all explored.

Candlin, C. N. and H. G. Widdowson (series eds.) *Language teaching: A scheme for teacher education.* Oxford: Oxford University Press.

Designed to involve language teachers in their own professional development through "critical appraisal of ideas and the informed application of these ideas in their own classrooms" (introduction to the series), this integrated series is organized in three sub-themes of inquiry and practice in language teaching and learning: 1) language knowledge, dealing with linguistic description (pronunciation, vocabulary, grammar, and discourse); 2) modes of behavior, applying that knowledge in the teaching of the four language skills (speaking, listening, reading, and writing); and 3) modes of action, operationalizing knowledge and behavior in language teaching (syllabus design, language-course content, methodology, and evaluation). Each volume is organized into three sections: 1) explanation (theoretical background); 2) demonstration (the application of that theory), and 3) exploration (small-scale classroom-centered research activities for teachers to undertake). Titles in the series include:

Anderson, A. & T. Lynch. *Listening.*
Batstone, R. *Grammar.*
Bygate, M. *Speaking.*
Cook, G. *Discourse.*
Dalton, C. & B. Seidlhofer. *Pronunciation.*
McCarthy, M. *Vocabulary.*

Nunan, D. *Syllabus design.*
Rea-Dickins, P. & K. Germaine. *Evaluation.*
Tribble, C. *Writing.*
Wallace, C. *Reading.*
Wright, T. *Roles of teachers and learners.*

Freeman, D. (series ed.) *TeacherSource series.* Boston: Heinle and Heinle.

This series positions the teacher's voice at the center of language-teacher development, focusing on the teacher's point of view in coming to understand aspects of teaching and learning. Each volume consists of three strands: 1) teachers' voices, where practicing language teachers in various settings talk about their experiences with the topic; 2) frameworks, which lay out key concepts and issues related to the topic; and 3) investigations, which provide activities to engage readers to relate the topic to their teaching contexts. Titles in the series include:

Anderson, N. *Exploring second language reading: Issues and strategies.*
Bailey, K. *Learning about language assessment: Dilemmas, decisions, and directions.*
Campbell, C. *Teaching second-language writing: Interacting with text.*
Becker, H. *Teaching ESL K–12: Views from the language classroom.*
Freeman, D. *Doing teacher research: From inquiry to understanding.*
Graves, K. *Designing language courses: A guide for teachers.*
Irujo, S. *Teaching bilingual children: Beliefs and behaviors.*
Johnson, K. E. *Understanding language teaching: Reasoning in action.*
Larsen-Freeman, D. *Teaching language: From grammar to grammaring.*
Moran, P. *Teaching culture: Perspectives in practice.*
Scovel, T. *Learning new languages: A guide to second language acquisition.*
Stevick, E. *Working with teaching methods: What's at stake?*
Johnson, K. E. *Teachers understanding teaching.* [CD–ROM]

Freeman, D. and K. E. Johnson (eds.) 1998a. *Research and practice in English language teacher education.* [Special issue of *TESOL Quarterly.* 32.3.]

Perhaps no other volume in the last decade better portrays the major concerns in language teacher education than this special issue of the *TESOL Quarterly.*

Following a lead article by the editors on "reconceptualizing the knowledge-base of language teacher education, subsequent articles explore issues of research, practice (especially 'best practice'), and collaboration in teacher education." The issue concludes with a number of thematic reviews of teacher education books and series.

Freeman, D. and J. C. Richards. 1993. Conceptions of teaching and the education of second language teachers. *TESOL Quarterly.* 27.193–216.

In their attempt to answer the question: "What is an appropriate theory of effective language teaching?" the authors analyze a range of ESL/EFL approaches and methodologies, using Zahorik's (1986) tripartite division of teaching conceptions: 1) science/research conceptions, which operationalize learning principles, follow a tested model, or base their notion of what effective teachers do on empirical studies; 2) theory/ philosophy conceptions, which rely on rational or values-based explanations, rather than empirical evidence; and 3) art or craft conceptions, which take an eclectic approach to both methodology and techniques and place more emphasis on the teacher than on the methodology. The authors point out that no teacher teaches according to just one of these; no one conception of teaching is superior to another (myth of supremacy); nor does a teacher consciously select a teaching conception at some point in training (myth of correct choice). There is also no evidence that teachers go through stages of professional development, accepting and then rejecting one conception (for example, science/ research) only to embrace another. Their analysis of teacher training programs suggests that teacher educators take one of three positions with regard to these conceptions of teaching: 1) noncompatibility, accepting one and rejecting others; 2) eclecticism, treating all conceptions as equal and encouraging teachers to choose among them; and 3) developmental, viewing different conceptions as appropriate at different stages of professional development.

Freeman, D. and J. C. Richards (eds.) 1996. *Teacher learning in language teaching.* Cambridge: Cambridge University Press.

"In order to better understand language teaching, we need to know more about language teachers... what they know about language teaching, how they think about classroom practice, and how that knowledge and those thinking processes are learned through formal teacher education and informal experience on the job" (p. 1).

The 15 studies in this collection offer insights into the thinking and experiences of teachers and their responses to training and teaching from three perspectives: the usefulness of preservice training, the importance of learning in the practice of teaching (teacher decision-making during teaching), and the role of teacher education in teaching practices.

Hartman, D. K. (ed.) 1998. *Stories teachers tell: Reflecting on professional practice.* Lincolnwood, IL: National Textbook Co.

This collection of presentations from the 1998 Northeast Conference on Foreign Languages is the first to be authored by classroom teachers and presented in narrative form. These 40 "professional stories," grouped into "beginnings," "evolution," "revelation," and "extinction," are written by and for novice or experienced foreign- and heritage-language teachers teaching in a wide range of kindergarten through university contexts. The contributors spent a weekend together in a writers workshop where they discussed, wrote, rewrote, and edited their contributions together. One of the most interesting stories for teacher educators is that of a student teacher whose creativity and confidence in the Spanish classroom is nearly destroyed by one supervising teacher, only to re-emerge when the student is assigned to another. G. Richard Tucker, in his review of the stories at the end of the collection, identifies "...strong correspondences between classroom practice and current language education theory... ," with teachers incorporating "...exemplary practices into their classrooms on a continual basis" (218–219). But he also notes a discordant discrepancy between how teachers present themselves in these stories ("anxious, creative, empathetic, ingenious, and sensitive") and the exemplary ways ("highly focused, intellectually confident, productive, and task-oriented") in which language researchers, policy makers, and administrators present teachers (220).

Head, K. and P. Taylor. 1997. *Readings in teacher development.* Oxford: Heinemann.

Written by two language teachers and teacher trainers with extensive experience in English language teacher development, this collection of readings and activities is designed to inspire and help teachers in their own development. The book begins by defining teacher development and then explores ways in which teachers can learn about themselves in relation to the learners in their classrooms and their interactions with colleagues. The final chapters focus on personal wellbeing, including coping with challenges and potential burnout, managing change, and assessing one's own progress. The book draws upon a wide range of sources (general educational theory and practice, psychology, and group dynamics, as well as language teaching and teacher development) in the brief text excerpts; it then provides a "jigsaw" of activities which can be undertaken alone or with others to promote greater self-awareness, confidence, willingness to experiment and change, and personal growth as a teacher.

> Lee, J. L. and B.VanPatten (series eds.) *The McGraw-Hill foreign language professional series: Directions in second language learning*, and *Perspectives on theory and research*. New York: McGraw Hill.

These two related series of texts for second and foreign language teachers, teacher educators, and researchers explore the relationship between second language acquisition research and second and foreign language teaching. The "Directions" series focuses on classroom instruction and management and is intended for teacher educators and teachers, while the "Perspectives" series is primarily for researchers of second language acquisition and teaching. Titles in the two series include:

> Bardovi Harlig, K. & B. Hartford (eds.) *Beyond methods: Components of second language teacher education.*
> Lee, J. F. & B. VanPatten. *Making communicative language teaching happen.*
> Musumeci, D. *Breaking tradition: An exploration of the historical relationship between theory and practice in second language teaching.*
> Sauvignon, S. J. *Communicative competence: Theory and classroom practice.*

> Richards, J. C. 1990. *The language teaching matrix*. Cambridge: Cambridge University Press.

With a goal of engaging "...teachers and teachers-in-training, as well as teacher educators, in the investigation of classroom teaching and learning ..." (ix), this collection introduces the "matrix," Richards' metaphor for an "... interactive and multidimensional view of language teaching...," consisting of a number of factors, including teachers, learners, the curriculum, methodology, and materials. Chapters address curriculum development, the design of instructional materials, and particular issues in the teaching of listening comprehension, spoken conversation, reading, writing, and content-based instruction (the latter written with Daniel Hurley). Throughout, the emphasis is upon a bottom-up description of the processes of teaching and learning (methodology), rather than a top-down approach to methods or products, consistent with the approach that Richards outlines in the second chapter, "Beyond methods." Much of what Richards discusses in his last chapter, on directions for language teacher education, is occurring today, including a shift from "training" to "education" perspectives; an emphasis on research in both preservice and inservice development; an inquiry, discovery-oriented, and reflective approach to teaching and learning; and an increased dependence on educational research and theory (especially curriculum and instruction) and reduced dependence on linguistics and language theory in language-teacher development.

Richards, J. C. and D. Nunan (eds.) 1990. *Second language teacher education.* Cambridge: Cambridge University Press.

A goal of this collection is to help prospective teachers develop critical decision-making skills and self-awareness as a teacher. The first chapter, by Richards, discusses the need for a "theory of effective teaching." He considers both a micro approach, looking at individual teacher behaviors such as questioning, pacing, or wait time, and a more macro or holistic approach, looking at teacher-student interaction in the classroom, including turn-taking, task organization, and classroom management. Also included are chapters by Nunan on "Action research in the classroom" and by Bartlett on "Teacher development through reflective teaching," one of the earliest discussions of the place of reflective teaching in ESL/EFL teacher education.

Underhill, A. (series ed.) *The teacher development series.* Oxford: Heinemann.

Intended for teachers, trainers, and academic managers, this series is focused not only on "...subject matter and teaching methods...," but also on the "...people who are working with the subject and using the methods." The goal of the series is to widen the perspective of language teaching and to encourage teachers to become students of their own learning. Titles in the series include:

Bowen, T. & J. Marks. *Inside teaching.*

Head, K. & P. Taylor. *Readings in teacher development.*
Impey, G. & A. Underhill. *The ELT managers' handbook.*
Scrivener, J. *Learning teaching.*
Underhill, A. *Sound foundations.*

Wallace, M. J. 1991. *Training foreign language teachers: A reflective approach.* Cambridge: Cambridge University Press.

After discussing two traditional models of language teacher education (craft and applied science), Wallace focuses on a third, involving reflection, which he develops throughout the book. He describes ways for teachers to recall their experiences and engage in reflection, suggesting the use of a number of media (audio, video, teacher logs), as well as approaches to recording, coding, and interpreting the findings.

William, M. and R. L. Burden. 1997. *Psychology for language teachers.* Cambridge: Cambridge University Press.

This educational psychology text for language teachers reviews major developments in psychological theories and discusses their relevance for language teaching and learning. Beginning with a review of behaviorism, humanism, and cognitivism, the authors then focus on integrating a social-interactionist perspective with a social-constructivist approach to learning, discussing in detail Feurestein's concept of mediation, Vygotsky's zone of proximal development, the role of attribution theory to individual learner variables, learner training, and the importance of context (both outside and inside the classroom) on teaching and learning. A final chapter reviews 10 basic principles for language teachers which emerge from the previous discussion.

UNANNOTATED BIBLIOGRAPHY

Allwright, D. and K. M. Bailey. 1991. *Focus on the language classroom: An introduction to classroom research for language teachers.* Cambridge: Cambridge University Press.

Anthony, E. M. 1963. Approach, method, and technique. *English Language Teaching Journal.* 17.63–67.

Bailey, K. 1992. The processes of innovation in language teacher development: What, why and how teachers change. In J. Flowerdew, M. Brock, and S. Hsia (eds.) *Perspectives on second language teacher education.* Hong Kong: City Polytechnic of Hong Kong. 253–282.

Bardovi-Harlig, K. and B. Hartford (eds.) 1997. *Beyond methods: Components of second language teacher education.* New York: McGraw-Hill.

Bartlett, L. 1990. Teacher development through reflective teaching. In J. C. Richards and D. Nunan (eds.) *Second language teacher education.* New York: Cambridge University Press. 202–214.

Bax, R. 1995a. Principles for evaluating teacher development activities. *English Language Teaching Journal.* 49.262–271.

——— 1995b. Appropriate methodology: The content of teacher development activities. *System.* 23.347–357.

Blair, R. W. (ed.) 1982. *Innovative approaches to language teaching.* Rowley, MA: Newbury House.

Braine, G. (ed.) 1998. *Non-native educators in English language teaching.* Mahwah, NJ: L. Erlbaum.

Brown, H. D. 1994. *Teaching by principles: An interactive approach to language pedagogy.* Englewood Cliffs, NJ: Prentice Hall Regents.

Bruner, J. 1986. *Actual minds, possible worlds.* Englewood Cliffs, NJ: Prentice Hall Regents.

——— 1990. *Acts of meaning.* Cambridge, MA: Harvard University Press.

Burns, A. 1995. *Collaborative action research for language teachers.* Cambridge: Cambridge University Press.

Casanave, C. P. and S. R. Schecter (eds.) 1997. *On becoming a language educator: Personal essays on professional development.* Mahwah, NJ: L. Erlbaum.

Celce-Murcia, M. (ed.) 1991. *Teaching English as a second or foreign language.* 2nd ed. Rowley, MA: Newbury House.

Chaudron, C. 1988. *Second language classrooms: Research on teaching and learning.* New York: Cambridge University Press.

Cook, V. 1999. Going beyond the native speaker in language teaching. *TESOL Quarterly.* 33.185–209.

Crandall, J. A. 1993. Professionalism and professionalization of adult ESL literacy. *TESOL Quarterly.* 27.497–515.

——— 1994. Strategic integration: Preparing language and content teachers for linguistically and culturally diverse classrooms. In J. E. Alatis (ed.) *Strategic interaction and language acquisition: Theory, practice, and research.* Washington, DC: Georgetown University Press. 255–274.

——— 1995. Reinventing (America's) schools: The role of the applied linguist. In J. E. Alatis (ed.) *Linguistics and the education of language teachers: Ethnolinguistic, psycholinguistic, and sociolinguistic aspects.* Washington, DC: Georgetown University

Press. 412–427.

Crandall, J. A. 1996. Teacher professionalism in TESOL. *MEXTESOL Journal.* 19.11–26.

——— 1998. A delicate balance: Theory and practice in teacher education. *TESOL Teacher Education Interest Section Newsletter.* 13.3–4.

Darling-Hammond, L. 1994. *Professional development schools: Schools for developing a profession.* New York: Teachers College Press.

Day, R. R. 1990. Teacher observation in second language teacher education. In J. C. Richards and D. Nunan (eds.) *Second language teacher education.* Cambridge: Cambridge University Press. 43–61.

Doff, A. 1988. *Teach English: A training course for teachers.* Cambridge: Cambridge University Press.

Doyle, W. 1986. Classroom organization management. In M. C. Wittrock (ed.) *A handbook of research on teaching.* New York: Macmillan. 392–431.

Edge, J. and K. Richards (eds.) 1993. *Teachers develop teachers research.* Oxford: Heinemann.

Fanselow, J. 1987. *Breaking rules.* New York: Longman.

——— 1992. *Contrasting conversations.* New York: Longman.

Flowerdew, J., M. Brock and S. Hsia (eds.) 1992. *Perspectives on second language teacher education.* Hong Kong: City Polytechnic of Hong Kong.

Freeman, D. 1989. Teacher training, development, and decision making: A model of teaching and related strategies for language teacher education. *TESOL Quarterly.* 23.27–45.

——— 1991. Three view to teachers' knowledge. *IATEFL Teacher Development Newsletter.* December, 1–4.

——— 1996. Redefining the relationship between research and what teachers know. In K. M. Bailey and D. Nunan (eds.) *Voices from the language classroom.* Cambridge: Cambridge University Press. 88–115.

——— 1998. *Doing teacher-research: From inquiry to understanding.* Boston: Heinle and Heinle.

——— and S. Cornwell (eds.) 1993. *New ways in teacher education.* Alexandria, VA: TESOL.

——— and K. E. Johnson. 1998b. Reconceptualizing the knowledge base of language teacher education. *TESOL Quarterly.* 32.397–417.

Graves, K. 2000. *Designing language courses: A guide for teachers.* Boston: Heinle and Heinle.

Hammadou, J. and E. Bernhardt. 1987. On being and becoming a foreign language teacher. *Theory into Practice.* 26.301–306.

Hayes, D. 1995. In-service teacher development: Some basic principles. *English Language Teaching Journal.* 49.252–261.

Holliday, A. 1994. *Appropriate methodology and social context*. Cambridge: Cambridge University Press.

Holmes Group. 1986. *Tomorrow's teachers*. East Lansing, MI: Holmes Group. [ED 270 454.]

Johnson, K. E. 1992. Learning to teach: Instructional actions and decisions of preservice ESL teachers. *TESOL Quarterly*. 26.925–944.

——— 1994. The emerging beliefs and instructional practices of preservice English as a second language teachers. *Teaching and Teacher Education*. 10.439–452.

——— 1996a. The role of theory in L2 teacher education. *TESOL Quarterly*. 30.507–535.

——— 1996b. The vision versus the reality: The tensions of the TESOL practicum. In D. Freeman and J. C. Richards (eds.) *Teacher learning in language teaching*. Cambridge: Cambridge University Press. 30–49.

——— 1996c. Portfolio assessment in second language teacher education. *TESOL Journal*. 6.11–14.

——— 1999. *Understanding language teaching: Reasoning in action*. Boston: Heinle and Heinle.

Kahmi-Stein, L., E. Lee and C. Lee. 1999. How TESOL programs can enhance the preparation of nonnative English speakers. *TESOL Matters*. 9.1–5.

Kennedy, C. 1987. Innovating for a change: Teacher development and innovation, *English Language Teaching Journal*. 41.163–170.

Kleinfield, J. 1992. Learning to think like a teacher: The study of cases. In J. H. Shulman (ed.) *Case methods in teacher education*. New York: Teachers College Press. 31–49.

Kramsch, C. 1997. The privilege of the non-native speaker. *Publication of the Modern Language Association*. 112.359–369.

Kral, T. (ed.) 1994. *Teacher development: Making the right moves: Selected articles from the English Teaching Forum 1989–1993*. Washington, DC: English Language Programs Division, United States Information Agency.

Larsen-Freeman, D. 1986. *Techniques and principles in language teaching*. New York: Oxford University Press.

——— 1990. On the need for a theory of language teaching. In J. E. Alatis (ed.) *Linguistics, language teaching, and language acquisition: The interdependence of theory, practice, and research*. Washington, DC: Georgetown University Press. 261–270.

Lave, J. 1988. *Cognition in practice*. New York: Cambridge University Press.

Li, D. C. S., D. Mahoney and J. C. Richards (eds.) 1994. *Exploring second language teacher development*. Hong Kong: City Polytechnic of Hong Kong.

Lortie, D. 1975. *Schoolteacher: A sociological study*. Chicago: University of Chicago Press.

Medgyes, P. 1992. Native and non-native: Who's worth more? *English Language Teaching Journal*. 46.340–349.

Medgyes, P. 1994. *The non-native teacher.* London: Macmillan.
Nunan, D. 1989. *Understanding language classrooms: A guide for teacher-initiated action.* London: Prentice Hall.
———— 1991. *Language teaching methodology.* New York: Prentice Hall.
———— 1999. *Second language teaching and learning.* Boston: Heinle and Heinle.
———— and C. Lamb. 1996. *The self-directed teacher.* Cambridge: Cambridge University Press.
Oller, J. W. (ed.) 1993. *Methods that work: Ideas for literacy and language teachers.* Boston: Heinle & Heinle.
———————— and P. Richard-Amato (eds.) 1983. *Methods that work: A smorgasbord of ideas for language teachers.* Rowley, MA: Newbury House.
Omaggio Hadley, A. 1993. *Teaching language in context.* Boston: Heinle and Heinle.
Pennington, M. C. 1990. A professional development focus for the language teaching practicum. In J. C. Richards and D. Nunan (eds.) *Second language teacher education.* Cambridge: Cambridge University Press. 132–151.
Plaister, T. 1993. *ESOL case studies: The real world of L2 teaching and administration.* Englewood Cliffs, NJ: Regents/Prentice Hall.
Polio, C. and C. Wilson-Duffy. 1998. Teaching ESL in an unfamiliar context: International students in a North American MA TESOL Practicum. *TESOL Journal.* 7.24–29.
Richards, J. C. 1996. Teachers' maxims in language teaching. *TESOL Quarterly.* 30.281–296.
——————(ed.) 1998. *Teaching in action: Case studies from second language classrooms.* Alexandria, VA: TESOL.
—————— and G. Crookes. 1988. The practicum in TESOL. *TESOL Quarterly.* 22.9–27.
——————and C. Lockhart. 1994. *Reflective teaching in second language classrooms.* Cambridge: Cambridge University Press.
——————and T. S. Rodgers. 1982. Method: Approach, design and procedure. *TESOL Quarterly.* 16.153–168.
———————————————— 1986. *Approaches and methods in language teaching.* Cambridge: Cambridge University Press.
Rivers, W. 1981. *Teaching foreign-language skills.* 2nd ed. Chicago: University of Chicago Press.
Roberts, J. 1998. *Language teacher education.* London: Arnold.
Sachs, G. T., M. Brock and R. Lo (eds.) 1996. *Directions in second language teacher education.* Hong Kong: City Polytechnic of Hong Kong.
Schon, D. A. 1983. *The reflective practitioner.* New York: Basic Books.
———— 1987. *Educating the reflective practitioner.* San Francisco: Jossey-Bass.
Shulman, J. (ed.) 1992. *Case methods in teacher education.* New York: Teachers College Press.

Stevick, E. W. 1980. *Teaching languages: A way and ways*. Rowley, MA: Newbury House.

——————— 1998. *Working with teaching methods: What's at stake?* Boston: Heinle and Heinle.

Stoynoff, S. 1999. The TESOL practicum: An integrated model in the U.S. *TESOL Quarterly*. 33.145–151.

van Lier, L. 1988. *The classroom and the language learner: Ethnography and second language classroom research*. London: Longman.

Widdowson, H. G. 1990. *Aspects of language teaching*. Oxford: Oxford University Press.

——————— 1997. Approaches to second language teacher education. In G. R. Tucker and D. Corson (eds.) *Encyclopedia of language and education, Volume 4. Second language education*. Dordrecht, Netherlands: Kluwer. 121–129.

Wideen, M., J. Maya-Smith and B. Moon. 1998. A critical analysis of the research on learning to teach: Making the case for an ecological inquiry. *Review of Educational Research*. 68.130–178.

Woods, D. 1996. *Teacher cognition in language teaching*. New York: Cambridge University Press.

Woodward, T. 1991. *Models and metaphors in language teacher training: Loop input and other strategies*. Cambridge: Cambridge University Press.

Wright, T. 1987. *Roles of teachers and learners*. Oxford: Oxford University Press.

——————— 1992. L2 classroom research and L2 teacher education: Towards a collaborative approach. In J. Flowerdew, M. Brock and S. Hsia (eds.) *Perspectives on second language teacher education*. Hong Kong: City Polytechnic of Hong Kong. 187–209.

LANGUAGES FOR
SPECIFIC PURPOSES

LANGUAGES FOR SPECIFIC PURPOSES

John M. Swales

SOME BRIEF HISTORICAL PERSPECTIVE

Thirty-five years ago, three leading British linguists published a landmark volume entitled *The linguistic sciences and language teaching* (Halliday, McIntosh and Strevens 1964). The careful wording of the title of this book was something of a clarion call; in effect, the authors promised to usher in a Brave New World of a stronger descriptive base for pedagogical materials. As far as Language for Special Purposes (LSP) is concerned, the key passage (which is well worth revisiting after all this time) is the following:

> Only the merest fraction of investigation has yet been carried out into just what parts of a conventional course in English are needed by, let us say, power station engineers in India, or police inspectors in Nigeria; even less is known about precisely what extra specialized material is required.
> This is one of the tasks for which linguistics must be called in. Every one of these specialized needs requires, before it can be met by appropriate teaching materials, detailed studies of restricted languages and special registers carried out on the basis of large samples of the language used by the particular persons concerned (1964:189–190).

This forthrightly-expressed agenda proved very attractive to most of the small band of LSP practitioners working in the 1960s as well as to many of the increasing numbers of others who have become involved in the LSP movement in each succeeding decade. The reasons for this attractiveness are not hard to find. The research would be descriptive (with no "literary" stylistic criticisms of the target discourses); it would deal with "normal" discourse (and not that provided by famous figures in the respective fields); it would be synchronic (with no need to look back at shaping historical forces); it would be basically textual or transcriptal (with little attempt to investigate such matters as authorial motives for linguistic choices); and it would rely on functional grammar, as primarily developed by Halliday, and also make use of some version of the "neo-Firthian" model of contextual factors affecting language choices.

In retrospect, we can see that the great appeal of this approach lay in the fact that it seemed eminently *manageable* to early LSP practitioners, who were often working in underprivileged environments and who were also having to administer programs, develop teaching materials, and do a fair amount of teaching. First, the 1964 "manifesto" offered a simple relationship between linguistic analysis and pedagogic materials. Second, there was no strong emphasis on the need for practitioners to have any of the following types of expertise: Expert content knowledge of the fields or professions they were trying to serve; real understanding of the rhetorical evolution of the discourses central to those fields or professions; or advanced anthropological training in "fly on the wall" ethnography. Third, the ways and means of studying registers and special languages were often taught in graduate courses and were familiar territory for LSP practitioners (although less so in the United States). The early LSP practitioners were thus well equipped to carry out relatively "thin" descriptions of their target discourses. What they principally lacked was a perception of discourse itself and of the means for analyzing and exploiting it—*lacunae* that were largely rectified by the 1980s.

We can usefully view the thirty-five years of Languages for Specific Purposes since the publication of *The linguistic sciences and language teaching* as a response (even if often inadvertent) to this opening scenario. On the one hand, there has been a solid tradition of work that has continued this descriptive textual tradition, albeit with shifts in focus from language to discourse to genre, and perhaps now to activity theory (Russell 1997). For example, many of the articles in the leading journal *English for Specific Purposes* fall into this category, as do many LSP master's theses from many parts of the world, and as do two of the collections selected for the Annotated Bibliography of this review (Duszak 1997, Fortanet, *et al.* 1998).

On the other hand, all of these founding tenets have been challenged at one time or another. The challenge to a simplistic relationship between linguistic analysis and classroom activities has long been one of Widdowson's major contributions to ESP (e.g., Widdowson 1998), and perhaps it reached its fullest earlier expression in Hutchinson and Waters (1987). More recently, the debate about this relationship has re-emerged in the context of how to handle in class the new masses of linguistic data being produced by corpus linguistics (Partington 1998). The second issue (what should practitioners know) has also become more complex. Part of this issue simply derives from the massive amount of new information that is now available; for example, we now have several studies that can tell us much about the evolution of professional discourse—in economics (Gunnarson 1997a, Henderson, Dudley-Evans and Backhouse 1993), in physics (Bazerman 1988), and in the life and health sciences (Atkinson 1999a, Salager-Meyer 1997, Valle 1999). Further, new approaches to understanding professional discourse have been developed, ranging from "shadowing" individual professionals as they go about their work (Dudley-Evans and St John 1998); to investigations into textual biographies (Swales 1998); to deeper perceptions of text construction, reception, and evaluation (Prior 1998); to various kinds of study of workplace discourse (Gunnarson, Linell and Nordberg 1997); and on to ideological critiques (Huckin 1997). However, if understanding discourse is so complexly situated in all these potentially various ways, then LSP practitioners are today forced into some kind of informal cost-benefit analysis as they struggle to come to terms with how much they need to know *before* they can offer what they have learned to their students. In this climate of competing models, exhaustive explorations, growing internationalization, and an exploding literature, it is not altogether surprising that the *simplicity* of purely textual studies based on mid-sized corpora continues to have appeal, perhaps especially in studies that attempt to compare texts in English with those of another language (Connor 1996).

LSP: A PROFESSION, A DISCIPLINE, OR NEITHER?

ESP/LSP has a rather peculiar relationship with other branches of applied linguistics. Its closest connection is certainly with discourse analysis and pragmatics (including cross-cultural pragmatics); indeed, in some sense, it can be argued that in many ways LSP *is* the prime realization of applied discourse analysis. (And this is not to disregard comparable and important developments in business and technical communication in North America and in the training of translators in Europe.) It also has good connections with language assessment and communicative language teaching. On the other hand, it has very few points of contact with second language acquisition (SLA). Indeed, in this context it is probably not a chance event that last year's *ARAL 19* had an opening section entitled "Second Language Acquisition" and a distinct second one entitled "Language Use in Professional Contexts." These two intellectual worlds thus continue to be socially constructed poles apart, perhaps because SLA continues to focus on grammar and its acquisition by young and often beginning learners. However, if these kinds of field-imposed restrictions are a cause of regret to the LSP movement, it is also true that LSP has been insufficiently concerned with how and how well its students acquire or do not acquire the communicative and literacy skills that they need. One thin strand of inquiry that has attempted to bridge this gap has been investigations into the transfer of academic skills (Johns 1997), and whether this learning is primarily articulated through content, through knowledge of a particular discourse domain (Douglas and Selinker 1994, Whyte 1995), or through the "formal" knowledge of how different genres are co-constructed and internally articulated. More work in this area would be welcome.

A major consequence of this picture is that LSP has a highly variable status as both a discipline and a profession in different parts of the world. The disjunction between ESP/LSP and language acquisition, basic FL methodology, psycholinguistics, and sociolinguistics has in the United States left very little space in graduate programs for ESP work. Apart from some individual efforts to change this situation, such as those by Peter Master and Denise Murray at San Jose State, the lack of opportunity for professional preparation has had deleterious effects on research and program quality. Elsewhere, the situation is much rosier because of the emergence of Departments of Applied Language Studies (or close terminological cousins), especially in places like Australia, Brazil, Britain, Hong Kong, and Scandinavia. Although these units are not always primarily interested in ESP/LSP, they tend to be favorably disposed to its aspirations. Finland, for example, in 1999 launched a nationally-funded Ph.D. program in applied language studies to be centered at the University of Jyväskylä.

The ESL/FL field as a whole, and as seen internationally, is known for having "a long tail." In other words, there are very few senior (professorial) positions but many lecturers, adjuncts, and part-timers. This situation is also largely true of ESP/LSP where traditional forces in language, literature, and linguistics departments have operated to preserve senior posts for established areas of scholarship, and where many LSP practitioners have unstable careers as independent consultants. As a partial consequence of this, ESP/LSP has yet to establish itself as either a full profession or as clear sub-discipline in the language sciences. The import of this uncertain status for the potentially globalized language situation in the new century is hard to ascertain, but the lack of institutional structure will probably be seen as more of a deficit than will its more optimistic interpretation—entrepreneurial flexibility—be believed to be an asset.

LSP AND SCIENCE, MEDICINE, AND LAW

In the spirit of Bakhtin's work on intertextuality (Bakhtin 1986), which has been so influential in studies of academic and professional discourse, I can open this short section by referring interested readers to the comprehensive surveys of the following areas in *ARAL 19*: Atkinson (1999b) on language and science; Gibbons (1999) on language and the law; and Hyden and Mishler (1999) on language and medicine. In consequence, I will be mostly concerned here with some LSP amplification and some minor updating.

As Atkinson (1999b) reveals, there have been numerous rhetorical and linguistic accounts of the contemporary scientific style, especially as it is encoded in the research article—that master academic narrative of recent decades. Montgomery (1996) offers an elegant recent synopsis:

> Scientist or not, one hears the voice of univocity, unbroken statement, the single voice of the scientific style. But how achieved? How constructed? For the most part, through a series of grammatical and syntactic strategies that attempt to depersonalize, to objectify all premises, such that they seem to achieve the plane of ahistorical essence: "recent advances have shown..." ; "Analyses were performed..." ; "The data, therefore, indicate..." . The narrative is driven by objects, whether these be phenomena, procedures, earlier studies, evidence, or

whatever (1996:13).

Meanwhile we know from the classic early laboratory studies, from Berkenkotter and Huckin (1995), from Prior's (1998) case studies, and from *The mangle of practice* (Pickering 1995), that matters on the investigative ground are much more contingent, haphazard, and interpersonally complex. Although focus on such compressed and depersonalized accounts has concentrated for good reason on methods sections, Dressen and Swales (in press) explore the suppression of field experience in introductions to geology articles. They show that petrologists no longer offer any descriptions of their expeditions to inhospitable settings, which are now replaced by a part-genre usually called "Geological Setting." Expertise in the locale is communicated via a condensed, expert, and conventionalized description and interpretation of the site's geological record, which has thus come to function as surrogate for the silenced voice of geological authority. In effect, their findings nicely reflect Montgomery's observation that "the narrative is driven by objects, whether these be phenomena, procedures, earlier studies, evidence, or whatever" (Montgomery, op. cit.). As Huckin trenchantly observes, "those of us interested in the cultural aspects of genre study would do well...to include textual silence in the list of features to be analysed" (Huckin 1997:76). For LSP in its more applied aspects, there would seem to be an important lesson here. If our students need various kinds of help as they acculturate into their chosen scientific or technical cultures, then they need to see that contemporary specialized texts are distanced reconstructions of mangled experience. If they do not, they will tend to believe that published authors have, in comparison to their own messy and preliminary excursions, been blessed by some unlikely combination of skill, magic, or luck to get everything seemingly so exactly right. EAP teaching and support materials might therefore do better by giving more attention to false starts, abandoned leads, and various types of revision and correction.

Although Johns (1997), Dudley-Evans and St John (1998), and Atkinson (1999a) all do a creditable job in describing and explaining the rise of genre-based approaches, they all stop short of conceptualizing genres as more than independent entities. Doubtless, taking a genre as a separable class of texts was a sensible practice in the early days of the genre movement, but pioneering studies by Bazerman (1995) on patents and by Devitt (1991) on tax accountancy communications reveal how genres are networked and reticulated. It is not clear at the moment how best to characterize these relationships, whether any kind of single characterization will work, or whether possible answers lie more in theory or in empirical investigation. At one extreme there are linear orderings such as in patent law, whereby genre X is prerequisite for the instantiation of genre Y, and Y a necessary precursor for genre Z. Here, as Bazerman argues, we could indeed envision some system of genres. At the other end, in the academy, the relationships among conference presentation or poster, publication, and thesis or dissertation have no necessary chronological relationship, even though there may be orderings in the sub-systems of supporting but "occluded" genres: A conference abstract is submitted, a committee reviews it, they find it acceptable and require a short summary for the program booklet, and the presentation event actually takes place. However, in academic situations in general, we might be better advised to think of genre relationships in terms of sets. While both of the above cases share a requirement for the selection of specific genres, still looser arrangements are possible in which, at many decision-points, communicative action can be realized by potentially different genres. For example, a request for an academic paper may be communicated by a departmental "reprint request" card, a formal letter, an e-mail, or a phone call. One option in this situation might be to conceive of the network as consisting of repertoires (or menus) of genres that can be drawn upon according to circumstance.

There are, I believe, several advantages that accrue to LSP research from these expansions of the role of genre. First, as Gunnarsson (1997b) persuasively argues, we now have a powerful way of reintegrating spoken and written professional discourse. Second, we can now more easily see how genres evolve and why, and not only under the pressures of technological developments. Third, our support materials can offer a more realistic mapping of the universe of discourse for which we might be preparing a particular group of students. In ongoing efforts to increase this understanding, useful recent contributions have been published on submission letters (Swales 1996), academic book reviews (Motta-Roth 1998), recommendation letters (Precht 1998), journal acknowledgment sections (Giannoni 1998), and research grant applications (Connor and Mauranen 1999).

Last year's *ARAL* chapters on Law and Medicine only need some minor rounding out via reference to work directed at the non-native speaker. Bhatia continues to be active in the area of legal discourse, especially in comparing legal with other disciplinary texts (e.g., Bhatia 1998). Harris (1992; 1997), originally a lawyer himself, is excellent on explaining non-native speaker (NNS) difficulties in legal educational settings; Fredrickson (1996) usefully shows how broader features of legal systems have their narrow discoursal effects; and Trosberg (1997) uses modifications of speech act theory to reveal differences in legislation, contracts, and conversation. A recent study by Feak, Reinhart and Sinsheimer (in press) offers an innovative analysis of the student-written but published "Law Review Note" in American law schools. However, despite the efforts of a few individuals, this is not an area of LSP that has particularly thrived in recent years; that said, one promising development is the international project on the discourses of commercial transactions under development at the City University of Hong Kong. LSP work in medicine has been particularly thin in recent years, except for synchronic and diachronic discoursal investigations of medical research articles, which *au fond* are really part of English for Academic Purposes. One of the few recent contributions is the needs analysis of medical students in Taiwan (Chia, *et al*. 1999).

LANGUAGES FOR BUSINESS PURPOSES

In recent years, Languages for Business Purposes has become a major growth area in LSP, many of the pedagogical consequences of which are well described by Dudley-Evans and St John (1998). The causes of this growth are multiple. First, this area has been historically under-researched (especially in discourse terms) in comparison to science or technology. Second, internationalization and the new globality (globaloney?) has drawn many more business people into bilingual and multilingual occupational settings. Third, the new business climate (wherein turbulence is the likely norm) has made it more and more obvious that traditional business language teaching materials (such as translating commercial letters) are becoming increasingly obsolete in today's multi-media business world. Fourth, the emerging recognition of an international marketplace has done something to bring together the strengths of the North American business-communications research tradition and the investigative and curricular skills and practices of a predominantly European tradition of languages for business.

Following the much-cited paper by Yates and Orlikowski (1992) on the genres of organizational communication (with its clever integration of structuration theory), genre and genre study has become a major starting point for analyzing and explaining these universes of discourse. However, much of the more successful work in this field has also adopted a number of additional (and triangulating) techniques such as linguistic auditing (Reeves and Wright 1996), interpretive ethnography (Smart 1998), familiarity analyis (Charles 1996), "fly on the wall" shadowing of business persons as they go about their daily routines (Louhiala-Salminen 1999), compuational analysis of a text corpus (Fox 1999), and user reactions to business discourses (Rogers in press). It seems clear that these innovative and comprehensive studies have largely heeded Devitt's admonition that "we need to find ways to keep genre embedded and engaged within context while also keeping our focus on learning about genre and its operations" (Devitt 1996:611). And here it is worth observing that in EAP we can often obtain some inkling of the reception-history of a particular text by seeing where it was published and how it was cited. In the business world (aside from focus-groups in advertising), we rarely have such traces. As Rogers (in press) points out, studies of genres have tended to conceptualize communicative purposes in terms of the strategies of the speakers or writers. She then goes on to argue that, at least in organizational contexts, such purposes cannot be fully understood without some sense of how those "purposes" are evaluated by their audiences. Hence, there is a need to incorporate user-based analyses; a superb example of this kind of work is Locker's recent study of responses to various forms of negative letters and the consequences of these findings for business communication textbooks and classes (Locker 1999).

Dudley-Evans and St John note a further important difference between English for academic and business purposes:

> EAP operates within a world where the fundamental concern is the acquisition of knowledge by individuals, while in EBP the purpose is not centered on the learner as an individual but as a member of a transactional world where the fundamental concern is the exchange of goods and services (1998:72).

As we gain increasing access to this (international) transactional world, a number of factors have emerged as being potentially relevant. First, Charles (1996) has convincingly shown that a key factor for the resulting discourse is whether participants are attempting to establish a new business relationship or merely consolidating a prior one. Second, the mode of communication (letter, phone, fax, e-mail, etc.) is also significant, as indeed we might expect (Akar and Louhiala-Salminen 1999, Nickerson 1998). Third, the primary power in the business is typically complementary to that of the academic setting: In the business relationship, the power relationship typically turns out to be with the potential buyer rather than the potential seller (Yli-Jokipii 1994). Fourth, the corporate or sectorial culture ("the way we do things around here") is quite different from the academic culture. This distinction is exemplified by Smart (1998) for the Federal Bank of Canada, Bilbow (1999) for a Hong Kong airline, and Nickerson (1998) for a multinational oil company. Finally, national cultural values and expectations add further variability and here much can be learned from Scollon and Scollon (1995) for east Asia, and Tebeaux (1999) for Mexico. These last efforts are both historically rich and subtle studies which salubriously steer their readers away from facile stereotyping.

Although it might be premature to conclude that Languages for Business has overtaken Language for Academic Purposes as the lead area in the field, there is equally no doubt that the quality gap has narrowed very considerably. One reason for this growth in Languages for Business has been a fine series of doctoral dissertations based (at least in part) on Scandinavian business settings, although good work has covered other geographical areas such as Akar (1998) for Turkish business communications and Barbara, et al. (1996) for Brazilian ones. Another contribution to this strength has come from a useful accumulation of particularistic genre analyses starting with Devitt (1991) on taxation correspondence and Bhatia (1993) on sales letters, and moving on to cover such disparate discourses as corporate mission statements (Swales and Rogers 1995), "chair talk" in business meetings (Bilbow 1999), and faxes (Akar and Louhiala-Salminen 1999). Basic research in this area positions LSP well for the new millenium, although there remain—as in EAP—significant issues with regard to what Language-for-Business-Purposes instructors need to know, how they are to be trained or helped to come to that knowledge, and how those insights can be parlayed into effective pedagogic delivery systems.

ENGLISH ENGLISH EVERYWHERE

One of the ironies of the emergent field of ESP is that its very success in catering to the needs of nonnative speakers has contributed to the overpowering position of English in today's worlds of science, scholarship, and business. Part of the irony is that those interested in comparing Anglo-American research rhetoric with comparable rhetorics in other languages are having increasing trouble locating sufficient numbers of those other-language texts. Indeed, there has been a massive conversion over the last two decades from other-language journals to English-medium ones, and, as far as I can see, almost all of the many new journals that have been springing up have an English-only submission policy. We are facing a real loss in professional registers in many national cultures with long scholarly traditions.

Crystal (1997) believes this trend to be a benign phenomenon, one inevitably linked with 'progress' and one that will lead to a more harmonious world. Others (Phillipson 1999, Swales 1997) strongly disagree with Crystal's excellently-written but ultimately triumphalist account. There are of course wider and important issues here that cannot be discussed in this chapter; nevertheless, the decline and disappearance of other major scholarly languages, as well as the stunted growth of aspiring new ones in developing countries, has at least one immediate consequence for LSP. Immense power is now concentrated in the hands of American academic gatekeepers; Wayt Gibbs (1995) calculated that, in 1994, 31 percent of all papers published in the world's leading journals emanated in the United States, and even five years later that percentage has probably moved upward. We are faced in effect with a growing linguistic and rhetorical monopoly and monoculture against which we need to consider offering 'cultural rainforest' arguments of the following type: "Insofar as rhetorical practices embody cultural thought patterns, we should encourage the maintenance of variety and diversity in academic rhetorical practices—excessive standardization may counteract innovation and creative thought by forcing them into standard forms" (Mauranen 1993:172). One small but direct way in which the field can resist this standardization is to transfer some of the resources and expertise that exists in ESP to lesser understood professional languages.

FINAL CONSIDERATIONS

One of the clearest signs that ESP/LSP has played its full part in the emergence of Applied Linguistics as a discipline is that the space constraints of a single short chapter prevent full coverage of the field. For instance, I have not been able to do full justice to the lively area that usually goes by the name of Contrastive Rhetoric, wherein scholars are now going beyond simply showing rhetorical differences between languages to now attempting to explain them. Nor have I adequately covered some other recent developments. One is the tremendous interest in corpus linguistics and its great, if uncertain, potential for LSP work of all kinds. Another is the rather belated recognition that many professional texts have an important visual structure that parallels that of the written word (Johns 1998, Miller 1998). Yet other developments include the impact of new forms of electronic communication, the current state of the art with regard to actual LSP pedagogic materials, recent developments in translation studies, and the question of whether ESP has been overly neutral in terms of its ideology and its attitudes toward its NNS clientele (Pennycook 1997).

Overall, we can see that LSP has a number of structural problems such as weaknesses in institutional recognition and uncertain provision of professional training. Chile, for example, a great pioneer in ESP in the 1970's, has been unable to recruit a younger generation of specialists to replace its retiring experts (Horsella, personal communication). Furthermore, although LSP has, in *English for Specific Purposes*, a flagship journal, regular attempts to get it included in the Social Science Citation Index have always failed. On the positive side, it is much more of a truly international field than most areas of applied linguistics, as this chapter has tried to show and as the provenance of papers in *English for Specific Purposes* impressively demonstrates. Its alliance with and contribution to discourse analysis is also impressive, but legitimate questions can be asked about the "applied" nature of some of these investigations, since it is not always clear how the findings are to be transmuted into teaching or study materials. All in all, though, the field has responded well to the 1964 "call to arms," both in terms of the envisioned types of linguistic analyses and in greatly extending and enriching them.

ANNOTATED BIBLIOGRAPHY

[Introductory Note: For this section, I have selected only book-length items published after 1994. In so doing, I have made a conscious effort to include some volumes that represent important and relevant work done outside the ESP mainstream, both in terms of provenance and in terms of orientation.]

Bargiela-Chiappini, F. and C. Nickerson. 1999. *Writing business: Genres, media and discourses.* London: Longman.

This volume offers a strong collection of articles that show the current vibrancy of this LSP sub-field, especially in western Europe; it is a showcase of this sub-field's strengths in both research and application.

Belcher, D. and G. Braine (eds.) 1995. *Academic writing in a second language: Essays on research and pedagogy.* Norwood, NJ: Ablex.

This book is the key collection on the topic of academic writing, now nicely complemented by Candlin and Hyland (1999). The volume contains some outstanding case studies of academic writing situations, and throughout there is a careful balance between social and cognitive demands, and between resistance to and acceptance of typified features of academic discourse.

Biber, D., S. Conrad and R. Reppen. 1998. *Corpus linguistics: Investigating language structure and use.* Cambridge: Cambridge University Press.

This book is a comprehensive and helpful introduction to a relatively new field. Of particular interest to users of this chapter will be Part II (Investigating the characteristics of varieties). The volume as a whole is strongly influenced by Biber's multi-dimensional model of register.

Candlin C. N. and K. Hyland (eds.) 1999. *Writing: Texts, processes and practices.* London: Longman.

This recent volume offers a wide variety of approaches to writing in a variety of academic and professional settings, not all of them involving non-native speakers. However, the papers cohere around a general acceptance that institutional practices and percepts strongly influence both the construction and interpretation of written texts. Another strong feature of this volume is the serious attention given to the relation between research and practice.

Dudley-Evans, T. and M. J. St John. 1998. *Developments in English for specific purposes.* Cambridge: Cambridge University Press.

As might be expected from the authors, this volume is a model of clarity and good sense. It provides a comprehensive overview of the field and, perhaps for the first time, offers a proper assimilation of work in English for academic purpose and English for business purposes, two sub-areas that traditionally have gone their rather separate ways. As a volume in the Cambridge Language Teaching Library series, it is full of textbook extracts and has a well-constructed series of tasks for student completion. It is probably the best introduction to the field now available, even if it tends to steer clear of a number of controversial topics.

Duszak, A. (ed.) 1997. *Culture and styles of academic discourse.* Berlin: Mouton de Gruyter.

This volume is an excellent contribution to the fast-growing area of contrastive rhetoric as applied to academic discourse. Part One deals with attitudes and values, Part Two with the expression of interpersonal meaning, and Part Three with variation in genres. Duszak's own contributions, both in the introductory chapter and in her paper on "digressiveness" in Polish texts, are exceptionally good. The volume as a whole showcases recent work from Eastern Europe.

Fortanet, I., S. Posteguillo, J. C. Palmer and J. F. Coll (eds.) 1998. *Genre studies in English for academic purposes.* Castello, Spain: Universitat Jaume I.

This collection presents a strong "normal science" contribution, generally showing excellent knowledge of the literature and high-level analytic skills. Since half the contributors come from Spain, the volume demonstrates the rapid development of a strong EAP tradition in this country. The volume may not turn out to be as well known as it deserves to be because of its relatively obscure provenance.

Grabe, W. and R. B. Kaplan. 1996. *Theory and practice of writing.* London: Longman.

This is a substantial volume (of close to 500 pages) that examines all aspects of writing from an applied linguistics perspective. The chapters of greatest interest and relevance to LSP are those devoted to contrastive rhetoric, writing for professional purposes, and teaching writing at advanced levels.

Gross, A. G. and W. M. Keith (eds.) 1997. *Rhetorical hermeneutics: Invention and interpretation in the age of science.* Albany, NY: State University of New York Press.

As the title might intimate, this is a challenging volume, but one of great interest to all those seriously interested in analyzing the language of science. Among the important issues the contributors discuss are the agency of the author, whether our clever analyses of technical texts reflect authorial intent or merely our own close reading, and whether at these higher levels of interpretation we are essentially staring into the mirror of our own imagination. The volume is something of a slugfest among contemporary rhetoricians, and engaging for that additional reason, although McCloskey clearly goes over the top. The editors provide an authoritative and intriguingly self-reflexive introduction.

Gunnarsson, B.-L., P. Linell and B. Nordberg (eds.) 1997. *The construction of professional discourse.* London: Longman.

This wide-ranging volume covers many fields, such as law, medicine, science, and social work. A number of the chapters provide instructive accounts of discourse in specialized communities of practice, how this discourse is socially constructed, and how it operates to validate and reify the values of the institution within which that discourse is situated.

Johns, A. M. 1997. *Text, role and context.* New York: Cambridge University Press.

Like several of its predecessors in the well-known Cambridge Applied Linguistics series, this volume is important for both its theoretical and practical contributions. Johns' chosen territory is the acquisition of academic literacy by incoming university students from disadvantaged backgrounds, and she succeeds in showing how a complex approach drawing on genre, community, and multiple modes of apprenticeship can be made to work. This book is one of few recent volumes to fully integrate research, theory, and practice.

Jordan, R. R. 1997. *English for academic purposes: A guide and resource book for teachers*. Cambridge: Cambridge University Press.

For this volume, Jordan has pulled a vast amount of material together, and manages to do so in such a way that research, pedagogical application, and practical illustration are well indicated. However, the volume somewhat over-favors British work and tends to avoid certain contemporary theoretical and ideological issues.

Louhiala-Salminen, L. 1999. *From business correspondence to message exchange: The notion of genre in business communication*. Jyväskylä, Finland: University of Jyväskylä.

This study integrates the theoretical framework of genre analysis and traditional notions of business communications. It then views the traditional business letter and the new genres of fax and e-mail through this lens. This monograph can serve as an exemplar of the quality of current studies in LSP business communications.

Miller, T. (ed.) 1997. *Functional approaches to written text: Classroom applications*. Washington: USIA. [Originally *THE Journal*. 2/3. Paris: TESOL France. 1995.]

Tom Miller of the USIA has here succeeded in pulling together a group of (mostly) leading specialists in their fields in order to demonstrate how discourse analysis can be put into practical effect. The coverage is particularly wide (reading, writing, critical discourse analysis, genre, grammar, concordancing, etc.) but the overall effect is remarkably coherent. This volume is one of the best volumes on applied discourse analysis available.

Prior, P. A. 1998. *Writing/disciplinarity: A sociohistoric account of literate activity in the academy*. Mahwah, NJ: L. Erlbaum.

This volume is a culmination of a long series of studies conducted by the author in recent years. If Johns (1997) is concerned with the enculturation of undergraduates, Prior is concerned with that of graduates. *Inter alia*, he is able to demonstrate, via extremely detailed casework, that this process is much more complex and multi-faceted than the field had hitherto imagined. Because of his striking findings, this important work needs replicating in other fields of endeavor, such as science, engineering, and medicine.

Swales, J. M. 1998. *Other floors, other voices: A textography of a small university building*. Mahwah, NJ: L. Erlbaum.

This is the first book by this author which is not directly concerned with LSP issues. Rather, it explores discoursal life in a small academic building, and then examines the textual lives of seven individuals, four botanists and three applied linguists. One of the book's main purposes is to re-examine—and perhaps rehabilitate—the concept of discourse community.

Valle, E. 1999. *A collective intelligence: The life sciences in the Royal Society as a scientific discourse community*. Turku, Finland: University of Turku. [Anglicana Turkuensia No 17.]

This volume is the latest is a fine series of discourse-based studies showing the evolution of scientific discourse. Once again, we find here a complex methodology ranging from standard historical research to very fine-grained studies of citations and modes of reporting the work of others. The author concludes that while the discourses she examined have remained dialogic over the last 300 years, that dialogue has consistently become more centered on the public rather than the private domain.

UNANNOTATED BIBLIOGRAPHY

Akar, D. 1998. Patterns and variations in contemporary written business communications. Ann Arbor: University of Michigan. Ph.D diss.

―――― and L. Louhiala-Salminen. 1999. Toward a new genre: A comparative study of business faxes. In F. Bargiela-Chiappini and C. Nickerson (eds.) *Writing business: Genres, media and discourses*. London: Longman.207–225.

Atkinson, D. 1999a. *Scientific discourse in sociohistorical context: The philosophical transactions of the Royal Society of London, 1675–1975*. Mahwah, NJ: L. Erlbaum.

―――― 1999b. Language and Science. In W. Grabe, *et al.* (eds.) *Annual Review of Applied Linguistics, 19. Survey of applied linguistics*. New York: Cambridge University Press. 193–214.

Bakhtin, M. M. 1986. *Speech genres and other late essays*. Austin: University of Texas Press.

Barbara, L., M. A. A. Celani, H. Collins and M. Scott. 1996. A survey of communication patterns in the Brazilian business context. *English for Specific Purposes*. 15.57–71.

Bazerman, C. 1988. *Shaping written knowledge.* Madison, WI: University of Wisconsin Press.

——————— 1995. Systems of genre and the enactment of social intentions. In A. Freedman and P. Medway (eds). *Genre and the new rhetoric.* London: Taylor and Francis. 79–101.

Berkenkotter, C. and T. Huckin. 1995. *Genre knowledge in disciplinary communication.* Hillsdale, NJ: L. Erlbaum.

Bhatia, V. K. 1993. *Analysing genre: Language use in professional settings.* Harlow, UK: Longman.

——————— 1998. Generic conflicts in academic discourse. In I. Fortanet, *et al.* (eds.) *Genre studies in English for academic purposes.* Castello, Spain: Universitat Jaume I. 15–28.

Bilbow, G. T. 1999. Look who's talking: An analysis of "chair-talk" in business meetings. *Journal of Business and Technical Communication.* 12.157–197.

Charles, M. 1996. Business communications: Interdependence between discourse and the business relationship. *English for Specific Purposes.* 15.19–36.

Chia, H.-U., R. Johnson, H.-L. Chia and F. Olive. 1999. English for college students in Taiwan: A study of perceptions of English needs in a medical context. *English for Specific Purposes.* 18.107–119.

Connor, U. 1996. *Contrastive rhetoric: Cross-cultural aspects of second language writing.* New York: Cambridge University Press.

——————— and A. Mauranen. 1999. Linguistic analysis of grant proposals: European Union research grants. *English for Specific Purposes.* 18.47–62.

Crystal, D. 1997. *English as a global language.* Cambridge: Cambridge University Press.

Devitt, A. 1991. Intertextuality in tax accounting: Generic, referential and functional. In C. Bazerman and J. Paradis (eds.) *Textual dynamics of the professions.* Madison: University of Wisconsin Press. 337–357.

——————— 1996. Genre, genres, and the teaching of genre. *College Composition and Communication.* 47.605–616.

Douglas, D. and L. Selinker. 1994. Native and nonnative teaching assistants: A case study of discourse domains and genres. In C. G. Madden and C. L. Myers (eds.) *Discourse and performance of international teaching assistants.* Alexandria, VA: TESOL. 221–230.

Dressen, D. F. and J. M. Swales. In press. "Geological setting/cadre geologique" in English and French petrology articles: Muted indications of explored places. In A. Trosberg (ed.) *Analysing professional genres.* Amsterdam: Benjamins.

Feak, C. B., S. M. Reinhart and A. Sinsheimer. In press. A preliminary analysis of law review notes. *English for Specific Purposes.*

Fox. R. 1999. The social identity of management ergolect. *English for Specific Purposes.* 18.261–278.

Fredrickson, K. M. 1996. Contrasting genre systems: Court documents from the United States and Sweden. *Multilingua.* 15.275–304.

Giannoni, D. S. 1998. The genre of journal acknowledgements: Findings of a cross-disciplinary investigation. *Linguistica e filologia.* 6.61–83.

Gibbons, J. 1999. Language and the law. In W. Grabe, *et al.* (eds.) *Annual Review of Applied Linguistics, 19. Survey of applied linguistics.* New York: Cambridge University Press. 156–173.

Gunnarsson, B.-L. 1997a. On the sociohistorical construction of scientific discourse. In B.-L. Gunnarsson, P. Linell and B. Nordberg (eds.) *The construction of professional discourse.* Longman: London. 99–126.

——— 1997b. The writing process from a sociolinguistic viewpoint. *Written Communication.* 14.139–188.

Halliday, M. A. K., P. Strevens and A. McIntosh. 1964. *The linguistic sciences and language teaching.* London: Longman.

Harris, S. 1992. Reaching out in legal education: Will EALP be there? *English for Specific Purposes.* 11.19–32.

——— 1997. Procedural vocabulary in law case reports. *English for Specific Purposes.* 16.289–308.

Henderson, W., A. Dudley-Evans and R. Backhouse (eds.) 1993. *Economics and language.* London: Routledge.

Huckin, T. 1997. Cultural aspects of genre knowledge. *AILA Review.* 12.68–78. Hutchinson, T. and A. Waters. 1987. *English for specific purposes.* London: Longman.

Hyden, L.-C. and E. G. Mishler. 1999. Language and medicine. In W. Grabe, *et al.* (eds.) *Annual Review of Applied Linguistics, 19. Survey of applied linguistics.* New York: Cambridge University Press. 174–192.

Johns, A. M. 1998. The visual and the verbal: A case study in macroeconomics. *English for Specific Purposes.* 17.183–197.

Locker, K. O. 1999. Factors in reader responses to negative letters: Experimental evidence for changing what we teach. *Journal of Business and Technical Communication.* 13.1.5–48.

Mauranen, A. 1993. Cultural differences in academic discourse: Problems of a linguistic and cultural minority. In L. Lofman (ed.) *The competent intercultural communicator: AfinLA Yearbook.* Helsinki: AfinLA. 157–174.

Miller, T. 1998. Visual persuasion: A comparison of visuals in academic texts and the popular press. *English for Specific Purposes.* 17.29–46.

Montgomery, S. L. 1996. *The scientific voice.* New York: The Guilford Press.

Motta-Roth, D. 1998. Discourse analysis and academic book reviews: A study of text and disciplinary cultures. In I. Fortanet, *et al.* (eds.) *Genre studies in English for academic purposes.* Castello, Spain: Universitat Jaume I. 29–58.

Nickerson, C. 1998. Corporate culture and the use of written English within British subsidiaries in the Netherlands. *English for Specific Purposes.* 17.281–294.

Partington, M. 1998. *Patterns and meanings: Using corpora for English language research and teaching.* Amsterdam: J. Benjamins.

Pennycook, A. 1997. Vulgar pragmatism, critical pragmatism, and EAP. *English for Specific Purposes.* 15.85–103.

Phillipson, R. 1999. Voice in global English: Unheard chords in crystal loud and clear. *Applied Linguistics.* 20.265–272.

Pickering, A. 1995. *The mangle of practice: Time, agency, and science.* Chicago: The University of Chicago Press.

Precht, K. 1998. A cross-cultural comparison of letters of recommendation. *English for Specific Purposes.* 17.241–265.

Reeves, N. and C. Wright. 1996. *Linguistic auditing: A guide to identifying foreign language communication needs in corporations.* Clevedon, UK: Multilingual Matters.

Rogers, P. S. In press. CEO presentations in conjunction with earning announcements: Extending the construct of organizational genre through competing values profiling and user-needs analysis. *Management Communication Quarterly.* 13.3.

Russell, D. 1997. Rethinking genre in school and society: An activity theory analysis. *Written Communication.* 14.501–554.

Salager-Meyer, F. 1997. Books vs. articles: A diachronic study of referencing in written medical prose. *The ESPecialist.* 18.4.147–183.

Scollon, R. and S. W. Scollon. 1995. *Intercultural communication.* Oxford: Basil Blackwell.

Smart, G. 1998. Mapping conceptual worlds: Using interpretive ethnography to explore knowledge-making in a professional community. *The Journal of Business Communication.* 35.1.111–127.

Swales, J. M. 1996. Occluded genres in the academy: The case of the submission letter. In E. Ventola and A. Mauranen (eds.) *Academic writing: Intercultural and textual issues.* Amsterdam: J. Benjamins. 45–58.

———— 1997. English as Tyrannosaurus rex. *World Englishes.* 16.373–382.

———— and P. S. Rogers. 1995. Discourse and the projection of corporate culture: The mission statement. *Discourse and Society.* 6.223–242.

Tebeaux, E. 1999. Designing written business communication along the shifting cultural continuum: The new face of Mexico. *The Journal of Business and Technical Communication.* 13.1.49–85.

Trosborg, A. 1997. Contracts as social action. In B.-L. Gunnarsson, P. Linell and B. Nordberg (eds.) *The construction of professional discourse.* London: Longman. 54–75.

Wayt Gibbs, W. 1995. Lost science in the third world. *Scientific American.* (August). 92–99.

Whyte, S. 1995. Specialist knowledge and interlanguage development: A discourse domain approach to text construction. *Studies in Second Language Acquisition.* 17.153–183.

Widdowson, H. G. 1998. Communication and community: The pragmatics of ESP. *English for Specific Purposes.* 17.3–14.

Yates, J. and W. Orlikowski. 1992. Genres of organizational communication: A structurational approach. *Academy of Management Review.* 17.296–325.

Yli-Jokipii, H. 1994. Requests in professional discourse: A cross-cultural study of British, American and Finnish business writing. Helsinki: University of Helsinki. Ph.D. diss.

LSP IN NORTH AFRICA: STATUS, PROBLEMS AND, CHALLENGES

Mohamed Daoud

INTRODUCTION

This chapter presents a survey of recent developments in teaching Languages for Specific Purposes (LSP) in North Africa[1] and discusses current issues and future challenges. It devotes more space to ESP in this francophone environment given the greater demand for English, as opposed to other languages, and the more abundant ESP activity in terms of practice, research, and publications.

In Northern Africa, the challenges for the next decade and beyond are considerable but exciting: First, while the demand for LSP, and ESP in particular, is clear and the political discourse which reflects such a demand is unequivocal, there is a lack of policy and planning commitments to ensure the professional development and delivery of LSP services. The obstacles, in this case, include central control, institutional inertia, and, with respect to ESP in particular, continuing resistance to the spread of English in a French-dominant educational and economic system. Second, current ESP/LSP practice is largely ad hoc, lacking in course design, teacher training, sufficient instruction time, and proper evaluation. The challenges, in this respect, involve developing true specific-purpose curricula (based on learners' needs) which would provide the appropriate context for sustainable language programs. Third, as in other parts of the world, there is an increasing demand for language training for occupational business and vocational purposes added to the established instruction in English for Academic Purposes (EAP). The additional challenges, in this case, include the provision of good teacher-education programs (necessarily post B.A.) which require that the universities that offer such training open up to the professional and vocational sectors and learn to work with them. This demand will, of course, have an impact on the content and methodology of applied linguistics degree programs. Fourth, there are theoretical challenges which will keep applied linguists who are interested in ESP/LSP oscillating between theoretical pursuits and practical applications. Theoretical frameworks for ESP course design and teaching, in particular, have to be adaptable to the local contexts where LSP programs are needed. At the same time, localized LSP practice, which is socioculturally embedded, must inform theoretical developments. In all of these challenges, mainstream (Anglo-American) and local ESP practitioners have every reason to work together.

THE NORTH AFRICAN CONTEXT

The language of everyday communication in North Africa is the oral dialect of the country (Tunisian, Algerian, and Moroccan Arabic), together with Berber in Algeria and Morocco, where the Berber population is around 15 percent and 30 percent, respectively. Modern Standard Arabic (MSA), which is taught at school, is the language of instruction in elementary and early secondary education. It is later restricted to teaching the humanities and social science subjects through college. French is well established as a second language, although it is officially labeled the first foreign language. It is taught no later than the third year of elementary education and becomes the medium of instruction of math, science and technology, and business subjects in late secondary education and at the university level. Thus, it competes with, or predominates over, both MSA (in government administration, private business, and the media) and the local dialects, particularly among the educated (Battenberg 1997, Daoud 1991b, Walters 1999).

English is taught as a foreign language for up to six years in secondary education at the rate of 2-4 hours a week; then it becomes a required subject in all the tracks of vocational training and higher education. Other foreign languages (e.g., German, Italian, Spanish) are taught as additional optional languages in late secondary education and the university level, but their spread is not at all comparable to English.

ESP practice started in North Africa in the early 1960s, much as it may have arisen in other countries in the Middle East, Asia, and Latin America, with expatriates teaching English to engineering students. The first major ESP event on record in North Africa was *The Hammamet Conference on English for Special Purposes*, held in Tunisia in February 1975 (Payne 1979). It brought together over fifty ESP practitioners including teachers from Tunisia, Algeria, Morocco, and Libya; expatriate teachers from Egypt and Sudan; specialist speakers from Britain and the U.S.; and aid agency representatives. In the conference resolutions, the local participants commented: "We recognize the increasing role of English in our countries and the urgent need for a shift towards more appropriate language programs, tailored to the needs of the area." However, they noted with regret that "no North African scholars read papers at this conference, which was at times too theoretical and not immediately relevant to this area" (Payne 1979:95).

The last remark remains, although to a lesser degree, a characteristic of ESP in this EFL context and a challenge to mainstream and local ESP practitioners. For even though ESP instruction is now assured by local teachers, the region continues to draw heavily on guest speakers, research references, and textbooks from the U.K. and the U.S. Local practitioners, who are mindful of the linguistic and sociocultural characteristics of local learners and their educational/work environment, are acutely aware of the need to develop ESP locally to ensure a reasonable degree of effectiveness and professionalism.

The next major development was the establishment in the early 1980s of ESP resource-center projects (ESPRCP) which were funded by the British Overseas Development Administration (ODA) (Bencherif 1993, Kennedy 1985, Thomas 1993). Such projects helped set up advisory units for in-service teacher training and materials design and encouraged local discussion and research of ESP through seminars and conferences (e.g., *the Maghreb ESP Conference*, a biennial event held in 1993, 1995, and 1997) and publications (*Tunisia ESP Newsletter* and conference proceedings).

The measure of success of these projects was the development of long term sustainability through local staffing and funding (Kennedy 1985, Seymour and Bahloul 1992). The Tunisian ESPRCP has survived. With the end of ODA funding in 1995, it gained official recognition as a department for the promotion of ESP and has now grown to reach a large ESP teacher/researcher population (over 600 regular users) and to help sustain an M.A. program in Applied Linguistics/ESP (Daoud, *et al.* 1999). The Algerian ESPRCP faded in the mid-1990s in spite of the hard work and commitment of local practitioners (see separate reports by Meliani, Belkenshir, and Bensouiki in *Maghreb ESP Conference* 1993) as a result of political instability in the country. ESP activity in Morocco was judged not substantial enough (El-Haddad 1993, Najbi 1997) to receive ODA support for a similar project.

Thus, ESP has been growing, although in jumps and starts. In Tunisia, it has become a required subject at various levels of education and vocational training (Daoud 1996a; 1998a; 1998b). It is also in great demand in the public and private sectors (Daoud and Labassi 1996).[2] However, questions remain about whether what is being offered is true ESP given the lack of proper needs analysis, teacher training, and evaluation (Daoud 1999, Seymour 1993). It seems that these questions will stand for the foreseeable future for a number of reasons which are explored later in this chapter.

It is important to note, however, that ESP is not the sole issue in LSP concerns in North Africa. Issues involving other languages also need to be reviewed in order to assess fully the role of LSP in the region. The reader will soon realize that the current problems and future challenges relative to ESP readily apply to other languages, which lag far behind in terms of practice and research.

THE CURRENT STATE OF LSP

The experience of the *Institute Bourguiba des Langues Vivantes* (IBLV) in Tunis, in terms of developing LSP, is unique in North Africa and may, therefore, be described as the best case scenario for LSP development in the region. Since its founding in 1964, this institution has taught several foreign languages to the general public as well as to clients with specific needs from the public and private business/industrial sectors. It even developed B.A.-level programs combining at least two languages and focusing on business communication skills and translation (*Maîtrise combinée de langues, M.C.L.*). These languages include Italian, Spanish, German, Russian, Chinese, and Japanese, in addition to French and Arabic for professional and business purposes.

Given the greater demand for these languages, the M.C.L. (which was abandoned in the 1980s) was reborn in 1996–1997 as the *Maîtrise de langues vivantes appliquées* (*M.L.V.A.*) [B.A. in modern applied languages[3]], with specific application to business communication and practices (Department of Languages 1996). The curriculum involves language and discourse practice, translation, cultural awareness raising through lectures and seminars run by language and business specialists, on-site visits and training, and case studies. In the same year, the IBLV also started a diploma program in translation involving the three main languages (MSA, French, and English), with an applied orientation to market demands.

The main justification for these programs is twofold: 1) to supply businesses with operational language users in specific domains as Tunisia gears up for economic partnership with the European Union (which takes effect in 2007), and 2) to help language-degree holders find jobs in the socio-economic sector (government, banking, tourism, NGOs, etc.) as opposed to joining the saturated ranks of language teachers. ESP practitioners should note with interest that English is required in all of these LSP programs.

The IBLV has also proposed to offer a professional diploma in French for Specific Purposes (FSP) [*Diplôme d'études supérieures spécilaisées (D.E.S.S.) en français à des fins spécifiques*], which departs from the traditional literature/civilization track prevailing in the university system. The degree program has four goals:

1. Address learners' needs for French for professional purposes,
2. Help employees secure promotion through a higher level of functional literacy in the language,
3. Promote the teaching of French for academic and occupational purposes in the educational system, and
4. Develop appropriate teaching materials for FSP.

The proposal concludes with the blunt statement that "the specific framework for the mastery (of FSP) and for research leading to this mastery is non-existent" (Department of French 1999:2, translation from the original French). The French department has already taken steps to model this program after the ESP program already in place since 1995 and to support it with an FSP resource center.[4]

POLICY AND PLANNING FOR ESP

ESP in North Africa has always suffered from a status problem. It has been sustained through the commitment of ESP teachers, the enthusiasm of certain deans and subject-specialist teachers, and the financial assistance of foreign aid agencies representing U.K. and U.S. interests. The official attitude, although unstated, is something like the following: "It's their (U.K. and U.S.) language; if they want to promote it like the French promote their language, they will help us financially." Paradoxically, the official discourse has been unequivocal about the need for English, but there has never been an official provision to structure ESP activity in the various higher education institutions. The Tunisian government has probably gone the furthest in the region in generalizing the teaching of English in the educational sector; however, it has failed to provide the resources to design proper ESP curricula or the incentives to motivate ESP practitioners to teach ESP and investigate it. Over 95 percent of the ESP teachers are on loan from secondary schools and thus receive little or no recognition from university faculty, while those who undertake postgraduate studies in ESP are promoted out of ESP instruction and into traditional English departments (Daoud 1998b; 1999, Daoud, et al. 1999; but note that such a state is not uncommon elsewhere, cf. Swales 1984; 1994).

This situation stems from a lack of policy and planning commitments to ensure the professional development and delivery of ESP services, which may be explained by several factors, including central control, institutional inertia, and continuing resistance to the spread of English in a French-dominant educational and economic system. With respect to central control, the agencies in charge of curriculum planning have a top-down approach. They do not listen to the practitioners in the field, allocate too little time for ESP instruction, and set common examination criteria that are at odds with the nature of ESP practice.

As for institutional inertia, it is reflected in the statements, beliefs, and perceptions of many top decision makers, deans, and even university faculty relative to ESP: 1) *"anybody with an English degree can teach ESP,"* 2) *"learning ESP takes a short time,"* and 3) *"designing ESP course materials is easy and costs nothing."* In the private sector, where the notion of a long-term language program is not palatable, the common practice is to hire someone with an English degree, expect him/her to quickly learn about the business, and then act as a translator/communication facilitator with English speaking clients, rather than invest in training the relevant personnel in ESP. Inertia also leads to poor planning such that, when the teaching of ESP was generalized to all students in the latest reform of higher education in Tunisia (Daoud in press b), no measures were taken to design ESP courses, retrain practicing teachers, or recruit enough new ones. Instead, the Ministry required practicing teachers to teach 50 percent more hours and instructed deans to hire part-time teachers for the remaining groups.

A further explanation for the lack of commitment to ESP may be a resistance to the spread of English, especially from the *Centre culturel français*, which seems to counter efforts that may undermine the position of French in the region (Battenberg 1997). This resistance is also felt among French-educated administrators and faculty who seem to be concerned about losing their influence (Daoud 1991b). However, what is sometimes perceived as resistance to English may simply be linguistic realism relative to the promotion of other languages, given the greater economic activity between Tunisia and other non-English speaking countries in the European Union (France, Italy, Germany, etc.), with the U.K. and the U.S. coming later in order of importance (cf. Kaplan and Baldauf 1997, ch.6, on the language policy and planning dichotomy).

It is interesting to note that the mainstream ESP literature hardly addresses these issues. In the last seven years, *English for Specific Purposes: An International Journal* published no articles on the matter and only one book review (Kaplan 1998). Dudley-Evans and St John (1998), Johns and Dudley-Evans (1991), and Robinson (1991), the defining references on ESP, do not discuss these important obstacles in the way of ESP as an international movement. In his review of Robinson's book, Markee (1993) notes this oversight and states:

> ...[O]ne of the most useful current developments in ESP which is showing signs of being picked up by the wider profession is the interest in treating language curricula as innovations whose development has to be carefully managed. I predict that by the time Robinson writes the third edition of this book in the year 2000, an entire chapter on this topic may well be necessary (1993:265).

The year 2000 is upon us and yet ESP teacher-training programs are only beginning to address these issues. Among the twelve ESP degree/

certificate programs listed in Holden (1998), only one offers a language policy course, while another offers a course on the management of change in teaching situations. Daoud (1999) discusses some of the obstacles to ESP growth in Tunisia in terms of the management of innovation and concludes by questioning the commitment of Tunisian educational policy makers to ESP development:

> One is led to wonder whether English is truly desired in the official school system in spite of official and semi-official (media) pronouncements about its importance. If English is desired, even as a commodity in this global business and technological era, then there is an urgent need for a clear policy, a coherent structure and adequate resources for curriculum development and innovation (1999:135).

These issues are occasionally addressed by international ESP guest speakers in local contexts (e.g., Grabe 1996, Swales 1993; 1994); however they are given more attention in the language policy and planning literature (Kaplan and Baldauf 1997, chapters 6 and 9, and Hornberger and Ricento 1996) and in references dealing with the management of change, innovation, and quality control in ELT (cf. Christison and Stoller 1997, O'Dwyer 1996, and the literature stemming from the *Best Practices* work on EPP/EOP, Lomperis 1997).

The challenge for ESP practitioners is to influence language policy and planning, with the bulk of this responsibility falling to local practitioners who are more attuned to the political culture of their country rather than to the occasional guest speaker or foreign aid agency representative. Local ESP program coordinators and project directors need to learn the appropriate communication and negotiation skills to get through to decision makers and curriculum planners. This goal requires understanding that the decision makers may not necessarily be opposed to ESP, but simply working under their own political, financial, and other constraints. The practitioners' negotiating positions would be strengthened by the professionalism they would show in doing their work; however, this professionalism may not be easy to achieve because one is rarely afforded the resources for self-improvement (e.g., attending management courses and professional conferences).

CURRENT ESP PRACTICE AND HUMAN RESOURCE DEVELOPMENT

Current ESP practice in this part of the world is largely ad hoc, lacking in proper needs analysis, appropriate course design, materials production resources, teacher training, sufficient instruction time, and assessment and evaluation guidelines. Daoud (1999) finds that while general EFL practice in basic and secondary education benefits from an established institutional structure in the Ministry of Education, ESP is left in the hands of individual teachers who may be appropriately called "islands." Seymour, who managed the ESPRCP in Tunisia from 1989 to 1995, draws their profile:

> Most are Tunisians who have Tunisian degrees in "English" studied through the medium of English. However, few have been trained as teachers and most have never studied TEFL at all, let alone TESP. Many have traditional attitudes to teaching and learning and tend to concentrate on reading and *explication de texte*. This seems to consist mainly of giving students *textes*, chosen only because of their subject content, and setting comprehension questions. There is rarely any real teaching, just practice (Seymour 1993:19).

As the number of ESP teachers grow in several higher education institutions, coordinators are designated to run what are called *ESP sections*, for they were refused departmental status. With a few exceptions, coordination remains cosmetic, leading to the production of sketchy syllabi of little relevance to the learners' needs. This probably arises because the coordinators are not trained for syllabus design, nor are they given the authority and resources to do it.

Nonetheless, the ESPRCP has succeeded in establishing and sustaining an in-service training scheme for ESP teachers in higher education through professional events (three national ESP seminars per year, a summer school program, and the Maghreb ESP Conference) as well as the provision of up-to-date reference materials and on-site advice. It also helps sustain pre-service training in two advanced degree programs offered by the IBLV—*D.E.S.S.* [specialized higher education diploma in ESP] and the *Diplôme d'études approfondies (D.E.A.) en linguistique appliquée* [M.A.in Applied Linguistics/ESP]; it awards scholarships to do postgraduate studies in ESP; and it makes available to students adequate research references as well as a computer station with statistics and concordancing software and an Internet connection (Daoud, 1998a, Daoud, *et al.* 1999).

This coordinated effort is shoring up the professionalism of practicing teachers and producing a new generation of trained practitioners and able researchers in such areas as genre analysis (e.g., Labassi 1996; to appear), classroom research on reading strategies (Dhieb-Henia to appear), writing processes (Mahfoudhi 1999), contrastive lexical research (Annabi 1997), program evaluation (Oueslati 1998; see Daoud, *et al.* 1999), as well as materials production and evaluation (Daoud, *et al.* 1998/1999). The postgraduate program in ESP and the ESPRCP have helped to create a research environment suitable for informed discussion of ESP and the promotion of teamwork. Nevertheless, more work remains to be done.

Local experience has shown that the availability of international ESP textbooks for teachers to photocopy for their students only helps to promote ad hoc ESP practice. It often happens that a textbook off the shelf quickly supplants a sketchy syllabus which may have taken much effort to produce. Because individual ESP teachers are the ones who deliver the teaching in the classroom, they are ultimately the ones who determine the success or failure of ESP courses. Thus, teacher (re)education will remain a condition for the promotion of ESP in North Africa, for it will allow ESP teachers to make informed decisions at every level of practice, including the adoption or adaptation of international textbooks.

The English for Occupational Purposes (EOP) textbook series, which was designed for the Ministry of Professional Training and Employment (Daoud, *et al.* 1998/1999) has, for example, proven to be a suitable context for promoting several aspects of ESP practice in the local environment, which makes it worthy of duplication for higher education. It has served as a context for, among other things, 1) improved communication and negotiation with policy makers, 2) better collaboration with subject specialists and a deeper understanding of their discourse communities and communicative culture, 3) hands-on teacher education concerning theoretical developments in ESP research which informed materials design, and 4) constructive feedback on teachers' classroom performance while the materials were being piloted, bearing in mind that most of the teachers were co-authors of the textbook series.

This work was inspired by mainstream genre analysis research, task-based curricula, and strategy training, and by more recent ethnographic research in specific discourse communities (see references below). This approach is in line with the *Best Practices* literature (Lomperis 1997), which sets the trend for future curriculum design, particularly in light of the growing demand for English for Occupational Business Purposes (EOBP), English for Professional Purposes (EPP), and EOP, in both pre-employment vocational training and workplace retraining (cf. Dudley-Evans and St John 1998). The *Best Practices* work sets specific criteria for planning, implementing, and evaluating EOP/EPP curricula, but it also incorporates non-traditional aspects of ESP practice from the business and management culture, such as communication and negotiation skills, market research, marketing, and independent consultancy.

The evolving branches and sub-branches of ESP and the incorporation of business principles in the planning and delivery of ESP services present enormous challenges for practitioner training programs. (I would even argue that the label "ESP teacher" no longer seems appropriate for anyone involved in the field, because of the multiple roles required by this job, which in turn requires multidisciplinary knowledge and a variety of skills.) ESP practitioner training, then, requires that the universities offering such training open up to the business and occupational sectors and learn to work with them. These issues are addressed by Eustace (1996) on changing business communication practices vs. classroom practice, Louhiala-Salminen (1996) and Lumley (1998) on language-trained vs. occupational experts' ratings of EOP proficiency, and Jacoby and McNamara (1999) on the variable assessment of communicative ability in EOP and on the use of peer training for academic presentations. This expansion will, of course, have an impact on the content and methodology of Applied Linguistics/ESP degree programs.

THE FUTURE OF ESP: INTERNATIONAL SCOPE, ANGLO-AMERICAN PARADIGM, LOCALIZED PRACTICES

There is a general consensus in the ELT profession and in the broader field of Applied Linguistics that ESP is international in scope (Johns and Dudley-Evans 1991), regardless of whether English is called an *international language*, a *world language*, or a *lingua franca* (Kachru 1997). Initial ESP practice in the early 1960s, together with some of the earliest textbooks and research on English for Science and Technology (EST) (see Swales 1988), all attest to this international outlook (e.g., the predominant use of English in international journals of science and technology and medicine [Gibbs 1995], as well as the more recent surge in Business English [St John 1996]).

In North Africa, no one questions the international *scope* of ESP, but many question its international *nature*. There are two concerns in particular: 1) the relevance of ESP ideas and practices from the "inner circle" to this part of the world in the "expanding circle" (Kachru 1997), and 2) the local contribution to these ideas and practices.[5] The appraisal of the first ESP conference in North Africa—regretting that no local practitioners presented papers and commenting that the conference "was at times too theoretical and not immediately relevant to this area" (Payne 1979:95)—is still echoed by local ESP practitioners even though 99 percent of the teachers are now North African and a growing number of local practitioners are producing appropriate teaching materials and reliable research.

Rather than blaming mainstream ESP experts for failing to adapt their theories and practical solutions to the North African context, this appraisal is meant to call local practitioners to the task of contributing to ESP research and practice. There is a heightened sense that local awareness of learners' linguistic, educational, and cultural backgrounds (Daoud 1991a; 1996b, Hemissi 1987; 1993, Labassi 1995; 1996, Lowe 1992; 1996), together with knowledge of the local political, financial, and administrative constraints (Daoud 1998b; 1999), favors the design of appropriate responses by local ESP practitioners.

It should be clear, though, that just as such responses draw on the mainstream ESP/Applied Linguistics research literature, it is possible that mainstream research is augmented by the localized responses and the processes underlying them. This interaction is, in fact, what would make ESP truly international in nature. International ESP experts often testify to the superior quality of localized ESP projects and practices and regret that they never appear in international publications (e.g., Johns and Dudley-Evans 1991). Local practitioners must publish then and let the so-called gatekeepers do their duty.

There are legitimate reasons for local practitioners to question the relevance of mainstream ESP research and practice, and they would be unwise not to do so. For instance, (Hemissi 1993) argues that the linguistic background of North African

ESP learners results in a variable degree of proficiency in MSA and French, but no native speaker mastery or awareness of either one. For this reason, mainstream ESP materials and teaching approaches that were originally designed for ESL audiences may be helpful, but not necessarily suitable for these learners, and they would have to be adopted only with great caution and flexibility.

For other local practitioners, *in situ* investigations of needs indicate that the literature and materials produced in the U.K. and the U.S. may not suit these needs. Local studies have called for teaching specific skills and strategies such as translation skills[6] to help researchers read and publish in English (Labassi 1995; 1996). These skills include: 1) raising awareness of the variable use of symbols and other non-verbal devices in English and French scientific discourse (Lowe 1992; 1996) as well as prefixes in medical discourse (Annabi 1997), 2) promoting cross-linguistic rhetorical and genre awareness in processing EST discourse (Daoud 1991a; 1996b), and 3) developing metacognitive strategies to aid expeditious and careful reading (Dhieb-Henia to appear, cf. Weir 1997). On the other hand, Daoud (in press a) shows that subject-specific teaching, learning, and evaluation practices in this educational environment have an impact on the motivation of ESP learners, and these practices require specific training for ESP teachers if teachers are to motivate not only their students but also their subject-specialist colleagues and deans.

On a more abstract level, the theoretical paradigm for ESP research[7] seems to us very Anglo-American (or rather "American-Anglo"), always with English as the language of reference (see Swales 1993; 1997). This emphasis is true of the growing number of EAP studies on dissertation writing which promote the Anglo-American model of exposition. Yet we know that in academic contexts, as well as in professional and occupational ones, interlocutors are more and more likely to be non-native speakers of English (Johns and Swales 1998).

ESP, and applied linguistics in general, would gain from a truly international investigation of ESP learners' communicative uses of the languages they already know (see Johns 1997, Barbara, *et al.* 1996) in order to inform ESP research and practice. The international nature of ESP would only be strengthened if more projects involved American/British and international ESP practitioners. This partnership would help us all understand, for instance, how multilingual discourse communities function in specific academic/occupational domains, how sociocultural variables in NNS-NNS domain-specific interaction in English influence communication (e.g., in terms of amount and patterns of communication, degree of accommodation to the interlocutor, etc.), how the nature of strategic behavior can vary in oral/written interaction, and how the transfer of strategies can be promoted across language backgrounds.

These complex questions will keep applied linguists who are interested in LSP oscillating between theoretical pursuits and localized practical applications. Theoretical frameworks for LSP program design and implementation have to be adaptable to the local contexts where LSP is needed. At the same time, localized LSP practices, which are socio-culturally embedded, must inform theoretical development.

CONCLUDING REMARKS

This survey has discussed issues of language policy and planning and the viability of the ESP/LSP movement in North Africa more than the pragmatic aspects of ESP research and practice. Some of the more pragmatic theoretical issues that will retain our attention in the next decade include further investigation of such common notions as communicative competence, genre, and discourse community. These notions are still in need of empirical definition and socio-cultural validation. Subject specialists have perceptions of communicative competence and ratings of language proficiency that are different from ours (cf. Jacoby and McNamara 1999, Lumley 1998). They may belong to a specific discourse community, but they also participate effectively in other communities based on shared goals, cultural norms of communication, and the principle of interdisciplinarity, indicating an overlap of communities and an extensive use of strategies for switching discourse modes and communication styles (Bazerman 1998). Subject specialists also use/produce genres with a degree of flexibility that is only beginning to be examined in current applied linguistics research (Atkinson 1999, Bhatia 1997).

Improving our understanding of these notions for the sake of adequate application will require collaborating with subject-specialist informants and, when possible, doing ethnographic textography (Swales 1998). This evolution will also require further research at the macro-level (even though the macro/micro distinction is somewhat artificial) along the lines of contrastive rhetoric (cf. Mauranen 1993,

Swales, *et al.* 1997), sociocultural literacy (Johns 1997), diachronic studies of genres (Salager-Meyer 1999, Labassi to appear), and critical discourse analysis (Huckin 1997); at the micro-level, research will focus on grammar (e.g., Biber, *et al.* 1996) and vocabulary (Coady and Huckin 1997).

On the instructional side, classroom based research and reflective teaching will be more significant in the next decade and beyond in order to achieve a reasonable match between theoretical approaches and actual course design and teaching. Current reading research, for instance, is just beginning to address strategy training issues in real ESP teaching contexts (cf. Dhieb-Henia to appear, Grabe 1996, Weir 1997). With respect to teacher education, much remains to be done to help teachers incorporate in their lessons insights from research on grammar and style (e.g., Biber, *et al.* 1996) and vocabulary (Coady and Huckin 1997). On the other hand, practitioner education, particularly for ESP program coordinators and project managers, will receive more attention along the lines set out in O'Dwyer (1996) and Christison and Stoller (1997), although there again, the predominance of the Anglo-American model of management will have to be more sensitive to local political and educational cultures around the world.

This brief survey shows that the current theoretical and practical concerns of ESP practitioners are truly within the realm of applied linguistics, for they embrace issues of language policy and planning, language teaching and practitioner training, functional literacy skills in specific discourse communities, language assessment, program evaluation, and language program administration. Looking forward to the next decade and beyond, the multidisciplinary, and increasingly multicultural, nature of ESP will keep it in the forefront of applied linguistics research and maintain its trail-blazing role for general ELT and for the teaching/ learning of other languages for specific purposes. North African applied linguists will play their part in the global growth of ESP by designing localized solutions to present and future language-related problems.

NOTES

1. The label "North Africa" designates three countries in the Maghreb in particular: Tunisia, Algeria, and Morocco, because they have a very similar linguistic profile and educational structure. There has been substantial ESP activity

in this region for more than three decades, particularly in Tunisia and Algeria, although in the latter country it has been affected by the unstable political situation since 1991. In Morocco, ESP has not yet reached the same degree of official recognition and public awareness as in Tunisia and Algeria (El-Haddad 1993, Najbi 1997).

2. The demand for English is so unprecedented that the numerous providers are turning back clients. In Tunisia, providers include the *Institute Bourguiba des Langues Vivantes* (IBLV) which has branches countrywide, the British Council, AMIDEAST, the Tunisian American Chamber of Commerce, as well as many private educational institutions which are thriving on courses in English for business and management. This demand is also indicated by the increasing number of job ads appearing in English in a leading Tunisian newspaper published in French (Labassi in press). There is a project underway to survey the ESP needs of several business organizations, carried out by a group of graduate (M.A. level) students (Jabeur 1999).

3. Programs in other languages used around the Mediterranean are possible in the future, depending on public demand and the availability of qualified instructors: Greek, Turkish, Persian, Hebrew, Portuguese, etc.

4. The programs described in this section are now run by the *Institut Supérieur des Langues de Tunis* (ISLT) which separated from the IBLV in September 1999.

5. In North Africa, most ESP practitioners hold the moderate, pragmatic view that English is *the* international language of communication, particularly in science, technology, and trade. It should be promoted as a service language in as professional a manner as possible, but not to the exclusion of other languages (Walters 1999). A few hold an ideologically strong view which associates English with the hegemonic power of multinational/American companies and the impoverishing policies of the World Bank and the IMF (cf. Mchala 1999, Pennycook 1997). However, nobody really accepts the simplistic views that ESP/EAP is neutral (Allison 1996) or that English is innocent (Widdowson 1998).

6. Translation has received scant attention in mainstream ESP research, and in the collection of over 1,000 recently published ESP textbooks available at the ESP Resource Center in Tunis, I have not found any translation activities. This is an area worthy of attention as ESP practitioners feel the need to develop basic translation skills: University students often use English references, but they write their exams

and papers in French. More advanced researchers who want to publish in English or give presentations at international, and even national, conferences often write their papers in French then ask English teaching colleagues to translate their drafts. Those who feel confident enough to write originally in English often produce French-sounding prose (Daoud in press a, Daoud and Labassi 1996, Labassi 1996). Translation training is also critically needed by business professionals and administrators, as demonstrated rather dramatically by the Tunisian president's 1995 visit to South Africa with leading Tunisian businessmen, only to discover that they did not have the adequate English proficiency to achieve the aims of the visit.

7. Shulman defines a paradigm in terms of "principles of regularity and cannons of evidence" (Shulman 1988:9).

ANNOTATED BIBLIOGRAPHY

Daoud, M., *et al.* 1998/1999. *English for professionals.* Tunis: CENAFFIF, Ministère de la Formation Professionnelle et de l'Emploi. *Level one: English for professionals; Level two (a): English for professionals: Introduction to technical culture, Level two (b): English for professionals: Introduction to business culture; Level three:* (5 volumes) *English for professionals: Electrical engineering, Civil engineering, Mechanical engineering, Textiles and leather,* and *Business administration.*

This is a 100 percent Tunisian EOP textbook series for students seeking to obtain a vocational certificate or diploma for employment in more than 150 different specialties. The series includes eight volumes, three for the first year (levels 1 and 2), and five for the second year (level 3). This product is unique in Tunisia not only because of the quality of the materials (which are in some respects superior to international textbooks), but more importantly because of the process that was involved in producing them. This process started with needs analysis and syllabus design (in 1996–97), and is now concluding with materials evaluation and revision in light of classroom observation and teacher feedback. This project has served as an appropriate context for interacting professionally with the various stakeholders in the Tunisian vocational training system, and for educating teachers about the various roles they have to play in course design, lesson planning, classroom practice, learner assessment, and materials evaluation. The project has had the added advantage of promoting team work.

Dudley-Evans, T. and M. J. St John. 1998. *Developments in English for specific purposes: A multi-disciplinary approach.* Cambridge: Cambridge University Press.

This book is a state-of-the-art volume on ESP, long-awaited after Hutchinson and Waters (1987) and Robinson (1991). Its main strengths include: 1) updating the reader on major developments in the field which has become more multidisciplinary than ever before as it continues to seek distinction within ELT, and 2) defining the various roles that the ESP teacher/practitioner must perform professionally. Its main weakness, though, is that it avoids language policy and planning issues and avoids an ideological stance on ESP as an international phenomenon.

Kaplan, R. B. and R. B. Baldauf Jr. 1997. *Language planning: From practice to theory.* Clevedon, UK: Multilingual Matters.

Two sections in this book are of special interest to the applied linguist/ESP practitioner (chapters 6 and 9). However, the rest of the book makes very interesting reading as well for those who want to understand the wider political context which constrains practice. The book defines the discipline of language policy and planning, discusses various international examples of practice, and from a review of practice attempts to define a theory: Hence the subtitle, *From practice to theory*. In this sense, the book sets the ground rules and techniques for the localized investigation of language policy and planning and for writing a series of books on the subject in various parts/countries of the world.

UNANNOTATED BIBLIOGRAPHY

Allison, D. 1996. Pragmatist discourse and English for academic purposes. *English for Specific Purposes.* 15.85–103.

Annabi, T. 1997. The language of medicine in English and French: Prefixes and their degree of constancy. Tunis: Faculty of letters, Manouba. D.E.A. thesis.

Atkinson, D. 1999. Language and science. In W. Grabe, *et al.* (eds.) *Annual Review of Applied Linguistics, 19. Survey of applied linguistics.* New York: Cambridge University Press. 193–214.

Barbara, L. M., *et al.* 1996. A survey of communication patterns in the Brazilian business context. *English for Specific Purposes.* 15.57–71.

Battenburg, J. D. 1997. English vs. French: Language rivalry in Tunisia. *World Englishes.* 16.281–290.

Bazerman, C. 1998. Charles Bazerman on John Swales: An interview with Tony Dudley-Evans. *English for Specific Purposes*. 17.105–112.

Bencherif, M. O. 1993. Presentation of the Algerian universities ESP project. In *Maghreb ESP conference: Current initiatives in ESP in the Maghreb and future perspectives*. London: The British Council. 12–13.

Bhatia, V.K. 1997. Genre-mixing in academic introductions. *English for Specific Purposes*. 16.181–195.

Biber, D., S. Conrad and R. Reppen. 1996. Corpus based investigations of language use. In W. Grabe, *et al.* (eds.) *Annual Review of Applied Linguistics, 16. Language and technology*. New York: Cambridge University Press. 115–136.

Christison, M. A. and F. L. Stoller (eds.) 1997. *A handbook for language program administrators*. Burlingame, CA: Alta Book Center.

Coady, J. and T. Huckin (eds.) 1997. *Second language vocabulary acquisition*. Cambridge: Cambridge University Press.

Daoud, M. 1991a. The processing of EST discourse: Arabic and French native speakers' recognition of rhetorical relationships in Engineering texts. Los Angeles: University of California. Ph.D. diss.

——— 1991b. Arabization in Tunisia: The tug of war. *Issues in Applied Linguistics*. 2.1.7–29.

——— 1996a. English language development in Tunisia. *TESOL Quarterly*. 30.598–605.

——— 1996b. Discourse analysis and reading instruction: Background knowledge variables in reading EST discourse. Paper presented at the annual TESOL conference. Chicago, March 1996.

——— 1998a. ESP teacher training: Establishing professional standards. Paper presented at the annual TESOL conference. Seattle, WA, March 1998.

——— 1998b. Le point sur l'enseignement de l'anglais de spécialité. [The state of teaching ESP.] Report presented to the Minister of Higher Education at a seminar on the teaching of English and French for Specific Purposes, computer skills, and human rights. Tunis, June 1998.

——— 1999. The management of innovation in ELT in Tunisia. In M. Jabeur, A. Manai and M. Bahloul (eds.) *English in North Africa*. Tunis: TSAS Innovation Series, TSAS and the British Council. 121–137.

——— In press a. Teaching, learning and testing in the disciplines as motivational factors in ESP. In M. Bahloul and M. Triki (eds.) *Proceedings of the Second Maghreb ESP Conference*. Sfax, Tunisia: Faculté des Lettres et Sciences Humaines.

——— In press b. Education in Tunisia. In *Education in the Arab world*, Volume II. Washington, DC: America-Mideast Educational and Training Services.

LSP IN NORTH AFRICA: STATUS, PROBLEMS AND, CHALLENGES 107

Daoud, M. and T. Labassi. 1996. ESP and the real world: Some answers to new requirements. Paper presented at the 2nd National ESP Seminar, Tunis, March 1996. [To appear in *Tunisia ESP Newsletter* 13.]

────────── *et al.* 1999. *Evaluation of the English for Specific Purposes Resource Center Project in Tunisia: Executive summary.* Tunis: The ESP Resource Center, Institut Bourguiba des Langues Vivantes.

Department of French. 1999. *Projet de mise en place d'un D.E.S.S. en français a buts spécifiques.* [Project for setting up a specialized diploma of higher education in French for specific purposes.] Tunis: Institut Bourguiba des Langues Vivantes.

Department of Languages. 1996. *Demande d'habilitation: Maîtrise de langues vivantes appliquées.* [Application for certification: B.A. in modern applied languages.] Tunis: Institut Bourguiba des Langues Vivantes.

Dhieb-Henia, N. To appear. The effect of metacognitive strategy training on EFL students' reading scientific research articles. Tunis: Faculty of Letters, Manouba. Doctoral diss.

El-Haddad, M. 1993. Specificity of ESP in the Maghreb countries. In *Maghreb ESP conference: Current initiatives in ESP in the Maghreb and future perspectives.* London: The British Council. 14–18.

Eustace, G. 1996. Business writing: Some aspects of current practice. *English for Specific Purposes.* 15.53–56.

Gibbs, W. W. 1995. Trends in scientific communication: Lost science in the Third World. *Scientific American.* August, 92–99.

Grabe, W. 1996. Reading in an ESP context: Dilemmas and possible solutions. *ESP Malaysia.* 4.1–28.

Hemissi, H. 1987. Which ESP for Tunisia? *Tunisia ESP Newsletter.* 3.2.10–14.

────────── 1993. Specificity of ESP in the Maghreb countries. In *Maghreb ESP conference: Current initiatives in ESP in the Maghreb and future perspectives.* London: The British Council. 21–24.

Holden, P. 1998. An overview of degree, diploma, certificate and credential programs for teacher training in English for specific purposes. *English for Specific Purposes.* 17.219–225.

Hornberger, N. H. and T. K. Ricento (eds.) 1996. *Language planning and policy.* [Special issue of *TESOL Quarterly.* 30.3.]

Huckin, T. 1997. Critical discourse analysis. In T. Miller (ed.) *Functional approaches to written text: Classroom applications.* Washington, DC: English Language Programs, USIA. 78–92.

Hutchinson, T. and A. Waters. 1987. *English for Specific Purposes: A learning-centred approach.* Cambridge: Cambridge University Press.

Jabeur, M. 1999. English, globalization and Tunisia. In M. Jabeur, A. Manai and M. Bahloul (eds.) *English in North Africa.* Tunis: TSAS Innovation Series, TSAS and the British

Council. 13–31.
Jacoby, S. and T. McNamara. 1999. Locating competence. *English for Specific Purposes.* 18.213–241.
Johns, A. M. 1997. *Text, role and context: Developing academic literacies.* Cambridge: Cambridge University Press.
———————— and T. Dudley-Evans. 1991. English for specific purposes: International in scope, specific in purpose. *TESOL Quarterly.* 25.297–314.
———————— and J. M. Swales. 1998. Past imperfect continuous: Reflections on two ESP lives. *English for Specific Purposes.* 17.15–28.
Kachru, B. B. 1997. World Englishes and English-using communities. In W. Grabe, *et al.* (eds.) *Annual Review of Applied Linguistics, 17. Multilingualism.* New York: Cambridge University Press. 66–87.
Kaplan, R. B. 1998. Review of Language and development, by T. Crooks and G. Crewes (eds.). *English for Specific Purposes.* 17.317–320.
Kennedy, C. (ed.) 1985. *ESP in Tunisia.* Corvallis, Oregon: ELI, Oregon State University. [*English for Specific Purposes* 96.]
Labassi, T. 1995. Interview with John Swales. *Tunisia ESP Newsletter.* 12.6–11.
———————— 1996. A genre-based analysis of nonnative chemistry research article introductions. Tunis: Faculty of Letters, Manouba. D.E.A. thesis.
———————— In press. ESP: a market-oriented approach. In M. Bahloul and M. Triki (eds.) *Proceedings of the second Maghreb ESP conference.* Sfax, Tunisia: Faculté des Lettres et Sciences Humaines.
———————— To appear. The evolution of scientific abstract writing: The case of chemical abstracts 1900–1995. Tunis: Faculty of Letters, Manouba. Doctoral diss.
Lomperis, A. E. 1997. Best practices in English for occupational purposes/English for professional purposes (EOP/EPP): Toward a final document. Paper presented at the annual TESOL conference. Orlando, FL, March 1997.
Louhiala-Salminen, L. 1996. The business communication classroom vs. reality: What we should teach today. *English for Specific Purposes.* 15.37–51.
Lowe, I. 1992. Scientific language at pre-university level between French and English. Surrey: University of Surrey. Ph.D. diss.
———————— 1996. Non-verbal devices in pre-university science: The extent of correspondence between English and French. *English for Specific Purposes.* 15.217–232.
Lumley, T. 1998. Perceptions of language trained raters and occupational experts in a test of occupational English language proficiency. *English for Specific Purposes.* 17.347–367.
Maghreb ESP Conference. 1993. *Maghreb ESP conference: Current initiatives in ESP in the Maghreb and future perspectives.* London: The British Council.

Mahfoudhi, A. 1999. Writing processes of Tunisian EFL students in argumentative essays. Tunis: Faculty of Letters, Manouba. D.E.A. thesis.

Markee, N. P. 1993. Review of ESP today: A practitioner's guide, by P. Robinson. *English for Specific Purposes.* 12.263–266.

Mauranen, A. 1993. *Cultural differences in academic rhetoric.* Frankfurt-am-Main: Peter Lang.

Mchala, N. 1999. The free economy of English: A tale. In M. Jabeur, A. Manai and M. Bahloul (eds.) *English in North Africa.* Tunis: TSAS Innovation Series, TSAS and the British Council. 77–94.

Najbi, M. 1997. Editorial: All effective language teaching is ESP. *MATE Newsletter.* 17.3.1. [Newsletter of the Moroccan Association of Teachers of English (MATE).]

O'Dwyer, J. (ed.) 1996. Quality management and the management of change: Paper presented at an international conference on management in English Language teaching. Ankara, Turkey, Bilkent University School of English Language, and IATEFL, November, 1995.

Oueslati, Z. 1998. An attempt to design a questionnaire to evaluate ESP teachers' use of the resources for teaching and research. Tunis: Institut Bourguiba des Langues Vivantes. D.E.S.S. Mémoire.

Payne, R. M. (ed.) 1979. *Papers on English for special purposes.* Tunis: Institut Bourguiba des Langues Vivantes.

Pennycook, A. 1997. Vulgar pragmatism, critical pragmatism, and EAP. *English for Specific Purposes.* 16.253–269.

Robinson, P. 1991. *ESP today: A practitioner's guide.* Englewood Cliffs, NJ: Prentice Hall.

Salager-Meyer, F. 1999. Referential behaviour in scientific writing: A diachronic study (1810–1995). *English for Specific Purposes.* 18.279–305.

Seymour, A. 1993. ESP in Tunisia. In *Maghreb ESP conference: Current initiatives in ESP in the Maghreb and future perspectives.* London: The British Council. 19–20.

——— and Bahloul, M. 1992. Project sustainability: A case study of the Tunisia ESP project. *ELT Management.* 8.2–6. [Newsletter of the IATEFL Management Special Interest Group.]

Shulman, L. 1988. The disciplines of enquiry in education: An overview. In R. Jager (ed.) *Complementary methods of research in education.* Washington, DC: American Educational Research Association.

St John, M. J. 1996. Business is booming: Business English in the 1990s. *English for Specific Purposes.* 15.3–18.

Swales, J. 1984. A review of ESP in the Arab world 1977–1983: Trends, developments and retrenchments. In J. Swales and H. Mustafa (eds.) *English for specific purposes in the Arab world.* Birmingham, UK: The Language Studies Unit, University of Aston in Birmingham.

——— 1988. *Episodes in ESP.* Hemel Hempstead, UK: Prentice Hall.

Swales, J. 1993. The English language and its teachers: Thoughts past, present, and future. *English Language Teaching Journal.* 47.283–291.

———— 1994. Human resource development in and for ESP. Paper presented at the 3rd National ESP Seminar 1994–95. Tunis: Ecole nationale d'ingénieurs. [Also published under the title: ESP in and for human resource development. *ESP Malaysia.* 2.1–18.]

———— 1997. English as Tyrannosaurus Rex. *World Englishes.* 16.373–382.

———— 1998. *Other floors, other voices: A textography of a small university building.* Mahwah, NJ: L. Erlbaum.

———— , B. Melander and K. Fredrickson. 1997. Journal abstracts from three academic fields in the United States and Sweden: National or disciplinary proclivities? In A. Duszak (ed.) *Intellectual styles and cross cultural communication.* Berlin: Mouton de Gruyter. 251–272.

Thomas, A. 1993. Future perspectives on ESP in the Maghreb: Language, teacher training and management. In *Maghreb ESP conference: Current initiatives in ESP in the Maghreb and future perspectives.* London: The British Council. 65–69.

Walters, K. 1999. "New year happy" : Some sociolinguistic observations on the way to the "Anglicization" of Tunisia. In M. Jabeur, A. Manai and M. Bahloul (eds.) *English in North Africa.* Tunis: TSAS Innovation Series, TSAS and the British Council. 33–63.

Weir, C. J. 1997. The selection of texts and tasks for teaching and testing EAP reading. Plenary presentation at the 1st National ESP Seminar 1997–98. Sousse, Tunisia: Faculty of Medicine, November 1997.

Widdowson, H. G. 1998. Communication and community: The pragmatics of ESP. *English for Specific Purposes.* 17.3–14.

LITERACY

WRITING, LITERACY, AND APPLIED LINGUISTICS*

Ilona Leki

INTRODUCTION

The first charge to the contributors to this volume was to consider applied linguistics from the point of view of the subfield each of us represents. Such a formulation constructs writing and literacy research as subordinate to the superordinate domain of applied linguistics and this was not one that corresponded well with my own sense of my work in relation to applied linguistics. To investigate this issue further, I informally questioned other writing researchers about whether or not they consider themselves applied linguists and what they do to be applied linguistics.

The small set of answers revealed quite a split, with one group of writing/literacy researchers immediately embracing applied linguistics and defining themselves as applied linguists (even wondering what else they could be). The attitude of the other (mainly North American) group was more agitated, almost denouncing applied linguistics as pointlessly aspiring to be scientific, overly oriented toward quantitative research on narrow, decontextualized issues, ideologically naive, and yet profiting from the cachet of linguistics and of science such that calling oneself (however resentfully) an applied linguist lent credibility to the work of researchers otherwise thought of under the less prestigious rubric of ESL. (See Vandrick's [1997] suggestion that ESL teachers at the tertiary level in the U.S. may sometimes even hide their own identities and attempt to "pass" as English or writing teachers rather than ESL teachers, many of whom at this level are basically writing/literacy teachers.)

The reasons for such an odd configuration of allegiances are probably historical. Since structural linguistics viewed spoken language as core, teaching L2 writing and reading was long considered primarily a means of reinforcing oral language learning. Thus, as applied linguistics split away from linguistics in the 1940s and 1950s to focus less on the science of language and more on language teaching (Grabe 1992), it began with a legacy of interest in spoken rather than written form. Furthermore, research in SLA (at least among those who do discourse analysis) has continued to focus on oral language, despite the fact that probably most adult and many adolescent L2 learners depend heavily on written forms to further L2 language development.[1] This applied linguistics focus on oral forms created a potential for the separation of the two sister fields of applied linguistics and L2 writing/literacy research.

L2 writing/literacy research was soon also separated from another sister field, L1 English writing research. In his account of the decoupling of English L1 and L2 writing research in the U.S., Matsuda (1998; 1999) documents the initial links between English L1 and L2 writing practitioners at the tertiary level based on the English L1 practitioners' concern to serve all students in their classes who were not experienced in writing in English. The disintegration of those links coincided with the birth of TESOL in 1966, which underscored a perceived need for specialist (i.e., applied linguistics) training in order to teach L2 writing. Consequently, English L1 and L2 writing/reading focuses diverged. Matsuda describes the sad last meetings of the applied linguists at the Conference on College Composition and Communication (CCCC, an English L1 organization), as interest in L2 writing waned among English L1 professionals. The division of labor was symbolically completed (at least at the official macro-level) when no one attended the 1965 CCCC workshop on L2 writing, and the discouraged organizers abandoned plans for future workshops.

Most L2 literacy teachers at that time had no specific training in teaching reading or writing, and had they looked to research for insights, they would have found justification for a bottom up, sentence-level, and contrastive rhetoric orientation. Thus, L2 writing and reading continued to be taught throughout most of the 1970s with an applied linguistics (i.e., a formalist) orientation and those few who published work on L2 writing no doubt considered themselves something like applied linguists. In the meantime, however, in L1 English, research into L1 writers, texts, and composing processes (such as Emig 1971 and Shaughnessy

1977) was changing L1 English writing instruction, and a new generation of L2 writing teachers in North America, dissatisfied with what they were sensing as not a very fruitful way to teach and evaluate L2 writing at the tertiary level, soon began to turn away from a linguistic approach and look to L1 perspectives for insights. Articles by Zamel (1976) and Raimes (1979) encouraged L2 writing teachers to reject, even despise, what became characterized as an ineffective and punitive-seeming approach to L2 writing, where the focus was not on communication but on correctness and where the L2 writer was necessarily cast as deficient. L2 writing teachers were exhorted to become writing teachers, not language teachers (aka, applied linguists), who were stigmatized as excessively, even exclusively focused on structure and error. In the new process approaches imported into L2 from L1 writing instruction, language concerns were grudgingly addressed almost as an afterthought only at the end of the writing process. Applied linguistics became, and for many remain, tainted with the stain of the old error-focused approaches.

Throughout the 1980s, L2 writing researchers became increasingly aware of how much was at stake in teaching/learning L2 writing. Of all the language skills or functions, only writing creates a product that can be examined independent of the physical presence of the L2 learner, disclosing student vulnerabilities that can easily remain hidden in L2 reading, for example (Leki 1993). The potential serious risks for the L2 writer may be at the core of the contentiousness that has characterized L2 writing research over the last 15 years. Although at first, the points of contention appeared to be various pedagogical issues, since the beginning of the 1990s, the debates have taken an ideological turn, starting with Santos' (1992) description of the L2 English writing profession as resolutely non-ideological compared to English L1 because of its roots in applied linguistics, and with Canagarajah's (1993) criticism of L2 writing researchers for not addressing ideological questions. Since that time, among L2 writing researchers, debates on such topics as EAP (Allison 1996, Benesch 1996, and Pennycook 1997), critical pedagogy (Benesch 1993), voice (Ramanathan and Kaplan 1996 and Raimes and Zamel 1997), individualism (Ramanathan and Atkinson 1999), and plagiarism (Pennycook 1994a) have been distinctly ideological.

Despite spirited and convincing depictions of mainstream applied linguistics (Grabe 1994, Grabe and Kaplan 1992) as drawing on many social-science traditions, recent criticisms of applied linguistics, from within the discipline itself, also seem to home in on perceptions of narrowness and failure to see research issues as embedded within broader educational, sociocultural, and ideological frames. As Pennycook (1996b) comments:

> One of the areas in [sic] which TESOL/applied linguistics has been slow to acknowledge as a fast-moving, fascinating, contentious, and "happening" area of research and speculation is in literacy. Whereas work around L2 literacy continues by and large to focus on the mechanics of reading and writing, a large body of work has focused on literacy within a far broader social and political context, viewing literacy as a social practice, as a central part of how we read the world, and as connected therefore to cultural frameworks and political access (1996b:163).

Literacy as social practice might here be juxtaposed against the idea of writing as "technology," which appears to represent a more mainstream applied linguistics view of writing (Grabe and Kaplan 1996). That applied linguistics continues a focus on "the mechanics of reading and writing" whereas L2 writing and literacy work has become more interested in literacy as social practice is perhaps materially seen in the fact that relatively little writing research appears in the main applied linguistics periodicals and much of what does appear could be characterized as quantitative in its methodologies. In fact, even the ideologically aware work of the genre researchers in Australia that Pennycook was reviewing in the citation above has offered until quite recently a relatively mechanical, overly simple answer to questions of empowerment through literacy: a relentless focus on genre, a form of literacy study which is seen, and sees itself, as squarely situated at the core of applied linguistics.

Lazaraton (1998) further notes that, despite a sense among some that applied linguistics is moving from "an essentially unquestioned reliance on and preference for quasi-experimental studies employing parametric statistics in the 1980s, to a broader, multidisciplinary perspective on research methodology, as well as the nature of research itself, in the 1990s" (1998:3), applied linguistics periodicals, except for the *TESOL Quarterly*, do not reflect this change. "From 92 percent to 97 percent of the articles [in the three journals she reviewed besides the *TESOL Quarterly*] are quantitative in nature" (p. 3), a state of affairs that might in part be a cause of " ... our increasingly pointed questions about the significance of our [applied linguistics] research (e.g., Rampton 1997)" (1998:3).

The pointed questions clearly suggest a dissatisfaction with the traditional applied linguistics paradigm and perhaps ways to break out of it. Larsen-Freeman (1997) sees in applied linguistics "a certain turmoil, a field in search of a new paradigm" (91), and McGroarty (1998) urges applied linguistics to take a lesson from what she calls the "constructivists" and include in its formulations greater awareness of the constructed nature of knowledge. In other words, L2 writing and literacy researchers who are dissatisfied with applied linguistics are not alone.

With these contested characterizations of applied linguistics in mind, I would like to propose three key areas in L2 writing/literacy research which are likely to be influential into the next decade. Some of this work draws fairly directly on applied linguistics traditions; some of it, on the other hand, might usefully contribute to alternative perspectives in the move to "postmodernize" applied linguistics. Finally, I will note areas where applied linguistics traditions might enhance L2 writing/ literacy research.

Because *ARAL* regularly reviews current work in L2 language teaching, rather than repeat the material in its 1998 volume, I refer readers to excellent review articles by Hudson and Cumming covering theoretical perspectives in reading and writing, Bamford and Day (reading) and Raimes (writing) on teaching, and Perkins (reading) and Kroll (writing) on testing. In proper postmodern fashion, in this review I do not claim to cover the range of contributions to L2 writing/ literacy research in some objective way that would somehow capture all its multiple facets. Nor can I feel confident that my choices would be those of others involved in L2 writing/literacy research. Rather I embrace the position that the perspective apparent in my choices here, as well as the views expressed, is contingent, dynamic, and necessarily limited by my own situatedness as an L2 writing researcher in North America.

NEEDS ANALYSIS

Within education more generally, and so also within applied linguistics, traditional needs analysis explores the context for literacy acquisition by examining the target. Genre studies overlap with needs analysis through their attempt to describe target texts (Swales 1990), although researchers like Berkenkotter and Huckin (1995), as well as Swales (1990) and Johns (1997), also situate genres within social contexts and as a response to them. Contrastive Rhetoric too is often a form of needs analysis, anathema to some L2 writing researchers because of its propensity to essentialize cultures (see discussion of identity, below), partly through its static representation of their written products and its implication that L2 writers too are little more than products of a static culture (see, for example, Kubota 1997; 1999). While Contrastive Rhetoric has become more subtle and its analyses more sophisticated and sensitive in its later years (Connor 1996), Scollon (1997) suggests that Contrastive Rhetoric is a misnomer since Contrastive Rhetoric has in fact never really engaged in a rhetorical analysis which would focus on persuasion and so encompass an analysis of audience. Such an analysis would of necessity include more sensitivity to context, and to shifting contexts, which would likely loosen the stasis of simply comparing one set of textual patterns to another, which Scollon terms contrastive poetics.

Within the context of academic writing, needs analyses like Leki and Carson (1994) and Carson, *et al.* (1992) attempt to determine the kinds of literacy demands L2 writers face at the tertiary level, presumably to then create L2 literacy classes more responsive to those needs. A very positive feature of these investigations is their inclusion of students' own views on their needs through surveys and interviews. However, needs analysis of this kind has been subject to cogent criticism by Benesch (1993; 1996), who in effect asks whose needs are actually served by the more traditional needs analyses and proposes, instead, a consideration of the broader political issues that created the "needs." In her analysis, for example, cutbacks in funding for education at her institution resulted in larger classes which, in turn, resulted in L2 learners having a more difficult time following a psychology professor's lectures. A traditional needs analysis would have led to the students being offered extra work on, perhaps, listening comprehension or vocabulary. In the critical needs analysis Benesch describes, it is the large class sizes and funding cutbacks that need to be addressed. The economic and political context, not the students, is the problem.

But problematizing traditional views takes other angles as well. Ramanathan and Kaplan (1996), for example, question the usefulness of the unexamined transfer from L1 to L2 writing instruction of the highly prized concept of voice. Similarly Atkinson (1997) deconstructs the notion of critical thinking in relation to L2 learners. (See also three responses to Atkinson by Davidson [1998], Gieve [1998], and Hawkins [1998].) In fact, the whole notion of literacy in L1 or L2 as an unblemished good has been severely challenged in several quarters (Grabe and Kaplan 1996, Purcell-Gates 1998, Street 1993, Stuckey 1991). In L2 settings, this negative perspective on literacy has dovetailed with Phillipson's (1992) applied linguistics work on linguicism and Pennycook's (1994b) challenge to the view that the acquisition of English worldwide is a neutral act, disengaged from political exigencies.

Within the L2 writing classroom, arguably the most potent aspect of the context for learning is the writing teacher's response to the students' writing. Ferris' (1997) and Ferris, et al.'s (1997) detailed studies of both L2 writing students' responses to teachers' markings and the revisions that subsequently resulted are important and extremely useful works, with direct applications to classroom teaching. But in a less traditional applied linguistics mode, and in keeping with recent moves toward seeing more closely the humans who are the central actors in L2 literacy acquisition (and toward the growing consciousness of the complex variability across these humans and over time), Hyland (1998) and Severino (1993) use qualitative and context-sensitive research methodologies which counterbalance the inadequacies of a more distanced, and more generalizable, approach. In Hyland's (1998) case study of two L2 writers in New Zealand, we meet Samorn, who requested of her writing teacher a particular focus on grammatical errors but who (unrecognized by the teacher) became increasingly discouraged when her teacher in fact did as she asked. Severino (1993), on the other hand, demonstrates three different approaches (encouraging resistance, accommodation, or assimilation) she used in a writing center to respond to differing needs of three students. We see from this work that "needs" are complex, difficult to sort out, and may require a variety of responses.

Like the Ferris/Hyland/Severino explorations, particularly useful to developing an understanding of the intersection of theoretical issues, historical forces, and students' lives are combinations of studies that illuminate these intersections from different points of view. Pennycook's (1996a) historical examination of plagiarism in the Western literacy tradition and Currie's (1998) naturalistic study of one student's use of plagiarism to help her get through her course work at a Canadian university, mutually illuminate the terrain, grounding theoretical discussion in a real life.

Finally, from applied linguistics' traditional domain of error correction, Truscott (1996) reviews the published research and comes to the rather untraditional conclusion that error correction is probably useless and potentially harmful to L2 writing students. Here too, although Truscott does not pursue the angle, what is at issue is needs analysis, but no longer constructed as the mold into which students must be squeezed by instruction. What is implied in a rejection of error correction is that there is room for differential attainments at differential speeds.

Thus, the traditional domain of needs analysis, coming from education and overlapping in a variety of ways with applied linguistics research, has become more complex with the realization of competing needs and vested interests in defining and meeting those needs.

IDENTITY

A second theme of recent L2 writing/literacy research that will surely be expanded upon in the coming decade is related to identity issues. Identity "... will be a preoccupation in any period of intense change..." (Fairclough 1997:14) and probably becomes a particularly contested terrain whenever an individual moves into any new context. In a special issue of the *TESOL Quarterly* guest edited by Norton (1997) and devoted to L2 learner identity, Thesen (1997) calls into question critical discourse analysis of individuals as the hapless sites of struggles of competing discourses (although Critical Discourse Analysis has recently incorporated a greater interest in identity as well; see Fairclough 1997). With her intention to emphasize individual human agency in these struggles, her in-depth interviews with a group of students in South Africa show how multiple home literacies inform the development of academic literacy in play with the learners' strategic positioning of themselves in relation to the dominant target (here academic) discourse. The learners are central actors. They actively engage in calculating and manipulating just how far they want to go in pushing a particular identity for themselves. Ivanic (1998) too describes an adult learner who intermingles both active resistance to and acceptance of a particular kind of literacy (academic) in favor of another kind (professional) even within the same text, underscoring the hybridity of both texts and identities. These kinds of studies, because they are sensitive to context, work to complicate views of learners and work against the kind of essentializing that has been noted, sometimes vehemently, as a danger in cross-cultural studies. (See for example, Kubota 1997; 1999, Spack 1997c, Susser 1998; see also Atkinson, to appear, for a response.)

One potentially fruitful but underrepresented type of study is in-depth interviews and observational investigations by researchers who speak the same language as the research participants. Riazi (1997) explores the initiation of a group of Farsi-speaking graduate students into discourse and literacy demands of a Canadian college of education, and Kanno and Applebaum (1995) interview Japanese speaking students on their experiences of marginalization in a Canadian high school. Further such studies conducted in students' L1s can be anticipated and will be welcome.

In addition to examining others' identities, a perhaps growing trend has been to examine one's own identity conflicts both as a literacy learner (Bell 1995) and as a literacy teacher (Spack 1997b, Vandrick 1997). Studies like these potentially offer rich and intimate perceptions.

LONGITUDINAL STUDIES AS EXTENSIONS OF IDENTITY WORK

Portrayals of individuals' struggles with L2 literacy are greatly enhanced, as well as less liable to the dangers of overly simple cultural explanations of behaviors, when studies are conducted over time, allowing investigators and readers to see transitions to and shifts among different identities in response to different environmental pressures. Although such research is time consuming, a bank of studies focusing on real students, with names, over time, is developing (Mlynarczyk 1998, Smoke 1994).

Harklau's (1999; in press) study of four students' experiences in a U.S. high school poignantly describes their transition from being considered model students (obedient, quiet, respectful, cooperative) in high school to being labeled, instantly upon moving into tertiary education, ESL students, their whole identities summed up in their writing and language skills. We also see the teachers' misguided attempts to draw on the experiences of the students in the ESL writing class by encouraging them to contrast their experiences in the U.S. with their experiences at home. For Harklau's four students, home was the U.S.; they had no real experience of their previous residences to draw on, but by repeatedly pointing them toward those residences, their teachers constructed them as outsiders they did not feel they were.

Spack (1997a) follows the on-going development of academic literacy for a Japanese college student. Initially ascribing her difficulties to some sort of Japanese approach to education, this student comes to see and demonstrate her own multiple literacies reinforcing and interweaving with each other as she confronts a variety of literacy demands in college.

My own (Leki 1999) five-year study of the literacy experiences of a Polish-speaking student shows dramatically how his educational experiences, first in a U.S. high school and then in a university, served to create an approach to education that might be called self-defeating or perhaps opportunistic. As the student, Jan, struggles to negotiate what he increasingly intensely comes to see as meaningless institutional obstacles, he cynically learns to play whatever game it takes to pass courses.

While studies like these can be extremely illuminating, they inevitably entail serious issues of representation as students' identities are created in the text for readers by researchers. The constructed nature of knowledge is most easily apparent in such studies and, it is to be hoped, promotes sensitivity to the constructed nature of all forms of knowledge, including quantitative work. (See Mortensen and Kirsch 1996 for enlightening reflections on the ethics of reporting on in-depth studies.)

Oddly underrepresented in longitudinal research are in-depth, over-time studies of students' experiences in L2 literacy classes themselves, which would focus not on increased control over the language but on the whole experience— the interaction with other students, with the material, and with the teacher. We get a glimpse of one such set of experiences in Malicka (1996), where students' initial enthusiasm for the L2 writing course changed to boredom and irritation, changes the teacher remained unaware of. (See Villalobos 1996; also see Toohey 1998 for an example with 5-7-year-olds.)

APPLIED LINGUISTICS' CONTRIBUTIONS TO L2 LITERACY RESEARCH

While mainstream applied linguistics itself has lamented the overrepresentation of English and monolingual English-speaking countries in its work, writing research probably suffers from this flaw even more so. Silva, Leki, and Carson (1997) chide L1 academic literacy researchers for their ethnocentric discussions of writing theories and processes, universalizing Western literacy contexts, and basing their conclusions about writing on the experiences of 18-year-old U.S. college students. They also assert that L2 studies can offer L1 academic literacy studies access to an expanded universe of literacy development (see also Muchiri, *et al.* 1995). But in fact, L2 literacy studies, like applied linguistics, are also far too English oriented. Clearly material conditions of scholarship that Canagarajah (1996) discusses play a role in creating the lopsided overemphasis on English from monolingual English-speaking countries. But mainstream applied linguistics, particularly in its consideration of language planning issues, has a great deal to offer literacy studies, helping to develop in literacy investigators a sense of the international contexts for literacy development both in L1 and L2. Parry and Su's (1998) book, for example, consists almost entirely of student-written explorations of literacy issues in China and combines information on language policy and planning with these graduate students' reflections on their own experiences as language learners and English teachers in technical training schools.

Efforts like the special issue of the *Journal of Asian Pacific Communication*, guest edited by Kaplan (1995), and devoted to literacy and language planning in countries of the Pacific rim, and Brock and Walter's (1993) volume also focusing on that part of the world, need to be expanded and supplemented with information from additional areas of the world and with more grounded descriptions of students' actual experiences. Dubin and Kuhlman (1992) represents an effort in this direction as does Purves' (1992) IEA study, one in reference to which Cumming and Riazi (1996) feel more L2 literacy researchers need to position their own work.

Finally, more traditional mainstream work in applied linguistics continues to bring detailed insights into writing processes (Roca de Larios, Murphy and Manchon 1999, Zimmermann in press), focusing particularly on how and when L1 is tapped during L2 text production. In spite of such progress, however, Cumming and Riazi (1996) remind us that we are as yet still in the embarrassing situation of having no suitable model for inquiry to inform educational practices, including writing instruction.

CONCLUSION

Parks and Maguire assert that in applied linguistics, context has been "evoked but not explored" (1999:144). It seems reasonable to expect that the next decade will bring about greater attention to the multiplicity and complexity of literacy acquisition, at least partly through more detailed, "thicker" descriptions of individual acquirers within specific and carefully specified contexts: These descriptions should include both immediate contexts of educational settings and personal histories (where, it is to be hoped, the voices—the words—of these acquirers will be heard much more than they have been to this point) as well as more distanced contexts of social, cultural, economic, political, and ideological environments. (See Pennycook 1997 and Benesch 1996 for discussions of excessively limited ideas about context.)

The acquisition of literacy, like the acquisition of English, is risky, and not an implicitly beneficial or even neutral undertaking. While education by its nature inevitably entails change, obviously not all change brought about by education is for the benefit of everyone. Some are left behind and excluded from political power and a variety of social and material benefits, often on the basis of differential literacy acquisition. Initiation into the literate worlds of alien cultures and technologies can also, for example, promote education in and knowledge about inappropriate technologies, ones that may be useful in the metropolitan countries of origin but (imported into non-urban countries by their own educated elite and oriented toward concerns of the center) are useless to the periphery. This type of change creates societies that are made "... permanent parasites on the developed countries for knowledge and information ... " (Pattanayak, p. vi, cited in Pennycook 1994b:21). Literacy acquisition can also create disjuncture between individuals' local or home culture and their new literate or academic culture. Maintaining a critical awareness of the dangers of literacy activities, that is, holding carefully and reflectively in mind the political and power-relation consequences of literacy activities means, as has been said many times before in the critical pedagogy literature, asking fundamental questions: Why are these people learning to read and/or write this language? What are they giving up? Who stands to benefit? Who will lose?

It seems essential that new applied linguists be carefully and thoroughly acquainted with the various critical discourses that probe and contest otherwise unexamined meaning-making structures like classrooms and educational institutions. The spread of English and the spread of literacy cannot be assumed to be benign. Without such exposure to critical discourses, applied linguists will be in unconscious complicity with the status quo, in effect, working to reproduce unjust social, economic, and political arrangements. Since the discourses that reproduce such structures are readily available (Pennycook 1997) and therefore tempting, and since the discourses that work against reproducing those structures are far less available and are often difficult to understand, an essential role for senior applied linguists is to help expose future applied linguists to contestatory discourses and, if necessary, help demystify the sometimes dense language that can discourage novices and lead to their dismissal of these points of view.

While I earlier characterized debates surrounding academic literacy issues as contentious, it is to be hoped, nevertheless, that debate can continue but also that the most powerful voices will not drown out or silence quieter contributions in pursuit of a single correct outlook. (See Belcher 1997 on the issue of nonadversarial argumentation.) While I am not suggesting some neoliberal acceptance of everyone's happy voices and native costumes, like biodiversity, ideational diversity permits the mutations that create new questions and options, and that, in turn, can lead toward a desirable "pluralisation of knowledge" (Pennycook 1997:263).

NOTES

* I would like to thank Dwight Atkinson for his challenging and insightful reading of this manuscript.

1. I am indebted to Linda Harklau for sharing her insights on this point with me. Although SLA has drifted away from the core of applied linguistics to follow an independent course with somewhat different preoccupations (Grabe and Kaplan 1992), its interest in oral forms remains influential in applied linguistics more generally.

ANNOTATED BIBLIOGRAPHY

Benesch, S. 1996. Needs analysis and curriculum development in EAP: An example of a critical approach. *TESOL Quarterly*. 30.723–738.

For readers wishing a lucid introduction to the project of critical pedagogy, Benesch offers a clear and compelling example from her own writing class. Although thoroughly grounded in theoretical issues, Benesch's account avoids the dense theoretical language of critical work, making her account accessible even to newcomers.

Harklau, L. In press. From the "good kids" to the "worst": Representations of English language learners across educational settings. *TESOL Quarterly*. 34.

Harklau offers a moving and convincing portrayal of a group of students in transition between high school and college in the U.S. whose identities are actively constructed for them by the institutions in which they find themselves. The construction of these students as foreigners, though well-meaning, contradicts and undermines their own developing sense of themselves as complex individuals and cultural hybrids.

Ivanic, R. 1998. *Writing and identity*. Philadelphia: J. Benjamins.

Through extensive interview and textual analysis, Ivanic explores the case of a writer between identities: her personal sense of herself as a budding social worker and an academic identity being pushed upon her as a student. Here again the account is eminently readable yet clearly conversant with pertinent theoretical issues.

Mortensen, P. and G. Kirsch. 1996. *Ethics and representation in qualitative studies of literacy*. Urbana, IL: National Council of Teachers of English.

This collection of reflections reporting on qualitative research cuts to the core of what it means to represent someone else publically in writing (and profit by it, if only in terms of professional esteem and promotion). It raises concerns about colonizing the other, confronting research participants with negative evaluations of themselves, and a number of other provocative issues.

Norton, B. (ed.) 1997. *Language and identity*. [Special issue of *TESOL Quarterly*. 31.3.]

This special-topic issue touches on a number of questions related to how identities are constructed and reconstructed through the process of language learning.

Pennycook, A. 1996a. Borrowing others' words: Text, ownership, memory and plagiarism. *TESOL Quarterly.* 30.201–230.

Pennycook offers here an example of the kind of work applied linguists might do that would work toward critical perspectives on teaching and research in L2 writing contexts. L2 professionals are called upon to see themselves as the cultural workers that they are and to embrace that identity through efforts such as this one, whose project is to demystify the unexamined assumptions in the West about plagiarism, that greatest of literary sins, which nevertheless has thrived throughout Western academic and literary life.

UNANNOTATED BIBLIOGRAPHY

Allison, D. 1996. Pragmatist discourse and English for academic purposes. *English for Specific Purposes.* 15.85–103.

Atkinson, D. 1997. A critical approach to critical thinking in TESOL. *TESOL Quarterly.* 31.71–94.

——— 1999. TESOL and culture. *TESOL Quarterly.* 33.625–654.

Bamford, J. and R. Day. 1998. Teaching reading. In W. Grabe, *et al.* (eds.) *Annual Review of Applied Linguistics, 18. Foundations of second language learning.* New York: Cambridge University Press. 124–141.

Belcher, D. 1997. An argument for nonadversarial argumentation: On the relevance of the feminist critique of academic discourse to L2 writing pedagogy. *Journal of Second Language Writing.* 6.1–21.

Bell, J. 1995. The relationship between L1 and L2 literacy: Some complicating factors. *TESOL Quarterly.* 29.687–704.

Benesch, S. 1993. ESL, ideology, and the politics of pragmatism. *TESOL Quarterly.* 27.705–717.

Berkenkotter, C. and T. Huckin. 1995. *Genre knowledge in disciplinary communication.* Hillsdale, NJ: L. Erlbaum.

Brock, M. and L. Walters (eds.) 1993. *Teaching composition around the Pacific rim.* Philadelphia: Multilingual Matters.

Canagarajah, S. 1993. Comment on Ann Raimes's "Out of the woods: Emerging traditions in the teaching of writing"; Up the garden path: Second language writing approaches, local knowledge, and pluralism. *TESOL Quarterly.* 27.301–306.

——— 1996. "Nondiscursive" requirements in academic publishing, material resources of periphery scholars, and the politics of knowledge production. *Written Communication.* 13.435–472.

Carson, J. 1998. Cultural backgrounds: What should we know about multilingual students?

TESOL Quarterly. 32.735–740.

Carson, J., N. Chase, S. Gibson and M. Hargrove. 1992. Literacy demands of the undergraduate curriculum. *Reading Research and Instruction.* 31.25–50.

Connor, U. 1996. *Contrastive rhetoric.* New York: Cambridge University Press.

Cumming, A. 1998. Theoretical perspectives on writing. In W. Grabe, *et al.* (eds.) *Annual Review of Applied Linguistics, 18. Foundations of second language teaching.* New York: Cambridge University Press. 61–78.

────── and A. Riazi. 1996. Building models of adult second-language writing instruction. Paper presented at the seminar: Second Language Acquisition and Writing. University of Southampton, July 1996.

Currie, P. 1998. Staying out of trouble: Apparent plagiarism and academic survival. *Journal of Second Language Writing.* 7.1–18.

Davidson, B. 1998. A case for critical thinking in the English language classroom. *TESOL Quarterly.* 32.119–123.

Dubin, F. and N. Kuhlman (eds.) 1992. *Cross-cultural literacy: Global perspectives on reading and writing.* Englewood Cliffs, NJ: Prentice Hall.

Emig, J. 1971. *The composing process of twelfth grader.* Urbana, IL: National Council of Teachers of English.

Fairclough, N. 1997. Discourse across disciplines: Discourse analysis in researching social change. *AILA Review.* 12.3–17.

Ferris, D. 1997. The influence of teacher commentary on student revision. *TESOL Quarterly.* 31.315–339.

────── , S. Pezone, C. Tade and S. Tinti. 1997. Teacher commentary on student writing: Descriptions and implications. *Journal of Second Language Writing.* 6.155–182.

Gieve, S. 1998. A reader reacts ... *TESOL Quarterly.* 32.123–129.

Grabe, W. 1992. Applied linguistics and linguistics. In W. Grabe and R. Kaplan (eds.) *Introduction to applied linguistics.* Reading, MA: Addison-Wesley. 35–58.

────── 1994. Applied linguistics. In A. Purves (ed.) *Encyclopedia of English studies and language arts.* New York: Scholastic Leadership Policy Research. 60–62.

────── and R. Kaplan (eds.) 1992. *Introduction to applied linguistics.* Reading, MA: Addison-Wesley.

────────────── 1996. *Theory and practice of writing.* New York: Longman.

Hawkins, M. 1998. Apprenticing nonnative speakers to new discourse communities. *TESOL Quarterly.* 32.129–132.

Hudson, T. 1998. Theoretical perspectives on reading. In W. Grabe, *et al.* (eds.) *Annual Review of Applied Linguistics, 18. Foundations of second language teaching.* New York: Cambridge University Press. 43–60.

Hyland, F. 1998. The impact of teacher-written feedback on individual writers. *Journal of Second Language Writing.* 7.255–286.

Johns, A. 1997. *Text, role, and context.* New York: Cambridge University Press.

Kanno, Y. and S. Applebaum. 1995. ESL students speak up: Their stories of how we are doing. *TESL Canada Journal.* 12.32–49.

Kaplan, R. (ed.) 1995. *The teaching of writing in the Pacific basin.* [Special issue of *Journal of Asian Pacific Communication.* 6.1/2.]

Kroll, B. 1998. Assessing writing abilities. In W. Grabe, *et al.* (eds.) *Annual Review of Applied Linguistics, 18. Foundations of second language teaching.* New York: Cambridge University Press. 219–240.

Kubota, R. 1997. A reevaluation of the uniqueness of Japanese written discourse. *Written Communication.* 14.460–480.

———— 1999. Japanese culture constructed by discourses: Implications for Applied Linguistics research and ELT. *TESOL Quarterly.* 33.9–35.

Larsen-Freeman, D. 1997. Impressions of AILA 1996. *AILA Review.* 12.87–92.

Lazaraton, A. 1998. Research methods in Applied Linguistics. *TESOL Research Interest Section Newsletter.* 5.2.3.

Leki, I. 1993. Reciprocal themes in ESL reading and writing. In J. Carson and I. Leki (eds.) *Reading in the composition classroom: Second language perspectives.* Boston: Heinle & Heinle. 9–32.

———— 1999. "Pretty much I screwed up" : Ill-served needs of a permanent resident. In L. Harklau, K. Losey and M. Siegal (eds.) *Generation 1.5 meets college composition.* Mahwah, NJ: L. Erlbaum. 17–43.

———— and J. Carson. 1994. Students' perceptions of EAP writing instruction and writing needs across the disciplines. *TESOL Quarterly.* 28.81–101.

Losey, K. 1997. *Listen to the silences.* Norwood, NJ: Ablex.

Malicka, A. 1996. Tasks, interaction, affect, and the writer's development: A descriptive study of an ESL composition class. Indiana University of Pennsylvania. Ph.D. diss.

Matsuda, P. 1998. Situating ESL writing in a cross-disciplinary context. *Written Communication.* 15.99–121.

———— 1999. Composition studies and ESL writing: A disciplinary division of labor. *College Composition and Communication.* 50.699–721.

McGroarty, M. 1998. Constructive and constructivist challenges for Applied Linguistics. *Language Learning.* 48.591–622.

Mlynarczyk, R. 1998. *Conversations of the mind.* Mahwah, NJ: L. Erlbaum.

Nelson, G. 1998. Categorizing, classifying, labeling: A fundamental cognitive process. *TESOL Quarterly.* 32.727–735.

Parks, S. and M. Maguire. 1999. Coping with on-the-job writing in ESL: A constructivist-semiotic perspective. *Language Learning*. 29.143–175.

Parry, K. and X. Su (eds.) 1998. *Culture, literacy, and learning English*. Portsmouth, NH: Boynton/Cook.

Pennycook, A. 1994a. The complex contexts of plagiarism: A reply to Deckert. *Journal of Second Language Writing*. 3.277–284.

———— 1994b. *The cultural politics of English as an international language*. New York: Longman.

———— 1996b. TESOL and critical literacies: Modern, Post, or Neo? *TESOL Quarterly*. 30.163–171.

———— 1997. Vulgar pragmatism, critical pragmatism, and EAP. *English for Specific Purposes*. 16.253–269.

Perkins, K. 1998. Assessing reading. In W. Grabe, *et al.* (eds.) *Annual Review of Applied Linguistics, 18. Foundations of second language teaching*. New York: Cambridge University Press. 208–218.

Phillipson, R. 1992. *Linguistic imperialism*. Oxford: Oxford University Press.

Purcell-Gates, V. 1998. Literacy at home and beyond. Paper presented at the Watson Conference on Rhetoric and Composition. Louisville, KY, October 1998.

Purves, A. 1992. *The IEA study of written composition*. New York: Pergamon Press.

Raimes, A. 1979. *Problems and teaching strategies in ESL composition*. Arlington, VA: Center for Applied Linguistics.

———— 1998. Teaching writing. In W. Grabe, *et al.* (eds.) *Annual Review of Applied Linguistics, 18. Foundations of second language teaching*. New York: Cambridge University Press. 142–167.

———— and V. Zamel. 1997. Response to Ramanathan and Kaplan. *Journal of Second Language Writing*. 6.79–81.

Ramanathan, V. and D. Atkinson. 1999. Individualism, academic writing, and ESL writers. *Journal of Second Language Writing*. 8.45–75.

———— and R. Kaplan. 1996. Audience and voice in current L1 composition texts: Some implications for ESL writers. *Journal of Second Language Writing*. 5.21–34.

Rampton, B. 1997. Second language research in late modernity. *Modern Language Journal*. 81.329–333.

Riazi, A. 1997. Acquiring disciplinary literacy: A social-cognitive analysis of text production and learning among Iranian graduate students of education. *Journal of Second Language Writing*. 6.105–137.

Roca de Larios, J., L. Murphy and R. Manchon. 1999. The use of restructuring strategies in EFL writing: A study of Spanish learners of English as a Foreign Language. *Journal of*

Second Language Writing. 8.13–44.

Santos, T. 1992. Ideology in composition: L1 and ESL. *Journal of Second Language Writing.* 1.1–15.

Scollon, R. 1997. Contrastive rhetoric, contrastive poetics, or perhaps something else? *TESOL Quarterly.* 31.352–358.

Severino, C. 1993. The sociopolitical implications of response to second language and second dialect writing. *Journal of Second Language Writing.* 2.181–201.

Shaughnessy, M. 1977. *Errors and expectations.* New York: Oxford University Press.

Silva, T., I. Leki and J. Carson. 1997. Broadening the perspective of mainstream composition studies. *Written Communication.* 14.398–428.

Smoke, T. 1994. Writing as a means of learning. *College ESL.* 4.1–11.

Spack, R. 1997a. The acquisition of academic literacy in a second language. *Written Communication.* 14.3–62.

———— 1997b. The (in)visibility of the person(al) in academe. *College English.* 59.9–31.

———— 1997c. The rhetorical construction of multilingual students. *TESOL Quarterly.* 31.765–774.

Street, B. (ed.) 1993. *Cross-cultural approaches to literacy.* New York: Cambridge University Press.

Stuckey, J. 1991. *The violence of literacy.* Portsmouth, NH: Boynton/Cook.

Susser, B. 1998. EFL's othering of Japan: Orientalism in English language teaching. *JALT Journal.* 20.49–82.

Swales, J. 1990. *Genre analysis.* New York: Cambridge University Press.

Thesen, L. 1997. Voices, discourse, and transition: In search of new categories in EAP. *TESOL Quarterly.* 31.487–511.

Toohey, K. 1998. "Breaking them up, taking them away": ESL students in Grade 1. *TESOL Quarterly.* 32.61–84.

Truscott, J. 1996. The case against grammar correction in L2 writing classes. *Language Learning.* 46.327–369.

Vandrick, S. 1997. The role of hidden identities in the postsecondary ESL classroom. *TESOL Quarterly.* 31.153–157.

Villalobos, J. 1996. Process-oriented approach to writing: A case study of a writing class in English as a second language (ESL) at the college level. Iowa City, IA: University of Iowa, Ph.D. diss.

Zamel, V. 1976. Teaching composition in the ESL classroom: What can we learn from research in the teaching of English. *TESOL Quarterly.* 10.67–76.

Zimmermann, R. In press. Formulating in L2 writing: Towards an empirical model. *Learning and Instruction.* 10.

DESIGN AND PRACTICE: ENACTING FUNCTIONAL LINGUISTICS

James R. Martin

LINGUISTICS AS SOCIAL ACTION

I have tried to practice linguistics as a form of social action, a practice which Halliday (e.g., 1985) has suggested cannot be other than ideologically committed. This practice dissolves the linguistics vs. applied linguistic opposition which has evolved in response to the hegemony of American formalism—whose idealizing reductivity comes nowhere near serving the needs of language users and their aids around the world. In its stead, linguistics as social action engages theory with practice in a dialectic whereby theory informs practice which, in turn, rebounds on theory, recursively, as more effective ways of intervening in various processes of semogenesis are designed (Martin 1997; 1998a). My own experience of this engagement has been mainly in the field of literacy, especially of writing development in primary and secondary school. Accordingly, I'll draw on this experience to address the sub-field 'Writing and Literacy,' writing as a linguist working across what is generally read and has been increasingly institutionalized as an applied vs. theoretical frontier.

WRITING DEVELOPMENT

The transdisciplinary literacy research to which I am referring evolved as an action research project in and around Sydney from 1979 (reviewed in Christie 1992, Cope and Kalantzis 1993, Martin 1993; 1998b, Rothery 1989; 1996), involving at key stages the Linguistics Department at the University of Sydney and the Metropolitan East Region of the New South Wales Disadvantaged Schools program.

Our goal, as educational linguists, was to intervene in the process of writing development in primary and secondary school across various depths of time. As far as logogenesis was concerned, we attempted to provide students with knowledge about language (Carter 1996) that they could use in reading, writing, and editing. As for ontogenesis, we worked with teachers on the design of curriculum (learner pathways) and pedagogy (classroom activity). Finally, with respect to phylogenesis, we were committed to a redistribution of literacy resources and critical language awareness (Fairclough 1992) which we hoped would emancipate the meaning potential of the students we were working with, with a view to giving them ways of redesigning their world. To date, we have had some impact on the first two of these frames for intervention; only time will tell the extent to which the work has been socially empowering for the non-mainstream students involved.

To inform our interventions, we drew on the functional model of language in social context evolving around the work of Halliday (1994), especially the notion of genre (Martin 1992).[1] Genre was used to redesign both curriculum and pedagogy. As far as curriculum was concerned, we worked in secondary schools for example, to map disciplines as systems of genres (e.g., Coffin 1996; 1997, Veel and Coffin 1996 for secondary school history). From these maps, we developed learner pathways[2] as a guide for moving students through the uncommon sense discourses of the discipline. Our secondary school history pathway is outlined in Table 1.

The pathway begins with various recount genres designed to reconstruct personal and vicarious experience; it moves on through genres concerned with explaining cause and effect; it continues with argumentative genres; and it culminates with Foucauldian genealogy. (The general stages in each genre are indicated in brackets.) One critical factor in this development is the mobilization of grammatical metaphor (Halliday 1994; 1998, Halliday and Martin 1993, Martin 1993, Martin and Veel 1998)—resources for nominalizing processes, qualities, and modal assessments and resources for realizing logico-semantic connections inside the clause. Our work in this project convinced us that learning to read and write discourse heavily dependent on grammatical metaphor was the main linguistic task for teachers and students in secondary school; it is through grammatical metaphor that every discipline and institution we considered evolves the discourses which construe specialized knowledge and regulate populations (Christie and Martin 1997).

Table 1: Learner pathway for secondary school history genres (by genre [including staging] and language features)

GENRE [staging]	INFORMAL DESCRIPTION	KEY LINGUISTIC FEATURES (Halliday 1994, Martin 1992)
personal recount [Orientation^Record]	agnate to story genres; what happened to me	sequence in time; 1st person; specific participants
autobiographical recount [Orientation^Record]	borderline - agnate to story & factual genres; story of my life [oral history]	setting in time; 1st person; specific participants
biographical recount [Orientation^Record]	story of someone else's life	setting in time; 3rd person (specific); other specific & generic participants
historical recount; [Background^Record]	establishing the time line of the grand narrative	setting in time; 3rd person; mainly generic participants (but specific great 'men')
historical account; [Background^Account]	naturalizing linearization rendering the grand narrative inevitable	incongruent external causal unfolding; 3rd person; mainly generic participants; prosodic judgement
factorial explanation [Outcome^Factors]	complexifying notion of what leads on to/from what	internal organization of factors; factors externally linked to outcome; 3rd person; mainly generic participants
consequential explanation [Input^Consequences]	complexifying notion of what leads on to/from what; hypothetical variant - if x, then these outcomes	internal organization of factors; consequences externally linked to input; 3rd person; mainly generic participants
exposition - one-sided; promote [Thesis^Arguments]	problematic interpretation that needs justifying	internal conjunction keying on thesis

continued

challenge-one-sided; rebut [Position^Rebuttal]	someone else's problematic interpretation that needs demolishing	internal conjunction keying on thesis
discussion - multi-sided; adjudicate [Issue^Sides^Resolution]	more than one interpretation considered	internal conjunction keying on thesis; + internal organization of points of view
deconstruction [Foucault]	avoiding reductive temporal & causal linearization into grand narrative, effacing voices of the 'other' ...	replace naturalizing time/cause explanation with 'spatial' discursive formation realizing episteme

As for pedagogy, in order to provide the scaffolding needed to move learners along pathways of this kind, a teaching/learning cycle was developed, and refined for secondary school along the lines of Figure 1 (from Rothery and Stenglin 1994:8). In this model, setting up the social context of the genre and building field-knowledge are generalized across all stages of the model (Deconstruction, Joint Construction, and Independent Construction). The point of this cycle is to emphasize the instrumentality of shared understandings about disciplines/institutions in their cultural contexts for scaffolding to proceed effectively (Martin 1998b). In order to establish effective zones of proximal development, in other words, the knowledge that teachers and students can all assume is vital.

In addition, the goal of the model is explicitly oriented to both control of, and a critical orientation to, the discourse under consideration. This goal reflects a concern that genres be taught as part of a critical language awareness program (Fairclough 1992, Hasan and Williams 1996) which gives students opportunities to critique and renovate genres alongside mobilizing them to interrogate power relations in the culture (Christie and Misson 1998).

Bernstein's work on pedagogic discourse (Bernstein 1990, Christie 1998) provides a model for considering this pedagogy in relation to alternative positions in their idealized form, as reviewed for *ARAL* in Martin (1993).

Janks (in press) suggests a comprehensive framework for assessing language in education interventions of this kind, organized around the issues of access,

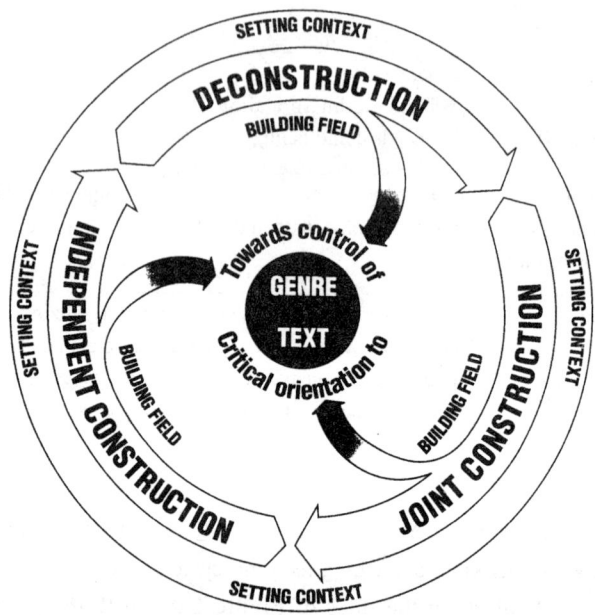

Figure 1. A teaching/learning cycle for secondary school
(from Rothery and Stenglin 1994:8)

dominance, diversity, and design. In relation to genre-based initiatives, access focuses attention on the extent to which pedagogy and curriculum redistribute control of genres to non-mainstream groups. Dominance deals with issues of power—which genres are selected, how critically is their social function addressed? Diversity considers the range and hybridity of subjectivities involved in institutional learning, for example, divergent orientations to literacy, and the problem of valuing non-mainstream discourses at the same time as offering access to mainstream ones. Design takes up the question of creativity and innovation: Does renovation indeed depend on mastery of a genre, and how do we provide opportunities for students to rework genres in line with their interests and goals? Our experience is that the approach to curriculum and pedagogy outlined above is flexible enough to address issues of this kind (Callow 1999). Naturally, some measure of redesign is to be expected as it is recontextualized in new social environments, for example, the challenge of reconstruction in South Africa, as outlined by Janks.

BEYOND GENRE

Functional linguistics is concerned with relating language to the social in a motivated way. The utility of genre theory in language education derives from its articulation as recurrent configurations of meanings, so that the social (genres) can be naturally related to language (meanings). Interventions in Australia have tended to move into education from the genre, and then move on to look more closely at meaning as resources permit. Underpinning genre with functional grammar has turned out to be a vexing political issue, with the print and electronic media and politicians voicing a variety of reactionary concerns (see Martin 1997 for discussion). And not much progress has been made with bringing discourse analysis (e.g., cohesion, following Martin 1992) and register analysis (e.g., Christie and Martin 1997, Eggins and Slade 1997, Martin and Veel 1989) into schools by way of mediating the connection between grammatical meaning and genre. Clearly, the next phase of intervention will have to address the problem of constructing functional grammar, discourse analysis, and register analysis as tools for teachers and students to use when relating language to the social, whether as part of literacy programs, or as subject-specific learning across the curriculum. Hasan's elaboration of Bernstein's work on coding orientations (e.g., Hasan 1996) will also have a critical role to play, especially in relation to Janks' diversity issue noted above.

Strong contributions are also to be expected in the area of evaluative language (Martin 1999b on appraisal), where frameworks have now been developed that systematically account for the construction of value in texts. This focus on attitude (embracing affect, ethics, and aesthetics) helps balance the ideational bias which often colors discourse analysis, especially where factual writing is concerned. It also calls into focus the issue of subjectivity and reading position, since evaluative language is so patently sensitive to class, gender, ethnicity, and generation; as such, it provides additional scope for incorporating critical language awareness into language-in-education programs (as encouraged by the various papers in Fairclough 1992).

Alongside appraisal, multimodal text analysis is generating considerable interest (following Kress and van Leeuwen 1996, van Leeuwen 1999). Callow (1999) shows how a concern with both the verbiage and the image can be incorporated in various ways into the primary-school curriculum. Once we add sound and music to the picture, then a rich framework for considering texts from a wide range of registers inside and outside the school is enabled. One of the intriguing developments in this work has been the use of image analysis as a way into the analysis of language, especially functional grammar. The pedagogical implications of this reorientation should be a fertile area of Australian action research in the next decade.

Alongside the expansion of resources for analysis, new sites for intensive intervention seem to be emerging as we struggle to rebuild our post-colonial world. One Australian site has to do with English literacy for indigenous people; Brian Gray, Wendy Cowey, and David Rose are currently developing relevant curricula and pedagogy as part of a well-funded federal initiative, initially in South Australia (Gray and Cowey 1999). The South African challenge of providing access to education to the 'lost generation' is also of immense significance (Hart 1999). I would expect these sites of reconstruction and reconciliation, and related sites around the world, to pose challenges for the dialectic of theory and practice in language education. The dialectics will reshape our conception of what language education is about and how educational linguistics can help out.

DIALOGUE

We have been asked to comment on obstacles to our field (by the editor), and I can sum up my perspective in this regard around the theme of dialogue. For linguistics as social action to be effective, it has to evolve—to be recontextualized in relation to new problems and in relation to informing theories (Martin 1998a). To get this kind of dialectic working, we have to communicate across frontiers, as part of transdisciplinary initiatives. Based on past experiences, an interdisciplinary endeavour is unsatisfactory. Dividing up a problem so that it can be addressed by different theories doesn't encourage the dialogue we need. Rather, we need to move beyond difference towards overlapping and intruding expertise (Martin 1997). In Australia, for example, our efforts thrived in proportion to the amount of linguistics our educators could learn, and the amount of educational theory and practice our linguists could absorb. We tried to develop a linguistic theory of learning (genre-based pedagogy) and a linguistic theory of knowledge (genre-based curriculum); or, turning this around, we had to reconceive language development as pedagogy and social context as curriculum for purposes of institutionalized learning.

Looking forward (Wells 1994), ideal partners in a transdisciplinary dialogue of the kind I have in mind here would be systemic functional linguistics (SFL) and neo-Vygotskyan learning theory (the Mind, Culture, and Activity group [MCA] anchored by Cole and Wertsch). The SFL community starts with language and tries to interpret activity, image, and sound as meaning; the MCA group starts with action, and tries to interpret language as activity (with genres as cultural artifacts for example; Kamberelis and Bovino 1999). SFL and Critical Discourse Analysis (CDA) would also be promising partners. To the extent that regionality, technicality, and power-infested human foibles of various kinds discourage dialogue of this kind, then, to that extent, the evolution of linguistics as social action will be impeded—at the expense of those it is trying to serve. I see the lack of dialogue as our major obstacle.

The emergence of the field of applied linguistics itself is a major problem in this regard, since it symbolizes the alienation of formal linguistics from the needs of the community. I personally find it hard to imagine how a centripetal formalist linguistic discourse, however hegemonic it now appears, can withstand the marketing pressures of economic rationalism. For me, it puts the discipline of linguistics itself at risk—leaving it perhaps to applied linguists to rebuild departments a generation hence. This dialogic gulf is fraught with challenges and needs to be faced by linguists looking back to the examples of Fries and Pike and Firth for inspiration so that some disciplinary reconciliation might get under way (a kick-start is probably overdue).

One final obstacle I would like to highlight, concerns the lack of what I call positive discourse analysis (Martin 1999c). By this, I mean discourse analysis, however informed, which focuses on social change and how it comes about. It seems to me that we have no end of critical discourse analysis which focuses on power and how it oppresses. What we are lacking is a complementary focus on how social subjects design change—how Mandela and the ANC achieved their goals, how feminists have renovated our world, how Irish Catholics in Australia mobilized across social class, and so on. If we understood change for the better, then we could use these understandings to inform our interventions in whatever practice is undertaken. We could stop being so monologically depressing all the time when talking about language and power. More Foucault please, complementing Gramsci. We need to take heart in pursuit of our ideals.

METALANGUAGE

I also would like to comment on the training and development of future generations. I have strong views in this regard, and they run against the grain of current practice, which tends to emphasize eclecticism. This practice seems to be driven by the idea that no single theory can serve all needs; and so practitioners need to take a little speech act theory here, a little conversation analysis there, some critical discourse analysis here, a little variation theory there, some language acquisition here, a little gender analysis there...until a range of pressing problems are somehow addressed. The problem with this catholic approach is that applied linguists end up as pidgin speakers of a range of theories, with theory so divorced from practice that any possibility of creolization is pretty much foreclosed. For eclecticists, the possibility of a genuine theory/practice dialectic is simply out of reach. Ultimately, this approach de-professionalizes the applied linguistics community as a whole.

Alternatively, perhaps complementing eclecticism, we could encourage the institution of a metalinguistic lingua franca, a common theoretical language shared across the community for purposes of working together on problems and feeding practice back into theory. For this investment to be worthwhile, the theory selected will have to repay the costs of both its technicality and the boundaries it places on what can be thought. In this regard, we should perhaps recall Kenneth Pike and the development of tagmemics in relation to bible translation around the world. Two critical properties of Pike's designs were (i) extravagance (a model of language in relation to a unified theory of the structure of human behavior), and (ii) fractality (redeployment of theoretical concepts across levels and modalities).

Currently, the model which most clearly partakes of these properties and which is already emerging as a lingua franca for discourse-oriented applied linguistics is Systemic Functional Linguistics, as developed by Halliday and his colleagues around the world. The best resourced part of this framework is Halliday's functional grammar (1994), which I would therefore recommend as part of the training and development of future applied linguists. The concepts on which this grammar is based are mobile ones, and can be redeployed across languages (Caffarel, *et al.* in press), across levels (including phonology, discourse, and context), and across modalities (including image, sound, music, and action). The model has also proven itself to be a practical one, regularly redeployed across an expanding range of practices (e.g., language teaching, forensics, museology, psychosis, computational linguistics, and so on; see Unsworth 1999.) Over time, I believe, the cost of learning the new terminology and theoretical design of SFL can be repaid.

In our post-Fordist information society, training has to include re-training: Pre-training is simply an initiation into a lifetime of in-service education. This expectation puts an additional pressure of adaptability on any *lingua franca* we promote. Future applied linguists need a flexi-theory they can adapt to new concerns; pre-training can't cover all contingencies, and it's just too costly to learn a new theory on the go for each new job.

Alongside SFL, how many serious contenders do we have for the lingua franca that I think we need? If none, why none? How can we encourage their development if SFL isn't up to the job?

Developing an adaptive framework for applied linguistics is one great challenge for a new millennium! The other great challenge, along with keeping their own house in order, is that applied linguists will have the job of resuscitating linguistics as a discipline—one with a more socially responsible role to play in a post-colonial, post-modern world.

NOTES

1. Our social perspective on genre evolved from 1980 in ways that resonate with work by Berkenkotter and Huckin (1993), Kamberelis and Bovino (1999), Miller (1984), Russell (1997), and Swales (1990); the development of the model is reviewed in Martin (1999a).

2. We would not argue that every student follow this pathway precisely, but we would point out that genres further along tend to presuppose resources in preceding genres and that this meaning potential has to be developed in other ways if the genres in question are in some sense 'skipped.'

UNANNOTATED BIBLIOGRAPHY

Berkenkotter, C. and T. N. Huckin. 1993. Rethinking genre from a sociocognitive perspective. *Written Communication.* 10.475–509.

Bernstein, B. 1990. *Class, codes and control 4: The structuring of pedagogic discourse.* London: Routledge.

Caffarel, A., J. R. Martin and C. M. I. M. Matthiessen (eds.) In press. *Language typology: A functional perspective.* Amsterdam: J. Benjamins.

Callow, J. 1999. *Image matters: Visual texts in the primary classroom.* Sydney: Primary English Teacher Association [PETA].

Carter, R. 1996. Politics and knowledge about language: The LINC project. In R. Hasan and G. Williams (eds.) *Literacy in society.* London: Longman. 1–28.

Christie, F. 1992. Literacy in Australia. In W. Grabe, *et al.* (eds.) *Annual Review of Applied Linguistics, 12. Literacy.* New York: Cambridge University Press. 142–155.

─────── (ed.) 1998. *Pedagogy and the shaping of consciousness: Linguistic and social processes.* London: Cassell.

─────── and J. R. Martin. 1997. *Genres and institutions: Social processes in the workplace and school.* London: Pinter.

─────── and R. Misson. 1998. *Literacy and schooling.* London: Routledge.

Coffin, C. 1996. *Exploring literacy in school history.* Sydney: Metropolitan East Disadvantaged Schools Program.

─────── 1997. Constructing and giving value to the past: An investigation into secondary school history. In F. Christie and J. R. Martin (eds.) *Genres and institutions: Social processes in the workplace and school.* London: Pinter. 196–230.

Cope, W. and M. Kalantzis (eds.) 1993. *The powers of literacy: A genre approach to teaching literacy.* London: Falmer. [Distributed in the U.S. by University of Pittsburg Press.]

Eggins, S. and D. Slade. 1997. *Analysing casual conversation.* London: Cassell.

Fairclough, N. (ed.) 1992. *Critical language awareness.* London: Longman.

Gray, B. and W. Cowey. 1999. *Book orientation: The potential (Scaffolding literacy with indigenous children in school).* Canberra: Schools and Community Centre, University of Canberra.

Halliday, M. A. K. 1985. Systemic Background. In J. D. Benson and W. S. Greaves (eds.) *Systemic perspectives on discourse. Volume 1: Selected theoretical papers from the 9th International Systemic Workshop.* Norwood, NJ: Ablex. 1–15.

─────── 1994. *An Introduction to functional grammar.* 2nd ed. London: Edward Arnold.

─────── 1998. Things and relations: Regrammaticising experience as technical knowledge. In J. R. Martin and R. Veel (eds.) *Reading science*. London: Routledge. 185–235.

Halliday, M. A. K. and J. R. Martin. 1993. *Writing science: Literacy and discursive power*. London: Falmer.

Hart, M. 1999. Opening doors: A genre-based introduction to academic literary for first-year South African university students (University of Natal). Paper presented at the 27th International Systemic Functional Congress. Singapore, 1999.

Hasan, R. 1996. *Ways of saying: Ways of meaning: Selected papers of Ruqaiya Hasan* (Edited by C. Cloran, D. Butt and G. Williams). London: Cassell.

——— and G. Williams (eds.) 1996. *Literacy in society*. London: Longman.

Janks, H. In press. We re-wrote the book: Constructions of literacy in South Africa. In R. Wodak, *et al.* (eds.) *Functional il/literacy*. Vienna: Verlag der Akadamie der Wissenschaften.

Kamberelis, G. and T. D. Bovino. 1999. Cultural artifacts as scaffolds for genre development. *Reading Research Quarterly*. 34.138–170.

Kress, G. and T. van Leeuwen. 1996. *Reading images: The grammar of visual design*. London: Routledge.

Martin, J. R. 1992. *English text: System and structure*. Amsterdam: J. Benjamins.

——— 1993. Genre and literacy: Modelling context in educational linguistics. In W. Grabe, *et al.* (eds.) *Annual Review of Applied Linguistics*, *13. Issues in teaching and learning*. New York: Cambridge University Press. 141–172.

——— 1997. Linguistics and the consumer: Theory in practice. *Linguistics and Education*. 9.409–446.

——— 1998a. Practice into theory: Catalysing change. In S. Hunston (ed.) *Language at work*. Clevedon, UK: Multilingual Matters. 151–167.

——— 1998b. Mentoring semogenesis: 'Genre-based' literacy pedagogy. In F. Christie (ed.) *Pedagogy and the shaping of consciousness: Linguistic and social processes*. London: Cassell. 123–155.

——— 1999a. Modelling context: The crooked path of progress in contextual linguistics (Sydney SFL). In M. Ghadessy (ed.) *Context: Theory and practice*. Amsterdam: J. Benjamins. 25–61.

——— 1999b. Beyond exchange: Appraisal systems in English. In S. Hunston and G. Thompson (eds.) *Evaluation in text: Authorial stance and the construction of discourse*. Oxford: Oxford University Press. 142–175.

——— 1999c. Grace: The logogenesis of freedom. *Discourse Studies*. 1.31–58.

——— and R. Veel (eds.) 1998. *Reading science: Critical and functional perspectives on discourses of science*. London: Routledge.

Miller, C. R. 1984. Genre as social action. *Quarterly Journal of Speech*. 70.151–167.

Rothery, J. 1989. Learning about language. In R. Hasan and J. R. Martin (eds.) *Language development: Learning language, learning culture*. Norwood, NJ: Ablex. 199–256.

———— 1996. Making changes: Developing an educational linguistics. In R. Hasan and G. Williams (eds.) *Literacy in society*. London: Longman. 86–123.

———— and M. Stenglin. 1994. *Spine-chilling stories: A unit of work for Junior Secondary English*. Sydney: Metropolitan East Disadvantaged Schools Program.

Russell, D. 1997. Rethinking genre in school and society: An activity theory analysis. *Written Communication*. 14.504–554.

Swales, J. 1990. *Genre analysis: English in academic and research settings*. Cambridge: Cambridge University Press.

Unsworth, L. (ed.) 1999. *Researching language in schools and communities: Functional linguistics approaches*. London: Cassell.

van Leeuwen, T. 1999. *Speech, music, sound*. London: Macmillan.

Veel, R. and C. Coffin. 1996. Learning to think like an historian: The language of secondary school history. In R. Hasan and G. Williams (eds.) *Literacy in society*. London: Longman. 191–231.

Wells, G. 1994. The complementary contributions of Halliday and Vygotsky to a 'language-based theory of learning.' *Linguistics and Education*. 6.41–90.

LANGUAGE POLICY AND LANGUAGE ASSESSMENT

LANGUAGE POLICY AND PLANNING

Sauli Takala and Kari Sajavaara

INTRODUCTION

The field of language policy and planning is clearly a sub-field within applied linguistics. It generally does not draw heavily on formal linguistics, except for aspects of corpus and status planning. However, it does draw extensively from a range of disciplines in order to plan, implement, and evaluate language policies that respond to the needs of stake holders of various types. Despite continuous development of the field, aspects of language policy and planning need to be developed further. One of the key areas where policy can be enhanced considerably is in the area of policy and planning evaluation. This direction of inquiry is also relevant to a number of other areas within applied linguistics.

In the present article, we will be concerned primarily with foreign language planning, that is, planned changes in foreign language instructional systems and in uses of languages in different social contexts (with special reference to the Nordic and Baltic countries). These planned changes may result from language policy decisions by relevant authorities and institutions. We have also chosen to focus, in particular, on the relationship between language planning and evaluation. The article will close with brief summaries of language policy developments in Nordic and Baltic countries.

At the outset, it should be pointed out that language planning decisions and language policies are not the only reason for the growth of a nation's total language capital. There are at least three more general reasons for such growth. First, globalization has resulted in an increased need and use of foreign languages. The most important factors include internationalized labor markets, communication media, internet, data banks, various types of international collaboration, foreign trade, and professional needs and training. It is quite evident that a fair amount of this activity centers around a small number of major languages, primarily English. For example, globalization of various industries and foreign trade has meant that many companies have adopted English as the language of their internal communication. A number of institutions have had a direct impact on the need and use of foreign languages. In Europe, the most important of these is the European Union, which has eleven official languages. This setting means that less widely used languages, such as Finnish for instance, have been assigned unprecedented functions in European community activities.

Second, explicit decisions by public authorities or various types of institutions have resulted in changes in policies. In 1995 in its White Book, the European Union, for instance, adopted an obective according to which all European citizens should learn at least two European languages in addition to their mother tongues. In Finland, such a decision was made in connection with the introduction of the Comprehensive School system in the early 1970s: All comprehensive school pupils have to study, in addition to their mother tongues, the other national language of the country and a foreign language. This language policy decision was not derived from language planning considerations; it was an outcome from a purely political deal between representatives of the Finnish Cabinet and the party representing a Swedish speaking minority in Finland. Similarly, all Finnish university graduates have to pass a test in the non-native domestic language which authorizes them to function as civil servants in bilingual areas in Finland. In this institutional category, we could also include various European Union exchange and cooperation programs which result in raised levels of foreign language competence through increased cross-language interactivity. This emphasis on bilingualism is an institutionalized counterpart to migration due to, for instance, unemployment, poverty, and restricted human rights.

Third, language capital is increased through people's private decisions to travel and migrate without any intervention by authorities. Tourism and employment abroad often result in prolonged interaction with speakers of other languages and in steady interest in other cultures, which may be a source of a more profound motivation to learn the languages concerned.

It is obvious, however, that language policy and planning efforts have become increasingly institutionalized activities because, as noted by a Finnish language planning committee in the early 1990s, political conflicts/issues can often be simultaneously language conflicts/issues and political conflicts/issues.

ISSUES IN LANGUAGE POLICY AND PLANNING

Applied linguistics has incorporated language policy and language planning as one of its many domains. The *Annua Review of Applied Linguistics* has made a valuable contribution by taking up the theme regularly (together with issues of bilingualism and multilingualism) in several volumes (at least in Volumes 2, 6, 10, 14, and 17). There have also been important pioneers in this field, including Haugen (1966), Kloss (1969), Tauli (1968), and Fishman (1974), to mention only a few prominent scholars. However, the field is not yet well-established and needs further development. It is posited here that language policy and language planning should, more systematically than in the past, draw on the work of policy studies in general and forge closer links with evaluation. It is argued that good planning needs good evaluation to inform it.

Planning can take many forms. Common sense suggests that some planning is better than other planning and some plans better than others. This raises the question of *criteria* that can be properly used to evaluate planning and plans. It is not possible to elaborate on this topic here. It can only be briefly noted that criteria involve at least the following four issues: 1) the set-up of the planning system (stakeholder perspective); 2) the principles, values, and procedures applied during planning (e.g., equality, fairness, factual and comprehensive data, hearing of experts); 3) public review and discussion of plans; and 4) adequate monitoring and evaluation of plan implementation and of potential unplanned (and undesirable) side effects.

Planning can take place in a variety of settings. One possible way of looking at the situation is a typology suggested some thirty years ago by Thompson and Tuden (1959). Parties involved may either agree or disagree on facts and on values. If there is agreement on values and facts, programmatic plans/decisions can be made, basically in a bureaucratic structure. This is hardly a common situation, however, as far as language policy and planning is concerned. If there is agreement on values but not on facts, pragmatic plans/decision can be made, often in a collegial structure. If there is agreement on facts but not on values, bargained plans/decisions can be made in a representative structure. If there is no agreement on either values or facts, plans/decisions are largely ad hoc in an anomic structure.

Another aspect worth considering—as implied by Kaplan (1994), for example—is to try to proceed from country and regional analyses to "universal" analysis in order to discover similarities and differences, leading to useful typologies and perhaps ultimately universal principles. In fact, Kaplan, in collaboration with Baldauf has recently made considerable progress in this direction in the recent volume, *Languag planning: From practice to theory* (1997), which represents a major contribution to the field of language policy and planning. The comprehensiveness of the book in terms of content and literature covered deserves acclaim.

In planning, a general distinction should be made between strategic planning and operational planning. Main tasks in strategic planning are problem analysis, stakeholder analysis, analysis of objectives, analysis of inputs, analysis of external influencing factors, and analysis of the responsible organizations (e.g., Dale 1998). Operational planning consists of the formulation of a detailed guide for implementation. This requires an elaboration of more specific objectives, procedures, tasks, time scales, and budgets.

LINKING LANGUAGE PLANNING AND EVALUATION

The consequences of plans and their implementation need to be evaluated. Planned and systematic action presupposes that evaluation is an inherent part of it. The plan itself can be critically examined in terms of appropriate criteria. The implementation of the plan can be monitored on a continuous basis for information needed for follow-up purposes. This is called formative evaluation. At the point where the plan needs to be more systematically reviewed, summative evaluation is needed (Scriven 1967).

Language planning can be carried out more or less explicitly or implicitly, but always draws on prior activities and prior views. Language planning means making decisions. It requires monitoring to determine the impact of the decisions. In order to progress as a form of social activity, language planning needs conceptual frameworks to advance professionalism in the domain. What is said above suggests that a possible framework is one which links decisions and monitoring in a systematic manner. The literature of program evaluation contains several models (Shadish, Cook and Leviton 1991), but the model presented by Stufflebeam (1975) is one that does this more systematically than any other model. Consequently it will be used as the organizing framework for the following discussion. The purpose is to explore the feasibility of the model in the domain of language planning. The original model is presented in Table 1.

Table 1: The CIPP model of evaluation (Stufflebeam 1975, Stufflebeam, *et al.*1971)

	INTENDED	ACTUAL
ENDS	PLANNING DECISIONS Supported by CONTEXT EVALUATION	RECYCLING DECISIONS Supported by PRODUCT EVALUATION
MEANS	STRUCTURING DECISIONS Supported by INPUT EVALUATION	IMPLEMENTING DECISIONS Supported by PROCESS EVALUATION

The acronym CIPP comes from the initial letters of four types of evaluation: context, input, process, and product. From the decision-making point of view, a corresponding acronym PSIR might be derived to reflect the four types of decision: planning, structuring, implementing, and recycling.

Briefly stated, context evaluation serves planning decisions to determine aims. Input evaluation serves structuring decisions to determine program designs. Process evaluation serves implementing decisions to control program and project operations. Finally, product evaluation serves recycling decisions to judge and react to program and project attainments.

In the CIPP model, context evaluation is the most basic kind of evaluation. Its purpose is to provide a rationale for determining objectives. In the domain of language planning, this evaluation would include careful definition of the relevant language community, description of the desired and actual conditions pertaining to the language environment, identification of unmet needs and unused opportunities, and diagnosis of the problems that prevent or interfere with the fulfilment of needs or restrict the full use of existing opportunities. The diagnosis of problems provides an essential basis for developing objectives whose attainment will result in improved language policies.

The CIPP model suggests that context evaluation begins with a conceptual analysis to identify and define the limits of the domain to be served as well as its major subparts. This view seems to apply also to language planning quite well. Next, empirical studies—surveys and other types of research—are carried out to identify unmet needs and unused opportunities. Then context evaluation involves both empirical and conceptual analyses, as well as appeal to theory and authoritative opinion, to aid udgements on the basic problems which must be solved. According to Stufflebeam, identification of the problems to be solved is equivalent to identification of the objectives to be achieved. In language planning, the situation is seldom so straightforward.

In the CIPP model, the purpose of input evaluation is defined as the provision of information for determination of the kind and amount of resources needed and the manner in which they will be utilized to achieve program and project objectives. In language planning, this would mean identification and assessment of: 1) relevant capabilities of the responsible agency, 2) strategies for achieving planned objectives, and 3) designs for implementing a selected strategy. Alternative language planning options are assessed in terms of the following:

1. their resource, time, and budget requirements;
2. their potential procedural barriers;
3. the consequences of not overcoming these barriers;
4. the relevance of the designs to project obectives; and
5. the overall potential of the design to meet project objectives.

Stufflebeam sees this information as essential in program evaluation, and this view seems to be relevant also for language planning.

Stufflebeam suggests that input evaluation can vary from highly structured to quite informal procedures. In language planning, common practices would include committee deliberations, professional literature, interest-group submissions and reports, and the experiences of other countries/contexts. Pilot experiments in a limited number of contexts may even be carried out. Major changes in language policy normally require extensive efforts to provide the information which is not available but needed if proected objectives are to be attained.

When the implementation of the new language plans has begun, process evaluation is needed to provide periodic feedback to persons responsible for implementing plans and procedures. This kind of evaluation has three main functions: 1) to detect and predict defects in the procedural design or its implementation during the implementation stages, 2) to provide information for future decisions, and 3) to maintain a record of procedures as they occur.

Finally, product evaluation is intended to measure and interpret outcomes not only at the end of a program or a project cycle but as often as necessary during the process. In language planning, this evaluation would mean a major review of the state of achieved language planning goals.

As language policy and planning literature has long recognized, there are several actors with a stakeholder interest in the activities to be carried out (see Haugen 1966, Ingram 1989, Kaplan and Baldauf 1997). Kaplan and Baldauf present a comprehensive view of the theme and summarize their discussion in a very illuminating figure (1997: 6) which posits national resource development planning as the overarching concept, dividing it into natural resource development planning and human resource development planning. Under the latter is placed language planning and other planning, and language planning is elaborated further to include government agencies, education agencies, non/quasi-governmental organizations, and other organizations. Each of these elements is specified in some detail. Figure 1 relates the basic language planning model of Kaplan and Baldauf to the CIPP evaluation model.

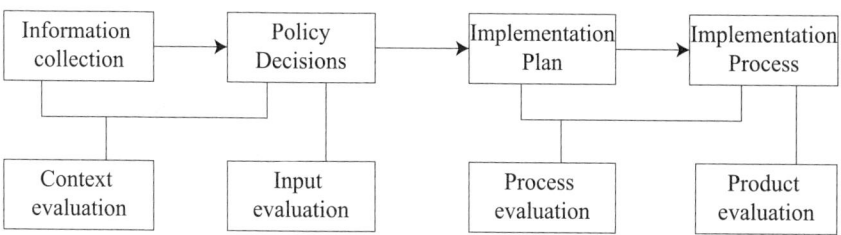

Figure 1 Basic language planning model in relation to an evaluation model (adapted from Kaplan and Baldauf 1997 and Stufflebeam, *et al.* 1971).

In the following Tables (2 and 3), the same conceptual approach is applied, relating the CIPP model to decisions and evaluations made by various stake holders. This mapping is an attempt to test the feasibility of the model in the context of language planning and policy.

Table 2: Types of decisions related to levels of decision making (stakeholders)

Level of decision making	Types of decision			
	Context	Input	Process	Product
Individual - Parents - Minors - Adults/ citizens	Individual language goals, language choices	Decisions concerning individual input in terms of - Time - Energy - Investment	Decisions concerning how individuals monitor their progress toward individual goals	Decisions concerning how individuals assess outcomes in terms of individual goals
Associations/ organizations, interest groups	Group's language goals	Decisions concerning group's support for goal attainment	Decisions concerning how group monitors progress toward the group's goals	Decisions concerning how group assesses outcomes in terms of its goals
Local government	Language planning goal at the local level	Decisions concerning local input for goal attainment in terms of - facilities - staff - programs	Decisions concerning how local government monitors progress toward its language planning goals	Decisions concerning how local government assesses outcomes in terms of its goals
Regional government	Language planning goal at the regional level	Decisions concerning regional support for goal attainment in terms of - facilities - staff - programs	Decisions concerning how regional government monitors progress toward its language planning goals	Decisions concerning how regional government assesses outcomes in terms of its goals

continued

National government	Language planning goal at the national level	Decisions concerning national support for goal attainment in terms of - facilities - staff - programs	Decisions concerning how national government monitors progress toward its language planning goals	Decisions concerning how national government assesses outcomes in terms of its goals
Supranational agencies	Declarations/ recommendations on goals	Recommendations on input	Recommendations on process monitoring	Recommendations on how to assess outcomes of recommended goals
Research community	Critical analysis of plans and goals	Critical analysis of the planned input	Critical analysis of the planned process	Critical analysis of the planned product

Table 3: Types of evaluation related to levels of decision making (stakeholders)

Level of decision making	Types of evaluation			
	Context	Input	Process	Product
Individual - Parents - Minors - Adults/ citizens	Survey of goals	Survey of what goal achievement presupposes of individuals - Time - Energy - Investment	Survey of how progress toward individual goals is made	Survey of outcomes in terms of individual goals
Associations/ organizations, interest groups	Analysis/critique of current goals, proposals, expert goal discussions	Survey of the goal attainment conditions of the group	Survey of how progress of the relevant group is made	Survey of outcomes in terms of the group's goals
Local government	Survey of the local situation, local language plans	Survey of what the attainment of goals imposes on local - facilities - staff - programs	Survey of how progress toward local goals is made	Survey of outcomes in terms of local language planning goals

continued

Regional government	Survey of the regional situation, regional language plans	Survey of what the attainment of goals imposes on regional - facilities - staff - programs	Survey of how progress toward regional goals is made	Survey of outcomes in terms of regional language planning goals
National government	Survey of the national situation, national language plans	Survey of what the attainment of goals imposes on national - facilities - staff - programs	Survey of how progress toward national goals is made	Survey of outcomes in terms of national language planning goals
Supranational agencies	Declarations/ recommenda- tions on goals	Recommenda- tions on input	Survey of how progress toward recommended goals is made	Survey of outcomes in terms of recom- mended language planning goals
Research community	Critical analysis of the actual context	Critical analysis of the actual input	Critical analysis of the actual process	Critical analysis of the actual product

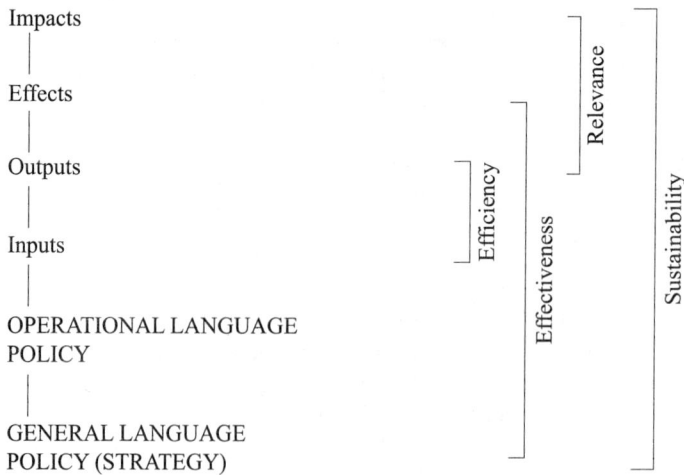

Figure 2 Language policy in an evaluation framework (adapted from Dale 1998).

The evaluation perspectives can vary in terms of their scope (e.g., Dale 1998, Scheerens and Bosker 1997) (see Figure 2). Efficiency is usually related to how productively the inputs (resources) have been converted into outputs (results). Effectiveness is a broader concept and has to do with the extent to which the planned outputs, immediate objectives, and long-term impacts are achieved. *Relevance* addresses the question of how the high priority goals of key stakeholders/beneficiaries are being met (e.g., Nikki 1992). Impact refers to longer-term, largely indirect, consequences of the plan/program for the intended beneficiaries and for societal change in general. *Sustainability* has to do with how the planned (and hopefully achieved) improved state of affairs can be maintained.

A BRIEF LOOK AT THE NORDIC AND BALTIC REGION

In the following sections, we will discuss briefly some recent developments in Scandinavia and the Baltic. The discussion is related to recent language policy documents prepared and adopted under the auspices of the Council of Europe, which has a long and recognized role in issues related to human rights and language rights. The discussion is purposefully limited to the Nordic and Baltic regions to highlight the current, dramatically different, situations in two adjacent regions.

1. The Nordic states

In July 1999, the Swedish Government submitted a proposal to the parliament concerning measures that needed to be taken for Sweden to be able to ratify the Council of Europe Framework Convention for the Protection of National Minorities (approved and opened for signatures on February 1, 1995). This proposal would mean that Swedish national minorities and their languages are recognized and that the minority languages will be given the support they need to stay alive. The groups covered by the proposed law are the Sami people, Swedish-Finns, Tornedal-inhabitants, Romanis, and Jews. The minority languages are Sami, Finnish, Meänkieli (Tornedal-Finnish), Romani Chib, and Yiddish. Of these languages, Sami, Finnish, and Meänkieli are recognized to possess a historical geographical basis, which means that they are entitled to broader support than the other languages. In practice, this designation has to do with the right to use these three languages in court and in administrative matters in those areas where the languages have been traditionally used and are still widely used. The bill is proposed to take effect in April, 2000.

More generally, the European Framework Convention entered into force on February 1, 1998 when it was initially ratified by twelve countries. The countries that were among the first to ratify the convention were: Austria, Croatia, Cyprus, the Czech Republic, Denmark, Estonia, Finland, Germany, Hungary, Italy, Liechtenstein, Macedonia, Malta, Moldavia, Norway, Rumania, Russia, San Marino, Switzerland, Slovakia, Slovenia, Spain, the Ukraine, and the United Kingdom.

The European Charter for Regional or Minority Languages, open for signatures since November 5, 1992, took effect on March 1, 1998 when five countries initially ratified it. Among the first countries to have ratified it were Croatia, Finland, Germany, Hungary, Liechtenstein, The Netherlands, Norway, and Switzerland. Norway was actually the first to ratify the minority language charter. The only minority language mentioned is Sami and it applies to the approximately 35,000 Sami-speaking citizens. The Norwegian language groups were not eager to be labeled minorities in the manner specified in the earlier convention, and thus, this document has not been ratified for them. Its principles are, however, adhered to by Norway.

In Finland, national minority language legislation traditionally covers Swedish (1922) and Sami (1992). Finland ratified the Charter on Regional or Minority Language as the second country in 1994 (and also ratified the Framework Convention in 1997). Finland has ratified the Framework Convention for Sami, Swedish, Romani, and other non-territorially bound languages, following consultation with the recognized bodies representing these language groups. This wording also means that Finland may later decide to award minority language status to other languages. Groups to be consulted would represent Jews, Tatars, and "old Russians."

In Finland, the current language laws stem from 1922 (based on paragraph 14 of the 1919 constitution). It designates Finnish and Swedish as national languages, and it requires that they and their speakers are treated with full equality (a revised constitution is expected to take effect in early 2000). Other laws specify, for instance, the language requirements for various categories of civil servants. There have been complaints that practice does not always correspond to the principles as far as the Swedish speaking minority is concerned. The Ombudsman of the Parliament has issued a statement in which the complaint is confirmed and the Cabinet Office has reminded the various ministries about the obligations of the language laws. A government committee has been appointed recently to draft the new language laws and related legislation. The new laws are expected to be in effect not later than in four years.

Denmark ratified the Framework Convention in 1997. It applies to the German-speaking minority in Southern Jutland. Denmark did not ratify the Charter on Regional or Minority Language at the same time.

2. The Baltic states

The Baltic States were independent from 1918 to 1940. Before the First World War they had a mixed history of German, Swedish, Polish, and Russian rule and influence. From 1944 to 1991 they all were under Russian rule.

The language policy developments in the Baltic States after the collapse of the Soviet Union are a good example of how the ethnic constitution of the population, in addition to the past history of the country, can be reflected in language attitudes and decision-making. The three Baltic States—Estonia, Latvia, and Lithuania—have adopted policies that differ from each other and are directly dependent on the proportion of the non-local population in each country.

In all three states, the language legislation is basically the same, with the local majority language being the state language, obliging state employees to use the language for their services. Yet Lithuania, where only one fifth of the population is non-Lithuanian, has adopted practices which give less emphasis to the promotion of the state language than the ones in use in Latvia and Estonia, where two fifths of the population are non-local. Interestingly, the attitudes of the Latvian population have gradually become stricter, where the non-local population has been more willing to learn the state language than in Estonia.

Before World War II, the Baltic States had their own school systems, cultural organizations, publications, and other elements of cultural autonomy. During the Soviet period, a Leninist principle of the equality of languages was originally adopted, which was also meant to solve the problem of illiteracy. At the same time, however, Russian was promoted as a language of wider communication and international contacts, while the national language was considered a communication instrument and not an integral element of identity. Russian was gradually given more emphasis, and a special kind of idea of bilingualism was developed through the introduction of the concept of *Homo Sovieticus*. Gradually, particularly during the Brezhnev years, the use of the local language became restricted: Services in Russian were to be available throughout the Soviet Union and local people were expected to comply with this requirement.

After the Baltic States gained their new independence in 1991, new legislation was developed which was fully implemented at a rather rapid pace. Generally speaking, the new laws included the following provisions: The local language was to be the official state language, which meant that all state operations and various other uses of language, such as signing, names, etc., were to be in the official language. Staff employed by the state were to be able to use the national language. Citizenship was acknowledged only for people who were citizens in 1940 and their descendants.

Language requirements were also imposed on citizenship. Naturalization was made possible on the basis of time of residence and demonstrated competence in the official language of the country. The national language requirement has an impact on the status of speakers of Russian. In the early 1990s, the percentages of monolingual Russian speakers were high in all of the three states, and national language requirements excluded many of them from citizenship.

<u>Latvia</u>: At present, the largest proportion of non-local population lives in Latvia. In 1998, out of the 2.43 million inhabitants, a total of 647, 000 (24 percent) are non-citizens, which means that 76 percent of the total population are citizens. A total of about 400, 000 of the citizens are of non-Latvian origin, that is, persons who have passed the tests for naturalization. The 1989 language law set rules for the use of the Latvian language in state institutions, corporations, educational establishments, and public meetings. Language inspectors were appointed who had the right to fine persons in breach of the rules. A new stricter law was adopted by the Latvian parliament in 1998, adding self-employed persons to the list of those who have to use the state language. If a foreign language is used at meetings, the organizers have to provide translation into the state language. This law applies also to private enterprises and meetings held at the workplace. Codification of the Latvian language has been given an important role: New terms

can be used only after they have been approved by a state terminology commission. The new law was not accepted by the Latvian President, one of the reasons being the fact that the law did not sufficiently promote the inclusion of national minorities into Latvia's society, so it was sent back to the parliament for reconsideration.

As many as 90 percent of the non-Latvians believe that it is very important or fairly important for Latvian residents to know Latvian well. Between 1992 and 1997, a total of 388,000 people passed the Latvian language proficiency examinations administered by the State Language Centre. The development of the Latvian language test for citizenship purposes has drawn largely on the work done under the Council of Europe auspices (e.g., the Threshold concept), and the development teams have been consulting several European institutions with recognized expertise in testing and assessment.

Estonia: Estonia's population is slightly less than 1.5 million. Non-ethnic Estonians constitute 37 percent of the total population, approximately 28 percent being ethnic Russians. According to Estonian legislation, state employees have to be proficient in Estonian. A fairly large number of state employees have been dismissed since the law took effect in 1993. If inhabitants are in a district where more than one-half of the population speak a language other than Estonian, they are allowed to receive information in that language and the local government can conduct business in that language. From 1999, knowledge of the Estonian language is obligatory for all state, municipal, and other functionaries and for people who work in the area of public services. Estonia emphasizes an integration program. Its objective is to cut down the number of people with undetermined citizenship, step up the teaching of Estonian, and increase non-Estonians participation in Estonian society. All persons resident in Estonia are allowed to vote in local elections, but only Estonian citizens can stand as candidates. Russian language schools will be discontinued from 2000. Only 42 percent of those who were naturalized between 1992 and 1996 have passed the language examination. According to the present legislation, naturalization without Estonian proficiency is no longer possible. Children born in Estonia after 26 February 1992 have been granted an easier access to citizenship. Between 1992 and 1998, a total of 103,000 persons were naturalized.

Lithuania: In Lithuania, 80 percent of the population of 3.72 million are Lithuanians, and only 20 percent represent minorities, the largest being Poles (9 percent) and Russians (8 percent). The Lithuanian language is the state language, and it is to be used in the activities of state and public bodies, as well as in educational, cultural, scientific, industrial, and other institutions, enterprises, and organizations. State employees have to be proficient in Lithuanian. Lithuanian authorities have indicated that no one should be dismissed solely because of an inability to meet the language requirement. It is to be considered a moral incentive for people to learn Lithuanian. The 1991 Lithuanian law on nationality has made it possible for the authorities to grant citizenship to all persons resident in Lithuania, regardless of their origins, previous residence, or ability to speak Lithuanian. Some 90 percent of persons belonging to the minorities have Lithuanian citizenship. There are no plans to constrain education in minority languages, and in higher education, minorities have been given their own quotas.

THE OUTLOOK

As has been suggested in this survey, we believe that systematic effort should be taken to develop professionalism in the area of language policy and language planning. The dawn of the new millenium seems to be a particularly opportune moment to reflect on the new challenges that are facing us. Reference has already been made to the importance of linking planning and evaluation—they are like two sides of the same coin. Those involved in language policy and language planning could pursue the disciplinary development of evaluation by seeking to establish it as a distinct academic sub-field with its own degree programs or perhaps as oint degree programs that utilize the potential of the Internet, preparing, as ajoint effort, standards for the practice of language policy making and language planning. There exist standards for evaluation of educational programs, projects, and materials which are continuously revised to reflect changes in the discipline. The evaluation standards cover four broad areas: utility standards, feasibility standards, propriety standards, and accuracy standards. The first three would be quite relevant also for language policy and language planning.

In the spirit of the present article, it is suggested that there should be systematic attempts to monitor and evaluate the efficiency, effectiveness, impact, relevance, and sustainability of language policies and plans. Another area of study would involve the critical study of public discourse and debate on language policy and planning.

A desirable development would also include a tradition of recurrent regional and international conferences and seminars on language planning. The authors of this article contributed to arranging one such conference and the experience was both useful and rewarding. Hopefully, joint conferences would lead to joint studies by international teams of experts.

ANNOTATED BIBLIOGRAPHY

Baker, C. and S. Prys Jones. 1998. *Encyclopedia of bilingualism and bilingual education.* Clevedon, UK: Multilingual Matters.

This is a comprehensive volume that covers a range of issues on bilingualism. It deals with individual bilingualism, bilingualism in society, languages in contact, and bilingual education. There is also a chapter on bilingualism and language policies. The volume is unquestionably a major contribution to the field of bilingualism.

Cenoz, J. and F. Genesee (eds.) 1998. *Beyond bilingualism: Multilingualism and multilingual education.* Clevedon, UK: Multilingual Matters.

This edited book of twelve articles incorporates a multilingual perspective and looks at multilingualism from both a global and an individual perspective. It also examines educational implications of multilingualism, presenting six case studies in multilingual education.

Kaplan, R. B. and R. B. Baldauf, Jr. 1997. *Language planning: From practice to theory.* Clevedon, UK: Multilingual Matters.

This important book deals with key concepts and issues in language planning, presenting a general framework for planning. The ambitious aim of the book, as the title suggests, is to make a contribution to the theory of language planning. It does this by conceptualizing language planning in terms of key elements and issues. Several case studies in language planning are also presented. The book should be required reading for all engaged in language policy and language planning.

Lambert, R. D. (ed.) 1994. *Language planning around thd world: Contexts and systemic change.* Washington, DC: National Foreign Language Center.

The papers in this volume deal with recent planned changes in the foreign language instructional systems of a variety of countries (the Netherlands, Sweden, Finland, England, Israel, and Australia) and address problems and prospects for planning in the American context. In most of the countries covered, the language planning issues address concerns at the national level, and the value of learning foreign languages is unquestioned. In the United States, in contrast, the minimal planning that exists takes the form of dispersed isolated decisions. The themes that recur in the volume include: 1) differences in the context on planning, 2) recommendations for change in specific features of the language-instructional system, and 3) the process of planning and systemic change.

McKay, S. L. and N. H. Hornberger (eds.) 1996. *Sociolinguistics and language teaching.* Cambridge: Cambridge University Press.

This edited book contains highly informative articles by a number of well-known scholars. Sections deal with language and variation, language and interaction, language and culture, and there is a chapter specifically on language and education. In the section on language and society, there is a 45-page article on language planning and policy by Terrence G. Wiley. Among several topics covered, the discussion of various approaches to language planning in particular stands out as a valuable contribution.

Paulston, C. B. and D. Peckham (eds.) 1998. *Linguistic minorities in central and eastern Europe.* Clevedon, UK: Multilingual Matters.

This edited volume, of great topical interest, contains an integrating introduction by Paulston and ten case studies. The case studies cover a wide geographic region: Austria, minorities in the Balkans, Bulgaria, the Caucasus, the Czech Republic, Hungary, Latvia, Romania, Russia, and Slovakia.

Saavaara, K., R. D. Lambert, S. Takala and C.A. Morfit (eds.). 1993. *National foreign language planning: Practices and prospects.* Jyväskylä: Institute for Educational Research, University of Jyväskylä.

This collection of papers originated from a conference that brought together experts on foreign language teaching and learning from North America and from western, central, and eastern Europe. It focuses primarily on a comparison across countries and continents of the domains, directions, and processes of language planning. The papers provide both a sense of national differences in the contexts in which language planning is carried out and an in-depth analysis of particular substantive domains relating to language planning such as language choice, teacher training, and assessment. A number of domains of language policy in which the Europeans and Americans have relevant experience are identified, and it is hoped that these domains provide useful guidance for future planning.

Schiffman, H. E. 1996. *Linguistic culture and language policy.* London: Routledge.

This book is a strongly culturally—anchored view of language policy. It represents a systematic approach to analyzing language policies and presents several typologies that implement this view. It also presents detailed analyses of language policies in different parts of the world. The discussion on the language policies in France may be singled out as presenting new and interesting reflections.

Spolsky, B. and E. Shohamy. 1999. *The languages of Israel: Policy, ideology and practice.* Clevedon, UK: Multilingual Maters.

The authors of the book provide a thorough and timely analysis of the linguistic scene and linguistic policy in the truly multilingual state of Israel. The authors note that the book appears close to two anniversaries: just over 100 years since the decision to revive Hebrew was made and 50 years since the establishment of the state of Israel and its policy to maintain Hebrew and Arabic as official languages and languages of instruction. The book describes and analyzes the developments during the half century up to the present time, including the 1995–96 Policy for Language Education. It gives a thoughtful appraisal of the developments and the current state and prospects of true linguistic diversity. The book is a valuable and welcome contribution to the rapidly evolving field of language policy studies.

Wodak, R. and D. Corson (eds.) 1997. *Encyclopedia of language planning and education. Volume 1: Language policy and political issues in education.* Dordrecht: Kluwer Academic Publishers.

This edited volume contains a number of articles, each about ten pages in length. Five articles deal with theoretical issues; another five address minorities and education; eight articles present language policy in various countries and regions; and five articles address practical and empirical issues. One unifying feature of the articles is that they discuss future directions in the areas covered.

UNANNOTATED BIBLIOGRAPHY

Chelimsky, E. and W. R. Shadish (eds.) 1997. *Evaluation for the 21st century.* Thousand Oaks, CA: Sage.

Dale, R. 1998. *Evaluation frameworks for development programmes and projects.* New Delhi: Sage.

Fishman, J. (ed.) 1974. *Advances in language planning.* The Hague: Mouton.

Haugen, E. 1966. Linguistics and language planning. In W. Bright (ed.) *Sociolinguistics.* The Hague: Mouton. 50–71.

Kaplan, R. B. 1994. Language policy and planning: Fundamental issues. In W. Grabe, et al. (eds.) *Annual Review of Applied Linguistics, 14. Language policy and planning.* New York: Cambridge University Press. 3–19.

Kieliohjelmakomitean mietintö. 1979. Helsinki. [Report of the Commission on Language Teaching Policy.]

Kloss, H. 1969. Research possibilities on group bilingualism. A report. Quebec: Center for Research on Bilingualism.

Nikki, M.-L. 1992. *The implementation of the Finnish national plan for foreign language teaching.* Jyväskylä: University of Jyväskylä. [Jyväskylä studies in education, psychology and social research 87.]

Patton, M. Q. 1997. *Utilization-focused evaluation.* 3rd ed. Thousand Oaks, CA: Sage.

Rist, R. C. (ed.) 1995. *Policy evaluation: Linking theory to practice.* Aldershot: Elgar Publishing.

Scheerens, J. and R. Bosker. 1997. *The foundations of educational effectiveness.* Oxford: Pergamon.

Scriven, M. 1967. The methodology of evaluation. *AERA Monograph Series on Curriculum Evaluation.* No. 1, 39–83.

Shadish Jr., W. R., T. D. Cook and L. C. Leviton (eds.) 1991.*Foundations of Program Evaluation.* Newbury Park, CA: Sage.

Stufflebeam, D. K. 1975. *The CIPP model of evaluation.* Kalamazoo, MI: Western Michigan University, Evaluation Center.

Stufflebeam, D. K., W. J. Foley, W. J. Gebhart, E. Guba, R. L. Hammond, H. O. Merriman and M. Provus. 1971. *Educational evaluation and decision making.* Itasca, Illinois: F. E. Peacock Publishers.

Tauli, V. 1968. *Introduction to a theory of language planning.* Stockholm: Almqvist and Wiksell. [Acta universitatis Upsaliensis: Studia Philologiae Scandinaviae Upsaliensia 6.]

Thompson, J.D. and J. D. Tuden. 1959. Strategies, structures and processes of organizational decisions. In J. D. Thompson (ed.) *Comparative studies in administration.* Pittsburg: University of Pittsburg Press. 182–215.

ASSESSMENT AND TESTING

Caroline Clapham

INTRODUCTION

In this brief article, I discuss the relationship between language testing and the other sub-disciplines of applied linguistics and also the relationship, as I see it, between testing and assessment. The article starts with a brief exploration of the term 'applied linguistics' and then goes on to discuss the role of language testing within this discipline, the relationship between testing and teaching, and the relationship between testing and assessment. The second part of the article mentions some areas of current concern to testers and discusses in more detail recent advances in the areas of performance testing, alternative assessment, and computer assessment. One of my aims in this article is to argue that the skills involved in language testing are necessary not only for those constructing all kinds of language proficiency assessments, but also for those other applied linguists who use tests or other elicitation techniques to help them gather language data for research.

APPLIED LINGUISTICS AND THE ROLE OF ASSESSMENT

It is usually the case with new disciplines that they go through periods of adjustment as the limits of the discipline are realigned. Applied linguistics is going through such a stage at present as its scope widens and its subfields start to impinge on those of other disciplines.

The term 'applied linguistics' appears first to have been used in the late 1940s when the discipline embraced the teaching and learning of second and foreign languages (Johnson and Johnson 1998), but since then the discipline has expanded to cover a wider range of sub-disciplines or 'subfields' as they are called by Bachman and Cohen (1998). In 1980, Henry Widdowson said, "...applied linguistics yields descriptions which are projections of actual language which explore linguistic theory as illumination..." (p. 169), and in 1997, Chris Brumfit defined applied linguistics as "...the theoretical and empirical investigation of real-world problems in which language is the central issue" (p. 93). (See also Ben Rampton's [1997] introduction to the special issue of *Applied Linguistics* in which Brumfit's article appeared; this issue of *Applied Linguistics* focused on the concept of 'applied linguistics.')

In 1999, Richard Hudson, in an e-mail to the LAGB (Linguistics Association of Great Britain) listserve, said:

The main distinguishing characteristic of AL (Applied Linguistics) is its concern with professional activities whose aim is to solve 'real-world' language-based problems, which means that research touches on a particularly wide range of issues—psychological, pedagogical, social, political and economic as well as linguistic. As a consequence, AL research tends to be interdisciplinary (Hudson 1999).

Language assessment plays a pivotal role in applied linguistics, operationalizing its theories and supplying its researchers with data for their analysis of language knowledge or use. It has itself become a sub-discipline of applied linguistics, which is in some ways unfortunate, since it is has tended to become compartmentalized (Bachman and Cohen 1998) and does not interact as much as it should with the other sub-disciplines. Bachman and Cohen (1998) decry the compartmentalization of second language acquisition (SLA) and language testing, saying that most mainstream researchers in the two sub-disciplines are unaware of research taking place in the other. However, they hope that this lack of awareness may now be changing. (For other discussions of the relationship between testing and SLA, see Shohamy 1998, Upshur and Turner 1998.)

A key point, which perhaps not all applied linguists appreciate, is that language testing is by no means limited to assessing the linguistic proficiency of L2 students. Many areas of linguistic research use elicitation instruments to gather data, and these instruments often take the form of tests or tasks (see, for example,

Robinson 1997, Skehan and Foster 1999). If the results of such data elicitation techniques are to be credible, they need to be prepared with as much rigor as proficiency tests, and they therefore have to be valid and reliable (Alderson and Banerjee in press). Crudely, a valid elicitation technique is one that accurately elicits what it is intended to elicit, and a reliable technique is one that produces consistent results. (For discussions of validity, see Chapelle 1999, Messick 1989; 1996, Shepard 1993; and for comments on the relationship between validity and reliability, see Moss 1994.) Although Messick (1989) subsumes reliability under validity, since any valid measure must, by definition, be reliable, it is useful here to distinguish between validity and reliability since the assessment of an instrument's reliability is often neglected in elicitation procedures. If research is to have credibility, data gathering instruments must not only be carefully designed to ensure that they will elicit the type of language required, they must also be pre-tested to check that the measures do indeed elicit such language practice and that any rating or coding system is workable and capable of producing consistent results (see North and Schneider 1998). Since it is generally expected that subjects in an investigation produce similar kinds of language regardless of when the task is done, and that this language can be analyzed in a similar manner regardless of when and by whom it is assessed or coded, the reliability of the elicitation techniques must be given careful consideration.

ASSESSMENT AND LANGUAGE TEACHING

There has been much discussion about how language testing fits into applied linguistics and how it relates to language teaching (see, for example, Bachman and Palmer 1996). In general, it seems clear that "...language testing benefits from insights from applied linguistics as a discipline..." (Alderson and Clapham 1992:164) but that it is sometimes necessary for testing to lead the way:

> We believe that language testers can serve linguistic theory by examining the way in which their tests work, how their different components interrelate, and what they reveal about candidates' language proficiency. Insights from such an analysis of test results should contribute to the development of a better understanding of what is involved in knowing and using language (1992:164).

It seems, indeed, that each affects the other: Methods of assessment may affect teaching in the classroom (Cheng 1997, Wall 1996; 1997), while new theories of language learning and teaching lead to changes in testing practices (Spolsky 1995).

THEORIES OF LANGUAGE TESTING

With the advent of communicative teaching in the late 1970s, there was a need for testers to devise new theories of language testing. Canale and Swain (1980), whose model applied to both teaching and testing second and foreign languages, included grammatical, sociolinguistic, and strategic competence in their description of the domains of language use. In 1990, Bachman added psychophysiological mechanisms and proposed four components in his model: grammatical, textual, illocutionary, and sociolinguistic competence. Bachman and Palmer (1996) elaborated on this model further to include both affective and metacognitive factors. Bachman and Palmer's model of communicative language ability is used as the theoretical basis for tests such as the International English Language Testing System (IELTS) test, and it provides the basis for many current research projects (e.g., Hasselgren 1998). (See McNamara 1996 for a discussion of language testing models.)

ASSESSMENT AND TESTING

The term 'assessment' is used both as a general umbrella term to cover all methods of testing and assessment, and as a term to distinguish 'alternative assessment' from 'testing.' Some applied linguists use the term 'testing' to apply to the construction and administration of formal or standardized tests such as the Test of English as a Foreign Language (TOEFL) and 'assessment' to refer to more informal methods such as those listed below under the heading 'alternative assessment.' For example, Valette (1994) says that 'tests' are large-scale proficiency tests and that 'assessments' are school-based tests. Intriguingly, some testers are now using the term 'assessment' where they might in the past have used the term 'test' (see, for example, Kunnan 1998). There seems, indeed, to have been a shift in many language testers' perceptions so that they, perhaps subconsciously, may be starting to think of testing solely in relation to standardized, large-scale tests. They therefore use the term 'assessment' as the wider, more acceptable term.

Since, for the remainder of this article, I wish to comment on differing attitudes between 'testers' and 'assessors,' I shall use the term 'testers' for those who concern themselves with requirements of validity and reliability, and 'assessors' for those who are not consciously guided by such constraints. I must emphasize, though, that while I am giving the two terms distinct meanings, I do not think that there is a fundamental difference between them, and in other publications (e.g., Clapham 1997; to appear), I use the two terms interchangeably.

Unfortunately, although 'assessors' and 'testers' have the same aims, there is less dialogue than there should be between them, possibly because many of them tend to think of 'testing' and 'assessment' as being categorically different (see Hill and Parry 1994) instead of being on a continuum with at one end those 'testers' who deliver carefully validated multiple choice tests, and at the other end, 'assessors' who prepare real-life tasks for their students and candidates but who do not concern themselves with how well these tasks actually work. 'Assessors' appear to distrust extreme 'testers' because they feel that these 'testers' are so wedded to the numerical analysis of data that they are not sufficiently concerned with the content and administration of their tests. Such 'assessors' tend to be concerned that these 'tests' are not 'communicative,' and that they may lead to negative washback (Brown and Hudson 1998). In contrast, many 'testers' are concerned with the fact that, although the 'assessors' methods of assessment may be novel and interesting, the tasks are not pre-tested to see whether they work as intended or whether the assessments can be delivered and marked in a consistent manner. In short, they distrust 'assessors' because 'assessors' do not appreciate the importance of investigating the validity and reliability of their instruments. Brown and Hudson (1998) quote Huerta-Macias (1995) who says that it is unnecessary to evaluate the validity and reliability of methods of alternative assessment because they are already built into the assessment process. Brown and Hudson make the point that it is not enough to build validity and reliability into the measures; the measures must also be trialed to see whether or not they are valid and reliable in practice. (See also Johnstone [in press] and Rea-Dickens [in press].)

Another source of distinction between 'tests' and 'assessments' is that some educators and applied linguists feel that 'high stakes' tests, which have a direct bearing on students' immediate futures, need to have validity and reliability built into them, but that 'low stakes' tests such as classroom tests, which do not have such an obvious impact on students' futures, do not (Davidson, *et al.* 1997). This division of tests into high- and low-stakes types seems to me to be misguided: Tests do not fall neatly into one or the other category. Whether a test is 'high-' or 'low-stakes' is surely a question of degree; a test may be deemed to be more 'high-stakes' than another if students' futures are more clearly at stake, but all tests which assess students' proficiency levels, whether in the examination hall or the classroom, are in reality high-stakes. Even if the results of a classroom test do not affect a student's immediate future, the results may become self fulfilling; for example, a student with a low score may be considered by both teacher and student to be a poor language learner, and this may have a damaging effect on the student's future performance. If students are to have an accurate idea of their proficiency, they should, where possible, be given tests which are valid and reliable. Even classroom tests, therefore, should, at least from time to time, be checked to see whether the skills being assessed are those intended, whether the marking scheme is appropriate and can be used consistently, and whether the results tally with other views of the student's proficiency.

This apparent dichotomy between 'testers' and 'assessors' has, however, become less marked as the move towards 'authenticity' (see Bachman 2000) in text and task has led 'testers' towards the increased use of performance tests. In addition, there is a trend at present, perhaps partly due to the influence of Messick (1989), for 'testers' to be more concerned with the construct validity than simply with the reliability of their measures. It is also the case, possibly due to the influence of post modernism, that many 'testers' are rejecting the positivist principle that there is an "...independently existing reality that can be discovered (or measured) using objective, scientific methods..." (Hamp-Lyons and Lynch 1998). The desire to question former 'truths' has led many 'testers' to trust standard statistical procedures less than they used to. Some 'testers' are also now expressing concerns about the ethicality of testing (see Kunnan in press).

CURRENT AREAS OF CONCERN IN TESTING

Areas that are attracting attention in the testing literature at present have, in a number of cases, been the subject of recent *ARAL* reviews. Performance testing was covered by Shohamy (1995), alternative assessment by Hamayan (1995), advances in the use of the computer for testing by Chalhoub-Deville and Deville (1999) and the interface between tasks and assessment by Skehan (1998) and McNamara (1998). Other areas of current interest include test washback (Alderson and Wall 1993; 1996, Wall 1997) and the ethics of language testing (Davies 1997, Hamp-Lyons 1997, Kunnan in press, Norton 1997). (For more about these and other areas of current concern, see Bachman 2000, Brindley in press; see also Clapham and Corson 1997.) In the remainder of this article, I will update the *ARAL* articles on performance testing, alternative assessment, and the use of computers for testing. I will, at the same time, relate these three areas to real or imaginary differences between 'testers' and 'assessors.'

1. Performance testing

As Shohamy (1995) points out, alternative assessment and performance testing have much in common. Indeed, the major difference between the two seems to be that performance testers agonize about the validity and reliability of their instruments while alternative assessors do not (Hamayan 1995). Both, however, are concerned with asking students to create or produce something, and both focus on eliciting samples of language which are as close to real life as possible (see Kormos 1999, Lynch and McNamara 1998, Papajohn 1999, Upshur and Turner 1998). McNamara (1996) states that a defining characteristic of performance testing is that "the assessment of the actual performances of relevant tasks are required of candidates, rather than the more abstract demonstration of knowledge, often by means of paper-and-pencil tests" (McNamara 1996:6; see also McNamara 1997). The same could well be said of methods of alternative assessment.

2. Alternative assessment

'Alternative assessment' is one of the terms used to refer to informal assessment procedures such as those often used in the classroom. Typical examples of such methods involve portfolios (Hamp-Lyons 1996), learner diaries or journals, and interviews with teachers (Genesee and Upshur 1996). Such procedures may be more time-consuming and difficult for the teacher to administer than 'paper-and-pencil' tests, but they have many advantages. They produce information that is easy for administrators, teachers, and students to understand; they tend to be integrated;

and they can reflect the more holistic teaching methods being used in the classroom (Hamayan 1995). A problem with methods of alternative assessment, however, lies with their validity and reliability: Tasks are often not tried out to see whether they produce the desired linguistic information; marking criteria are not investigated to see whether they 'work'; and raters are often not trained to give consistent marks (see Brown and Hudson 1998). As Hamayan (1995) says, such alternative methods of assessment will not be considered to be part of the mainstream of language assessment until they can be shown to be both valid and reliable.

Methods of alternative assessment are not, of course, solely used for classroom purposes. Many alternative assessment schemes are initiated by local or national government agencies (see Brindley 1998, Stansfield 1994) with aims such as comparing students' levels of linguistic ability or comparing levels of instruction across institutions. Governments (sometimes in a hurry) wish to use the results for their own aims (Brindley 1998). They do not appreciate the need for careful trialing, and therefore they do not always allow researchers the time to try out the assessment instruments. Some types of assessment used in these circumstances may have high face validity—they may look excellent to the uninformed—but they may be marred by inappropriate marking schemes and rating inconsistencies. Trialing such measures is essential if the final tools are to be valid and reliable, but unfortunately such pre-testing and subsequent editing of materials takes time, and time is often in short supply. Inevitably, the ensuing tasks and marking schemes are not valid and reliable (Brindley 1998), and such schemes, therefore, launched with much fanfare, may produce invalid results which are unfair to students and teachers alike. If all assessors appreciated the importance of trialing in the construction of all assessment procedures, they might be able to work together to tell governments and other funding bodies that test development requires more time if assessors are to devise satisfactory assessment instruments.

The present move towards the inclusion of more performance testing in examinations (see for example the University of Cambridge Local Examinations Syndicate examinations) is also likely to bring 'testing' and 'assessment' closer together, but, unfortunately, because of financial and practical constraints, some large-scale tests are likely to remain much as they are, with uncontextualized, multiple choice items. There is a danger that the authors of such large-scale tests will be marginalized, and that their thorough work on pre-testing their items will not be appreciated because of perceived weaknesses in test content. Indeed, it is possible to envisage a day when performance testers and alternative assessors align themselves against the producers of large-scale tests. Such a division must not be allowed to occur.

3. Advances in computer assessment

It is probably too early to say whether advances in the use of computer technology for testing will have a positive or a negative effect on testing and whether computer administered tests will be distrusted by 'assessors.' Until recently, computer testing tended to fossilize existing objective testing methods because objectively marked items such as multiple-choice questions and gap-filling tasks were straightforward to answer on the computer and were easy to mark mechanically. Any attempts to introduce interesting new methods of assessment and testing were foiled by limitations in the memory size and processing speed of the computers. The move of the TOEFL towards computer based testing too has, at least in the short run, extended the use of multiple choice and other easy-to-mark objective items in computer tests. However, it seems that the promised testing revolution may at last be on its way. The expanding use of video conferencing and video interviews, the comparative ease with which videos and listening extracts can now be downloaded from the Web, the improvement in the computer's ability to recognize sounds and letters, the expanding uses of language corpora for teaching and testing, and the increasing and more rapid storage capacity of modern computers are all widening the scope of computer administered tests (see Burstein, *et al*. 1996, Drasgow and Olson-Buchanan 1998, Ordinate Corporation 1998). These advances will not only increase the efficiency of standardized tests, but will increase the scope of other elicitation techniques.

One project that has the potential to produce interesting and yet easy-to-deliver-and-mark tests is DIALANG, which aims to produce diagnostic tests in 14 different European foreign languages (DIALANG 1997). The tests will be delivered on the world wide web; they will be computer adaptive (see Chalhoub-Deville and Deville 1999); and students, after taking their chosen test, will receive instant diagnostic information about the strengths and weaknesses of their performance. At present, compositions written for DIALANG will be marked by hand, but this may not always be the case as there are now research projects looking into the computer marking of tests of language production (see Burstein and Chodorow 1999). Although it is hard to imagine computers ever replacing human markers, and we might not wish them to, it is possible that they will take some of the drudgery away from subjective marking and will thus make the marking task easier and more interesting for the raters.

There will thus, in the near future, be great advances in computer testing. However, we cannot yet know whether or not there is still a danger that the use of computers will limit rather than expand the kinds of tests that will be used.

CONCLUSION

One of my aims in this article has been to discuss the need to bring 'testers' and 'assessors' closer together, and I expect that over the next decade any differences between them will become less and less marked. 'Testers,' I hope, will become more open to ideas of different kinds of assessment, and 'assessors' will be more willing to accept that even the most carefully designed task or set of marking criteria needs to be trialed. If 'testers' and 'assessors' can each see that they are aiming for the same goal, they will perhaps start a dialogue which might transform both tests and assessments. Similarly, on a larger scale, the basic issues of testing and assessment are important in all areas of applied linguistics that call on the use of elicitation techniques to collect data. All such elicitation techniques should be reliable and valid. Understanding this connection, however, will only be possible if all putative applied linguists (and all potential language teachers) are introduced during their training to the vital tenets of testing so that they can be more critical of the elicitation techniques they use.

ANNOTATED BIBLIOGRAPHY

Alderson, J. C. and D. Wall. 1993. Does washback exist? *Applied Linguistics*. 14.115–129.

This article opened language testers' eyes to the fact that, although the expression 'washback' was freely used in language teaching and testing communities, and although there was plenty of anecdotal evidence as to its existence, there had been few serious attempts to define it or to investigate its existence and possible effects. The authors reported on the few existing studies of language testing washback and listed fifteen washback hypotheses which, they said, should be investigated. This article led to a flurry of investigations into test washback, and the results of the first of these studies are now being published.

Bachman, L. F. 2000. Modern language testing at the turn of the century: Assuring that what we count counts. *Language Testing.* 17.1.

This is a state-of-the-art article on language testing in the year 2000. After a brief overview of testing in the 1980s, Bachman comments on some of the main areas of interest in the 1990s: criterion referenced measurement, generalizability theory, item response theory, structural equation modeling, qualitative research approaches, testing cross-cultural pragmatics, testing language for specific purposes, testing vocabulary, computer based assessment, and research into factors that affect performance. He also discusses recent theories of language testing and the concept of communicative testing. He concludes his overview of the 1990s with discussions of test washback and test ethics, and then turns to what lies ahead.

Bachman, L. F. and A. Cohen. 1998. Language testing—SLA interfaces: An update. In L. F. Bachman and A. Cohen (eds.) *Interfaces between second language acquisition and language testing research.* Cambridge: Cambridge University Press. 1–31.

This chapter serves as a useful introduction to the book, *Interfaces between second language acquisition and language testing research.* It discusses the reasons why SLA and language testing were for some time viewed as totally distinct, and it gives reasons why in recent years the two fields seem to have moved closer together. Bachman and Cohen describe areas of common interest between SLA and language testing and make recommendations for future joint areas of research.

Bachman, L. F. and A. Palmer. 1996. *Language testing in practice.* Oxford: Oxford University Press.

This book, which is a key textbook in language testing at present, is composed of three parts: Part 1 discusses the conceptual basis of test development and includes the Communicative Language Ability model, which is used as the basis of much current research in language testing; Part 2 describes the stages of language test development; and Part 3 describes a set of ten illustrative test development projects ranging from a placement test used in a U.S. university to a syllabus based test for primary school children.

Brindley, G. 1998. Outcomes-based assessment and reporting in language learning programmes: A review of the issues. *Language Testing.* 15.45–85.

In this article, Brindley discusses national standards, frameworks, and benchmarks of various kinds. He shows that the introduction of such systems has sometimes been problematic because of political, practical, and technical factors. Brindley discusses what the problems are and makes suggestions for how future systems might be more successfully implemented.

Brown, J. D. and T. Hudson. 1998. The alternatives in language assessment. *TESOL Quarterly.* 32.653–675.

The main purpose of Brown and Hudson's article is to help language teachers decide what types of language tests they should use in the classroom. The article discusses the concepts of validity and reliability, and lists the different kinds of tests that teachers might use. The authors group tests under various headings such as 'selected response' and 'performance assessments' and describe the advantages and disadvantages of each type.

Clapham, C. and D. Corson (eds.) 1997. *Language testing and assessment, Vol. 7. The encyclopedia of language and education.* Dordrecht, Holland: Kluwer Academic.

This volume contains 29 chapters on different aspects of first and second language testing and assessment. Each chapter presents a state-of-the-art description of one aspect of language assessment and provides a bibliography of about 30 references for future researchers in the field. The book is divided into four sections covering the testing of individual skills, methods of assessment, quantitative and qualitative approaches to test validation, and the ethics and effects of testing and assessment.

McNamara, T. 1996. *Measuring second language performance.* London: Longman.

This highly readable book starts with a discussion of communicative testing and defines what McNamara means by performance testing. This discussion is followed by a valuable discussion of the influential models of communicative language testing that have been devised since Dell Hymes introduced his theory of communicative competence in 1972. In the second part of the book, McNamara starts by describing a performance test, the Occupational English Test, and then devotes most of the rest of the book to a discussion of the use of Rasch multi-faceted measurement for research into the assessment of second language performance.

Messick, S. 1996. Validity and washback in language testing. *Language Testing.* 13.241–256.

This article focuses on washback and the consequential aspects of construct validity. Messick relates washback to his overall conception of validity and, in doing so, explains his ideas about validity more clearly and concisely than he did in his seminal 1989 article.

Shepard, L. 1993. Evaluating test validity. *Review of Research in Education.* 19.405–450.

This article discusses validity in educational measurement as a whole. Shepard starts by describing the evolution of the concept of validity over time and then devotes the second half of the article to a very clear explanation of Messick's theory of validity. She concludes the chapter with comments on the implications of this reconceptualizing of the term for new test standards.

Wall, D. 1996. Introducing new tests into traditional systems: Insights from general education and from innovation theory. *Language Testing.* 13.334–354.

This article describes several key concepts in educational innovation. The author applies these concepts to the teaching of English as a foreign or second language and relates them to a study she carried out into the washback of a new school examination in Sri Lanka. She shows how the belief that assessment and the curriculum would together affect teaching in the classroom turned out to be misplaced, partly because of discrepancies between the curriculum and the examination, and partly because of a lack of teacher training in the new 'communicative' methodology. In her conclusion, she makes suggestions as to how future investigations into washback should be carried out and how innovations in the classroom might be brought about more successfully.

UNANNOTATED BIBLIOGRAPHY

Alderson, J. C. and J. Banerjee. In press. Impact and washback research in language testing. In C. Elder, *et al.* (eds.) *Experimenting with uncertainty: Essays in honor of Alan Davies*. Cambridge: Cambridge University Press.

────────── and C. Clapham. 1992. Applied linguistics and language testing: A case study of the ELTS test. *Applied Linguistics*. 13.149–167.

────────── and D. Wall (eds.) 1996. *Washback in testing*. [Special issue of *Language Testing*. 13.1.]

Bachman, L. F. 1990. *Fundamental considerations in language testing*. Oxford: Oxford University Press.

Brindley, G. In press. Assessment. In R. Carter and D. Nunan (eds.) *The Cambridge ELT companion*. Cambridge: Cambridge University Press.

Brumfit, C. 1997. How applied linguistics is the same as any other science. *Applied Linguistics*. 7.86–94.

Burstein, J. and M. Chodorow. 1999. Automated essay scoring for non-native English speakers. Paper presented at the Association of Computational Linguistics and the International Association of Language Learning Technologies. [Available from http://www.ets.org/research/erater.html]

────────, T. Frase, A. Ginther and L. Grant. 1996 Technologies for language assessment. In W. Grabe, *et al.* (eds.) *Annual Review of Applied Linguistics, 16. Language and technology*. New York: Cambridge University Press. 240–260.

Canale, M. and M. Swain. 1980. Theoretical bases of communicative approaches to second language teaching and testing. *Applied Linguistics*. 1.1–47.

Chalhoub-Deville, M. (ed.) In press. *Issues in the computer adaptive testing of reading proficiency*. Cambridge: Cambridge University Press.

────────────────── and C. Deville. 1999. Computer adaptive testing in second language contexts. In W. Grabe, *et al.* (eds.) *Annual Review of Applied Linguistics, 19. Survey of applied linguistics*. New York: Cambridge University Press. 273–299.

Chapelle, C. 1998. Construct definition and validity enquiry in SLA research. In L. F. Bachman and A. Cohen (eds.) *Interfaces between second language acquisition and language testing research*. Cambridge: Cambridge University Press. 32–70.

────────── 1999. Validity in language assessment. In W. Grabe, *et al.* (eds.) *Annual Review of Applied Linguistics, 19. Survey of applied linguistics*. New York: Cambridge University

Press. 254–272.

Cheng, L. 1997. How does washback influence teaching? Implications for Hong Kong. *Language Education.* 11.38–54.

Clapham, C. 1997. Review of Hill, C. and Parry, K. (eds.) *From testing to assessment.* 1994. *Language and Education.* 11.222–223.

─────── To appear. Assessment. In M. Byram (ed.) *Encyclopedia of Language Teaching and Learning.* London: Routledge.

Davidson, F., C. E. Turner and A. Huhta. 1997. Language testing standards. In C. Clapham and D. Corson (eds.) *Language testing and assessment, Vol. 7. The encyclopedia of language and education.* Dordrecht, Holland: Kluwer Academic. 303–311.

Davies, A. (ed.) 1997. *Ethics in language testing.* [Special issue of *Language Testing.* 14.3.]

DIALANG. 1997. 'DIALANG: A new European system for diagnostic language assessment.' *Language Testing.* Update. 21.38–39. [http://www.jyu.fi/DIALANG]

Drasgow, F. and J. Olson-Buchanan (eds.) 1998. *Innovations in computerized assessment.* Mahwah, NJ: L. Erlbaum.

Genesee, F. and J. Upshur. 1996. *Classroom-based evaluation in second language education.* Cambridge: Cambridge University Press.

Hamayan, E. 1995. Approaches to alternative assessment. In W. Grabe, *et al.* (eds.) *Annual Review of Applied Linguistics, 15. Survey of applied linguistics.* New York: Cambridge University Press. 212–226.

Hamp-Lyons, L. 1996. Applying ethical standards to portfolio assessment of writing in English as a second language. In M. Milanovic and N. Saville (eds.) *Performance testing, cognition and assessment.* Cambridge: Cambridge University Press. 151–162.

─────── 1997. Ethics in language testing. In C. Clapham and D. Corson (eds.) *Language testing and assessment, Vol. 7. The encyclopedia of language and education.* Dordrecht, Holland: Kluwer Academic. 323–333.

─────── and B. Lynch. 1998. Positivistic versus alternative perspectives on validity within the LTRC. Unpublished manuscript.

Hasselgren, A. 1998. Small words and valid testing. Bergen, Norway: University of Bergen. Unpublished Ph. D. diss.

Hill, C. and K. Parry. 1994. *From testing to assessment.* London: Longman.

Hudson, R. 1999. E-mail message to the Linguistics Association of Great Britain (LAGB) listserve. [See http://www.phon.ucl.ac.uk/home/dick/AL.html]

Huerta-Macias. 1995. Alternative assessment—Responses to commonly asked questions. *TESOL Journal.* 5.8–11.

Johnson, K. and H. Johnson (eds.) 1998. *Encyclopedic dictionary of applied linguistics.* Malden, MA: Blackwell.

Johnstone, R. In Press. Context-sensitive assessment of modern languages in primary and early secondary education: Scotland and the European experience. *Language Testing.* 17.

Kormos, J. 1999. Simulating conversations in oral proficiency assessment: A conversation analysis of role play and non-scripted interviews in language exams. *Language Testing.* 16.163–188.

Kunnan, A. J. 1998. An introduction to structural equation modeling for language assessment research. *Language Testing.* 15.295–332.

────────── (ed.) 2000. *Fairness and validation in language assessment.* Cambridge: Cambridge University Press.

Lynch, B. and T. McNamara. 1998. Using G-theory and many-facet Rasch measurement in the development of performance assessments of the ESL speaking skills of immigrants. *Language Testing.* 15.158–180.

McNamara, T. 1997. Performance testing. In C. Clapham and D. Corson (eds.) *Language testing and assessment, Vol. 7. The encyclopedia of language and education.* Dordrecht, Holland: Kluwer Academic. 131–139.

────────── 1998. Policy and social considerations in language assessment. In W. Grabe, *et al.* (eds.) *Annual Review of Applied Linguistics, 18. Foundations of second language teaching.* 18.304–319.

Messick, S. 1989. Validity. In R. L. Linn (ed.) *Educational measurement.* New York: American Council of Education/Macmillan. 13–103.

Moss, P. 1994. Can there be validity without reliability? *Educational Researcher.* 23.8.5–12.

North, B. and G. Schneider. 1998. Scaling descriptors for language proficiency scales. *Language Testing.* 15.217–262.

Norton, B. 1997. Accountability in language Assessment. In C. Clapham and D. Corson (eds.) *Language testing and assessment, Vol. 7. The encyclopedia of language and education.* Dordrecht, Holland: Kluwer Academic. 313–322.

Ordinate Corporation. 1998. *PhonePass test validation report.* Menlo Park, CA: Ordinate.

Papajohn, D. 1999. The effect of topic variation in performance testing: The case of the chemistry TEACH test for international teaching assistants. *Language Testing.* 16.52–81.

Rampton, B. 1997. Retuning in applied linguistics. *Applied Linguistics.* 7.3–25.

Rea-Dickens, P. In press. Snares and silver bullets: Disentangling the construct of formative assessment. *Language Testing.* 17.

Robinson, P. 1997. Individual differences and fundamental similarities of implicit and explicit adult second language learning. *Language Learning.* 47.45–99.

Shohamy, E. 1995. Performance assessment in language testing. In W. Grabe, *et al.* (eds.) *Annual Review of Applied Linguistics, 15. Survey of applied linguistics.* New York: Cambridge University Press. 188–211.

Shohamy, E. 1998. How can language testing and SLA benefit from each other? The case of discourse. In L. F. Bachman and A. Cohen. (eds.) *Interfaces between second language acquisition and language testing research*. Cambridge: Cambridge University Press. 156–176.

Skehan, P. 1998. Task-based instruction. In W. Grabe, *et al.* (eds.) *Annual Review of Applied Linguistics, 18. Foundations of second language teaching*. New York: Cambridge University Press. 304–319.

———— and P. Foster. 1999. The influence of task structure and processing conditions on narrative retellings. *Language Learning*. 49.93–120.

Spolsky, B. 1995. *Measured words*. Oxford: Oxford University Press.

Stansfield, C. 1994. Developments in foreign language testing and instruction: A national perspective. In C. Hancock (ed.) *Teaching, testing and assessment: Making the connection*. Lincolnwood, IL: National Textbook Company. 43–67.

Upshur, J. and C. Turner. 1998. Systematic effects in the rating of second-language speaking ability: Test method and learner discourse. *Language Testing*. 16.82–111.

Valette, R. 1994. Teaching, testing and assessment: Conceptualizing the relationship. In C. Hancock (ed.) *Teaching, testing and assessment: Making the connection*. Lincolnwood, IL: National Textbook Company. 1–42.

Wall, D. 1997. Impact and washback in language. In C. Clapham and D. Corson (eds.) *Language testing and assessment, Vol. 7. The encyclopedia of language and education*. Dordrecht, Holland: Kluwer Academic. 291–302.

Widdowson, H. G. 1980. Models and fictions. *Applied Linguistics*. 1.165–170.

SECOND LANGUAGE ACQUISITON AND SECOND LANGUAGE PROCESSING

SECOND LANGUAGE ACQUISITION AND APPLIED LINGUISTICS

Diane Larsen-Freeman

INTRODUCTION

Just as applied linguistics (AL) may be said to be an emerging discipline, so too is one of its sub-fields, second language acquisition (SLA). The parallelism may not be surprising; after all, a difference of only about twenty years separates the points at which the two were identified as autonomous fields of inquiry.[1] Then, too, the two share central defining concepts. AL draws on multidisciplinary theoretical and empirical perspectives to address real-world issues and problems in which language is central (Brumfit 1997). SLA draws on multidisciplinary theoretical and empirical perspectives to address the specific issue of how people acquire a second language and the specific problem of why everyone does not do so successfully. Furthermore, the two share something else: At this juncture in the evolution of AL and SLA, both are grappling with fundamental definitional issues, ones even extending to the nature of language itself. (See Larsen-Freeman 1997a for how this is true of AL.) Should AL and SLA deal successfully with these challenges, both will have much to contribute in the decade to come. Should they instead succumb to internecine feuding and fragmentation, the future will not be as bright.

In this chapter, I will first make some introductory remarks about the SLA process and the differential success of second language learners. Next, I will discuss the fundamental challenges that this characterization faces. Then I will say what contributions I think SLA is capable of in the coming decade; I will also note the main obstacles confronting it. I will conclude by nominating topics for a training and development curriculum for future applied linguists from an SLA perspective.

THEORETICAL FOUNDATIONS OF SLA: THE ISSUE OF ACQUISITION AND THE PROBLEM OF DIFFERENTIAL SUCCESS

The disciplines that SLA draws on, and potentially contributes to, are many. Some of the more prominent include: first language acquisition, linguistics (e.g., issues of language transfer, UG), psychology (e.g., information processing, skill-learning, connectionism), sociolinguistics (e.g., variation, pragmatics, sociocultural theory), and education (e.g., immersion, input-based teaching approaches). It would be impossible to review here the many recent research findings that have contributed to our understanding of SLA from these disciplines; thankfully, it is also unnecessary. The previous volume of the *Annual Review of Applied Linguistics* featured up-to-date summaries of each of these areas (Foster-Cohen for first language acquisition, N. Ellis and Segalowitz & Lightbown for psychology, Young and Kasper & Rose for sociolinguistics, R. Ellis and Segalowitz & Lightbown for education; see also Mitchell and Myles 1998 for a recent review of these varied perspectives). The only discipline that was not specifically addressed in a separate chapter in last year's volume was linguistics; however, as Grabe (as Editor of the volume) noted in the Foreword, almost all of the authors that dealt with SLA issues felt obliged to address UG in their work, whether or not they accepted its tenets.

In place of a multidisciplinary research review, then, I will review the theoretical foundations of what has been referred to as "mainstream" SLA (Breen 1985). I do so in order to provide a backdrop for my later comments. My rendition will be brief, its brevity hopefully excusable because by now it is very familiar. Although admonished by Thomas (1998) to avoid "programmatic ahistoricity," most SLA researchers would agree that the autonomous study of SLA arose in modern times approximately thirty years ago (Gass, Fleck, Leder and Svetics 1998), born of observations concerning the systematicity of learners' language, which were inspired by the revolution taking place in linguistics and cognitive psychology at the time. In light of the status quo view that successful SLA was a matter of overcoming the habits of the first language, what was striking to researchers in those early days was the degree to which diverse learners' linguistic performance converged. To be sure, there were obvious individual differences and native language effects, with later studies bringing to light more subtle, yet widespread, L1 transfer. Still, the discovery of common morpheme accuracy or acquisition orders and common developmental sequences for basic syntactic structures generated a great deal of excitement. Even those who may not have accepted an innate LAD in its Chomskyan sense were impressed with the learners' creative construction and sought explanations for the shared features of learners' interlanguage (IL) by pointing to the learning and communicative strategies they employed, such as imitation of formulaic utterances, relexification, and incorporation. Clearly, learner performance was not just a reflex of the L1.

Due to SLA's pedigree, it is not surprising that a great deal of attention was given to the learners' developing morphosyntactic system. Learners were thought to be attempting to acquire the rules of the target language through an inductive hypothesis-formation process. Later, a more deductive process was proposed, one that was universal-grammar driven. Both processes were rendered possible when the input to learners was made comprehensible. This, in turn, was best accomplished when learners' negotiated meaning during communicative interactions. Understanding meaningful input and attempting to express meaning were hypothesized to stimulate interlanguage development.

However, learners needed to be at an appropriate developmental stage in order to benefit from any interaction. If they weren't able to process the input, interaction would not likely lead to IL restructuring. Even with favorable acquisition conditions, not all learners successfully traversed the IL continuum. L2 learners learned at different rates and ultimately attained different levels of proficiency. Many factors were posited to account for the differential success of L2 learners: motivation, attitude, aptitude, age, cognitive style, strategies, personality, hemisphericity, etc.

Recent research has centered on the role of input and interaction in SLA (see Gass 1997, Gass, Mackey and Pica 1998) and the facilitation of second language learning brought about by focusing learners' attention on linguistic form during communicative interactions (Doughty and Williams 1998, R. Ellis 1997, Spada 1997). Research on differential success has been extended recently by Schumann (1998) for neurobiology, Birdsong (1999) for the critical period hypothesis, and Breen (to appear) for other learner factors.

Of course, summarizing thirty years of SLA research, as I have done, is problematic for a number of reasons. First of all, I have omitted the names and individual contributions of many researchers. Second, it is a product of my own necessarily limited experience. Third, the coherence imposed by a retrospective perspective conceals disagreements along the way, many of which still exist, including at least the following:

- The extent of L1 influence on the L2,
- The role of formulaic utterances,
- The sufficiency of comprehensible input,
- The existence of free variation,
- The necessity of noticing,
- The value of explicit instruction,
- The feasibility of a non-interface position,
- The need for negative evidence,
- The existence of an age-related critical period,
- The teachability of "good language learner" learning strategies,
- The role of metalinguistic knowledge.

It is also common knowledge that, up to this point, SLA research has been rather limited. A great deal of the research has focused on the acquisition of European languages, the acquisition of second languages (as opposed to third, fourth, etc.), and, as I said earlier, mainly, although certainly not exclusively, on the acquisition of morphosyntax.[2]

However, in hindsight, and perhaps only because it is hindsight, it has seemed that these disagreements and limitations could be accommodated within the prevailing SLA paradigm. The disagreements have not all been resolved, nor all the limitations addressed; however, in theory, doing so might, for many of these issues, only require mid-course corrections or expansions. In contrast, at this point in its emergence, the sub-discipline of SLA is facing far more fundamental challenges. New theoretical perspectives have been advanced in the field without displacing established ones. This is not necessarily a problem, of course: In fact, it could be taken as a sign of vitality of the field. However, there has been a crescendo of dissonance accompanying the new perspectives which does not allow easy accommodation within the prevailing paradigm. I turn now to considering the dissonant perspectives.

CHALLENGES TO THE MAINSTREAM VIEW OF SLA

Challenges to the mainstream view have been issued concerning the language acquisition process, the language learner, and language itself. I will treat each of these in turn.

1. The language acquisition process

The most trenchant criticism of the characterization of the language acquisition process as I have just depicted it is that it fails to take into account the social reality: Mainstream SLA research is seen to be asocial (Breen 1985). While acknowledging the value of certain of its constructs (i.e., the learner's interpretation of meaningful input and the effort to express meaning as catalysts for language learning, the creative construction of interlanguage, and the use of learning and communicative strategies), Breen (1998) criticizes SLA research for being decontextualized. As he puts it, "Mainstream SLA research, in focusing upon the relationship between the learner and the language data, is conducted and reported on in ways that appear to overlook the social reality in which the research is actually conducted" (1998:116). The erroneous assumption, according to Breen, is that the interaction between the learner's mental resources and the features of linguistic input will provide a sufficiently adequate explanation of language learning. Crookes (1997) also points to SLA's individualistic, asocial orientation.

Others have found the highly cognitivist view of language acquisition to date to be a fundamental weakness, but have not been as circumspect as Breen and Crookes in their criticism. Firth and Wagner (1997) have proposed a radical reconceptualization of SLA study, asserting that language should be seen and studied as a social, contextualized phenomenon (Liddicoat 1997). In their critique, they reject fundamental concepts upon which mainstream SLA is based. For instance, they write, "...we are unable to accept the premises of 'interlanguage' —namely, that language learning is a transitional process that has a distinct and visible 'end' " (Firth and Wagner 1998:91). In the same vein, SLA researchers have been criticized for measuring learner performance against native speaker norms (Cook 1999, Klein 1998) so that learners are perceived as "failing" when they do not achieve them.

SLA researchers Lantolf and Appell (1994) and Hall (1997) have found in Vygotskyan ideas a theoretical stance to counter what they perceive to be a reductive cognitivism in the field. Vygotsky saw learning as embedded within, and inseparable from, social activity. These researchers propose an extension of investigations into SLA to include a "sociocultural" perspective. As Lantolf and Pavlenko (1995) put it:

> ...[sociocultural theory] situates the locus of learning in the dialogic interactions that arise between socially constituted individuals engaged in activities which are co-constructed with other individuals rather than in the heads of solipsistic beings. Learning hinges not so much on richness of input, but crucially on the choices made by individuals as responsible agents with dispositions to think and act in certain ways rooted in their discursive histories. Because of its insistence on the embeddedness of human activity, SCT allows us to observe learning in all of its fuzziness as it emerges from dialogic activity. This perspective is quite distinct from waiting for learning to crystallize into transitory or permanent steady states of IL competence (1995:116).

Mainstream SLA researchers have not been left defenseless. As Gass (1998), Kasper (1997), and Poulisse (1997) counter, social interaction has been studied, but since the focus of SLA is on language acquisition, not language use, it is natural to attend more to psycholinguistic variables than sociolinguistic ones. Long (1997) also makes this point, suggesting that the matter of the influence of social variables should not be subjected to polemics, but rather left to the results of empirical research to determine. A review of research findings thus far has led him (Long 1996) to conclude that whether or not learner interactions have occurred in "laboratory" or "natural" settings, the results have been very similar, Breen's (1996; 1998; to appear) conviction about the impact of contextual differences notwithstanding (see also Foster 1998, Tarone 1997).

2. The language learner

As for constructs of the language learner, they too have come under attack. Traditionally, the learner has been seen from an etic perspective, one that has led researchers, it is alleged, to see learners as idealized, autonomous language acquirers (Pennycook 1997). Perhaps, as Firth (1996), Firth and Wagner (1997), and Rampton (1997) argue, learner language forms are different from the target language structures, not because of incomplete L2 competence, nor fossilizations of IL forms, but rather because the marked or "deviant" forms are deployed by the learners for social purposes—they may be empathizing with their interlocutors, for example, or they may be reverting to earlier features of their interlanguage in order to signal that they are, in fact, learners (Rampton 1987). At the least, an emic perspective may sort out the motivation behind the use of such "deviant" forms. The position they seek to advance is that non-native speakers have multiple social identities, being a learner is just one of them.

The socioculturalists add that Activity Theory respects the agency of language learners, not depicting them as passive recipients of modified input, but as actively (co)constructing their own learning and identity in an L2 (Lantolf and Pavlenko 1995; to appear). In a similar vein, Norton and Toohey (to appear) challenge another long-standing concept of mainstream SLA by questioning the construct of "the good language learner" and the characteristics and behaviors associated with the concept by mainstream SLA researchers. Like Lantolf and Pavlenko, they argue that the construct fails to acknowledge the complex, social, cultural, and historical relationships and practices embedded in second language learning sites. The data they examine from two different contexts reveals how classroom practices and peer relationships shape the process and outcomes of learning for different learners.

Again, other SLA researchers have responded. Kasper (1997) points out that throughout social science, "...even disciplines such as anthropology that favor holistic and socially situated approaches to research, such as enthnography, construct their idealized agents by reducing away what seems trivial in terms of the adopted theory...." "The constructs 'nonnative speaker' and 'learner,' (rejected by Firth and Wagner [1997]) focus upon the aspect that is *common* to the studied agents, and relevant to the global research context (or discourse universe) of L2 generally and L2 acquisition (SLA) specifically" (1997:309). Long (1997) adds that Firth and Wagner's complaint—that SLA makes a distinction between native and nonnative speakers or learners while underestimating the importance of other social identities (father, friend, business partner, etc.)—is true; whether this is justified is a matter best left to empirical resolution.

3. Language

An additional challenge to the mainstream view of SLA is the nature of the property theory— "what a domain of knowledge is and how it is represented" (N. Ellis 1999:23). Gregg (1993:278) makes his position perfectly clear. To him, "...the overall explanadum is the acquisition (or non-acquisition) of L2 competence in the Chomskyan sense." Although not all SLA researchers would see explaining grammatical competence as the ultimate goal of SLA research, most SLA researchers have subscribed to the view, as I stated above, that language is a rule-governed phenomenon.

The theoretical underpinnings of the Chomskyan position are being increasingly challenged by empiricists who believe that language acquisition can be accounted for solely in terms of general learning and cognition, rather than a built-in UG (N. Segalowitz and Lightbown 1999; see also Robinson in press, Skehan 1998). Certain of them have looked to connectionist modeling of neural networks as representing a more plausible neural architecture than called for by an innate "language instinct" (Elman, *et al.* 1996, Quartz and Sejnowski 1997; cf. S. Segalowitz and Bernstein 1997). Significant for the prevailing SLA view, a connectionist explanation implies a non-rule, non-representation, activated node account of what is stored. Although connectionist networks exhibit behavior that could be described by rules, they are not rule-governed (N. Ellis 1998). Instead, artificial neurons extract regularities from masses of input data. Recent models have demonstrated that the acquisition of morphology (N. Ellis and Schmidt 1998) and syntax (MacWhinney 1997) may be accounted for by simple associative learning principles (N. Ellis 1998; 1999); in addition, such models have successfully simulated bilingual lexicons (Meara 1999b).

CONTRIBUTIONS TO, AND OBSTACLES CONFRONTING, SLA/AL IN THE COMING DECADE

1. Internal to the field

It seems to me that a major contribution that SLA/AL can make in the next decade will be to come to terms with these many challenges. How this mediation is to be accomplished remains to be worked out; however, it would be useful to consider certain alternative scenarios.

One option is to align oneself with one side of a debate and to adduce evidence (hopefully) to argue for its superiority. This approach is the normal *modus operandi* in science, of course—to subject disputes to empirical resolution. For instance, the debate over the goal of SLA research (to explain competence and/or performance) that ensued in 1990 (Gregg 1990, R. Ellis 1990, Tarone 1990; see also Brown, Malmkjær and Williams 1996) was one that would have had far-reaching consequences had one side triumphed. Upon subsequent review of the positions, however, Eckman (1994) concluded that the issue being debated was an empirical one and that more data were needed to adjudicate it. Eckman's conclusion illustrates this first option: Each side would be encouraged to pursue its own research agenda apart from the other(s): the psycholinguists separate from the sociolinguists, the innatists separate from the cognitivists/connectionists. Such an option, however, does not by itself respond to the charge made by Firth and Wagner (1998) that certain researchers, emphasizing the centrality of language acquisition over language use, erect "barriers, sealing off the area of SLA as a kind of intellectual 'private property' " (1998:91). In Firth and Wagner's view, "... SLA seems to be dominated by Chomskian thinking to such a degree that others' frames of reference for the understanding of language and cognition have become inconceivable" (1998:92).

It is importan to note, however, that with any dualism, the hegemony can extend in either direction. As Kirshner and Whitson (1997) point out, "the Vygotskyan tradition is similarly weighted toward a deterministic social plane. The source of this weighting is the central tenet that '...social relations or relations among people genetically underlie all higher [mental] functions and their relationships' " (Vygotsky 1981:163, in Kirshner and Whitson 1997:8). Since it is rather unlikely that empirical findings will resolve these debates once and for all, it seems the field will be subjected to repeated hegemonic pendulum swings. Givón (1999) quotes the eminent biologist Stephen Jay Gould with regard to the debate between an innate generative position and a input-driven emergent position: "...I doubt that such a controversy could have arisen unless both positions were valid (though incomplete)..." (Gould 1977:59). A better option, then, to breach the hegemony alleged by Firth and Wagner is to adopt a more complex, multifocal strategy.

A pluralistic stance might have it that both individual-cognitive and social-cultural perspectives have their place, as do innatist and empiricist positions. Both are necessary; both have something to contribute. Poulisse (1997), for example, though arguing for a psycholinguistic perspective, observes that there is room for both psycholinguistic and sociolinguistic research. And Firth and Wagner (1998) do acknowledge that Long and Kasper were right to point out the importance of acquisition. Certainly one reading of Firth and Wagner (1997) is that they are simply seeking balance: SLA is imbalanced in favor of cognitive-oriented theories and methodologies, they assert, at the expense of socially-oriented theories and methodologies.

Pienemann (1998) makes a reasonable case for this second option, and also suggests a way that it might be managed. Advocating for a modular approach to complicated issues such as the nature of SLA, he points out that a worthwhile research strategy is to break down the task of explaining SLA into discrete subtasks. Germane to the present discussion, Pienemann recommends separating the cognitive from the social as each "...have a degree of autonomy, each following its own logic" (1998:35). This would achieve more, in Pienemann's view, than an attempt such as Towell and Hawkins' (1994) to integrate a parametrization approach with a cognitive one, since such a synthesis does not permit tests of all of the issues. Pienemann is careful to add, however, that the modular approach he proposes works well "...as long as the different modules are able to communicate with each other and are theoretically consistent" (1998:33). In a related comment, Gass (1998) holds that few would disagree that it is a good thing for data to be considered from different perspectives; however, she adds that for this multifocal approach to be a tenable option, we have to be asking the same questions. It is not clear that we are.

Liddicoat (1997), for example, makes the case that rectifying the imbalance is not all it would take:

> What F[irth] & W[agner] propose in their call for rebalancing the field of SLA requires not only a rebalancing of the theoretical stance of the field, but has far reaching implications for the ways in which research in the field is designed and carried out at practical levels. Reconceptualizing SLA to take

into consideration language as a social and contextual phenomenon requires a concomitant reanalysis of the research methods used to collect the data used for SLA research to ensure that the adopted approaches do actually examine language in appropriate contexts (1997:316).

Without such a reconceptualization and a commitment to review and perhaps employ new research methodologies, then, it is not likely that we are going to meet Pienemann's conditions of communication and theoretical consistency. A third option, therefore, might be to reconceptualize the way we work—to deal with our differences by finding a way to transcend them. At the risk of overstating the need, I might even say that what is required is a paradigm shift (Gregg, Long, Jordan and Beretta 1997) or at least a shared epistemology.

It is my opinion that conceiving of language and its acquisition as complex, dynamical, nonlinear systems shows promise in this regard, providing a metaphorical lens through which diverse perspectives can be accommodated, indeed integrated (Larsen-Freeman 1997b; 1998; 1999). Innatism is reflected in such systems by the fact that they are very sensitive to their initial conditions, conditions following Chaos/Complexity Theory, which might be viewed as built-in fields of attraction. These systems can easily accommodate cognitive or connectionist perspectives as well as innatist views (MacWhinney 1998; 1999, Robinson in press). Computer implementations, at least, show that distributed dynamic systems with built-in attractors exhibit properties of adaptability, goal orientedness, self-repair, and efficient learning and recognition under noisy conditions (Mohanan 1992). These systems are also nonentropic. They are self-organizing, creating order where none existed before. They accomplish this both through an emergent process whereby individuals create new linguistic patterns or engage in morphogenesis, while at the same time, through an adaptation process, internal changes in their linguistic systems are subject to the pressure to conform or to adapt to those of other members of the community. Indeed, a social-interactive view of language acquisition is clearly compatible with this theory. (See, for example, Cameron 1999, Snow 1999.)

Obviously there are disadvantages to using such a wide-angle lens. First, if such an interpretation is ever to move beyond the metaphorical level, we run into problems with falsifiability due to its elaborate and integrated nature. For instance, a critical tenet of Chaos/Complexity Theory is that the behavior of the whole system emerges (i.e., it is not reflected in any one part, nor directed by a central executive). Second, importing a theory from one discipline into another is a risky business, particularly as the borrowing in this case is from a physical science to a social science. Third, this interpretation must still be subject to the same empirical rigor as any of the other perspectives—through model-building (Meara 1999a), laboratory-type research(Hulstijn and De Keyser 1997), qualitative research (Edge and Richards 1998), etc. Nonetheless, I am convinced that a major contribution of SLA/AL over the next decade lies in coming to terms with our differences—not so that we all agree, but so that the field can become more inclusive, when justified, and so that the complexity of the SLA process and learners is duly respected. A coherent epistemology would be a remarkable contribution of the next decade. Should we fail to accomplish this, I fear that we will experience continued internecine feuding and fragmentation.

2. External to the field

Besides getting our own house in order, it should not be forgotten that SLA deals with real-world issues and problems. As indicated in the review of mainstream SLA, many researchers continue to seek optimal solutions to nettle-some pedagogical dilemmas of classroom instruction. In addition, SLA has not had much to say yet on the use of technology in second language learning (but see van Lier 1999). Questions that need addressing include, for example, whether computers encourage a different type of learning from what transpires in a classroom—what Papert (1980) called "syntonic" learning, for instance, or Noblett (personal communication) refers to as "relational learning." There are many other real-life problems to contend with these days which cry out for an informed SLA/AL perspective. The controversy over the use of Ebonics for instructional purposes is one (e.g., Rickford 1999). The challenge bilingual education faces in California is another (Krashen 1999). A third is the recent situation at the City University of New York, in which the time given to non-native speakers of English for remediation was seriously curtailed.

An obstacle related to our external agenda is our relative inexperience in the political arena. We need to learn how to become more politically-savvy advocates for our constituents—language learners and teachers.

THE TRAINING AND DEVELOPMENT OF FUTURE APPLIED LINGUISTS

It follows from this review, then, that from an SLA perspective, AL students should become well-versed in the extant paradigm, but should also be introduced to non-paradigmatic points of view. Varying proposals should be vetted, with their strengths and limitations discussed. In addition, the full spectrum of research methods, qualitative and quantitative, should be taught, with ample opportunity for first-hand, supervised application. Finally, a social-justice perspective should be cultivated. We might even consider some training in political activism, with the limited goal of encouraging future applied linguists to provide a rational voice when second language acquisition potential is threatened by political realities.

NOTES

1. Howatt (1984) dates the first use of the term "applied linguistics" to the inauguration of the journal *Language Learning: A Journal of Applied Linguistics* in 1948. Most SLA researchers would claim that SLA was launched in 1967 with the publication of Corder's "The significance of learners' errors."

2. For this reason, research investigating other languages is very welcome and seems to be growing (e.g., in 1998, a number of articles report on the acquisition of Japanese as a second language: Mori, Shirai and Kurono, Rounds and Kanagy). Also a good sign is the fact that entire volumes of leading journals have been devoted to other subsystems of language recently: for example phonology (Major 1998, Leather 1999) and vocabulary (Wesch and Paribakht 1999). In addition, the influence of second languages on third language acquisition has recently been examined by Williams and Hammarberg (1998) and Dewaele (1998).

ANNOTATED BIBLIOGRAPHY

Breen, M. (ed.) To appear. *Learner contributions to language learning: New directions in research.* Harlow: Pearson Education.

The origin of this volume was the invited colloquium, "Constructions of the learner in second language acquisition research," presented at the 1998 Annual

Conference of the American Association for Applied Linguistics. This collection of papers addresses two themes: how learners are constructed by research(ers) or by the learning process, and how learners themselves construct language learning conceptually or through action. Issues addressed by the authors paint a picture of the learner's contribution to SLA and how certain of these contributions appear to be related to success in language learning. It also reveals the diverse nature of learner conceptualizations. This book provides useful reviews of previous research in a wide range of aspects of SLA. More provocatively, it also challenges some of the "givens" in mainstream SLA research.

Gass, S. M. 1997. *Input, interaction and the second language learner.* Mahwah, NJ: L. Erlbaum.

The stated goal of the author is "...to provide a view of the relationship among input, interaction, and second language acquisition." In other words, it provides a good review of many of the issues in mainstream SLA. In a balanced way, Gass presents the major issues in the field (e.g., the question of negative evidence, variability in the input, the functions of modified input) with treatments of different theoretical perspectives (e.g., UG, MacWhinney's competition model, Krashen's monitor model).

Kirshner, D. and J. Whitson (eds.) 1997. *Situated cognition: Social, semiotic, and psychological perspectives.* Mahwah, NJ: L. Erlbaum.

In their preface, the authors make the case that the shift within cognitive science to situated cognition theory is at least as profound as the shift from behaviorism to cognitivism some 35 years ago. They write that "...the opportunity to explore learning and knowledge as processes that occur in a local, subjective and socially constructed world is severely limited by behaviorist and cognitivist paradigms" (1997:vii). Situational cognitionists thus recognize the need for the integration of individual and social perspectives. Though there are no chapters on language acquisition, and only one chapter that deals with language (Gee's on reading), this book is relevant to mainstream SLA, which has, as I have indicated in this review, been accused of being asocial. There is also some interesting discussion on what new units of analysis would look like, a question I posed as an issue raised by a Chaos/Complexity Theory perspective (Larsen-Freeman 1997a).

MacWhinney, B. (ed.) 1999. *The emergence of language.* Mahwah, NJ: L. Erlbaum.

The chapters in this book were first delivered as papers in May 1997 at the 28th Carnegie Mellon Symposium on Cognition with the theme "Emergentist approaches to language acquisition." Although the papers mostly deal with first, not second, language acquisition, I like this volume for two reasons. First, although not all contributors subscribe to an explicit emergentist "party line," they are able to demonstrate the richness of seeing language and its acquisition from this perspective. Second, several of the chapters in this book walk the middle ground that I have here suggested might benefit SLA. As Editor, MacWhinney writes in his introduction: "Emergentism should not be interpreted as a radical rejection of either nativism or empiricism. On the contrary, emergentism views nativist and empiricist formulations as partial components of a more complete account. The traditional contrast between nativist and empiricism revolves around the fact that they describe developmental processes that operate across different time frames" (1999:xi). This is the same conclusion that I arrived at independently, which I applied to SLA in terms of discussing diachrony and synchrony in language, and acquisition and use in SLA (Larsen-Freeman 1999).

Mitchell, R. and F. Myles. 1998. *Second language learning theories.* London: Arnold.

The opening two chapters of this book introduce readers to key concepts in SLA and offer an account of its recent history. Six chapters follow, each surveying a different perspective on SLA: linguistic, cognitive, functional/ pragmatic, input/ interactional, sociocultural, and sociolinguistic. The authors include a balanced treatment of each, summarizing their strengths and weaknesses. They conclude by noting that grand synthesizing theories have not received much support in the field (although they do not mention which ones) and by emphasizing their impression that there is great diversity of perspectives. Writing a comprehensive account of the burgeoning SLA research at this point in time is a formidable undertaking, and so the authors probably chose wisely to approach it by discussing the various theoretical perspectives in the field. This is a valid and valuable way to make sense of the field. What is sacrificed in this representation, though, is much of the history and many of the details of the SLA research endeavor.

UNANNOTATED BIBLIOGRAPHY

Birdsong, D. (ed.) 1999. *Second language acquisition and the critical period hypothesis*. Mahwah, NJ: L. Erlbaum.

Breen, M. 1985. The social context for language learning: A neglected situation? *Studies in Second Language Acquisition*. 7.135–158.

——— 1996. Constructions of the learner in SLA research. In J. E. Alatis, C. A. Straehle, M. Ronkin and B. Gallenberger (eds.) *Georgetown University round table on languages & linguistics 1996*. Washington, DC: Georgetown University Press. 84–107.

——— 1998. Navigating the discourse: On what is learned in the language classroom. In W. Renandya and G. Jacobs (eds.) *On language and language learning*. Singapore: SEAMEO Regional Language Centre. 115–144.

Brown, G., K. Malmkjær and J. Williams (eds.) 1996. *Performance and competence in second language acquisition*. Cambridge: Cambridge University Press.

Brumfit, C. 1997. Theoretical practice: Applied linguistics as pure and practical science. *AILA Review*. 12.18–30.

Cameron, L. 1999. Aligning Vygotsky and complexity theory in the analysis of metaphor in interaction. Paper presented at the Chaos/Complexity Perspective on Applied Linguistics Colloquium, American Association for Applied Linguistics Conference. Stamford, CT, March 1999.

Cook, V. 1999. Going beyond the native speaker in language teaching. *TESOL Quarterly*. 33.209.

Crookes, G. 1997. SLA and second language pedagogy: A socioeducational perspective. *Studies in Second Language Acquisition*. 19.93–116.

Dewaele, J.-M. 1998. Lexical inventions: French interlanguage as L2 versus L3. *Applied Linguistics*. 19.471–490.

Doughty, C. and J. Williams (eds.) 1998. *Focus on form in classroom second language acquisition*. Cambridge: Cambridge University Press.

Eckman, F. R. 1994. The competence-performance issue in second-language acquisition theory: A debate. In E. E. Tarone, S. M. Gass and A. D. Cohen (eds.) *Research methodology in second-language acquisition*. Hillsdale, NJ: L. Erlbaum. 3–15.

Edge, J. and K. Richards. 1998. May I see your warrant please? Justifying outcomes in qualitative research. *Applied Linguistics*. 19.334–356.

Ellis, N. C. 1998. Emergentism, connectionism and language learning. *Language Learning*. 48.631–664.

——— 1999. Cognitive approaches to SLA. In W. Grabe, *et al.* (eds.) *Annual Review of Applied Linguistics, 19. Survey of applied linguistics*. New York: Cambridge University

Press. 22–42.

Ellis, N. C. and R. Schmidt. 1998. Rules or associations in the acquisition of morphology? The frequency by regularity interaction in human and PDP learning of morphosyntax. *Language and Cognitive Processes*. 13.307–336.

Ellis, R. 1990. A response to Gregg. *Applied Linguistics*. 11.384–391.

——— 1997. *SLA research and language teaching*. Oxford: Oxford University Press.

Elman, J., E. Bates, M. Johnson, A. Karmiloff-Smith, D. Parisi and K. Plunkett. 1996. *Rethinking innateness: A connectionist perspective on development*. Cambridge, MA: MIT Press.

Firth, A. 1996. The discursive accomplishment of normality: On "lingua franca" English and conversation analysis. *Journal of Pragmatics*. 26.1–23.

——— and J. Wagner. 1997. On discourse, communication, and (some) fundamental concepts in SLA. *Modern Language Journal*. 81.285–300.

——— 1998. SLA property: No trespassing! *Modern Language Journal*. 82.91–94.

Foster, P. 1998. A classroom perspective on the negotiation of meaning. *Applied Linguistics*. 19.1–23.

Gass, S. M. 1998. Apples and oranges: Or, why apples are not orange and don't need to be. *Modern Language Journal*. 82.83–90.

———, C. Fleck, N. Leder and I. Svetics. 1998. Ahistoricity revisited: Does SLA have a history? *Studies in Second Acquisition*. 20.407–421.

———, A. Mackey and T. Pica. 1998. The role of input and interaction in second language acquisition. *Modern Language Journal*. 82.299–307.

Givón, T. 1999. Generativity and variation: The notion "rule of grammar" revisited. In B. MacWhinney (ed.) *The emergence of language*. Mahwah, NJ: L. Erlbaum. 81–114.

Gould, S. J. 1977. *Ontogeny and phylogeny*. Cambridge: Harvard University Press.

Gregg, K. 1990. The variable competence model of second language acquisition and why it isn't. *Applied Linguistics*. 11.364–383.

——— 1993. Taking explanations seriously; or, let a couple of flowers bloom. *Applied Linguistics*. 14.276–294.

———, M. Long, G. Jordan and A. Beretta. 1997. Rationality and its discontents in SLA. *Applied Linguistics*. 18.538–558.

Hall, J. K. 1997. A consideration of SLA as a theory of practice. *Modern Language Journal*. 81.301–306.

Howatt, A. P. R. 1984. *History of English language teaching*. Oxford: Oxford University Press.

Hulstijn, J. and R. De Keyser (eds.) 1997. *Testing SLA theory in the research laboratory*. [Special issue of *Studies in Second Language Acquisition*. 19.2.]

Kasper, G. 1997. "A" stands for acquisition. *Modern Language Journal*. 81.307–312.

Klein, W. 1998. The contribution of second language acquisition research. *Language Learning.* 48.527–550.

Krashen, S. 1999. *Condemned without a trial: Bogus arguments against bilingual education.* Westport, CT: Heinemann.

Lantolf, J. and G. Appel (eds.) 1994. *Vygotskyan approaches to second language research.* Norwood, NJ: Ablex.

——— and A. Pavlenko. 1995. Sociocultural theory and second language acquisition. In W. Grabe, et al. (eds.) *Annual Review of Applied Linguistics, 15. Survey of applied linguistics.* New York: Cambridge University Press. 108–124.

——— To appear. Understanding second language learners as people. In M. Breen (ed.) *Learner contributions to language learning: New directions in research.* Harlow: Pearson Education.

Larsen-Freeman, D. 1997a. Chaos/complexity science and second language acquisition. *Applied Linguistics.* 18.141–165.

——— 1997b. Impressions of AILA 1996: Remarks delivered at the closing plenary session, 11th World Congress of Applied Linguistics. *AILA Review.* 12.87–92.

——— 1998. On the scope of second language acquisition research: "The 'learner variety' and beyond." *Language Learning.* 48.551–556.

——— 1999. Chaos/complexity theory: Blurring the boundaries. Paper presented at the Chaos/Complexity Perspective on Applied Linguistics Colloquium, American Association for Applied Linguistics Conference. Stamford, CT, March 1999.

Leather, J. (ed.) 1999. *Phonological issues in language learning.* [Special issue of *Language Learning.* 49. Supplement 1.]

Liddicoat, A. 1997. Interaction, social structure, and second language use. *Modern Language Journal.* 81.313–317.

Long, M. 1996. The role of the linguistic environment in second language acquisition. In W. Ritchie and T. Bhatia (eds.) *Handbook of second language acquisition.* San Diego, CA: Academic Press. 413–468.

——— 1997. Consruct validity in SLA research. *Modern Language Journal.* 81.318–323.

MacWhinney, B. 1997. Second language acquisition and the competition model. In A. M. B. de Groot and J. F. Kroll (eds.) *Tutorials in bilingualism: Psycholinguistic perspectives.* Mahwah, NJ: L. Erlbaum. 113–144.

——— 1998. Models of the emergence of language. *Annual Review of Psychology.* 49:199–227.

Major, R. (ed.) 1998. *Interlanguage phonetics and phonology.* [Special issue of *Studies in Second Language Acquisition.* 20.2.]

Meara, P. 1999a. Remarks as discussant. Chaos/Complexity Perspective on Applied Linguistics Colloquium, American Association for Applied Linguistics Conference. Stamford, CT,

March 1999.
Meara, P. 1999b. Self-organization in bilingual lexicons. In P. Broeder and J. Murre (eds.) *Language and thought in development*. Tübingen: Gunter Narr Verlag. 127–144.
Mohanan, K. P. 1992. Emergence of complexity in phonological development. In C. Ferguson, L. Menn and C. Stoel-Gammon (eds.) *Phonological development*. Timonium, MD: York Press, Inc. 635–662.
Mori, Y. 1998. Effects of first language and phonological accessibility on Kanji recognition. *Modern Language Journal*. 82.69–82.
Norton, B. and K. Toohey. To appear. Reconceptualizing "the good language learner." In M. Breen (ed.) *Learner contributions to language learning: New directions in research*. Harlow: Pearson Education.
Papert, S. 1980. *Mindstorms: Children, computers, and powerful ideas*. New York: Basic Books.
Pennycook, A. 1997. Cultural alternatives and autonomy. In P. Benson and P. Voller (eds.) *Autonomy and independence in language learning*. London: Longman. 35–53.
Pienemann, M. 1998. *Language processing and second language development*. Amsterdam: J. Benjamins.
Poulisse, N. 1997. Some words in defense of the psycholinguistic approach. *Modern Language Journal*. 81.324–328.
Prince, A. and P. Smolensky. 1997. Optimality: From neural networks to universal grammar. *Science*. 275.1604–1610.
Quartz, S. R. and T. J. Sejnowski. 1997. The neural basis of cognitive development: A constructivist manifesto. *Behavioral and Brain Sciences*. 20.537–556.
Rampton, B. 1987. Stylistic variability and not speaking "normal" English. In R. Ellis (ed.) *Second language acquisition in context*. Englewood Cliffs, NJ: Prentice Hall. 47–58.
——— 1997. Second language research in late modernity. *Modern Language Journal*. 81.329–333.
Rickford, J. 1999. A challenge for applied linguistics: The challenges confronting Ebonics speakers in schools and society. Plenary address delivered at American Association for Applied Linguistics Conference. Stamford, CT, March 1999.
Robinson, P. (ed.) In press. *Cognition and second language instruction*. Cambridge: Cambridge University Press.
Rounds, P. and R. Kanagy. 1998. Acquiring linguistic cues to identify AGENT: Evidence from children learning Japanese as a second language. *Studies in Second Language Acquisition*. 20.509–542.
Schumann, J. 1998. *The neurobiology of affect in language*. Malden, MA: Blackwell. [Also *Language Learning Monograph Series*. 48.]

Segalowitz, N. and P. Lightbown. 1999. Psycholinguistic approaches to SLA. In W. Grabe, *et al.* (eds.) *Annual Review of Applied Linguistics, 19. Survey of applied linguistics.* New York: Cambridge University Press. 43–63.

Segalowitz, S. and D. Bernstein. 1997. Neural networks and neuroscience: What are connectionist simulations good for? In D. Johnson and C. Erneling (eds.) *The future of the cognitive revolution.* New York: Oxford University Press. 209–216.

Shirai, Y. and A. Kurono. 1998. The acquisition of tense-aspect marking in Japanese as a second language. *Language Learning.* 48.245–279.

Skehan, P. 1998. *A cognitive approach to language learning.* Oxford: Oxford University Press.

Snow, C. 1999. Social perspectives on the emergence of language. In B. MacWhinney (ed.) *The emergence of language.* Mahwah, NJ: L. Erlbaum. 257–276.

Spada, N. 1997. Form-focused instruction and second language acquisition: A review of classroom and laboratory research. *Language Teaching.* 30.73–87.

Tarone, E. 1990. On variation in interlanguage: A response to Gregg. *Applied Linguistics.* 11.392–400.

―――― 1997. Analyzing IL in natural settings: A sociolinguistic perspective on second-language acquisition. *Culture & Cognition.* 30.137–150.

Thomas, M. 1998. Programmatic ahistoricity in SLA. *Studies in Second Acquisition.* 20.387–405.

Towell, R. and R. Hawkins. 1994. *Approaches to second language acquisition.* Clevedon, UK: Multilingual Matters.

van Lier, L. 1999. Computers and language learning: A case study in ecology and complexity. Paper presented at the Chaos/Complexity Perspective on Applied Linguistics Colloquium, American Association for Applied Linguistics Conference. Stamford, CT, March 1999.

Wesche, M. and S. Paribakht (eds.) 1999. *Incidental L2 vocabulary acquisition: Theory, current research, and instructional implications.* [Special issue of *Studies in Second Language Acquisition.* 21.2.]

Williams, S. and B. Hammarberg. 1998. Language switches in L3 production: Implications for a polyglot speaking model. *Applied Linguistics.* 19.295–333.

STILL WRESTLING WITH "CONTEXT" IN INTERLANGUAGE THEORY

Elaine Tarone

INTRODUCTION

One of the most intractable issues in the field of second-language acquisition (SLA) research has been the attempt to identify the role of social context in influencing (or not) the process of acquisition of a second language. The central question has been whether a theory of SLA must account only for the psycholinguistic processes involved in acquiring an interlanguage (IL), or, alternatively, whether social and sociolinguistic factors influence those psycholinguistic processes to such an extent that they too must be included in such a theory. It seems very clear that SLA is a psycholinguistic process. But to what extent are those psycholinguistic processes affected by social context? In 1985, Selinker and Douglas proposed a construct of "discourse domains" to show how social and psycholinguistic processes might be included in a theory of interlanguage; Young (1999) reviews that proposal and a recent attempt to test it, concluding that the results are still uncertain. After 15 years, this is still a lively issue in the field of SLA. Indeed, it is becoming a source of increasing conflict both within the field of SLA and within such areas of applied linguistics as second/foreign language teaching and second/foreign language teacher training. In this article, I will briefly summarize the problem, and review and summarize the current evidence being brought to bear upon this issue in the SLA research literature.

CRITICISM OF SLA RESEARCH FOR IGNORING SOCIAL CONTEXT

Criticisms have been advanced both by applied linguists working in other areas and by SLA researchers themselves. Applied linguists working in other fields have become increasingly vocal in their criticisms of the SLA research endeavor. One of their common themes is the charge that too much SLA research focuses on psycholinguistic processes in the abstract and does not consider the social context of L2 learning. It is said, for example, that IL data are typically gathered from L2 learners in artificial settings, removed from the social contexts in which they normally use and acquire the L2. As a consequence, it is argued that the results of such SLA research are irrelevant to the concerns of applied linguists who must deal with L2 learners in social context, not in the lab. For example, Firth and Wagner (1997) state that:

> SLA research takes a view of the learner that is too individualistic and mechanistic, and...fails to account in a satisfactory way for interactional and sociolinguistic dimensions of language. As such, it is flawed, and obviates insight into the nature of language, most centrally the language use of second or foreign language (S/FL) speakers (285).

The Firth and Wagner (1997) paper seems to have touched a sensitive spot with SLA researchers, generating several rejoinders in the same and subsequent issues of *Modern Language Journal* (Gass 1998, Kasper 1997, Long 1997; 1998, Poulisse 1997) and a reply from Firth and Wagner (1998). This article will not summarize that debate, but merely point out that it is not confined to the pages of the *Modern Language Journal*. Other applied linguists working in areas related to SLA have made a similar point, most notably Cook (in press) and Rampton (1995):

> The very undifferentiated portrait of the second language learner that emerges in SLA no doubt partly results from its tendency to thematise the learner's internal psychological condition. Rather than looking at interaction as a sociohistorically sensitive arena in which language learner identity is socially negotiated, SLA generally examines learner behaviour for evidence of the determining influence of psycholinguistic states and processes (Rampton 1995:293).

Rampton argues that one problem with this approach is that SLA researchers who have ignored social context in their studies cannot then claim that their results are generalizable to all social situations. Crucially wrong assumptions may be made in such studies about the social conditions which normally hold for L2 learners in society, and wrong generalizations may be made:

> In the 'root image' underlying SLA research, it is assumed that L2 learning generates situational anxiety, that progression along the route towards target language proficiency is (or should be) the learner's abiding preoccupation, and that learner status is fundamentally stigmatised. All of these characterisations may be true of some, or indeed many, situations, but they are certainly not invariable... (Rampton 1995:292).

And, indeed, Rampton (1995) shows in graphic and very convincing terms that these very characterizations are simply wrong for the adolescent L2 learners in his ethnographic study in Great Britain.

The criticism of SLA research for failure to include social context has become so pronounced that, at present, some influential second/foreign language teacher trainers are even taking the position that L2 teachers do not need to know the results of current SLA research. So, for example, when Freeman and Johnson (1998) "reconceptualize" the knowledge base which second/foreign language teachers must have, they do not include any knowledge of language learners and language acquisition/learning. They explain the omission this way:

> In general, due perhaps to its roots in L1 acquisition and cognitive psychology, the field of SLA has viewed language learning from an individualist perspective. Thus, until recently, the field has not examined language learning from the standpoint of socially negotiated, constructivist processes that may be at play.... From our point of view...a social constructivist view of language learning would seem to interface more directly with the nature of classroom language learning.... Because the research knowledge per se does not articulate easily and cogently into classroom practice, much current knowledge in SLA may be of limited use and applicability to practicing teachers (Freeman and Johnson 1998:411).

This position is taken by two leaders in language teacher education in the theme-setting initial paper in a collection in *TESOL Quarterly* in December of 1998. It suggests that schools of education will not be major consumers of SLA research in the coming century unless SLA researchers can either convert teachers to a more psycholinguistic mode of thinking or show that they do study the impact of social context on processes of SLA.[1]

If we examine the criticisms of the applied linguists outlined above in light of actual publications in SLA, those criticisms seem unwarranted. In fact, as already seen in the case of Selinker and Douglas (1985), there are some SLA researchers who have for some time taken the position that SLA theory and research should explore the relationship between social context and psycholinguistic processes of SLA. More recently, Preston (1996) proposes an alternative psycholinguistic model of SLA in which social factors can constrain grammatical marking, both in competence and performance. Larsen-Freeman's (1997) rather different proposal that interlanguage be studied as a complex dynamic system, using correlational research designs in natural settings, provides a very promising framework for SLA research relating social and cognitive factors in the L2 learner. But such models are merely proposals; where is the evidence?

The second half of this paper will review a small but growing subset of SLA research work which demonstrates an impact of social factors on psycholinguistic processes of L2 acquisition. It would be premature for other applied linguists to dismiss the entire field of SLA research out of hand without considering the evidence produced in that field—some of which was laid out in Young (1999) and in Bayley and Preston (1996)—arguing that social factors are related to systematic variation in interlanguage and to SLA itself.

But why, if this work is being done, is it relatively unmentioned by mainstream SLA researchers with a psycholinguistic orientation? As the next section will briefly show, these two streams of SLA research have not, as yet, affected one another. The problem is that there is minimal overlap between them.

THE SPLIT IN SLA: RESEARCH ON COGNITIVE FACTORS AND RESEARCH ON SOCIAL FACTORS

Research on second language acquisition that takes a sociolinguistic or even co-constructionist orientation typically focuses on L2 use in natural social contexts at a single point in time. Note that the emphasis is on interlanguage USE in such contexts, but not typically on the acquisition of new elements of the interlanguage. Further, such studies typically do NOT focus on discrete grammatical, morphological, or phonological elements in the interlanguage. Rather, they typically focus on general pragmatic or discourse patterns. For example, Peirce (1995) shows that Martina, while usually hesitant in speaking English with Canadian interlocutors, became much more fluent in her use of English L2 when she perceived a threat to her home and had to talk to her landlord. Thus, the interlocutor and Martina's roles (when speaking as low status immigrant or as mother defending her family) were shown to influence Martina's IL USE and fluency. However, the study provided no evidence of her acquisition of any features of IL due to the forces of either interlocutor or social role. Similarly, Platt and Troudi (1997) trace an ESL child's failure to learn to read in her L2 to such social factors as the teacher's instructional style (following from her beliefs about the way L2s are acquired) and fellow students' willingness to help the learner get by without reading for herself. Platt and Troudi show that such social factors influence an L2 learner's discourse patterns and overall success in reading, but they do not show how these social factors influence the development or fossilization of specific features in the learner's interlanguage. And so it goes. All the studies cited in Tarone (1988) and most of those in Bayley and Preston (1996) can be argued to suffer from the same general deficiency: They demonstrate the impact of social factors on interlanguage USE at a single point in time and do not show that those social factors affect the ACQUISITION of SPECIFIC linguistic features of IL over time.

To be fair, since sociolinguistic and co-constructionist studies take place in very complex natural settings and focus on the language input and output of just a few individuals in those settings, it would be very difficult and time-consuming to establish that the acquisition of new L2 forms has been influenced by identifiable social factors. Such an enterprise would involve longitudinal studies of those learners and the transcription of long stretches of conversation in which it would be very difficult to identify the new forms being acquired. Thus, while SLA researchers who take a sociolinguistic or co-constructionist orientation have a good deal of evidence showing that L2 learners' IL USE is variably affected by identifiable features of social context, they have usually not tried to show that those social features change the process of L2 ACQUISITION—specifically, the acquisition of an IL linguistic system—in any clear way. They have assumed it, and asserted it, but not often accumulated the evidence to prove it.

Research on second-language acquisition that takes a psycholinguistic, or cognitive orientation, whether it operates within a UG framework or not (cf. Long's [1998] assertion that most SLA cognitive research does not belong in a UG tradition), is clearly focused on the goal of explaining how an interlanguage grammar gets acquired over time. As Kasper (1997) says, in the acronym SLA, "the 'A' is for acquisition," not use. Tightly controlled studies are designed to identify particular grammatical features to be acquired and explore the impact of various cognitive factors on the acquisition process. Such research, exemplified in articles by de Bot (this volume) and Scovel (this volume), sets out to establish some clear causes for the acquisition (or fossilization) of very specific phonological and grammatical features of the L2. And since, in such studies, the social context is greatly controlled or reduced in complexity, and is usually fairly similar across university studies, such researchers have assumed that social factors are irrelevant for their work.

Thus, two strands of SLA research exist in parallel, but rarely focus on the same data or the same questions. The issue of the relationship between social factors and psycholinguistic processes of acquisition is, as Eckman (1994) points out, an empirical question, best resolved by the presentation of the right sort of data and not by argument alone. But neither strand of SLA research has consistently and systematically set out to gather the sort of data which might show whether social factors affect cognitive processes of acquisition in specific ways and thereby enable both strands to see how their work is related.

Long (1998) states the position of cognitively-oriented SLA researchers succinctly, and makes two assertions which can be empirically tested:

> Remove a learner from the social setting, and the L2 grammar does not change or disappear. Change the social setting altogether, e.g., from street to classroom, or from a foreign to a second language environment, and, as far as we know, the way the learner acquires does not change much either, as suggested, e.g., by comparisons of error types, developmental sequences, processing constraints, and other aspects of the acquisition process in and out

of classrooms... (Long 1998:93).

These two assertions seem to provide useful ways to structure the remainder of the present article. There is evidence in the recent SLA research literature which may address both of the above assertions.

RESEARCH EVIDENCE AT THE INTERFACE OF SOCIAL CONTEXT AND INTERLANGUAGE GRAMMAR

1. Remove the L2 learner from the social setting: Does the IL grammar change?

Let us assume that we are not talking about instantaneous changes—instantaneous acquisition of entirely new rules, or a switch to a completely different learner grammar—as the learner moves from the classroom to the hallway. Positing such switches from one grammar to another would certainly violate Occam's Razor. But we do know from research on English for Specific Purposes (Bhatia 1993, Swales 1990) that different social situations often require different registers of English, some of them with rules for grammatical usage that differ markedly from those for general English. For example, the rules for tense usage in academic research papers are distinctly different from those for general English. (See Swales 1990 for a review.) Active and passive aspect are patterned quite differently in astrophysics papers than in publications for researchers in other fields (Tarone, *et al.*, 1981 [1985; 1998]). We could assume that the IL grammar stays the same but is in fact variable, sensitive to social setting at any given point in time (a position consistent with studies in Bayley and Preston 1996, Preston 1996, Tarone 1988, and others). In this view, the entire IL grammar at any given time consists of a range of styles. As the learner moves from one social setting to another, the IL grammar does not change wholesale—the learner just accesses one or another style of a grammar that stays the same.

Perhaps a more empirically interesting way to paraphrase the question above is as follows: If two L2 learners acquire English in two different social settings, will those learners internalize two different IL grammars? The answer to this question, based on the research evidence, is surely yes. As just seen, ESP research shows that the TL rules to be learned vary in specific ways from one social situation to another. The classroom may expose L2 learners to only one rather formal register (Cohen 1997, Cohen and Tarone 1997, Tarone and Swain 1995). Tarone and Swain (1995) show that the immersion classroom provides input only in an academic register of L2, while an L2 adolescent vernacular register is only available in other social settings. Thus, it is well-established that, for any given target language, the L2 learner receives different input on the grammatical and lexical features to be acquired in different social situations.

But there are also other ways in which social context can influence the TL input given to learners. The degree to which native speakers adjust their language for learners may differ in different social contexts, and the amount of overall modeling and collaborative assistance given to learners may also differ in different social situations. For example, social context affects the degree to which interlocutors make linguistic and conversational adjustments for learners. It was initially claimed (Long 1980; 1983) in fairly general terms that all native speakers adjust the input they give to L2 learners. Based on his study of 16 elementary level non-native speakers of English performing six tasks with native speakers they had never met before in a lab at UCLA, Long identified a set of linguistic and conversational adjustments in the input given to the learners. Long's study and his review of the literature suggested to him that foreigner talk could be found in virtually all groups of people addressing speech to learners:

(1) in children as well as adults, (2) in upper-middle, middle and working-class adults, (3) individuals with or without prior FT experience, and (4) second language teachers, content-teachers and non-teachers.

...linguistic and conversational adjustments...appear to be immune to differences among groups/types of speakers (Long 1983:184).

More recently, however, Gass (1997) draws a different conclusion in reviewing the research on simplification of input to L2 learners. She cites several studies which show that some individuals in some social situations do not modify their speech, even for people experiencing obvious language difficulty. She notes two studies which document such "counter-accommodating behavior" : Arthur, *et al.* (1980) and Varonis and Gass (1985). Data from the latter study are discussed in Gass (1997:64–66), particularly a long telephone conversation between a native speaker at a TV repair shop and an L2 learner who believes he is calling a TV sales shop. In that conversation, which is fraught with misunderstandings, the native speaker does not make linguistic accommodations for the learner: She speaks rapidly, uses contractions and idiomatic language, and shows none of the conversational adjustments which are supposedly constant across social situation and interlocutor. Bondevik (1996) discusses similar findings in a more controlled study in a Minnesota electronics store. Each of four salesmen from Minnesota failed on three different occasions to accommodate to different L2 learner listeners by making linguistic and conversational adjustments; one even complexified his syntax after learners indicated noncomprehension. In subsequent interviews with the salesmen, one said that he felt it would have been insulting to simplify his speech in that context. Yet the listeners in Long (1980; 1983) did simplify their speech. Thus, the research evidence indicates that interlocutors in differing social situations provide L2 learners with differing amounts of adjusted TL input; some do not accommodate to learners by simplifying linguistic input at all. If simplified input is important to the SLA process, then we must conclude that the process of SLA is affected differently in these different social contexts.

But the input provided to learners in different social contexts differs in one more way: The overall modeling and collaborative assistance given to learners may also vary from one context to another. In conversation in certain formal institutional contexts, learners may not have direct access to the L2 input they need. Bardovi-Harlig and Hartford (1996) studied the sort of input which is available to L2 learners in the institutional setting of the university academic advising session. They described this session as "an unequal status encounter that by nature is a private speech event and cannot be observed by other learners." Thus, the L2 learner entered this encounter with no previous input or preparation on the sort of language that would be needed. Although the advisors attempted to guide the students in choosing courses for the coming term by teaching them that student suggestions are expected, and that certain types of content are appropriate for those suggestions, they did not teach the students appropriate linguistic forms for the invited speech acts, and they provided corrective feedback on meaning, not form.

When the higher-status, more powerful advisors tried to make suggestions for the students, those suggestions could not serve as direct models of appropriate language use for the students. Examples were "I'm going to have you take...," "we'll ask you to take...," and "I would suggest...." Additionally, learners whose mastery of tense-mood-aspect morphology did not enable them to mitigate as required would have had especial difficulty with this type of situation. In a similar study of interactions in institutional settings, Tarone and Kuehn (in press) taped L2 learners going through intake interviews in a welfare office. They showed that this too, as a private unequal status encounter, provided little or no useful input for L2 learners to use in order to know what applicants should say, or how they should say it. As a consequence, L2 learners had demonstrable difficulty understanding and responding to directives and suggestions being made by the welfare worker. Their attempts to communicate in this situation were not well supported.

In contrast with the restricted available input in these two institutional situations, there was very collaborative input and co-construction provided to L2 learners in social situations documented in two other recent studies. Parks and Maguire (1999) reported on the way in which francophone nurses, newly hired in an English-medium hospital in Montreal, acquired skill in writing nursing notes in English L2. In a highly collaborative process, the francophone learners observed more experienced nurses as they interacted with patients about to be discharged, interacted themselves under observation, solicited input from supervisors and co-workers, got and used advice given, and revised and produced notes in a highly collaborative process. Parks and Maguire concluded:

> ...when nurses had questions about language they did not have to rely solely on their internalized language resources but were able to have access to resources in the form of relevant documentation or more knowledgeable others, who confirmed or disconfirmed hunches or supplied genre-specific language. Indeed, all acts of language use, whether oral or written, are inherently social and context specific (1999:166).

The data provided in Parks and Maguire (1999) actually could allow us to move beyond language USE, since it shows how, over time, input provided by others gradually becomes incorporated into each new revision of nursing notes. Though the authors did not point this out, the data in the paper even show changes in a grammatical construction produced by the learner, from an initial erroneous "was been given" to a correct "was given." Co-construction is a central feature of another study: Swain and Lapkin (1998) recorded and analyzed the way in which two French immersion students worked together in a dyad to co-construct a story. In this study, the authors focused on ACQUISITION of L2 linguistic items. The learners worked together to help each other identify lexical and grammatical forms which they later used in their report; forms were proposed and then revised to become more target-like over the course of the learners' interactions. In this study, collaboration in this social context permitted the learners to focus on form and internalize specific new features of an IL grammar.

In summary, we have seen that L2 learners in different social contexts receive input which contains different grammar rules (cf. the ESP research), or which contains more or fewer linguistic/conversational adjustments, or which provides more or less explicit modeling and co-construction to support the acquisition process. Thus, because the TL input provided in different social situations is different, the IL grammars which can be acquired in those contexts must also be different.

2. Change the social setting altogether: Will the way the learner acquires L2 change much?

This second question focuses more specifically on certain types of change in acquisition processes that might arise due to different social settings. These processing changes might include error types, developmental sequences, processing constraints, and other aspects of the acquisition process. There is, in fact, research evidence that error detection, developmental sequences, and negotiation of meaning may all be sensitive to social context.

Kormos (1999), in an extensive review of processes of monitoring and self-repair in the use of an interlanguage, shows that while Levelt's perceptual loop theory of monitoring can account for monitoring in IL speech, it needs to be supplemented with recent research on consciousness, attention, and noticing if it is to account for mechanisms of error detection in using an IL. The studies she reviews suggest that error detection in L2 depends on several factors, some of them psycholinguistic, like the availability of attention. However, error detection also depends on social context factors such as the "accuracy demand of the situation" and "various listener-based discourse constraints" (1999:324). Kormos concludes that diverse results on the rate of well-formed repairs in studies with different research designs (cf. Levelt 1983, van Hest 1996) suggest that the well-formedness of corrections is both speaker-based and listener-based. "...[S]peakers will strive to produce well-formed repairs not only because their original speech plan needs to be encoded again, but also because they want to aid their interlocutors" (1999:330). We must assume that if the learner is correcting errors differentially in different social contexts to accommodate to different interlocutors, then the errors which remain uncorrected in those social contexts will be different.

Developmental sequences of SLA can also be influenced by factors of social context. Here we have only a small amount of intriguing research evidence, and a puzzling lack of attempt to obtain any more such evidence. Liu (1991), and Tarone and Liu (1995; see discussion in Young 1999) show that a 6-year-old Chinese boy acquiring English L2 in Australia over a two-year period acquired Pienemann and Johnston's (1987) six stages of interrogatives in a different order from that predicted. Stage 4 and 5 questions were acquired before Stage 3 questions. Each new stage of interrogative formation except for one was produced in conversation in a single social context: in play sessions with the researcher at the learner's home. Each new stage of question then gradually spread to other social contexts, appearing next in conversations with other peers in desk work at school, and last in conversations with the teacher in school. Liu (1991) argues that there was something about the social context of play sessions at home with the researcher which caused later-stage questions to emerge before earlier-stage questions in this learner's interlanguage. Aspects of input (Young 1999), and aspects of play (cf. Tarone 1999) have both been cited as possible characteristics of this social context that altered the sequence of acquisition of questions for this learner. To date, there have been no other reports of research studies which examine the impact of different social contexts on the sequence of acquisition of any phonological, morphological, or grammatical feature of interlanguage. This absence of studies designed to obtain relevant data on possible interactions between social context and sequence of acquisition is hard to account for. Certainly it represents a gap in the literature that needs to be addressed.

In contrast to the above, there have been many studies focusing on interaction and negotiation as a central process in second-language acquisition. Negotiation is important because it leads to the psycholinguistic event of noticing that a linguistic form needs to be acquired:

> The input-interaction view must take the position that noticing is crucial. In negotiation the learner is focusing on linguistic form, and that focus, or specific attention paid to linguistic form, is the first step toward grammar change (Gass 1997:101).

Several recent studies of negotiation show that the negotiation process can be highly sensitive to social context. Gass (1997), in her substantive review of input, interaction, and second language learner, states:

> It would be too simplistic to assume that these integral parts of negotiation sequences occur without influence from the context in which they appear. To the contrary, many factors affect the structure of conversation (Gass 1997:117).

She then reviews studies which show the following features of social context to be important factors affecting negotiation:

1. Task type (where a task requiring the exchange of information results in more negotiation; a task which is student-student involves more negotiation than one which is teacher-fronted),
2. Background knowledge and status differences (where great status differences inhibit negotiation, and gaps in background knowledge provide more opportunities for negotiation),
3. Familiarity (where conversation partners who know each other negotiate more), and
4. Gender (where same gender partners negotiate more).

Disturbingly, Foster (1998) has found that the social context of the ESL classroom may be one which promotes little negotiation of meaning. Foster observed 21 intermediate level ESL students as they worked in dyads vs. small groups, doing tasks with optional or required information exchange. She found that many learners in small groups did not speak at all, and many more in dyads and groups did no negotiated interaction. Very few modified their utterances on the basis of interaction. Lyster (1998) found that French immersion teachers also did not respond to learner errors in ways that allowed for much negotiation to occur. In particular, teachers did not promote negotiation that drew learners' attention to errors of form. Thus, in different social contexts, the degree of negotiation of meaning (or, in theory, of focus on form) may vary tremendously.

But to what extent do these differences in negotiation lead to differences in noticing, or in a focus on linguistic form? We are beginning to see research on the impact of negotiation on noticing of particular linguistic features. Mackey, *et al.* (in press) found that L2 learners who are given implicit negative feedback while in the process of negotiating for meaning do not always notice that feedback. Feedback on phonology and lexis is noticed readily, but feedback on morpho-syntax is not, nor is it incorporated into subsequent learner production. How does social context affect this process of noticing? Does one notice more linguistic form when one's interlocutor is a teacher, as opposed to when the interlocutor is a student? Research on style shifting suggests that learners certainly adjust their speech towards the IL norm more in the presence of a teacher (e.g., Blanco-Iglesias, Broner and Tarone 1995, Liu 1991), but studies on differential noticing in response to such features of social context as interlocutor do not seem to exist.

As Gass (1997) points out, negotiation for meaning is only one possible means of getting L2 learners to focus on form. Another means proposed more recently by Cook (1997; in press), Tarone (1999), and Tarone and Broner (1999) is language play, which occurs in some social contexts more than others. Play with L2 forms at all linguistic levels may be another contextually-influenced way of drawing L2 learners' attention to language forms that need to be acquired. Work on language play, the social contexts in which it occurs, and its impact on second-language acquisition is just beginning.

To conclude this section, there does appear to be evidence in the literature to suggest that if we change the social setting altogether, the way the learner acquires [L2] does seem to change, at least with regard to error correction, developmental sequences, and negotiation of meaning.

CONCLUSION

There are SLA researchers who are exploring the ways in which social context may affect the acquisition of specific L2 forms. It thus appears premature for other applied linguists, or for SLA researchers themselves, to assert that the field has no interest in examining SLA in its social context. But there is also a good deal of research study to be done, particularly in documenting the impact of social factors on the psycholinguistic processes of acquisition of specific interlanguage morphosyntactic, lexical, and phonological forms. And what might an SLA theory look like that incorporated both social and psycholinguistic factors? Two theoretical proposals, those of Preston (1996) and Larsen-Freeman (1997), appear especially promising in their capacity to bring the two strands of research, the psycholinguistic and the sociolinguistic, together in a single framework. Work in this area appears important, and quite promising.

NOTES

1. For one response to Freeman and Johnson (1998), see Yates and Muchisky (1999).

ANNOTATED BIBLIOGRAPHY

Bondevik, S.-G. 1996. Foreigner talk revisited: When does it really occur and why? Tromso, Norway: University of Tromso. MA thesis.

Exploring the factors which trigger foreigner talk, the researcher conducted a study in an American electronics store. Over a period of several weeks, three L2 learners and a native speaker customer entered the store at different times, and each one talked to each of five native-speaker salesmen. All of the "customers" indicated serious noncomprehension at similar points in the conversation, and the salesmen's subsequent speech was analyzed to see if they had made linguistic or conversational adjustments to help their customers understand. Results showed that four of the five Minnesota salesmen did not use foreigner talk with the learners, not even with one who looked foreign and had a pronounced accent, while the one salesman who had lived in California did. One Minnesotan even complexified his speech after noncomprehension had been indicated. In interviews, he said he felt it would have been insulting to simplify his speech to his customers.

Larsen-Freeman, D. 1997. Chaos/complexity science and second language acquisition. *Applied Linguistics*. 18.141–165.

The author outlines a number of ways in which interlanguages exhibit the features of complex nonlinear systems: IL is characterized by dynamic processes; it is complex, with many interacting factors that determine its developing trajectory; it does not develop in a linear fashion; and it is an open, self-organizing system with continued input. The author uses this perspective to examine five issues in SLA: mechanisms of acquisition, definitions of learning, the instability and stability of interlanguage, differential success, and the effect of instruction. Adoption of this perspective would discourage theory construction through the aggregation of simple univariate cause-effect links, underscore the importance of details, and encourage a focus on the whole process of SLA rather than just a part.

Long, M. H. 1998. SLA: Breaking the siege. *University of Hawai'i Working Papers in ESL*. 17.79–129.

The author responds to three published criticisms of SLA research—that too many SLA researchers (a) focus overly narrowly on learner-internal, cognitive processes; (b) use an outdated "realist" perspective, ignoring the insights of postmodernist scholars; and (c) claim implications for second-language teaching from their research when they do not exist. The author takes on one paper claimed to represent each critical position (papers written by Firth & Wagner, Lantolf, and Nunan respectively). He concludes, rather contentiously, that none of these positions has any validity at all. While this reviewer is sympathetic with some of Long's positions, his rhetoric in this paper appears too extreme. Unfortunately, Long concludes by suggesting that research journals in the field which publish such attacks on SLA research are thereby not maintaining high enough standards of scholarship.

Preston, D. 1996. Variationist perspectives on second language acquisition. In R. Bayley and D. Preston (eds.) *Second language acquisition and linguistic variation*. Amsterdam: J. Benjamins. 1–46.

The author states that sociolinguistics as a discipline has much to contribute to the field of SLA, but that several factors have prevented a healthy relationship between the two fields: 1) variationists have not advanced plausible psycholinguistic models of SLA; 2) SLA researchers do not understand the aims of sociolinguistics as a field, or its tools and methods; and 3) many SLA researchers tend to rely overmuch on a UG framework which is too narrow to account for SLA. A variable psycholinguistic model is proposed to account for SLA data, one based on the analogy of weighted coins being flipped, the "coins" being selection devices in competence and performance which are sensitive to linguistic and stylistic factors.

Tarone, E. and M. Broner. 1999. Is it fun? Language play in a fifth grade Spanish immersion classroom. Unpublished manuscript, University of Minnesota [under review].

The authors discuss two kinds of language play which appear in the discourse of fifth grade Spanish immersion students: private speech used for purposes of rehearsal of target forms and ludic speech used for purposes of self-amusement and creativity. Examples of both kinds of language play are identified in the natural classroom L2 discourse of three learners, observed and taped over a period of five months. Five criteria are used to distinguish effectively the two kinds of play in most cases. The paper concludes with a brief discussion of the differing possible roles of each kind of language play in the process of SLA.

UNANNOTATED BIBLIOGRAPHY

Arthur, B., R. Weiner, M. Culver, Y. J. Lee and D. Thomas. 1980. The register of impersonal discourse to foreigners: Verbal adjustments to foreign accents. In D. Larsen-Freeman (ed.) *Discourse analysis in second language research.* Rowley, MA: Newbury House. 111–124.

Bardovi-Harlig, K. and B. Hartford. 1996. Input in an institutional setting. *Studies in Second Language Acquisition.* 18.171–188.

Bayley, R. and D. Preston (eds.) 1996. *Second language acquisition and linguistic variation.* Amsterdam: J. Benjamins.

Bhatia, V. K. 1993. *Analysing genre: Language use in professional settings.* London: Longman.

Blanco-Iglesias, S., M. Broner and E. Tarone. 1995. Observations of language use in Spanish immersion classroom interactions. In L. Eubanks, L. Selinker and M. Sharwood Smith (eds.) *Festschrift for William Rutherford.* Amsterdam: J. Benjamins. 239–251.

Cohen, A. 1997. Developing pragmatic ability: Insights from the accelerated study of Japanese. In H. M. Cook, K. Hijirida and M. Tahara (eds.) *New trends and issues in teaching Japanese language and culture*. Honolulu: University of Hawaii, Second Language Teaching and Curriculum Center. 137–163.

Cohen, A. and E. Tarone. 1997. Language learning in an accelerated college program: A case study of a learner in search of the vernacular. Paper presented at the Second Language Research Forum (SLRF). East Lansing, Michigan, October 1997.

Cook, G. 1997. Language play, language learning. *ELT Journal*. 51.224–231.

——— In press. *Language play, language learning*. Oxford: Oxford University Press.

Eckman, F. R. 1994. The competence-performance issue in second-language acquisition theory: A debate. In E. Tarone, S. Gass and A. Cohen (eds.) *Research methodology in second-language acquisition*. Hillsdale, NJ: L. Erlbaum. 3–15.

Firth, A. and J. Wagner. 1997. On discourse, communication, and (some) fundamental concepts in SLA research. *Modern Language Journal*. 81.285–300.

——— 1998. SLA property: No trespassing! *Modern Language Journal*. 82.91–94.

Foster, P. 1998. A classroom perspective on the negotiation of meaning. *Applied Linguistics*. 19.1–23.

Freeman, D. and K. E. Johnson. 1998. Reconceptualizing the knowledge-base of language teacher education. *TESOL Quarterly*. 32.397–417.

Gass, S. 1997. *Input, interaction and the second language learner*. Mahwah, NJ: L. Erlbaum.

——— 1998. Apples and oranges; Or, why apples are not oranges and don't need to be. A response to Firth and Wagner. *Modern Language Journal*. 82.82–90.

Kasper, G. 1997. "A" stands for acquisition: A response to Firth and Wagner. *Modern Language Journal*. 81.307–312.

Kormos, J. 1999. Monitoring and self-repair in a second language. *Language Learning*. 49.303–342.

Lantolf, J. P. and G. Appel (eds.) 1994. *Vygotskyian approaches to second language research*. Norwood, NJ: Ablex.

Levelt, W. J. M. 1983. Monitoring and self repair in speech. *Cognition*. 33.41–103.

Liu, G.-Q. 1991. Interaction and second language acquisition: A case study of a Chinese child's acquisition of English as a Second Language. Melbourne, Australia: La Trobe University. Ph.D. diss.

Long, M. H. 1980. Input, interaction and second language acquisition. Los Angeles: University of California at Los Angeles. Ph.D. diss.

——— 1983. Linguistic and conversational adjustments to non-native speakers. *Studies in Second Language Acquisition*. 5.177–193.

——— 1997. Construct validity in SLA research: A response to Firth and Wagner. *Modern Language Journal*. 81.318–323.

Lyster, R. 1998. Recasts, repetition, and ambiguity in L2 classroom discourse. *Studies in Second Language Acquisition.* 20.51–81.

Mackey, A., S. Gass and K. McDonough. In press. How do learners perceive implicit negative feedback? *Studies in Second Language Acquisition.*

Parks, S. and M. Maguire. 1999. Coping with on-the-job writing in ESL: A constructivist-semiotic perspective. *Language Learning.* 49.143–175.

Peck, S. 1978. Child-child discourse in second language acquisition. In E. Hatch (ed.) *Second language acquisition: A book of readings.* Rowley, MA: Newbury House. 383–400.

Peirce, B. N. 1995. Social identity, investment, and language learning. *TESOL Quarterly.* 29.9–32.

Pienemann, M. and M. Johnston. 1987. Factors influencing the development of language proficiency. In D. Nunan (ed.) *Applying second language acquisition research.* Adelaide, Australia: National Curriculum Resource Centre. 45–141.

Platt, E. and S. Troudi. 1997. Mary and her teachers: A Grebo-speaking child's place in the mainstream classroom. *Modern Language Journal.* 81.28–49.

Poulisse, N. 1997. Some words in defense of the psycholinguistic approach. *Modern Language Journal.* 81.324–328.

Rampton, B. 1995. *Crossing: Language and ethnicity among adolescents.* London: Longman.

Rounds, P. and R. Kanagy. 1998. Acquiring linguistic cues to identify agent: Evidence from children learning Japanese as a second language. *Studies in Second Language Acquisition.* 20.509–542.

Selinker, L. and D. Douglas. 1985. Wrestling with "context" in interlanguage theory. *Applied Linguistics.* 6.190–204.

Swain, M. 1995. Three functions of output in second language learning. In G. Cook and B. Seidlhofer (eds.) *Principle & practice in applied linguistics: Studies in honour of H. G. Widdowson.* Oxford: Oxford University Press. 125–144.

———— and S. Lapkin. 1998. Interaction and second language learning: Two adolescent French immersion students working together. *Modern Language Journal.* 82.320–337.

Swales, J. M. 1990. *Genre analysis: English in academic and research settings.* Cambridge: Cambridge University Press.

Tarone, E. 1988. *Variation in interlanguage.* London: Edward Arnold.

———— 1998. A sociolinguistic perspective on an SLA theory of mind. *Studia Anglica Posnaniensia.* 23.431–444.

———— 1999. Getting serious about language play: Language play, interlanguage variation and second-language acquisition. Paper presented at the annual Second Language Research Forum. Minneapolis, MN, September 1999.

————, S. Dwyer, S. Gillette and V. Icke. 1981. The use of the passive in two astrophysics papers. *ESP Journal*. 1.123–140. [Reprinted in J. Swales (ed.) 1985. *Episodes in ESP*. Oxford: Pergamon. 191–205.] [Updated and reprinted, 1998. *English for Specific Purposes*. 17.113–132.]

Tarone, E. and K. Kuehn. In press. Negotiating the social services oral intake interview: Communicative needs of non-native speakers of English. *TESOL Quarterly*.

——— and G.-Q. Liu. 1995. Situational context, variation, and second language acquisition theory. In G. Cook and B. Seidlhofer (eds.) *Principle and practice in applied linguistics: Studies in honour of H. G. Widdowson*. Oxford: Oxford University Press. 107–124.

——— and M. Swain. 1995. A sociolinguistic perspective on second-language use in immersion classrooms. *Modern Language Journal*. 79.166–178.

van Hest, E. 1996. *Self-repair in L1 and L2 production*. Tilburg, The Netherlands: Tilburg University Press.

Varonis, E. and S. Gass. 1985. Miscommunication in native/non-native conversation. *Language in Society*. 14.327–343.

Yates, R. and D. Muchisky. 1999. On the status of disciplinary knowledge in language teacher education. Paper presented at the International Language Teacher Conference, University of Minnesota. Minneapolis, MN, May 1999.

Young, R. 1999. Sociolinguistic approaches to SLA. In W. Grabe, *et al.* (eds.) *Annual Review of Applied Linguistics*, 19. *Survey of applied linguistics*. New York: Cambridge University Press. 105–132.

FRENCH IMMERSION RESEARCH IN CANADA: RECENT CONTRIBUTIONS TO SLA AND APPLIED LINGUISTICS*

Merrill Swain

INTRODUCTION

This review chapter addresses two questions: What has the recent research conducted in French immersion programs in Canada contributed to our understanding of second language acquisition (SLA)? What has it contributed to the broader field of applied linguistics? In this chapter, I also consider briefly what the research contributions of the coming decade might be and discuss some of the obstacles that may be faced in Canada in continuing to conduct research concerned with French immersion education.

FRENCH IMMERSION EDUCATION AS A TYPE OF BILINGUAL EDUCATION

Bilingual education has been defined as "schooling provided fully or partly in a second language with the object in view of making students proficient in the second language while, at the same time, maintaining and developing their proficiency in the first language and fully guaranteeing their educational development" (Stern 1972). Depending on the social, linguistic, educational, and political contexts, these goals of bilingual education can be achieved in many ways, immersion education being one of them.

French immersion (Fi) education in Canada takes several forms, but the underlying common element is that students study content material such as mathematics, history, geography, and science for at least 50 percent of the school day using French, a language which they are also simultaneously learning. Learning through the medium of a second language (L2) is certainly not a new phenomenon, but a number of characteristics combine to make immersion education different from other forms of bilingual education. In addition to the L2 being a medium of instruction, a number of further characteristics, discussed in Swain and Johnson (1997), identify the Canadian immersion curriculum:

- The immersion curriculum parallels the local L1 curriculum;
- Overt support exists for the L1;
- The classroom culture is that of the local L1 community;
- Students enter with similar (and limited) levels of L2 proficiency;
- Exposure to the L2 is largely confined to the classroom;
- The teachers are bilingual;
- The program aims for additive bilingualism.

There are presently over 300,000 students enrolled in elementary or secondary French immersion programs in Canada (Office of the Commissioner of Official Languages 1996).

French immersion programs have prospered in Canada for over three decades, fostered by the educational, political, and economic motives of those involved. Simultaneously, research has contributed to the growth and development of FI by allaying the fears of anxious parents and educators with its positive findings (e.g., Genesee 1987, Lambert and Tucker 1972, Swain and Lapkin 1982) and by enhancing our understanding of aspects of second language acquisition and applied linguistics.

CONTRIBUTIONS OF FI RESEARCH TO APPLIED LINGUISTICS

The major contributions of FI research to the field of applied linguistics have been threefold. First, immersion education has heightened our recognition of the influence of societal conditions on the outcomes of bilingual education, in particular, of the importance of the distinction between minority and majority language groups. But it has also shown how a particular model of bilingual education can be adapted and extended by different groups in society to serve their own particular purposes. Johnson and Swain (1997) provide examples of immersion being used outside Canada by majority language groups to learn a minority language (e.g., Swedish in Finland), a foreign language (e.g., French in Australia), or a language of power (e.g., English in Singapore), and by minority groups for language revival and language support (e.g., Basque in Spain).

Second, the contributions of disciplinary knowledge and related research paradigms to applied linguistics have been amply demonstrated in the FI research literature. Recent work has drawn on a variety of disciplines, for example, linguistics (Warden 1997), psycholinguistics (Harley and Hart 1997), sociolinguistics (Tarone and Swain 1995), anthropology (Weber and Tardif 1991), and education (Kowal 1997). Correlational (Rehner and Mougeon in press), experimental (Day and Shapson 1991), observational (Lyster and Ranta 1997), and ethnographic and case study (Dagenais and Day 1998; in press) methodologies have all been used in reaching a deeper understanding of the processes and products of FI education.

Third, French immersion research has contributed directly to various subfields of applied linguistics. An annotated bibliography published by the Canadian Association of Immersion Teachers (CAIT) documents the range of issues which have been investigated concerning FI education in Canada. Tardif and Gauvin (1995) list theses and research projects that have been conducted between 1988 and 1994 by researchers based at Canadian universities. Recent research includes contributions to language policy (e.g., Hart, Lapkin and Swain 1998, Turnbull, Lapkin, Hart and Swain 1998), second language pedagogy (see Lyster 1995 and Harley 1998a for recent reviews; see also Swain 1996), and SLA. Its contributions to SLA form the basis of the next section.

CONTRIBUTIONS OF FI RESEARCH TO SLA

FI research has added to our understanding of SLA in several important ways. I will consider these under the following headings: 1) output and SLA; 2) negative feedback and SLA; 3) focus on form and SLA; 4) the role of L1 and SLA; 5) age and SLA; and 6) language testing and SLA. Immersion research provides a more controlled environment in which to study pedagogical issues than is typically the case in ESL research where outside exposure to the language may overwhelm classroom effects. This control gives added weight to immersion findings.

1. Output and SLA

The notion that output, not just input, is important for SLA derives largely from the research in FI. Across a number of studies, it has been shown that, in spite of considerable amounts of rich comprehensible input, immersion students' otherwise fluent oral and written French is markedly non-native, most obviously in its grammatical features. Swain (1985) suggested that this may be due, in part, to the relatively few opportunities students have to use their French: Producing French may force learners to pay more attention to (or to notice) how the language is used to express one's intended meaning than does comprehending it. That is, while attempting to produce the target language, learners may notice that they do not know how to say (or write) precisely the meaning they wish to convey, bringing to their attention something they need to discover about their second language. This need to know, in turn, triggers cognitive processes that might generate new linguistic knowledge or consolidate their existing knowledge (Swain 1995, Swain and Lapkin 1995).

Supporting evidence for this claim comes from an observational study conducted in three grade-two FI classes (Netten and Spain 1989). Of the three classes, one class (Class A) had a low average scholastic ability score (54th percentile) relative to the other two classes, yet performed unexpectedly well on a test of French reading comprehension and much better than Class C whose average scholastic ability score was much higher (73rd percentile). Observations in these classes revealed that, in Class A, students "...were constantly using, and experimenting with, the second language as they engaged in communications of an academic and social nature with their peers and the teacher...," whereas in Class C, students "...had limited opportunities to use the second language to engage in real communication acts" (1989:494).

A second way in which producing language may serve the language learning process is through hypothesis formation and testing. Swain and Lapkin (1995) provide examples in which grade-eight FI learners used their output as a means of trying out new language forms (hypotheses) in situations in which feedback from external sources was not available; thus, there was nothing to test their hypotheses against except their own internalized knowledge. In more usual circumstances, however, learners are able to obtain information from external sources about the accuracy of their hypotheses, leading them to modify their output. Swain (1993) suggested that this modified (reprocessed) output may be considered to represent the leading edge of a learner's interlanguage.

A third function of output is its metalinguistic function—learners use language to reflect on their own, or others', language use (Swain 1995). This metatalk is a surfacing of language used to solve linguistic problems encountered during language production, and, as such, represents language used for the cognitive purposes of learning language. Metatalk surfaces naturally when students collaborate on language production tasks (Swain and Lapkin 1998).

The above perspective on output has been instrumental in determining the sort of exploratory studies conducted recently in French immersion classes by researchers at the Ontario Institute for Studies in Education of the University of Toronto (OISE/UT) (Kowal 1997; 1998, Kowal and Swain 1994; 1997, La Pierre 1994, Spielman to appear, Swain 1998a; 1998b, Swain and Lapkin 1998). In these studies, we have begun to try out in grade-seven and grade-eight FI classes different tasks that are communicatively oriented, but in which communication is, in part at least, about language; that is, students engage in tasks in which they will talk about— and consciously reflect on—their own output. Our findings provide evidence that the metatalk students engage in represents second language learning in progress. In these studies, later language use has been traced back to dialogues occurring as the students worked collaboratively to express their intended meaning and carry out the language production task at hand. The study of the roles of output in SLA has thus evolved into the study of collaborative dialogue: These dialogues (in the first language or target language) engage speakers in linguistic problem solving and knowledge building (Swain in press).

2. Negative feedback and SLA

Lyster (1998a; 1998b; 1999, Lyster and Ranta 1997) has carried out a set of descriptive studies in primary (grades four and five) FI classes. His main purpose has been to identify different ways in which teachers provide corrective feedback to their students and the effectiveness of these types of feedback as indicated by immediate learner repair (uptake). His data (consisting of over 900 error sequences in 18 hours of recordings of French language arts and content classes) reveal that these FI teachers used a number of different correction techniques: recasts, explicit corrections, and what Lyster labels "negotiations of form" (i.e., elicitations, metalinguistic clues, clarification requests, and repetitions of error). Negotiation of form techniques "push" learners to reprocess their output; that is, teachers guide their students to draw on their own resources and repair their own (or other's) errors, thus actively engaging students.

Lyster examined which type of corrective feedback tended to be used with different types of student errors (grammatical, lexical, or phonological), and which type of feedback was most likely to lead to student uptake. He found that negotiation of form tended to follow lexical errors, while recasts tended to follow grammatical and phonologicial errors. Interestingly, negotiation of form led to more frequent immediate repair by learners than recasts or explicit corrections for lexical and grammatical errors. Phonological repairs, however, were more likely to follow recasts, suggesting that the various types of negative feedback may be differentially effective for different types of errors.

Lyster examined further the recasts (377 in all) in his classroom-based data, comparing their pragmatic functions to the teachers' much more frequent use of noncorrective repetition. His findings led him to question the potential of recasts to be noticed as negative feedback by students in these FI classes. Specifically, Lyster found that "...recasts and noncorrective repetition fulfill identical functions distributed in equal proportions" (1998b: 51). Furthermore, unlike other forms of negative feedback, recasts included indications of teacher approval (positive response to the content of students' ill-formed utterances) in a little over one quarter of all recasts. Approval also accompanied the same proportion of noncorrective repetitions and teacher topic-continuation moves immediately following errors when no corrective feedback was provided.

Lapkin and Swain (1996) also describe their observations in an immersion class. They were interested in examining how the teacher integrated language (particulary vocabulary) and content teaching. In this grade-eight class, while teaching a science lesson, the teacher pushed his students to make accurate and sophisticated use of target words and associated grammatical constructions. The corrective feedback provided in the context of this science lesson facilitated the students' attempts to express what they wanted to say at the very moment they were struggling to produce it, a particularly useful time to support language learning (Lightbown 1998). The reason we asked this teacher if we could observe in his class was because his students had outperformed students in other classes in French, all of whom were part of a large-scale evaluation of 26 grade-eight immersion classes (Lapkin, Hart and Swain 1991).

3. Focus on form and SLA

Each of the studies considered under the previous two headings could also be considered under this more general heading: Output and negative feedback are both thought to play a role in SLA precisely because they lead learners' to notice and attend to language form. Several additional studies have also considered this phenomenon. These studies differ from those mentioned above in that curriculum materials with form emphases were prepared in advance and were used to teach FI students over a prolonged period of time. The instructional materials emphasized a focus on form through enhanced input, drew particular attention to form/function links, ensured that students had opportunities to produce the language feature being focused on through group work and collaborative learning, and provided students with feedback about the correctness of their language use. The performance of FI students receiving the focused instruction has been compared with other FI students who did not receive it using oral and written pre-, post-, and delayed post-tests.

A number of early experiments followed this paradigm. Harley (1989) provided grade-six FI students with focused input and output opportunities over an eight-week period to promote the perception and accurate use of form/meaning distinctions between the imperfect and the compound past verb tenses. Day and Shapson (1991; 1996) focused on teaching grade-seven FI students the use of the conditional in hypothetical situations and in polite requests over a six-week period. Lyster (1994) focused on teaching grade-eight FI students sociolinguistic aspects of French over a five-week period. Findings are consistent in showing superior results with the experimental groups relative to the comparison groups. However, sometimes the superiority was not maintained in the long run, or was not evident for all measures.

More recent experiments include Harley (1998b), Harley, Howard and Hart (1998) and Warden (1997); the focus of instruction for these studies was grammatical gender at grades two and eleven respectively. Harley's study suggests that a focus on form can have an impact even on young children. The instructional materials included a variety of children's games designed so that success depended on getting the gender right. For example, students played "Simon Says" in which they performed contrasting actions according to the gender of the noun they heard. The treatment extended over a five-week period for about 20 minutes a day. The results showed that the students in the experimental classes became more accurate in assigning gender to familiar nouns than did the comparison students. However, the experimental students were not able to assign the correct gender to unknown nouns based on their characteristic endings, suggesting item learning rather than system learning. Harley (1998b) suggests that, perhaps because so many new words were presented to the children, they were preoccupied with learning and remembering their meaning and were thus unable to pay full attention to the formal aspects that were the intended focus of the experimental treatment. Perhaps, too, "learners base their formal generalizations on prototypical items rather than on a plurality of items, as was the assumption in this study" (Harley 1998b:170).

In Warden's (1997) study with grade-eleven students, the treatment was quite different, and one more appropriate for older students. Also, the issue was not so much a preventive one, but rather one of reversing fossilization: Gender errors were still prevalent in the spoken and written French of these grade-eleven students. The treatment period lasted approximately eight weeks and consisted of form-focused activities designed to make the students aware of word-ending regularities which serve as clues to the gender of French nouns and provide opportunities to use gender markings correctly. Activities included working in groups to find nouns in the dictionary with specific endings and creating and playing games focusing on gender. The experimental students' performance was superior to that of comparison students on discrete-point tests of grammatical gender, but not in a writing assignment or speaking task. However, a fine-grained analysis of the written assignment showed that the experimental students had become more accurate on the nouns whose specific endings were included in the treatment activities.

Overall, the set of experiments conducted in FI classes suggests that there is value in focusing on language form through the use of pre-planned curriculum materials in the context of content-based language learning. Yet, there are indications that if we knew more about how students were processing the target language while engaging in the activities, we might be better able to structure the learning materials. One route to such understanding is to listen to learners as they talk with each other while carrying out specific activities. Their collaborative dialogues can be a source of considerable insight (Spielman to appear, Swain in press).

4. The role of L1 and SLA

The role of L1 in SLA is typically considered from the perspective of its positive or negative influence on target language use. Harley (1992), for example, has examined patterns of French language development with cross-sectional samples of grade-one, -four, and -ten FI students. She focused on the French verb system and found considerable transfer from English in the students' production. Students tended to assume not only equivalence in verb meaning across English and French, but also in the constructions that verbs enter into. As Wright (1996) demonstrated with grade-four and grade-five FI students, increasing exposure to verbs through reading materials and related analytical activities, including explicit discussion of L1-L2 contrasts, may lead to lasting improvement in the use of the target verbs.

A different perspective on the role of the L1 in SLA is reflected in our own ongoing research with FI immersion grade-eight students as they work collaboratively on language-focused communicatively-oriented tasks (Swain 1999). As they do so, the students often use English, their L1. We have examined the transcripts of student pairs in an attempt to understand their use of L1. Working from the data, we have isolated three categories of L1 use: 1) using L1 to move the task along (working out the sequencing of the story being reconstructed, comprehending the meaning of parts of the story, and managing the task); 2) using L1 to talk about the L2 (searching for vocabulary, focusing on form, and translating); and 3) using L1 to establish and maintain interpersonal relations (agreeing/disagreeing and talking off-task). In the case of the first category, students were using their L1 to mediate their understanding of the task, both in its substantive content and in what was required of them to complete the task. In the case of the second category, the L1 was clearly mediating students' learning of French. And in the case of the third category, it would appear that English was being used to create the affective environment needed to get the task done.

5. Age and SLA

A recent study conducted by Harley and Hart (1997) tested the hypothesis that different components of language aptitude (associative memory, memory for text, and analytical ability) come into play in SLA, depending on the age at which second language learning begins. At the time of testing, all students in this study were enrolled in grade-eleven FI classes. Some of the students had begun learning French in grade one (early immersion group), others in grade seven (late immersion group). All students completed a set of L2 proficiency tests (vocabulary recognition, listening comprehension, cloze test, written production task, and an individual oral test). For the early immersion students, memory for text was the main predictor of proficiency scores; whereas for the late immersion students, analytical ability was the main predictor. These findings suggest that older learners rely on different cognitive abilities than early learners do, with analytical language ability being more closely associated with success in L2 learning for later learners. Additionally, as the L2 proficiency results of the younger and older learners were not substantially different, the results support other evidence that older learners are more efficient learners than younger learners (e.g., Genesee 1981) and do not support the contention (e.g., Felix 1985) that analytic, problem-solving abilities of older learners will interfere with their L2 learning success.

6. Language testing and SLA

Recently the interfaces between SLA and language testing have been questioned and explored in some detail by Bachman and Cohen (1998). In conducting our FI classroom-based research (e.g., Swain and Lapkin 1998), we have come to the full realization that tests used in SLA research can at best measure what researchers assume students will learn from a teacher's or researcher's intervention. However, what students actually learn may be quite different and will depend on a number of factors, including the learner's current knowledge and affective state. Although the tasks we used in our research encouraged students to pay attention to accuracy and form-function links, the students established their own goals and agenda as to what they focused on. Thus, it would seem crucial, if we are to measure the learning that occurs as a result of the research "treatment," that we tailor our tests to what happens during that treatment. Some of this adapting can be uncovered in the dialogue of students as they interact with their peers during task performance, providing insight into what it is that students do and do not know, and how they come to know it—the real goal of SLA research.

OBSTACLES TO FURTHER FI RESEARCH IN CANADA

Given the political situation in Canada three decades ago, the innovative FI immersion programs appeared promising as a way to reduce the gap between Canada's two linguistic and cultural solitudes. The federal government was interested in supporting their growth, and it, along with provincial governments across Canada which were concerned about the educational implications of FI, provided the financial support for many program evaluations and related research. However, recent decades have brought political change. The issues are complex and have much to do with Quebec's current moves to separate from the rest of Canada in order to preserve its linguistic and cultural distinctiveness. In this political climate, the goodwill which led many Anglophone parents to enroll their children in FI programs appears to be waning, and enrollments in FI programs have leveled off after a long period of continuous growth. Even the interest of the federal and provincial governments has decreased, as indicated by the considerably reduced amounts of financial support given to subsidize FI programs and to continue research projects. So, as perhaps with any innovation, the biggest threat to its continued existence is its "normalcy." FI programs have become a regular, accepted type of education in Canada, and although pedagogical and political issues still provide a background to their existence, they are no longer seen as exceptional with respect to their challenges, problems, and difficulties. As a result, it is more and more difficult to persuade funders that FI holds considerable promise in furthering our understanding of second language learning and teaching.

CONTRIBUTIONS OF FI RESEARCH IN THE COMING DECADE

Of course, it is impossible to predict with any certainty the contributions of FI research in the coming decade. However, I think it is likely that the studies reviewed in this chapter have paved the way for further research which will contribute in particular to our understanding of second language teaching and learning processes.

Lyster plans to follow up his classroom observational work with experimental studies: *"nous reconnaissons que l'effet de la négociation de la forme sur l'apprentissage du français langue seconde reste encore à démontrer et à préciser experimentalement"* (1999:378). [We recognize that the effect of negotiation of form on the learning of French as a second language still remains to be demonstrated with experimental rigour.] Harley is continuing her investigations of second language processing at different ages. For our part, we intend to continue to pay close attention to what learners say to each other as they carry out different tasks. Using stimulated recall and more precise measuring instruments, we hope to refine our understanding of FI students' perceptions of French and how they learn it. Our long-term goal, as with other FI teachers and researchers, is to enhance the learning context for FI immersion students.

There is other research that needs to be done. For example, given the origins of FI in Canada, it is important to know what use immersion graduates are making of their French in the workplace and in social situations with francophones (cf. MacFarlane and Wesche 1995)—we need to understand the "fit" between the reality of FI instruction and the expectation that FI would help to close the gap between Canada's English and French solitudes. And, we need to ask what has been the effect of immersion education in Quebec compared to the rest of Canada. These are highly complex and politically charged questions in the Canada of today, and having some answers would contribute to the growing discipline of applied linguistics.

NOTES

* My thanks to Alister Cumming, Birgit Harley, Sharon Lapkin, and Miles Turnbull for reading and commenting on an earlier version of this review.

UNANNOTATED BIBLIOGRAPHY

Bachman, L. and A. Cohen (eds.) 1998. *Interfaces between second language acquisition and language testing research*. Cambridge: Cambridge University Press.

Dagenais, D. and E. Day. 1998. Classroom language experiences of trilingual children in

French immersion. *Canadian Modern Language Review.* 54.376–393.

Dagenais, D. and E. Day. In press. Home language practices of trilingual children in French immersion. *Canadian Modern Language Review.* 56.

Day, E. and S. Shapson. 1991. Integrating formal and functional approaches to language teaching in French immersion: An experimental study. *Language Learning.* 47.25–58.

——————————— 1996. *Studies in immersion education.* Clevedon, UK: Multilingual Matters.

Felix, S. 1985. More evidence on competing cognitive systems. *Second Language Research.* 1.47–72.

Genesee, F. 1981. A comparison of early and late second language learning. *Canadian Journal of Behavioral Sciences.* 13.115–128.

——————————— 1987. *Learning through two languages: Studies of immersion and bilingual education.* Rowley, MA: Newbury House.

Harley, B. 1989. Functional grammar in French immersion: A classroom experiment. *Applied Linguistics.* 10.331–359.

——————————— 1992. Patterns of second language development in French immersion. *French Language Studies.* 2.159–183.

——————————— 1998a. French immersion research in Canada: The 1990's in perspective. *Mosaic.* 6.3–10.

——————————— 1998b. The role of form-focused tasks in promoting child L2 acquisition. In C. Doughty and J. Williams (eds.) *Focus on form in classroom second language acquisition.* Cambridge: Cambridge University Press. 156–174.

——————————— and D. Hart. 1997. Language aptitude and second-language proficiency in classroom learners of different starting ages. *Studies in Second Language Acquisition.* 19.379–400.

——————————— , J. Howard and D. Hart. 1998. Grammar in grade 2: An instructional experiment in primary French immersion. In S. Lapkin (ed.) *French second language education in Canada: Empirical studies.* Toronto: University of Toronto Press. 177–193.

Hart, D., S. Lapkin and M. Swain. 1998. Characteristics of the bilingual private sector job market with special reference to French immersion graduates: Exploratory studies. In S. Lapkin (ed.) *French second language education in Canada: Empirical studies.* Toronto: University of Toronto Press. 56–85.

Johnson, R. K. and M. Swain (eds.) 1997. *Immersion education: International perspectives.* Cambridge: Cambridge University Press.

Kowal, M. 1997. French immersion students' language growth in French: Perceptions, patterns and programming. Toronto: University of Toronto. Ed.D. diss.

——————————— 1998. Grade 8 immersion students' understanding of French: Insights and pedagogical implications. In S. Lapkin (ed.) *French second language education in Canada:*

Empirical studies. Toronto: University of Toronto Press. 144–176.

Kowal, M. and M. Swain. 1994. Using collaborative language production tasks to promote students' language awareness. *Language Awareness.* 3.73–93.

——— 1997. From semantic to syntactic processing:. How can we promote it in the immersion classroom? In R. K. Johnson and M. Swain (eds.) *Immersion education: International perspectives.* Cambridge: Cambridge University Press. 284–309.

Lambert, W. E. and G. R. Tucker. 1972. *The bilingual education of children: The St. Lambert experiment.* Rowley, MA: Newbury House.

La Pierre, D. 1994. Language output in a cooperative learning setting: Determining its effects on second language learning. Toronto: University of Toronto. M.A. thesis.

Lapkin, S., D. Hart and M. Swain. 1991. Early and middle immersion programs: French language outcomes. *Canadian Modern Language Review.* 48.11–40.

——— 1996. Vocabulary teaching in a grade 8 French immersion classroom: A descriptive case study. *Canadian Modern Language Review.* 53.242–256.

——— with S. Shapson. 1990. French immersion research agenda for the 90s. *Canadian Modern Language Review.* 46.638–674.

Lightbown, P. 1998. The importance of timing in focus on form. In C. Doughty and J. Williams (eds.) *Focus on form in classroom second language acquisition.* Cambridge: Cambridge University Press. 177–196.

Lyster, R. 1994. The effect of functional-analytic teaching on aspects of French immersion students' sociolinguistic competence. *Applied Linguistics.* 15.263–287.

——— 1995. *Instructional strategies in French immersion: An annotated bibliography.* Canada: Canadian Association of Immersion Teachers.

——— 1998a. Negotiation of form, recasts and explicit correction in relation to error types and learner repair in immersion classrooms. *Language Learning.* 48.183–218.

——— 1998b. Recasts, repetition, and ambiguity in L2 classroom discourse. *Studies in Second Language Acquisition.* 20.51–81.

——— 1999. La négociation de la forme: La suite...mais pas la fin. [The negotiation of form: The follow-up...but not the end.] *Canadian Modern Language Review.* 55.355–384.

——— and L. Ranta. 1997. Corrective feedback and learner uptake: Negotiation of form in communicative classrooms. *Studies in Second Language Acquisition.* 19.37–66.

MacFarlane, A. and M. Wesche. 1995. Immersion outcomes: Beyond language proficiency. *Canadian Modern Language Review.* 51.250–274.

Netten, J. E. and W. H. Spain. 1989. Student-teacher interaction patterns in the French immersion classroom: Implications for levels of achievement in French language proficiency. *Canadian Modern Language Review.* 45.485–501.

Office of the Commissioner of Official Languages (OCOL). 1996. 1995 Annual Report.

Ottawa: OCOL.

Rehner, K. and R. Mougeon. In press. Variation in the spoken French of immersion students: To "ne" or not to "ne," that is the sociolinguistic question. *Canadian Modern Language Review*. 56.

Spielman, S. To appear. Collaborative learning of the conditional in a grade eight French immersion classroom. Toronto: University of Toronto. Ph.D. diss.

Stern. H. H. 1972. Introduction. In M. Swain (ed.) *Bilingual schooling: Some experiences in Canada and the United States*. Toronto: OISE Press. 1–6.

Swain, M. 1985. Communicative competence: Some roles of comprehensible input and comprehensible output in its development. In S. Gass and C. Madden (eds.) *Input in second language acquisition*. Rowley, MA: Newbury House. 235–253.

———— 1988. Manipulating and complementing content teaching to maximize second language learning. *TESL Canada Journal*. 6.68–83. [Reprinted in R. Philipson, E. Kellerman, L. Selinker, M. Sharwood Smith and M. Swain (eds.) *Foreign/second language pedagogy research*. Clevedon, UK: Multilingual Matters. 234–250.]

———— 1993. The output hypothesis: Just speaking and writing aren't enough. *Canadian Modern Language Review, Golden Anniversary Issue*. 50.158–164.

———— 1995. Three functions of output in second language learning. In G. Cook and B. Seidlhofer (eds.) *Principle and practice in applied linguistics: Studies in honour of H. G. Widdowson*. Oxford: Oxford University Press. 125–144.

———— 1996. Integrating language and content in immersion classrooms: Research perspectives. *Canadian Modern Language Review*. 52.529–548.

———— 1998a. Focus on form through conscious reflection. In C. Doughty and J. Williams (eds.) *Focus on form in classroom second language acquisition*. Cambridge: Cambridge University Press. 64–81.

———— 1998b. The output hypothesis, second language learning and immersion education. In J. Arnau and J. M. Artigal (eds.) *Immersion programmes: A European perspective*. Barcelona: Universitat de Barcelona. 127–140.

———— 1999. The role of L1 in L2 learning. Paper presented at the Leeds symposium on task-based learning. Leeds: University of Leeds, January 1999.

———— In press. The output hypothesis and beyond: Mediating acquisition through collaborative dialogue. In J. Lantolf (ed.) *Sociocultural theory and second language learning*. Oxford: Oxford University Press.

———— and R. K. Johnson. 1997. Immersion education: A category within bilingual education. In R. K. Johnson and M. Swain (eds.) *Immersion education: International perspectives*. Cambridge: Cambridge University Press. 1–16.

———— and S. Lapkin. 1982. *Evaluating bilingual education: A Canadian case study*.

Clevedon, UK: Multilingual Matters.

Swain, M. and S. Lapkin. 1995. Problems in output and the cognitive processes they generate: A step towards second language learning. *Applied Linguistics*. 16.370–391.

————————— 1998. Interaction and second language learning: Two adolescent French immersion students working together. *Modern Language Journal*. 82.320–337.

Tardif, C. and F. Gauvin. 1995. *Répertoire de la recherche universitaire en immersion française au Canada: 1988 à 1994*. [*An annotated bibliography of the research on French immersion in Canada conducted by university researchers: 1988 to 1994.*] Ottawa: L'Association canadienne des professeurs d'immersion, Canada.

Tarone, E. and M. Swain. 1995. A sociolinguistic perspective on second language use in immersion classrooms. *Modern Language Journal*. 79.166–178.

Turnbull, M., S. Lapkin, D. Hart and M. Swain. 1998. Time on task and immersion graduates' French proficiency. In S. Lapkin (ed.) *French second language education in Canada: Empirical studies*. Toronto: University of Toronto Press. 31–55.

Warden, M. 1997. The effect of form-focused instruction on control over grammatical gender by French immersion students in grade 11. Toronto: University of Toronto. Ed.D. diss.

Weber, S. and C. Tardif. 1991. Culture and meaning in French immersion kindergarten. In L. Malave and G. Duquette (eds.) *Language, culture and cognition: A collection of studies in first and second-language acquisition*. Clevedon, UK: Multilingual Matters. 93–109.

Wright, R. 1996. A study of the acquisition of verbs of motion by grade 4/5 early French immersion students. *Canadian Modern Language Review*. 53.257–280.

A CRITICAL REVIEW OF THE CRITICAL PERIOD RESEARCH

Thomas Scovel

INTRODUCTION: THE CPH AND APPLIED LINGUISTICS

Two decades of international research in applied linguistics provides a large number and variety of topics from which to choose for this special anniversary edition, but certainly one of the most significant among these choices is the critical period hypothesis (CPH). Few topics in applied linguistics have continued to captivate the interests of researchers and practitioners so intensively and for such a long period of time as the CPH. Indeed, one could easily go back to reviewing three, not two decades of sustained research and continuous interest in this topic (Lenneberg 1967, Scovel 1969). If number and diversity of publications is indicative, the CPH has engendered even more interest and controversy now than in any previous decade. Why is this so?

First and foremost, for the general public, and for language learners and teachers in particular, the CPH taps an inherent fascination with perceived and real contrasts between young children and adults, a fascination which has given birth to the pervasive "the younger, the better" myth concerning second language acquisition (SLA). Although even proponents of at least some version of the CPH have attempted to dispute or at least qualify this belief (Scovel in press), its profuse popularity has fueled general interest in any evidence which suggests that younger learners are more successful than their adult counterparts. This public interest is encouraged by a constant stream of articles and stories in the media, often attributing the reputed linguistic precocity of infants to developmental neurology (Spinney 1999). This myth has also continued to encourage language teachers who believe that one of the best ways to teach a second language to older learners is to attempt to replicate child language acquisition. In fact, more than any other area of applied linguistics, the CPH has directly or indirectly led to the development of methods for teaching foreign languages. Finally, this conviction that younger is better has had an enormous impact on language planning over the past twenty years, where many countries have introduced English at earlier and earlier grade levels in the belief that this policy will ensure a pool of fluent ESL speakers in the future. Given the pervasiveness of this general interest then, perhaps no topic in applied linguistics so directly affects the popular consciousness and public policy than the CPH.

Among applied linguists themselves, especially those with a specific interest in SLA, the CPH has been and remains a seminal topic. Long (1999) has claimed that research on the critical period has been "critical" to all SLA theory construction. Bialystok and Hakuta write, "The debate over the critical period hypothesis embodies some of the most basic questions about second language acquisition, and indeed, language acquisition in general" (1999:163). And Birdsong talks about "...the unmistakable centrality of the CPH..." to SLA research (1999a:18). Virtually all introductions to SLA devote at least some discussion to CPH research (Cook 1991, Ellis 1994, Larsen-Freeman and Long 1991, Skehan 1998), and over the past twenty years, scores of articles have been published reporting on experiments which supposedly support, refine, or refute the hypothesis. Additionally, there have been several texts and anthologies which have focused specifically on the topic (Birdsong 1999b, Harley 1986, Krashen, Scarcella and Long 1982, Scovel 1988, Singleton and Lengyel 1995, Strotzer 1994).

INITIAL CLAIMS CONCERNING THE CPH

The early work on the CPH was not done by applied linguistics, but it can certainly still be considered as representative of linguistics applied. Though many scholars had written about the apparent advantages that young children enjoy in SLA, Penfield (1963), a Canadian neurosurgeon, was the first to link "the earlier, the better" view of foreign language learning to the plasticity of a child's developing brain. Because of his frequent public presentations and writings advocating early foreign language exposure, Penfield could justly be considered the father of immersion programs in Canada, thus demonstrating how even early on, the CPH has influenced foreign language pedagogy. Due to the relatively limited knowledge about developmental neurology forty years ago, and due to his own over enthusiastic promulgation of "the earlier, the better" approach to foreign language teaching, Penfield's contributions have diminished with time. They did serve, however, to encourage Lenneberg, a psycholinguist, to explore the relationship between age and acquisition more intensively. Lenneberg (1967) examined a wide number of brain changes in early life and correlated these with maturational milestones in child development, especially the development of speech and language. It was he who suggested that puberty was the approximate cutoff age for completely successful primary language acquisition and, furthermore, that this was the age when foreign accents emerged. Scovel (1969) summarized and narrowed Penfield's and Lenneberg's views on the CPH into three essential claims: 1) that adult native speakers can identify non-natives by their accent immediately and accurately, 2) that loss of brain plasticity at about the age of puberty accounts for the emergence of foreign accents, and 3) that a CPH is tenable only for speech (a native accent) and does not ultimately affect other areas of linguistic competence. Intensive research since that time, especially during the past twenty years, has refined these claims and has greatly broadened this initial base of inquiry. Over the past twenty years, applied linguists, especially those who specialize in SLA research, have attempted to resolve the following issues concerning the CPH.

1. Does the preponderance of evidence support the CPH?
2. Is there a CP for acquiring accentless speech?
3. Is there a CP for morphosyntactic competence?
4. If the answers to (1) and either or both (2) and (3) are affirmative, how can age-related differences be explained?

DOES THE PREPONDERANCE OF EVIDENCE SUPPORT THE CPH?

Since this question is the most central one of all, and since it entails the answers and the evidence encapsulated in the three other questions which have just been introduced, it is important to define the scope of this first question. Avoided here is a discussion of the differences that may exist between primary (mother tongue) language learning and the acquisition of an additional (second) language. This review focuses only on age-related constraints on second language acquisition. Still, it should be acknowledged that these constraints may be very similar to CP limitations on first language acquisition. Any discussion of age-related constraints on primary language learning introduces a host of additional topics, however, among them the evolution of animal communication (Hauser 1996), the uniqueness of human speech (Lieberman 1991), and studies of feral children and the so-called "linguistic apes" (Candland 1993, Savage-Rumbaugh, Shanker and Taylor 1998). Also avoided here, for a variety of reasons, will be a discussion of the exact age at which a CP ostensibly ends. For most studies, the CP is loosely defined as the period of time between birth and puberty, but there are several problems in demarcating puberty chronologically (Scovel 1988: Chapter 3). Additionally, there is great variation among researchers on which age spans they use to divide up their subjects, and there may be multiple critical periods at varying age levels for different linguistic modalities, a possibility raised early on by Seliger (1978) and discussed more recently by Eubank and Gregg (1999).

More than twenty years ago, several studies had already suggested that children were not necessarily superior to older learners in acquiring a second language, not even in the area of pronunciation (Olsen and Samuels 1973, Snow and Hoefnagel-Hohle 1978). The majority of researchers seemed skeptical about the existence of a CP (Clark and Clark 1977, McLaughlin 1978), and several explicitly denied its existence (Neufeld 1980, van Els, Bongaerts, Extra, van Os and Janssen-Dieten 1984). It is also important to point out that at that time, with the rare exception of a few studies (Patkowski 1980), virtually all of the discussion focused on the ability of post-pubescent learners to acquire native-like speech. Indeed, several of these early studies on the emergence of foreign accents spawned new methods of foreign language teaching for adults. For example, Asher and Garcia's (1969) survey eventually led to the development of Total Physical Response, and Krashen's (1973) paper laid the foundation for his well-known contrast between "learning" and "acquisition" which led to the evolution of the Natural Approach.

Now, more than twenty years later, it is my impression that, based on a general reading of the relevant literature in applied linguistics and psycholinguistics (especially writers such as Long [1990] and Pinker [1994]), the belief in some version of the CPH presently represents the majority opinion. Furthermore, this opinion seems buttressed by a constant succession of new research supporting some aspect of the CPH (Major 1999, Spadaro 1998). Conversely, skeptics like Bialystok and Hakuta (1999) and Bongaerts (1999) now appear to represent the minority view on this subject. If this cursory answer to the first question regarding the CPH is at all accurate, a major shift in thinking has taken place at the end of the century on a topic of significant import to applied linguistics.

IS THERE A CP FOR ACQUIRING ACCENTLESS SPEECH?

Recall that one of the earliest claims made about the CPH, based on the initial work of Penfield and Lenneberg, was the presumption that a CP existed only for "speech" and not for "language" (Scovel 1969). That is, the original speculations about the existence of a biologically based CP in humans that would be homologous to the profuse and well-documented manifestations of CP's in animal behavior concerned the ability to sound like a native speaker. A proliferation of early studies appeared to document the existence of a CP for human speech; language learned after puberty invariably could be identified as non-native by native speakers of that target language (Asher and Garcia 1969, Fathman 1975, Flege, Munro and MacKay 1995, Harada 1997, Major 1987, Oyama 1976, Seliger, Krashen and Ladefoged 1975, Tahta, Wood and Lowenthal 1981). Studies also suggest that bottom/up measures of a foreign accent (e.g., voice onset timing) correlate with more global, top/down judgments (e.g., "Does this person sound like a native speaker?") (Major 1987, Riney and Takagi 1999). Irrespective of how these results are interpreted, the answer to the second question appears to be resoundingly affirmative. Nevertheless, some of those who hold to the minority view on the first question do so because they believe they have evidence that the answer to this second query is negative. That is, some researchers believe that there are people who can learn a new language after puberty without any trace of a foreign accent.

Several applied linguists have devoted their attention to experiments which are designed to train (or to find) post-pubescent learners of a second language who can pass themselves off as native speakers of that target language to native-speaking judges. Neufeld and Schneiderman (1980) attempted to train a group of English speakers to speak a few brief phrases in three different languages so that they would sound like native speakers, and the authors concluded they were essentially successful in this endeavor. However, serious criticisms have been levied about their experimental design and the interpretation of their results (Scovel 1988). A more elegant study was performed by Bongaerts and his colleagues (Bongaerts, Planken and Schils 1995) using, among other groups of speakers, a number of highly proficient post-pubescent Dutch speakers of English, but the results of this experiment are vitiated by the fact that the judges, who were native speakers of British English, had difficulty consistently identifying even the native speaking controls (Scovel 1997). Bongaerts (1999) has reported a more recent and convincing set of experiments in which highly proficient Dutch speakers of French have been identified as speaking with a native accent by native speaking French judges. Even though only a few of the participants in these experiments were able to speak "accentless" French, they appear to be exceptions to the strong version of the CPH for speech espoused by Scovel (1969). Similarly, an exceptional adult learner is discussed by Ioup, *et al.* (1994): They describe an English speaker who first began to learn Egyptian Arabic at the age of twenty-one and eventually acquired such a high proficiency that she was consistently identified as a native speaker. And a more recent study of 24 adult, English-speaking learners highly proficient in German suggests that at least one of the subjects was judged to have native-like pronunciation in his second language (Moyer 1999).

Studies such as these force us to reconsider the answer to question two. It may be that for the vast majority of adult language learners, a native-like accent remains impossible. But for all natural populations, exceptions abound, and these rare examples of precocious pronunciation may represent the exceptions found within plus two or three standard deviations from the norm as speculated by Scovel (1988).

Despite the fact that foreign accents emerge in early adulthood and, with rare exception, remain indelible after puberty, adult learners can, should, and do improve their pronunciation and intelligibility in a second language. Applied linguists who have been influenced by work on the CPH have made promising contributions to this particular area of SLA (Derwing, Munro and Wiebe 1998, Munro and Derwing 1995).

IS THERE A CP FOR MORPHOSYNTACTIC COMPETENCE?

Except for Penfield (1963), most of the early research on the CPH was confined to exploring possible CP effects on pronunciation. Penfield alone was a proponent of "the earlier, the better" claim and assumed that young children were superior to adults in all aspects of SLA. But beginning with Patkowski (1980), there have been several studies conducted which appear to muster increasing evidence that age constraints may also affect morphosyntactic competence (Coppetiers 1987, Johnson and Newport 1989, Shim 1995, Spadaro 1998, White and Genesee 1996). It is instructive to point out that unlike the pronunciation research, which focused almost exclusively on binary or N-ary judgements by native speakers of the target language whether or not taped subjects spoke with a foreign accent, these morphosyntactic studies tap a range of abilities in both performance and competence (e.g., accurate use of irregular morphological inflections, accurate and fluent use of idiomatic lexical collocations, and ability to make accurate grammaticality judgments). It is therefore immediately obvious that at least two major differences exist between the phonological work on the CPH and experiments dealing with lexical and grammatical knowledge. The former relies solely on the linguistic performance of non-native speakers, while the latter depends on tapping skills in both performance and competence in the target language. Second, as Scovel (1988) has pointed out, the former provides evidence for a CP for speech; the latter supports the notion that there is a CP for language.

Because the grammaticality-judgment research has garnered the most attention (e.g., the Johnson and Newport [1989] study is the single most cited reference for the CPH in the SLA literature), and because this research paradigm used in applied linguistics is the one most directly related to research in formal linguistics, it seems fair to examine it most critically. Several authors have lodged a variety of criticisms about either the use of grammaticality judgments in SLA or the interpretation of the results of such studies (Birdsong 1992, Eubank and Gregg 1999, Scovel 1988). In addition, a study undertaken by Slavoff and Johnson (1995) quite surprisingly found no differences between younger learners (7–9) and children close to or into the age of puberty (10–12) in a replication of the earlier, well-known work by Johnson and Newport. The authors also found an unanticipated but significant gender effect with girls outperforming boys. All of this adds support to the suspicion that grammaticality judgment tasks tap a type of target language competence which is difficult to correlate with hypotheses about a CP. Finally, going back to the larger issue of the use of grammaticality judgments as a source of evidence for native speaking competence, many formal linguists hold serious reservations about this particular mode of linguistic inquiry (Schutze 1996).

HOW CAN AGE-RELATED DIFFERENCES IN SLA BE EXPLAINED?

Over the past twenty years, probably the greatest shift in direction in the debate about the CPH has been from the issue of whether or not age-related differences in SLA do indeed exist, to the question of what actually accounts for the attested discrepancies between child and adult second language learners. Here is where the greatest disagreement emerges among the many researchers who are attracted by this area of applied linguistic inquiry. In a telling metaphor, McLaughlin, referring to Hegel's description of Schelling's philosophy, has aptly described this murky arena of explanation as "a night where all cows are black" (McLaughlin 1978:59)!

Because the whole notion of critical periods comes directly from biology (both from genetics and from ethology), the original application of the term to language has strong biological underpinnings. This orientation is especially evident in the early work explaining the emergence of foreign accents as being linked to the completion of lateralization (hence brain plasticity) by the age of puberty (Lenneberg 1967, Scovel 1969). In a narrow sense, therefore, a CP for SLA can only be viewed as a biologically based explanation for the emergence of non-native speech and/or language after about the first decade of life. Because only pronunciation has a clear neuromotor etiology, it alone is affected by the loss of plasticity, evidenced in part by the completion of cerebral lateralization at the emergence of puberty. Note that this biologically based explanation for a CP speech does not seem to explain why there might very well be a CP for the acquisition of native-like morphosyntax as well.

Krashen (1973) was the first to criticize this biologically based explanation. From his interpretation of the neurological data, Krashen argued that lateralization (and brain plasticity) was completed at about the age of four, and so, if age constraints exist for SLA, they are not due to developmental neurology. Krashen's reinterpretation of the neurological data has itself been critiqued (Scovel 1988), and there has been a great deal of new evidence supporting the claim that the plasticity of the developing brain provides children with unique opportunities for learning up to the end of the first decade of life (Spreen, Risser and Edgell 1995: Chapter 8). Note, however, that a biological explanation for age constraints in SLA is not nearly as adequate in accounting for any limits in morphosyntactic learning by older adults. As has been already intimated, it is difficult to see how highly abstract concepts such as irregular morphology or the subjacency principle would be directly linked to loss of neuromuscular plasticity. Nevertheless, if we assume that all humans are born with an innate awareness of certain linguistic principles (UG), how can we account for age constraints in morphosyntax? A variety of explanations have been offered.

Several formal linguists believe that, for reasons not yet determined, UG is dismantled at about the age of puberty and therefore older learners lose their "natural" ability to acquire nativelike language competence (Bever 1981, Pinker 1994). On the other hand, Newport (1990) suggests that the relative cognitive immaturity of pre-pubescent children prevents them from over-analyzing the language(s) they are learning and helps contribute to native-like accuracy. Note that this explanation is quite similar to Krashen's claim that children "acquire" language, but adults tend to "learn" a new language. Bialystok and Hakuta (1999) voice a similar argument in their summary of the most massive study of age effects on second language learning (over 60,000 subjects). They claim that maturational factors and education continually intervene in ultimate SLA success, and so it is misleading to invoke biological explanations such as the CPH for limitations that appear in older second language learners. Finally, there are those such as Birdsong (1999a), who believe that there is nothing "critical" about pubescence and that, as far as morphosyntactic learning is concerned, an earlier age of exposure to a new language is always advantageous, even with adult learners.

SUMMARY

To return to the opening theme of this review, no single area of applied linguistics seems to be as pertinent to non-linguists and to public policy makers as the CPH, and by now, it should be equally apparent that research in this area has a long, diverse, and somewhat controversial history. From this review, it should be apparent that perspectives on the topic have shifted over the past twenty to thirty years thanks to the informative work by applied linguists and by scholars from other fields who have applied their expertise to this area of language behavior. It should also be obvious that, given the conflicting evidence and contrasting viewpoints that still exist, parents, educational institutions, or ministries of education should be exceedingly cautious about translating what they read about the CPH research into personal practice or public policy. If applied linguists have learned anything at this important juncture in history, we have learned to look at the critical period hypothesis a bit more critically.

UNANNOTATED BIBLIOGRAPHY

Asher, J. and R. Garcia. 1969. The optimal age to learn a foreign language. *Modern Language Journal*. 38.334–341.

Bever, T. 1981. Normal acquisition processes explain the critical period for language learning. In K. Diller (ed.) *Individual differences and universals in language learning aptitude*. Rowley, MA: Newbury House. 176–198.

Bialystok, E. and K. Hakuta. 1999. Confounded age: Linguistic and cognitive factors in age differences for second language acquisition. In D. Birdsong (ed.) *Second language acquisition and the critical period hypothesis*. Mahwah, NJ: L. Erlbaum. 161–181.

Birdsong, D. 1992. Ultimate attainment in second language acquisition. *Language*. 68.706–755.

——— 1999a. Introduction: Whys and why nots of the critical period hypothesis for second language acquisition. In D. Birdsong (ed.) *Second language acquisition and the critical period hypothesis*. Mahwah, NJ: L. Erlbaum. 1–22.

——— (ed.) 1999b. *Second language acquisition and the critical period hypothesis*. Mahwah, NJ: L. Erlbaum.

Bongaerts, T. 1999. Native-likeness of pronunciation in naturalistic post-critical period second language acquisition. Paper presented at the 12th World AILA Congress. Tokyo, August 1999.

———, B. Planken and E. Schils. 1995. Can late starters attain a native accent in a foreign language? A test of the critical period hypothesis. In D. Singleton and Z. Lengyel (eds.) *The age factor in second language acquisition*. Clevedon, UK: Multilingual Matters. 30–50.

Candland, D. 1993. *Feral children and clever animals*. Oxford: Oxford University Press.

Clark, H. and E. Clark. 1977. *Psychology and language: An introduction to psycholinguistics*. New York: Harcourt Brace Jovanovich.

Cook, V. 1991. *Second language learning and language teaching*. London: Edward Arnold.

Coppieters, R. 1987. Competence differences between native and near-native speakers. *Language*. 63.544–573.

Derwing, T., M. Munro and G. Wiebe. 1998. Pronunciation instruction for "fossilized" learners: Can it help? *Applied Language Learning*. 8.185–203.

Ellis, R. 1994. *The study of second language acquisition*. Oxford: Oxford University Press.

Eubank, L. and K. Gregg. 1999. Critical periods and (second) language acquisition: Divide et impera. In D. Birdsong (ed.) *Second language acquisition and the critical period hypothesis*. Mahwah, NJ: L. Erlbaum. 65–99.

Fathman, A. 1975. The relationship between age and second language productive ability. *Language Learning*. 25.245–253.

Flege, J., M. Munro and I. MacKay. 1995. Factors affecting degree of perceived foreign accent in a second language. *Journal of the Acoustical Society of America*. 97.3125–3134.

Harada, T. 1997. Is there a critical period for acquiring aspiration? Paper presented at the annual TESOL Convention. Orlando, FL, March 1997.

Harley, B. 1986. *Age in second language acquisition*. San Diego: College-Hil Press.

Hauser, M. 1996. *The biology of communication*. Cambridge, MA: MIT Press.

Ioup, G., E. Boutagui, M. El Tigi and M. Moselle. 1994. Reexamining the critical period hypothesis: A case study of successful adult SLA in a naturalistic environment. *Studies in Second Language Acquisition*. 16.73–98.

Johnson, J. and E. Newport. 1989. Critical period effects in second language learning: The influence of maturational state on the acquisition of English as a second language. *Cognitive Psychology*. 21.60–99.

Krashen, S. 1973. Lateralization, language learning, and the critical period: Some new evidence. *Language Learning*. 23.63–74.

——————, R. Scarcella and M. Long (eds.) 1982. *Child-adult differences in second language acquisition*. Rowley, MA: Newbury House.

Larsen-Freeman, D. and M. Long. 1991. *An introduction to second language acquisition research*. London: Longman.

Lenneberg, E. 1967. *Biological foundations of language*. New York: John Wiley and Sons.

Lieberman, P. 1991. *Uniquely human*. Cambridge, MA: Harvard University Press.

Long, M. 1990. Maturational constraints on language development. *Studies in Second Language Acquisition*. 12.251–285.

—————— 1999. Theories and theory change in SLA. Keynote address presented at the 12th

World AILA Congress. Tokyo, August 1999.

Major, R. 1987. Phonological similarity, markedness, and rate of L2 acquisition. *Studies in Second Language Acquisition.* 9.63–82.

——— 1999. *Foreign accent: The ontogeny and phylogeny of second language phonology.* Phoenix, AZ: Arizona State University. [Unpublished manuscript.]

McLaughlin, B. 1978. *Second-language acquisition in children.* New York: L. Erlbaum.

Moyer, A. 1999. Ultimate attainment in L2 phonology: The critical factors of age, motivation, and instruction. *Studies in Second Language Acquisition.* 21.81–108.

Munro, M. and T. Derwing. 1995. Foreign accent, comprehensibility, and intelligibility in the speech of second language learners. *Language Learning.* 45.73–97.

Neufeld, G. 1980. On the adult's ability to acquire phonology. *TESOL Quarterly.* 3.285–298.

——— and E. Schneiderman. 1980. Prosodic and articulatory features in adult language learning. In R. Scarcella and S. Krashen (eds.) *Research in second language acquisition.* Rowley, MA: Newbury House. 105–109.

Newport. E. 1990. Maturational constraints on language learning. *Cognitive Science.* 14.11–28.

Olsen, L. and J. Samuels. 1973. The relationship between age and accuracy of foreign language pronunciation. *Journal of Educational Research.* 66.263–268.

Oyama, S. 1976. A sensitive period for the acquisition of a nonnative phonological system. *Journal of Psycholinguistic Research.* 5.261–283.

Patkowski, M. 1980. The sensitive period for the acquisition of syntax in a second language. *Language Learning.* 30.449–472.

Penfield, W. 1963. *The second career.* Boston: Little, Brown.

Pinker, S. 1994. *The language instinct: How the mind creates language.* New York: Morrow.

Riney, T. and N. Takagi. 1999. Global foreign accent and voice onset time among Japanese EFL speakers. *Language Learning.* 49.275–302.

Savage-Rumbaugh, S., S. Shanker and T. Taylor. 1998. *Apes, language, and the human mind.* New York: Oxford University Press.

Schutze, C. 1996. *The empirical base of linguistics: Grammaticality judgments and linguistic methodology.* Chicago: University of Chicago Press.

Scovel, T. 1969. Foreign accents, language acquisition, and cerebral dominance. *Language Learning.* 19.245–253.

——— 1988. *A time to speak: A psycholinguistic inquiry into the critical period for human speech.* Rowley, MA: Newbury House.

——— 1997. Review of D. Singleton and Z. Lengyel, The age factor in second language acquisition. *Modern Language Journal.* 81.118–119.

——— In press. "The younger, the better" myth and bilingual education. In R. Gonzalez (ed.) *Language ideologies: Critical perspectives on the official English movement.* Urbana,

IL: NCTE.

Seliger, H. 1978. Implications of a multiple critical periods hypothesis for second language learning. In W. Ritchie (ed.) *Second language research: Issues and implications*. New York: Academic Press. 11–19.

———, S. Krashen and P. Ladefoged. 1975. Maturational constraints in the acquisition of a second language accent. *Language Sciences*. 36.20–22.

Shim, R. 1995. The sensitive period for language acquisition: An experimental study of age effects on universal grammar and language transfer. Urbana, IL: University of Illinois. Ph.D. diss.

Singleton, D. and Z. Lengyel (eds.) 1995. *The age factor in second language acquisition*. Clevedon, UK: Multilingual Matters.

Skehan, P. 1998. *A cognitive approach to language learning*. Oxford: Oxford University Press.

Slavoff, G. and J. Johnson. 1995. The effects of age on the rate of learning a second language. *Studies in Second Language Acquisition*. 17:1–16.

Snow, K. and M. Hoefnagel-Hohle. 1978. The critical period for second language acquisition: Evidence from second language learning. *Child Development*. 49.1112–1128.

Spadaro, K. 1998. Maturational constraints on lexical acquisition in a second language. Perth, Australia: University of West Australia. Ph.D. diss.

Spinney, L. 1999. Tongue tied. *New Scientist*. July 24, 38–41.

Spreen, O., A. Risser and D. Edgell. 1995. *Developmental neuropsychology*. Oxford: Oxford University Press.

Strozer, J. 1994. *Language acquisition after puberty*. Washington, DC: Georgetown University Press.

Tahta, S., M. Wood and K. Loewenthal. 1981. Foreign accents: Factors relating to transfer of accent from the first language to a second language. *Language and Speech*. 24.265–272.

van Els, T., T. Bongaerts, G. Extra, C. van Os and A. Janssen-Dieten. 1984. *Applied linguistics and the learning and teaching of foreign languages*. London: Edward Arnold.

White, L. and F. Genesee. 1996. How native is near-native? The issue of ultimate attainment in adult second language acquisition. *Second Language Research*. 12.238–265.

PSYCHOLINGUISTICS IN APPLIED LINGUISTICS: TRENDS AND PERSPECTIVES

Kees de Bot

INTRODUCTION

This article addresses the relationship between two major terms, psycholinguistics and applied linguistics, and in the process, explores key issues in multilingual processing. A straightforward definition of psycholinguistics is provided by Kess (1991:1): "The field of study concerned with psychological aspects of language studies." In the last decade, the definition has become more restricted, leaving out more social-psychological aspects like the study of attitudes in language use. Here, psycholinguistics will be further restricted to the study of processes of language production and perception (as opposed to acquisition and attrition).

Defining what applied linguistics (AL) is at the moment is less straightforward,[1] particularly when the simple interpretation of the application of linguistic theory is abandoned. In Europe, AL as a label for a whole field, is now gradually losing ground to the more general label 'Applied Language Studies.' This change of emphasis reflects a distancing from structural linguistics and an awareness that there is more to be known about language that is applied than just linguistics. Looking at the role of linguistics itself in studies on cognitive processing, there is a clear preference for Lexical Functional Grammar over other models (e.g., Levelt 1989, Pienemann 1998). In particular, the more recent minimalist approach in generative grammar seems to have lost contact with the study of language acquisition and language use, while earlier L2 research based on the principles and parameters model has lost contact with more recent theoretical developments (Cook 1997).

RELATING PSYCHOLINGUISTICS AND APPLIED LINGUISTICS

If we want to clarify the role psycholinguistics can or should play in AL, we need to narrow down the definition of the latter, or rather look at only a part of that vast field. *The acquisition and use of a second language* seem to be the appropriate chunk of AL in this context. This sub-area relates to many other parts of our field, but its core is, in my view at any rate, essentially psycholinguistic in nature. The psycholinguistic interest would be in the processing mechanisms involved in using more than one language and the acquisition of additional languages. The AL interest would be in understanding why language learners behave the way they do, or in other words, what the mechanisms are for L2 use and acquisition. Ultimately, interest also lies in interventions that change and improve those mechanisms. This interpretation means that multilingual processing can be defined as the intersection or shared interest across psycholinguistics and AL. In this intersection, there are many questions to be answered: How are different languages processed? What are the processing mechanisms of cross-linguistic influence? What is the impact of level of proficiency? Is there a limit to the number of languages the system can deal with before breaking down? Are there processing differences between different types of languages? To what extent do socio-psychological factors influence processing mechanisms?

In the last two decades, psycholinguistics, as a sub-field of cognitive science, has seen an enormous growth that cannot be captured in a few pages. Therefore, a selection of topics will be discussed here to show the potential of connecting theories and models from other fields to the psycholinguistic study of multilingual processing. In what follows, I want to concentrate on a few issues that I expect to be high on the psycholinguistic research agenda for the coming decade, including the following: cognitive processes and SLA, socio-psychological factors in language processing, language processing and language testing, sign language and multilingual processing, and the neuro-imaging of multilingual processing. Before addressing each topic in turn, three central issues from the current literature on bilingual processing are noted briefly in order to set the stage.

KEY ISSUES IN THE MULTILINGUAL PROCESSING

1. The structure of the bilingual lexicon

Of all the issues that have been addressed, the structure of the bilingual lexicon is no doubt the main issue in recent years. As surveys of this literature show (cf. Kroll and de Groot 1997), early proposals based on single/dual storage models are too simple and inadequate to explain experimental findings. There now seems to be agreement that a functional view of the lexicon—that is, models that clarify how lexical information can be accessed—is to be preferred. Following proposals by Paradis (1987), the now dominant model assumes that the words from different languages are organized as subsets in lexical memory. These subsets are formed through the co-occurrence of word relations as these words are used together. This process leads to networks of interrelated words. Since the words of specific languages quite naturally tend to be used together, language-specific subsets develop. This concept of the bilingual lexicon clearly is a dynamic one: New words will be added and, through non-use, connections between words will weaken to the point that the network falls apart. (See Meara 1999 for a mathematical approach to structural changes of the lexicon.)

In most models of the (bilingual) lexicon, three levels are distinguished: a conceptual level, a lexical level, and a phonological level. How languages come into play at these three levels raises other major issues: 1) Are there language specific representations on the conceptual level? 2) Are words organized on the basis of language? 3) Are there different sets of phonemes or syllables? None of these issues have really been resolved.

2. Language choice in production and perception

In both production and perception, there must be language specific processing, though the two processes will differ. In perception, characteristics of the input (e.g., sounds that are language specific) will trigger the system to 'expect' input in a given language. (See Grosjean 1997 for an overview of the literature.) Of course, there will also be information in the communicative setting that suggests the use of a particular language. So in perception, language choice is typically both a top-down (setting) and a bottom-up (language characteristics) process. In language production, language choice is essentially a top-down process: The speaker has to include in his/her communicative intention the language in which an utterance has to be encoded. In many situations, it is clear that one specific language has to be selected exclusively for production. In situations in which multilingual speakers are interacting, the use of more than one language is possible and may even be the preferred choice. Language switching can be a communicative tool to highlight specific information or express an attitude towards a topic of conversation. De Bot and Schreuder (1993) propose a 'language cue' to explain the wide variation in code switching that has been reported in the literature. (See also Milroy and Muysken 1995 for a collection of papers on code-switching.) They argue that for many individual switches, no linguistic or socio-psychological explanation can be given and indeed is needed because speakers set the cues for the languages to be used to a certain value, leading to the right mix of language in a given situation. The exact locus of the language cue is still a matter of debate (cf. Poulisse 1997 and Green 1998 for a model in which inhibition plays a crucial role).

3. The language mode

In several publications, Grosjean has developed the idea of a language mode to explain the various ways multilinguals use their languages. The language mode is defined as follows: "The state of activation of the bilingual's languages and language processing mechanisms, at a given point in time." The language mode is a continuum, ranging from a monolingual mode to a bilingual speech mode (Grosjean to appear). In the monolingual mode only one language is activated and the other languages in a multilingual are deactivated. The notion of a language mode is related to the issues of the language cue discussed above: The language mode is defined by the setting and the communicative intentions of a speaker. This is not to say that there is fully conscious control of the position on the mode. Several experimental studies have shown that even in a supposedly monolingual setting, the other language continues to play a role (e.g., in experiments with monolingual and bilingual presentation of stimuli). Results from such studies have shown that, with monolingual presentation of stimuli, there was interference from the other language because the subjects could not completely 'switch off' that language (Dijkstra, van Jaarsveld and ten Brinke 1998). Hermans, Bongaerts, de Bot and Schreuder (1998), carried out an experiment in which they tested the interference of the L1 in L2 experimental tasks. Using a picture word interference task, they assessed the activation over time of form and meaning characteristics. They showed that in the initial stages of activation of an English word, the Dutch name of the picture to be named is also activated. Their data show that bilingual speakers cannot suppress activation of their first language while naming pictures in a foreign language.

The notion of the language mode clearly needs to be developed further. In several descriptions, it seems that language mode is a metaphor for the levels of activation of language-specific subsets in different processing components. It is not clear whether languages as a whole should be activated more, or less, or whether only parts can be active; in other words, can a bilingual operate in a more bilingual mode in the phonological processing unit and in a more monolingual mode for the syntactic unit? Or should they all be on the same place of the continuum? It seems likely that these components are interrelated and activate each other through back-propagation, and the components are probably 'in tune' most of the time, possibly with some delay, depending on the part of the system that makes a request for more information.

In general, the idea that the language mode is a one-dimension continuum is problematic: Mode is a momentary position of an individual speaker in a multi-dimensional space. For all languages, there is a given level of activation, in some situations zero, or close to that; in other situations, much higher, and every position in this multidimensional space is possible, though maybe for very high levels of activity, an as-yet-undefined level of proficiency is called for.

FUTURE DEVELOPMENTS AND NEEDS

1. Cognitive processes and SLA

In the last decade, several researchers have tried to relate cognitive processing to SLA. Richard Towell and his colleagues (Towell and Hawkins 1994, Towell, Hawkins and Bazergui 1996) have been looking at learners of French from the perspective of the Levelt model for quite some time, trying to relate the Chomskyan approach to SLA. Pienemann's (1998) book is a further development of his earlier work on learnability, but it now includes a processing component. His approach is heavily based on Lexical Functional Grammar and, again, on the Levelt model. His main argument is that processing components and mechanisms put constraints on what can be processed at a specific stage of acquisition. In a recent paper, Doughty (in press) discusses various steps in the processing system and storage systems in language production and perception. Her main interest is to find ways to impact the processing mechanisms through interventions in order to improve language processing in language learners. One of the real issues here is how input is used to change the knowledge in the system. It has been suggested that recasts, corrected versions of learners utterances, may be the best way to change that information because a direct comparison can be made between output and input. This hypothesis opens up a whole discussion that goes beyond the present article. My reading of the psycholinguistic literature on processing leads me to believe that there is never a direct comparison between input and output because the input information is immediately processed and not stored in memory in that form. In language production, words, rules, and elements are drawn from memory at a considerable speed. Therefore, availability of information is an important factor. If we assume that the same storage systems are used for production and perception (as the findings of cross-modal experiments on picture naming with interfering written stimuli seem to suggest), the activation of an element in memory through the perceptual system will be slightly higher for some time, then it decays again. This enhanced level of activation of an element increases the chances of that element being selected again. Selection is always a trade-off between accuracy and speed, and in many situations, a word that may not be the perfect match, but comes very close, may be preferred over the best match, because it is easier to access.

With respect to Doughty's main concern (whether it is possible to have an impact on processing), I take the position that we cannot interfere with the ongoing process, but what we can do is manipulate the selection process. A crucial point is that we cannot erase information from our memory. What we can do, though, is add competing information that for various reasons wins in the rat-race. Thus, to influence processing, another option needs to be made a more attractive candidate in the selection procedure. If a learner systematically matches the wrong word with a concept that he/she wants to express (like 'mourir' rather than 'tuer' in

Swain and Lapkin 1995), we need to make another word the better candidate. We cannot do that 'on-line' during the immediate retrieval process, but various lexical tasks in which relevant conceptual and functional aspects of that verb are activated may give this word a 'push,' making it a better match for later processing and, more importantly, one that is accessed more easily. Once we succeed in having this candidate win the competition—every time a successful match is made—the connection between the concept and the related lemma is strengthened, making a correct choice more likely the next time.

If we can manage to turn our understanding of the processes of production and perception into interventions that provide learners with the right information at the exact time they need it, this would represent a real step forward. Given the possibilities of information technology, it is easier now to develop materials and techniques to make such well-timed interventions than it was in the past.

2. Language processing and language testing

While language testers are generally never slow nor reticent to tell the applied linguistic community what their moral standards and research methods should be, the major part of their work on testing language proficiency is basically built on the black box approach prevalent in the behaviorist era. While there now is quite some information on the various subprocesses of language production and language perception, most language testing is still geared towards the outcomes of the whole process. For real diagnostic testing, instruments have to be developed that are specifically aimed at assessing the workings of various subprocesses. In production, things can go wrong in many stages of the process. For example, in phonological encoding, segmental and suprasegmental information have to be combined to develop the phonetic plan. It is more or less known how this takes place, and accordingly, what can go wrong. Testing procedures are needed that will allow us to get specific information about problems in these substages of language production.

3. Socio-psychological factors in language processing

One of the big issues for future research is to determine the extent and the manner in which socio-psychological factors related to the minority status of a language may have an impact on language processing. It is in a way attractive to view our language production system purely as a language producing machine, but this is evidently too simple a picture: lexical access, grammatical complexity, and phonological encoding do not take place in a socio-psychological vacuum. Factors like status, self-esteem, and self consciousness are critical factors in all stages of the production and perception process. To give an example, when, in speaking, a specific word is needed, there will be a process of matching the meaning components of a lexical item and the communicative intention it is supposed to express. In that matching process, there is an evaluative moment in which many factors will come into play. (For example, is this word appropriate or good enough for this communicative situation? Am I using the right level of politeness? If I cannot use this word, should I continue or stop?) There is no absolute or mechanistic device that can make that decision for all words. Of course, not every single word is weighed in such a way in speaking, since that would lead to too much loss of speed. How such social-psychologically motivated mechanisms operate is far from clear, but, in particular for our understanding of language use in language learners, a better understanding of such mechanisms is vital.

4. Sign language and multilingual processing

There is very little research specifically aimed at the study of the bilinguality of sign language. As Padden (1999) points out, very few sign users use that code only. Many language-signers either mouth or even vocalize spoken language and combine sign language with other communicative means, such as additional gestures or facial expressions. Dufour's (1997) overview of the research on sign language and bilingualism shows that some of the research that has been done on the processing of sign language can be reinterpreted in terms of bilingual processing. An example is the study by Siple, Caccamise and Brewer (1982) on the encoding of signs. In this study, deaf and hearing signers with different levels of fluency in signing had to encode signs that differed in formational properties, meaning, and translation in English. Formational properties appeared to play a more important role than the influence of (spoken) English, which suggests an independent storage of signs.

On the basis of the literature available, Dufour (1997) proposes a model of processing in which three levels are distinguished, a conceptual level, a lexical level, and a third level for both (vocal) articulation and signing. One of the problems in Dufour's model is that there is no account of the processing of sign words and finger spelled words. This is not a trivial matter for a processing model. The decision either to use a sign or to finger spell has to be made at a fairly early stage of the production process because different mechanisms are involved. In sign language, there is vocabulary that alternates between finger spelled and signed forms. For example the signed LOVE and the finger spelled LOVE are different in grammatical class: the signed form is a verb and the finger spelled, a noun (Padden, personal communication). This distinction means that in the early stages of encoding, the decision either to sign or finger spell has to be taken. So far, no research seems to have been done on the relation between signing or fingerspelling on the one hand and the other languages (signed or other) of the signing-language user on the other.

Another element that is missing in Dufour's model is the fact that most signers support their signing with mouthing. What aspects of processing exactly are expressed in mouthing is unclear; the impression is that content words are more likely candidates than function words and that new information is highlighted through mouthing more than old information. In addition, some parts of the communicative intention are expressed in a non-verbal way (e.g., through nodding to add negation to a message). Messing (1994) adds a sociolinguistic perspective in her study on bimodal communication, examining the introduction of individual signs into spoken language or individual words into a signed conversation. Her data showed that there are register variations in the mix of spoken and signed language.

The many options signers have, such as switching across sign languages, or between vocal language and sign language, or combining signing and mouthing, present a real challenge for the psycholinguistics of bilingualism. It is obvious that present models of language processing cannot deal with the complexities of signing and bilingualism. An extensive research program will be needed to come closer to an understanding of what our language processing system can do. As Dufour (1997) concludes, "The difference in modalities between signed and spoken languages may have important and critical consequences for our understanding of language representation and processing in the bilingual mind" (p. 327).

5. Neuro-imaging of language processing

In the last two decades, our understanding of the functional organization of the human language capacity has increased enormously. At the same time, various new techniques have been developed to register neuro-physiological processes in the brain. There is a rapidly expanding field of research that aims at relating the cognitive architecture of language and those neurophysiological processes.

Although the relation between the cognitive architecture and the neural architecture of higher cognitive functions is by no means a simple and direct one, there is a growing awareness among cognitive scientists that they should construct models of cognitive functions in which neurobio-logical constraints are taken seriously... The rapidly developing field of cognitive neuroscience is therefore based on the conviction that findings at the neurobiological level of analysis should have real consequences for the psychological analysis, and, similarly, that the results at the psychological level should have substantial implications for our understanding of the neurobiological system (MPI-Booklet for Psycholinguistics 1998).

Different techniques to support this agenda include measures of invivo brain activity, including nuclear magnetic resonance imaging (MRI), positron emission tomography (PET-scans) and magnetoencephalography (MEG). These techniques provide information about brain structures and the time course of language-processing events with a high resolution in terms of milliseconds.

Neuro-imaging of bilingual processing is still in its infancy, and even for 'big questions,' such as the neural substrates of individual languages, the more refined techniques have not yet led to real conclusions.[2] While some studies (Klein, *et al.* 1994 and Yetkin, *et al.* 1996) report that the same areas of the brain are used to process L1 and L2, other studies (Dehaene 1997, Kim, *et al.* 1997) report a dissociation of the areas used by the two languages. Here we should refer to Paradis (1997) who warns against simplified over-generalizations with respect to neural substrates of languages. He points out that differences in proficiency may lead to the use of different strategies (e.g., pragmatic vs. lexical) which have been shown to be located in different parts of the brain. In addition, there is evidence that type of bilingualism (early vs. late) has an effect on cognitive processing, even for near native speakers of the second language (Neville, Mills and Lawson 1992). In the future, neuro-imaging may become a useful tool to understand changes in processing that are associated with learning or forgetting, and it may even help us determine whether what we present is actually processed, which brings us close to the input-intake discussion in SLA.

One of the main problems is going to be that, in order to make a real contribution to our understanding of the human-language-processing mechanism, applied linguists have to keep in touch with researchers from other fields, while at the same time these fields are becoming more complex and technically advanced, as experimental techniques and measurement procedures develop further. Bilingualism and SLA are not the prime interest of researchers working in cognitive science and neuro-imaging. If we want to maintain that the study of multilingual processing is at the heart of the study of the human language capacity, we need to become discussion partners informed about new developments and techniques. This requirement means staying current with pretty much a complete field of research apart from one's own.

CONCLUDING REMARKS

From the above, it is obvious that a thorough introduction in psycholinguistics should be part of the training of future applied linguists. Without denying the importance of sociolinguistic and pedagogical issues in SLA, we need to teach and understand foremost the processing mechanisms that play a role in acquisition and use.

There is no simple answer to the question of whether we should develop programs in applied linguistics that take into account developments in cognitive science. There seems to be little point in having programs focused solely on multilingual processing. A set-up in which a major in applied linguistics, with a substantial part of the program devoted to psycholinguistic aspects of bilingualism, combined with a specially tailored minor in cognitive science, may be a solution here, but that will take the applied linguistics program quite far from what for many people working in this field consider to be the core of our field.

One final point is that while psycholinguistics as a field is highly international, it is remarkable that so much of the work on multilingual processing is done in Europe. This pattern probably reflects two tendencies: One is that monolingual researchers will in general be less interested in studying multilingualism than researchers who speak more than one language. The other tendency is that, for the kind of research reported on here, fairly large numbers of multilingual subjects are needed, preferably partly second language learners, and partly foreign language learners. Since the European scene is more multilingual, maybe not so much in numbers as in attitudes and interests, it is likely to carry on more research on multilingualism. Such a trend will, in all likelihood, increase with the current internationalization trends in Europe for at least the next decade.

NOTES

1. At the 1999 Tokyo world congress of AILA (*Association Internationale de Linguistique Appliquée*), several sessions were devoted to somewhat *fin-de-siècle* discussions of what constitutes the field of applied linguistics.

2. The author is indebted to Laura Sabourin for providing him with information about this topic.

ANNOTATED BIBLIOGRAPHY

de Groot, A. and J. Kroll (eds.) 1997. *Tutorials in bilingualism: Psycholinguistic perspectives*. Mahwah, NJ: L. Erlbaum.

This edited volume is the most comprehensive set of papers on bilingual processing that is currently available. In particular, the papers by Poulisse, Paradis, Cook, Dufour, and Grosjean are relevant in this context. The introduction by de Groot and Kroll provides a very useful overview of current trends.

Doughty, C. In press. Cognitive underpinnings of focus on form. In P. Robinson (ed.) *Cognition and second language instruction*. Cambridge: Cambridge University Press.

This paper is one of the first to integrate processing mechanisms and SLA with the aim to develop interventions for language learners. The paper covers a wide range of issues related to processing and storage in memory, and usefully relates this information to what we know about SLA.

Green, D. 1998. Mental control of the bilingual lexico-semantic system. *Bilingualism: Language and Cognition.* 1.2.67–82.

This provocative paper builds on Green's long ranging interest in bilingual processing. It proposes an inhibitory control model to explain how bilinguals control their two languages systems. The paper is followed by eight peer comments and the author's reaction to these comments.

Grosjean, F. To appear. The bilingual's language modes. In J. Nicol (ed.) *One mind, two languages: Bilingual language processing.* Oxford, Blackwell.

This paper contains the fullest description of Grosjean's ideas about the Bilingual Language Mode available. Though the concepts used and the mechanics of how the language mode works in actual processing are not always clear, the idea of a language mode is very compelling, and researchers working on multilingual processing have to at least take a position on this issue.

Levelt, W. J. M. 1989. *Speaking: From intention to articulation.* Cambridge, MA: MIT Press.

While now 10 years old, this book still is as relevant as it was when it came out. It is the only full description of the language production system, integrating information ranging from concept formation to articulation. Its relevance for multilingual processing has been evidenced in many recent articles on multilingualism.

Levelt, W. J. M., *et al.* 1999. A theory of lexical access in speech production. *Behavioral and Brain Sciences.* 22.1.1–75.

This article contains the most recent version of the Levelt model for language production. It is clearly the state of the art in lexical access. This very rich paper is followed by peer commentaries in the BBS-tradition.

Padden, C. 1995. Early bilingual lives of deaf children. In I. Parasnis (ed.) *Cultural and language diversity and the deaf experience.* Cambridge: Cambridge University Press. 99–116.

This is a very useful overview of what makes sign users bilinguals or multilinguals. Based on her own extensive experience in sign language research,

Padden describes how the various languages of signers grow and interact.

Pienemann, M. 1998. Language processing and second language development. *Processability Theory*. Amsterdam: J. Benjamins.

In this book, Pienemann describes his Processability Theory, which is based on the idea that constraints of the processing system determine what can be acquired in SLA. This view is in marked contrast with the idea that linguistic aspects, as proposed in formal linguistic theories, determine the order of acquisition in a second language.

Schreuder, R. and B. Weltens (eds.) 1993. *The bilingual lexicon*. Amsterdam: J. Benjamins.

Though the field is moving so fast that some of the papers in this volume are becoming outdated, this edited volume is still one of the few in which various aspects (teaching, testing, acquisition, attrition, and storage) of the bilingual lexicon are brought together, and most of the contributions have not lost much of their relevance.

Towell, R. and R. Hawkins. 1994. *Approaches to second language acquisition*. Clevedon, UK: Multilingual Matters.

In contrast to Pienemann, Towell and Hawkins firmly believe in the relevance of Chomsky's Principles and Parameters model to explain language acquisition. In this book, an interesting attempt is made to combine the ideas of the P&P model with processing mechanisms as proposed in the Levelt model.

UNANNOTATED BIBLIOGRAPHY

Beauvillain, C. and J. Grainger. 1987. Accessing interlexical homographs: Some limitations of a language-selective access. *Journal of Memory and Language*. 26.658–672.

Bierwisch, M. and R. Schreuder. 1992. From concepts to lexical items. *Cognition*. 41.23–60.

Cook, V. 1997. The consequences of bilingualism for cognitive processing. In A. de Groot and J. Kroll (eds.) *Tutorials in bilingualism*. Mahwah, NJ: L. Erlbaum. 279–300.

de Bot, K. 1992. A bilingual production model: Levelt's Speaking model adapted. *Applied Linguistics*. 13.1–24.

―――― and R. Schreuder. 1993. Word production and the bilingual lexicon. In R. Schreuder and B. Weltens (eds.) *The bilingual lexicon*. Amsterdam: J. Benjamins. 191–214.

de Groot, A. and G. Nas. 1991. Lexical representation of cognates and non-cognates in compound bilinguals. *Journal of Memory and Language*. 30.90–123.

Dehaene, S., *et al.* 1997. Anatomical variability in the cortical representation of first and second language. *NeuroReport*. 8.3809–3815.

Dijkstra, T., H. van Jaarsveld and S. ten Brinke. 1998. Interlingual homograph recognition: Effects of task demands and language intermixing. *Bilingualism, Language and Cognition*. 1.51–66.

Dufour, R. 1997. Sign language and bilingualism: Modality implications for bilingual language representation. In A. de Groot and J. Kroll (eds.) *Tutorials in bilingualism*. Mahwah, NJ: L. Erlbaum. 301–330.

Grainger, J. 1993. Visual word recognition in bilinguals. In R. Schreuder and B. Weltens (eds.) *The bilingual lexicon*. Amsterdam: J. Benjamins. 11–26.

Grosjean, F. 1997. Processing mixed language: Issues, findings and models. In A. de Groot and J. Kroll (eds.) *Tutorials in bilingualism*. Mahwah, NJ: L. Erlbaum. 225–254.

Hermans, D., T. Bongaerts, K. de Bot and R. Schreuder. 1998. Producing words in a foreign language: Can speakers prevent interference from their first language. *Bilingualism: Language and Cognition*. 1.213–229.

Kess, J. 1991. *Psycholinguistics: Psychology, linguistics and the study of natural language*. Amsterdam: J. Benjamins.

Kim, K., *et al.* 1997. Distinct cortical areas associated with native and second language. *Nature*. 388.9938.171–174.

Klein, D., *et al.* 1994. Left putaminal activation when speaking a second language. *NeuroReport*. 5.2295–2297.

Kroll, J. and A. de Groot. 1997. Lexical and conceptual memory in the bilingual: Mapping form to meaning in two languages. In A. de Groot and J. Kroll (eds.) *Tutorials in bilingualism*. Mahwah, NJ: L. Erlbaum. 169–200.

Meara, P. 1999. Simulating recovery from bilingual aphasia. *International Journal of Bilingualism*. 3.1.45–54.

Messing, L. 1994. Bimodel communication, signing skill and tenseness. *Sign Language Studies*. 84.209–220.

Milroy, L. and P. Muysken (eds.) 1995. *One speaker, two languages: Cross-disciplinary perspectives on code-switching*. Cambridge: Cambridge University Press.

MPI. 1998. Booklet for Psycholinguistics: Neurocognition of language processing. http://www.mpi.nl/world/groups/neuro/neuro_intro.html.

Neville, H., D. Mills and D. Lawson. 1992. Fractionating language: Different neural subsystems with different sensitive periods. *Cerebral Cortex*. 2.244–258.

Padden, C. 1999. Practical applications of sign language research. Keynote address, AILA World Congress. Tokyo, August 1999.

Paivio, A. and A. Desrochers. 1980. A Dual-Coding approach to bilingual memory. *Canadian Journal of Psychology.* 34.388–399.

Paradis, M. 1987. *The assessment of bilingual aphasia.* Hillsdale, NJ: L. Erlbaum.

────── 1997. The cognitive neuropsychology of bilingualism. In A. de Groot and J. Kroll (eds.) *Tutorials in bilingualism.* Mahwah, NJ: L. Erlbaum. 331–354.

Poulisse, N. 1997. Language production in bilinguals. In A. de Groot and J. Kroll (eds.) *Tutorials in bilingualism.* Mahwah, NJ: L. Erlbaum. 201–224.

────── and T. Bongaerts. 1994. First language use in second language production. *Applied Linguistics.* 15.36–57.

Siple, P., F. Caccamise and L. Brewer. 1982. Signs as pictures and signs as words: The effects of language knowledge on memory for new vocabulary. *Journal of Experimental Psychology: Learning Memory and Cognition.* 8.619–625.

Swain, M. 1995. Three functions of output in second language learning. In G. Cook and B. Seidlhofer (eds.) *For H. G. Widdowson: Principles and practices in the study of language. A festschrift on the occasion of his 60th birthday.* Oxford: Oxford University Press. 125–144.

────── and S. Lapkin. 1995. Problems in output and the cognitive processes they generate: A step towards second language learning. *Applied Linguistics.* 16.371–391.

Towell, R., R. Hawkins and N. Bazergui. 1996. The development of fluency in advanced learners of French. *Applied Linguistics.* 17.84–119.

Woutersen, M. 1997. The organization of the bilectal lexicon. Nijmegen: University of Nijmegen. Ph.D. diss.

Yetkin, O., *et al.* 1996. Use of functional MR to map language in multilingual volunteers. *American Journal of NeuroRadiology.* 17.473–477.

CONCLUDING SUMMARY

CONCLUDING THOUGHTS: APPLIED LINGUISTICS AT THE JUNCTURE OF MILLENNIA

G. Richard Tucker

INTRODUCTION

As Peter Stearns, the noted social historian, observed in the preface to a recent monograph,

> However briefly and artificially, the turn of the century/millennium will create a mirror in which we may be able to see where we've been coming from and where we are heading and wish to head. That's what the last turn of the century offered with complex and instructive results (1998:xi).

I am personally delighted to have an opportunity to contribute "Concluding Thoughts" to this volume, prepared as it is at the juncture of millennia, since it provides a similar opportunity for reflection and prediction, and since for one reason or another I have been an active participant in, and observer of, developments in the field of applied linguistics for more than three decades. Indeed my own career path reflects clearly the permeability of traditional departmental or disciplinary boundaries that has at once contributed to the sense of excitement and potential in the field and simultaneously to its lack of rootedness (e.g., I have at various times held academic appointments in departments of psychology, linguistics, and modern languages as well as worked for a private philanthropic foundation and a mission-oriented non-profit organization).

I would like to preface these "Concluding Thoughts" by observing that our field owes a debt of great gratitude to Charles A. Ferguson (1921–1998) who from my perspective long demonstrated an influential and far-reaching vision of what applied linguistics is and can be (see, for example, Ferguson 1998). This vision, developed and articulated on numerous occasions, was exemplified, for instance, by his inaugural plenary address at the very first AAAL meeting in Boston in December 1978, by his lecture "Applications of linguistics: Issues and challenges for the linguistic community" on the occasion of the golden anniversary of the Linguistic Society of America, and by his plenary address on the occasion of AAAL's 10th anniversary meeting in San Francisco. Ferguson also contributed to our evolving discipline more broadly by his service as founding director of the Center for Applied Linguistics (1959–1966). In this latter capacity, he was uniquely responsible for bringing to the attention of educators and policy makers throughout the world the contributions of applied linguists to problems of educational and national development. Exemplary of his accomplishments were his work in shaping the five-country East African Survey of Language Use and Language Teaching and his convening of the series of Anglo-American–French dialogues which became the exceedingly productive International Conferences on Second Language Problems (the so-called ICSLP conferences).

When one thinks of distinguished scholarship in our field, it is hard to imagine a more productive or a more respected scholar. In addition to his generally acknowledged reputation as the world's leading authority on Bengali, and some would add Arabic as well, Ferguson helped to define the parameters of the field of language policy and planning through his publications and his work as codirector of the International Research Project on Language Planning Processes. In addition, his early work on caretaker speech and on child phonology remain benchmarks for those who have attempted to follow in his footsteps. He was, as well, among the first to push the frontiers of the field by analyzing forms of speech such as sports announcers' talk, an innovative direction at the time, but one which would not now seem out of mainstream at all today. So in a very real sense the depth and the breadth of the field as we know it today owe much to the scholarship, the vision, and the leadership of Charles Ferguson. It is fitting that he was the inaugural recipient of the AAAL Award for Distinguished Scholarship and Service and that he served us as a member of the Board of Editorial Directors of *ARAL*. I turn now to offer some integrative comments based upon the contributions to this volume.

OVERVIEW OF PROMINENT THEMES

Although each of the other 14 contributions to this volume stands alone and can profitably be consulted for specific and valuable information, the volume is also marked for me by the prominence of three themes: 1) a provocative and informative set of reflections on disciplinary development(s) (see, for example, Daoud, Kaplan and Grabe, Larsen-Freeman, Leki, Scovel, Takala and Sajavaara, Widdowson), 2) a clear articulation of a set of major concerns, and 3) a stimulating set of comments on likely future directions for the field (see, for example, Clapham, Crandall, de Bot, Kaplan and Grabe, Larsen-Freeman, Leki, Martin, Takala and Sajavaara, Widdowson). The second prominent theme above, the major concerns that were articulated, seem to me to be four in number: 1) a concern with the social contexts in which we conduct our research, develop our materials, teach our students, and contribute to policy formation (see, for example, Crandall, Larsen-Freeman, Leki, Martin, Swain, Takala and Sajavaara, Tarone); 2) an intersecting and overlapping concern with social identity and the ways in which an individual's multiple identities may affect factors such as language processing or the development of literacies (see, for example, de Bot, Larsen-Freeman, Leki); 3) a concern with neglect—whether it be the pervasive neglect of languages other than English (see, for example, Swales, Widdowson), neglect in the professional training of scholars from the so-called developing world (see, for example, Crandall, Daoud), or neglect for substantive areas such as sign language and signing that could benefit from our concentrated attention (e.g., de Bot); and 4) a concern with the need for adjusting or broadening the dominant *research paradigm* to include the collection of longitudinal data from multiple disciplinary perspectives (see, for example, Leki, Swain, Tarone). In the sections to follow, I will comment briefly on each of these three prominent themes.

1. Reflections on disciplinary development(s)

From my perspective, the tone for this theme, and for the complexity and importance of the underlying issues, is captured by authors' observations such as the following (excerpted verbatim in many of the observations to follow and often without direct attribution): With respect to applied linguistics *per se* we are told that the development of a disciplinary field is a messy undertaking, and that full disciplinary acceptance will occur only to the extent that applied linguistics responds to wider social needs and to the extent that its expertise is valued by people beyond the professional field. However, despite the ongoing discussions and debates to which Kaplan and Grabe and others refer, it seems clear that the trajectory and the momentum toward disciplinary recognition is positive. Given this development it is probably inevitable that discussion of the autonomy of subfields or specializations would follow, and thus it was instructive for me that a number of contributors wrote specifically about the emergence of their fields as autonomous sub-disciplines. Larsen-Freeman, for example, described developments in the field of SLA (Second Language Acquisition) and suggested the publication of Pit Corder's article (1967) as marking the point of demarcation for the two areas. Leki commented on the disintegration of links between those working within the areas of writing and literacy and those working within the domains of TESOL and applied linguistics while Swales, on the other hand, painted a very different picture for the "field" of LSP (Language for Special Purposes). He notes that the disjunction between ESP/LSP and language acquisition, basic FL methodology, psycholinguistics, and sociolinguistics has in the United States left little space in graduate programs for ESP work... and the lack of professional preparation has had deleterious effects on research and program quality... so that as a partial consequence ESP/LSP has yet to establish itself as either a full profession or as clear sub-discipline in the language sciences. In similar fashion, Takala and Sajavaara observed that systematic effort needs to be taken to develop professionalism in the area of LPLP (Language Policy and Language Planning) and that such professionalism could well involve emulation of the development of educational evaluation as a separate discipline leading ultimately to the autonomy of LPLP as a discipline. I was left with the distinct impression that the centrifugal forces at work will inevitably lead to continuing fragmentation of the field and enhance the likelihood posited by Martin that applied linguists could wind up as pidgin speakers of a range of theories, with theory so divorced from practice that any possibility of creolization is pretty much foreclosed.

2. A set of major concerns

As mentioned, I saw four cross-cutting concerns woven throughout the various contributions. These dealt with the importance of social context(s) and social identity, with issues of neglect, and with calls to broaden the prevalent research paradigms. Concern with the importance of attending to social context was ubiquitous. As Crandall noted in her review of teacher education, decontextualized theory fails to consider the multidimensionality and the unpredictability of the classroom environment. Takala and Sajavaara highlighted the centrality of context in their view of LPLP as a recursive cycle of CIPP (context, input, process, and product). Other contributors (e.g., Leki, Martin) spoke of literacy as social practice and of linguistics as social actions to be recontextualized in relation to new problems. Clearly the pendulum has swung over the past two decades as noted by Tarone and by Larsen-Freeman who observed that mainstream SLA is not (or at least is no longer) asocial and who described a growing body of research that demonstrates the importance of social factors in second language acquisition. For me personally, the most compelling invitation came from Martin who asserted that there is a plethora of critical discourse analysis which focuses on power and how it oppresses, but noted that what we are lacking is a complementary focus on how social subjects design change. If, Martin noted, we understood better the phenomenon of change in all of its multiple dimensions, then we could use this understanding to inform our social interventions—an observation that has profound implications for the training of future generations of applied linguists. In this regard, Swain provided a fascinating description of the ways in which a multifaceted program of research and evaluation of French Immersion programs—that was at once sensitive to and supportive of the complex social and political dynamics surrounding language education in Canada—has both led to educational change but may also atrophy as the experience become "normalized."

Several contributors voiced an intersecting and overlapping concern with social identity and the ways in which an individual's multiple identities may affect language processing or the development of literacies. De Bot, for example, speculated about the contributions of social psychological factors in language processing and wondered whether a speaker's status as minority or majority member affects the processes of perception and production. Larsen-Freeman reminded us that non-native speakers have multiple social identities that they bring to any situation and that being a language learner is only one of them, while Leki and others called our attention to the necessity to be aware of, and draw upon, the multiple home literacies that students in many of our classes bring with them and that will inform and either facilitate or inhibit the development of so-called academic literacy. Thus, those working within a sociocultural framework remind us that learners actively (co)construct their own learning and identity in adding another language to their repertoire and that we must be sensitive to such factors in our research, in our teaching, and in our theory building.

I found the concern with neglect to be the most poignant theme that underpinned many of the contributions. The multiple expressions of this theme were particularly distressing given the frequency with which they have been articulated in earlier editions of *ARAL*. So yet again, contributors remind us of the pervasive neglect of languages other than English. Swales decries, for example, the prospect of real loss of professional registers in many national cultures with long scholarly traditions; Larsen-Freeman calls attention to the paucity of research on the acquisition of non-European languages; Leki describes the absorption of writing researchers with English language contexts and with monolingual English-speaking countries. In a complementary vein, Daoud calls attention to our collective neglect in the professionalization or development of "local" researchers and scholars. He noted the conspicuous absence of host country nationals at the pioneering 1975 Hammemet Conference on Language for Specific Purposes and asserts, probably accurately, that the composition of the participants would likely not be very different today. Crandall, too, calls our attention to the need for extending socially, culturally, and pedagogically appropriate training programs to "non-native-speaking" teachers of language(s) who likely comprise numerically the most rapidly expanding pool of teacher candidates. Lastly, contributors expressed concerns for neglected areas—so, for example, de Bot devotes considerable attention to the area of sign language acquisition, processing, and use. In the aggregate, these areas of concern with neglect are profoundly depressing since they recur so regularly in our survey literature.

The fourth expressed concern in this category—that of broadening the dominant research paradigm—is quite different. This is more a call for ensuring that we provide graduate students with broad, as opposed to narrow, methodological training; that we encourage them to consider collecting, examining, and interpreting data from multiple perspectives; and that we stress the importance of collecting longitudinal data to provide a more comprehensive frame within which to examine conflicting claims (in this regard, see also, Tucker 1999a). Swain, for example, makes a cogent case for the necessity for "tracer" studies to examine the life choices pursued by the graduates of French Immersion programs, while Leki draws our attention to the value that can be added to our understanding by examining the acquisition of literacies over time.

3. Future directions for the field of applied linguistics

With respect to the third prominent theme, I will comment briefly on some of the thoughts expressed by contributors concerning future directions for our field. One consistent focus was a prediction of greater uses of technology in teaching and learning and the conduct of research (see, for example, de Bot on neuro-imaging; Clapham on assessment; and Kaplan and Grabe on implications for all aspects of our work as well as the remarks of Swales and Widdowson on the potential uses of corpus linguistics). Although I agree that we seem destined for presently inconceivable enhancements in this area, I have expressed concerns elsewhere (Tucker 1999b) as a result of my review of the extant educational literature and my continuing review of demographic trends and projections. These concerns combine to suggest that: 1) we must give concerted individual and collective attention to the problem of allocation and distribution of technological resources, and 2) we must implement as soon as is practical a multi-faceted and longitudinal research agenda to examine the value that is actually added for students who pursue some or all of their continuing education using innovative technologies.

In addition, there appeared to be broad agreement about the importance of collaboration in student learning, research, and research training (Kaplan and Grabe) and of ensuring that students are well versed in so-called paradigmatic as well as non-paradigmatic points of view (Larsen-Freeman). Nonetheless, Martin's caution that we not focus on training which features eclecticism stands in contrast to some of the other contributors and deserves our attention. Simultaneously, Crandall predicts the closer intersection of developments in teacher education with those in general teacher preparation while Clapham directs our attention to continuing developments in the areas of performance testing, alternative assessment, and a concern with ethical considerations in assessment and testing.

Clearly, the most striking cumulative impression for me was one of the vitality of the field. There are regular fora (e.g., the conferences of the *Association*

Internationale de Linguistique Appliquée, and the American Association for Applied Linguistics) devoted to facilitating communication among researchers, practitioners, and policy makers; there are numerous journals, reviews, or series uniquely devoted to publication of work in the area; and there are many new monographs published annually on diverse aspects of this topic. Although I believe that the question of financial support for work in the broad domain of applied linguistics remains problematic, it seems inevitable to me that, at some point, policy makers and prospective funders will come to realize the centrality of language issues for educational and national development.

CONCLUDING OBSERVATION

By way of conclusion, let me note that the United States continues to receive over a million immigrants, legal and illegal, each year and that the foreign born is the fastest growing segment of the population. The most accurate prediction that we can make is that this trend will continue for the foreseeable future together with an increase in the number of native born individuals who will speak English as a second language. In addition, it is estimated that approximately one third of the population in urbanized western Europe under 35 years of age will have an immigrant background by the year 2000. These indicators suggest that the importance of language as a critical component of educational and national development in settings throughout the world will persist and likely grow more pervasive.

A recent study commissioned by the British Council on the future of the English language (Graddol 1997) underscores the growing need for all individuals to develop bilingual proficiency in order to be able to participate effectively in our increasingly global society. This situation poses challenges and opportunities for the applied linguist to craft a truly *applied* research agenda that can examine longitudinally, and from multiple perspectives, some of the perplexing questions that persist (NCLE 1998): What is the role of native language oral and literate proficiencies in the acquisition of a second or later studied language? What instructional sequences and approaches work best, and with whom? How can technology be effectively utilized? What is the relationship between teacher development on the one hand and program quality and learner attainment on the

CONCLUDING THOUGHTS: APPLIED LINGUISTICS AT THE JUNCTURE OF MILLENNIA   283

other? What immediate and long-term impact can be expected from various types of adult instructed-language programs? Which extant assessment instruments can reliably and validly document change in learner proficiency and at which levels?

Hopefully, during the decade ahead—with support from various public and private philanthropic sources—collaborative groups of researchers, educators, policy makers, and administrators will begin to ask questions such as these and gradually begin to aggregate relevant qualitative and quantitative data to shed light on the underlying issues. From my personal perspective, the search for answers to questions such as these should be accorded an exceptionally high priority since the *stakes* are so high. Consider information such as the following:

- Nearly one-sixth of the 5.9 billion people in the world cannot read or write according to a survey published by UNICEF (as reported in *The New York Times*, December 9, 1998);
- Three of four children in the "poorest nations" in the world are not in school (excerpted from the United Nations Human Development Report as reported in the *New York Times*, September 27, 1998);
- The additional cost of achieving and maintaining universal access to basic education for all, basic health care for all, reproductive health care for all women, adequate food for all, and clean water and safe sewers for all is roughly $40 billion a year—or less that 4 percent of the combined wealth of the 225 richest people in the world (*New York Times*, September 27, 1998);
- Providing universal primary education for all would cost about $8 billion per year (of the $40 billion mentioned above) which equals:

About four days' worth of global military spending, Seven days' worth of currency speculation in international markets, The amount spent by Americans each year on cosmetics, Less than half of what Americans spend on toys for children each year, Less than the annual amount that Europeans spend on mineral water. (*Washington Post*, April 3, 1999)

I have long been struck by some remarks made by Courtney Cazden (Cazden, *et al.* 1990) in a report to UNICEF in which she noted: "...despite the centrality of language achievements in the developmental agenda of the [child], language issues are rarely in the forefront of thinking about how to plan environments for young children... The prevalence of multilingualism in the world adds a particular urgency to the recommendation to attend [to the quality of language instruction available to the child] (p. 48)." Alas, these remarks are as relevant today as they were nine years ago.

I think it appropriate to end with what I find to be an apt quotation from Charles Ferguson (1998):

> In this autobiographical sketch I have made a point of the tension in my career between activist or 'applied' problem-solving on the one hand and 'pure' linguistic analysis and theory building on the other. While I recognize some validity to this dichotomy, I have never been able to agree with the extreme valorization of either at the expense of the other. It has always seemed to me that a theory that has little or no practical problem solving capacity is ipso facto less good than one that does and that one of the best places to look for clues to theory is in situations of 'application' (p. 54).

Like most of us, I eagerly await the further elaboration and development of our discipline in the millennium that is just beginning.

UNANNOTATED BIBLIOGRAPHY

Cazden, C., C. E. Snow and C. Heise-Baigorria. 1990. Language planning in preschool education with "annotated bibliography." Report prepared for the Consultative Group on Early Childhood Care and Development. New York: UNICEF.

Corder, S. 1967. The significance of learner's errors. *International Review of Applied Linguistics.* 9.147–159.

Ferguson, C. A. 1998. Long-term commitments and lucky events. In E. F. K. Koerner (ed.) *First person singular III: Autobiographies of North American scholars in the language sciences.* Philadelphia: J. Benjamins. 39–57. [Amsterdam Studies in Theory and History of Linguistic Science.]

Graddol, D. 1997. *The future of English.* London: The British Council.

NCLE (National Center for Literacy Education). 1998. *Research agenda for adult ESL.* Washington, DC: Center for Applied Linguistics.

Stearns, P. N. 1998. *Millennium III, Century XXI: A retrospective on the future.* Boulder, CO: Westview Press.

Tucker, G. R. 1999a. An applied linguist reflects on SIL's role(s) and selected activities. *Notes on Sociolinguistics.* 4.3.77–99.

Tucker, G. R. 1999b. The applied linguist, school reform, and technology: Challenges and opportunities for the coming decade. *CALICO Journal.* 17.2.1–25.

图书在版编目(CIP)数据

剑桥应用语言学年度评论.2000:作为新兴学科的应用语言学＝Annual Review of Applied Linguistics 2000·Applied Linguistics as an Emerging Discipline:英文／(美)威廉·格拉伯(William Grabe)主编.—北京:商务印书馆,2016
(剑桥应用语言学年度评论)
ISBN 978-7-100-12536-9

Ⅰ.①剑… Ⅱ.①威… Ⅲ.①应用语言学—研究—英文 Ⅳ.①H08

中国版本图书馆 CIP 数据核字(2016)第 215216 号

所有权利保留。
未经许可,不得以任何方式使用。

剑桥应用语言学年度评论 2000·作为新兴学科的应用语言学
Annual Review of Applied Linguistics
2000·Applied Linguistics as an Emerging Discipline
主编 〔美〕William Grabe
导读 何 伟

商 务 印 书 馆 出 版
(北京王府井大街36号 邮政编码100710)
商 务 印 书 馆 发 行
北京市松源印刷有限公司印刷
ISBN 978-7-100-12536-9

2016 年 12 月第 1 版　　开本 880×1230　1/32
2016 年 12 月北京第 1 次印刷　印张 10 3/8

定价:32.00 元